*The Holy and the
Daemonic from
Sir Thomas Browne to
William Blake*

GRANDE PROFUNDUM EST IPSE HOMO, CUJUS ETIAM CAPILLOS TU, DOMINE, NUMERATOS HABES ET NON MINUUNTUR IN TE: ET TAMEN CAPILLI EJUS MAGIS NUMERABILES QUAM AFFECTUS EJUS ET MOTUS CORDIS EJUS.

Augustine, *Confessions*

⊓

The Holy and the Daemonic from Sir Thomas Browne to William Blake

R. D. STOCK

PRINCETON UNIVERSITY PRESS
PRINCETON, NEW JERSEY

To Barbara

JOCUNDITAS CORDIS HAEC
EST VITA HOMINIS

CONTENTS

PLATES

*The Holy and the
Daemonic from
Sir Thomas Browne to
William Blake*

The Demons and the Scholars

In view of some recent works on witchcraft, it seems only prudent to avow that I have no belief in the black art or in the interference of demons in the daily life of mortals.

GEORGE LYMAN KITTREDGE, *Witchcraft in Old and New England* (1928)

When one of the most erudite professors of English in the country publishes as a crowning achievement a book on witchcraft . . . something is fundamentally wrong with our conception of literary scholarship.

NORMAN FOERSTER, *The American Scholar* (1929)

I HAVE INDULGED HERE an interest in two subjects that may seem ill-sorted: the non-rational or supranatural side of religious experience and the "Age of Rationalism." Most experts on the eighteenth century trace there a lively campaign by some intellectuals to secularize man's view of himself and the world. God as First Cause or Clockmaker was tolerated — so long as he did not meddle with the cosmic machinery and was not required too often to wind the Clock. But the full depth and range of religious experience was rationalized away or derided as superstition and fanaticism. Modern scholars may celebrate this attempt, deplore it, or avow their indifference; but most of them, in the event, lay stress on the rationalist side of the eighteenth century.

This study is concerned, chiefly, with certain kinds of religious experience as recorded in seventeenth- and eighteenth-century literature. But as I shall have occasion now and then to disagree with critics whose opinions tend at present to be hegemonic, I shall take a moment to specify my dissatisfaction with those critics and to lay bare my own presuppositions.

[3]

Introductory: Demons and Scholars

In 1931 Herbert Butterfield rebuked a creature whom he called the whig (with a small "w") historian:

> The case against the whig historian lies in the fact that he brings the effort of [historical] understanding to a halt. He stops the work of imaginative sympathy at a point that could almost be fixed by a formula. It would not be untrue to say that, apart from specialist work of recent date, much greater ingenuity and a much higher imaginative endeavour have been brought into play upon the whigs, progressives and even revolutionaries of the past, than have been exercised upon the elucidation of tories and conservatives and reactionaries. The whig historian withdraws the effort in the case of the men who are most in need of it.[1]

There are whig critics as well as whig historians, and their incapacities are neatly resumed in Yeats's definition of whiggery in "The Seven Sages": "A levelling, rancorous, rational sort of mind / That never looked out of the eye of a saint / Or out of a drunkard's eye." The saint and the drunkard, the holy and the daemonic: these are terminals of human experience equally unappealing to the whig sensibility, for whom, in fact, both conditions are diseases. Even the great scholar Ernst Cassirer thus lapses into whiggery: " 'Reason' becomes the unifying and central point of the eighteenth century, expressing all that it longs and strives for, and all that it achieves." The essence of that age, for Cassirer, is its breaking with the superstitions and dogmas that have haunted and infested human history, and its heroes, for him, are Hume and Voltaire, not Swift or Johnson. Cassirer's views have been broadcast with an unfaltering devotion by writers such as Peter Gay, although dissentient voices have been raised here and there.[2] Carl Becker, for example, despite his own

[1]H. Butterfield, *The Whig Interpretation of History* (1931; rpt. London: G. Bell, 1951), 94-95. A good example of a non-whig specialist study is R. R. Palmer's *Catholics and Unbelievers in Eighteenth Century France* (Princeton, N.J.: Princeton Univ. Press, 1939).

[2]Ernst Cassirer, *The Philosophy of the Enlightenment* (Princeton, N.J.: Princeton Univ. Press, 1951), 5. See Peter Gay, *The Enlightenment: An Interpretation*, 2 vols. (New York: Alfred A. Knopf, 1966, 1969).

[4]

whiggish propensities, has noted the ligatures between the
Enlightenment rationalists or *philosophes* and earlier thinkers,
thereby palliating their iconoclasm and softening their rationalism; and he has ventured to suggest that they were but fashioning a new religion to replace a decrepit Christianity. The theory
that Voltaire and his company were merely trading in old dogmas for new is highly distasteful to votaries of the Enlightenment, but it has been pushed further by cultural historians such
as Eric Voegelin, who sees in the *philosophes*, not emancipators
of reason, but architects of that "pragmatically planning will"
leading directly to the oppressive positivism of Marx. Voltaire,
the champion of intellectual freedom for whig critics, "has done
more than anybody else to make the darkness of enlightened
reason descend on the Western world." But Basil Willey's opinion of the century remains the model: "It was 'indispensable' as
a period in which the dry light of reason was free to penetrate
to the furthest limits of the universe, scattering the yellow-
skirted fays and all the last enchantments of the Middle Ages."[3]
The light of reason, not its darkness, that is, its smug and bump-
tious pretensions, such is still the stress of the routine critical
survey.[4] Without wishing to lapse into an equally partial toryism, for both extremes have about them a very exasperating
nonchalance, I should like to offer a study that is a bit more
skeptical of Enlightenment skepticism.

[3]Eric Voegelin, *From Enlightenment to Revolution* (Durham, N.C.: Duke
Univ. Press, 1975), ed. John H. Hallowell, 299–302, 32; Basil Willey, *The Eighteenth Century Background* (1940; rpt. Boston: Beacon Press, 1961), 111. Carl
Becker's arguments are found in his well-known study, *The Heavenly City of
the Eighteenth-Century Philosophers* (New Haven: Yale Univ. Press, 1932).
His thesis that the Enlightenment thinkers simply devised a new religion is
attacked by Peter Gay, *The Party of Humanity* (New York: Knopf, 1964), 167–
70, and defended in *Carl Becker's Heavenly City Revisited*, ed. Raymond O.
Rockwood (n. p.: Archon Books, 1958), 88, 89–95, 126. Becker's position is for-
tified by such valuable works as Franklin L. Baumer's *Religion and the Rise
of Scepticism* (1960).

[4]Good specimens of recent whig criticism are found, on the popular level,
in Robert Anchor's *Enlightenment Tradition* (New York: Harper and Row,
1967) and, on the scholarly, in John Redwood's *Reason, Ridicule and Religion
. . . in England, 1660–1750* (London: Thames and Hudson, 1976).

Introductory: Demons and Scholars

Akin to the whig critic is the spiritist critic, who tries to seize the spirit, the "inner nature," the "inherent reality," the "personality" of the century.[5] But the age of Voltaire was also the age of Hume, Burke, and Johnson, all independent thinkers who naturally disagreed strongly one with another. If I have any theory, it is only that the religious experience, in its complete range, includes a sense of mystery, of transcendence, of the holy and the daemonic, and that this sense is ubiquitous, regardless of whether it is certified by the supposed official philosophy or spirit of a given time. If I have any ax to grind, it is that the "demons," the non-rational facets, of the eighteenth century have been less fully and less fairly treated than its whiggery. I have tried to find the most important and fundamental beliefs of the figures I discuss, and I have hazarded a comparison or two among them; but I offer mainly a gallery of diverse and, to me, interesting intellects. Generally I have avoided purely philosophical or theological works on the one extremity and popular literature or folklore on the other. Hence there is nothing much here on Berkeley, Swedenborg, or Tillotson; on the Hell Fire Club, the Cock Lane Ghost, or the celebrated Mary Toft, who gave birth to rabbits. I have but glanced at Milton, for whom only a full-dress study would have done, and about whom enough, perhaps, has already been written. I have scanted the drama, believing that what it had to offer my theme was better provided by the novel. On the whole I have chosen authors who occupy major intellectual positions and employ a variety of literary forms.

As a group, the first three chapters are introductory. The first discusses the experience of the holy and the daemonic and inquires: when in fact *does* an age of rationalism begin? Using as examples John Donne and the *Book of Job*, I try to show how

[5]The quoted phrases come from the Introduction to Ira O. Wade's *Intellectual Origins of the French Enlightenment* (Princeton, N.J.: Princeton Univ. Press, 1971). Whig bias often intrudes in this otherwise fine study: e.g., "the initial shift of the Enlightenment was from a system dominated by a religious order to one in which the individual accepted responsibility for making his world" (25).

modern criticism is so often baffled and distorting when it carries skeptical premises to traditional works. The next chapter takes up three thinkers whose volleys against seventeenth-century rationalism are still compelling and supply models to which I shall often refer. The third is the only chapter not centering on a few major writers; the controversies studied there are inherently fascinating and furnish a larger intellectual context for what follows. I have contrived the chapters so that even an unspecialized reader might be able to dip into only one or two; but the book is, I hope, more than a sum of its parts, and I have not scrupled to refer in one section to matters into which I have entered more fully in another. I have tried to aim at the generally educated reader as well as the specialist, but not, frankly, at the tyro for whom Thomas Browne is an unknown personage and *Deist* an esoteric term. I have attended more to the texts themselves than to social or biographical background, and my interpretations claim to be nothing more than treatments of particular aspects.

It is not so controversial, I suppose, for an academic to discuss such subjects nowadays as it was half a century ago when Kittredge wrote the disclaimer and Foerster the complaint printed at the head of this section. But then Kittredge was only dissociating himself from the credulous, egregiously tory, books of Montague Summers, while Foerster was bemoaning the absence of any literary criticism in Kittredge's masterly but austere study. Still, some modern academics writing on such matters seem over-fearful of being taken for cranks, one of them going so far as to stigmatize Summers, long resting in peace, as "benighted" — Summers, whose ax-grinding, compared to that of many a punctilious whig critic, is no more obtrusive and at least as candid.[6] Let it be known, then, that I am no theosophist and have the greatest respect for philosophical skepticism, especially for its most notable and subtle adherent, David Hume. But I am no rationalist either. The experience of the holy and

---

[6]See Wayne Shumaker, *The Occult Sciences in the Renaissance* (Berkeley: Univ. of California Press, 1972), 79–80.

the daemonic is rooted in the human character and shoots through the highest as well as the humblest literature and art, ancient and modern. Voltaire, who finally became quite a bore with his "Écrasez l'Infâme," could no more extirpate it than he could obliterate the reputation of that buffoon, William Shakespeare.

CHAPTER I

The Plurality of Brave New Worlds: the Numen and the Lumen

Canst thou draw out leviathan with a hook? or his tongue with a cord which thou lettest down?

Job

The assertions of Christianity, when freed from their mythological incrustations . . . happen unfortunately to be true. Our universe is the universe of Behemoth and Leviathan, not of Helvetius and Godwin.

ALDOUS HUXLEY

WHEN IN *The Tempest* Miranda marvels at the diversity of life beyond her island home, she exclaims: "O brave new world / That has such people in't!" "Tis new to thee," says Prospero, mingling paternal affection with a dulcet irony. Although his rejoinder is less often quoted than Miranda's interjection, one is apt to recall it when encountering yet another inventory of "new world-views" hatched by the Enlightenment, the Restoration, or the Renaissance. In fact the idea of a "brave new world" is nowadays seldom treated with much grandiosity or hopefulness. The title of Louis I. Bredvold's belligerent tory study, *The Brave New World of the Enlightenment*, is flagrantly ironic, as is that of Aldous Huxley's famous utopian nightmare, which shows the dehumanizing propensities of technological positivism. I tend to view the phrase ironically myself, partly because I am unable to share the whig critics' zeal for a world wrought by the *philosophes*. But it strikes me as ironic for a less private reason. I had originally thought to argue that in the eighteenth century there was a decisive break between an older supernatural and a newer naturalistic or positivist point of view. The more I studied, however, the more I realized that the incubative phase of the Enlightenment has

[9]

been pushed back further and further by scholars, some glimps-
ing it in the Restoration; some in the Renaissance with Montaigne's famous *Apologie de Raymond Sebond;* some in the Paduan school and its most exorbitant pupil, Giordano Bruno; some
in the fourteenth century when learning began to migrate from
monastery to urban university. Some, finally, have spied it in
the nominalism of Averroes (1120–1198), whose skepticism
influenced the Paduan school. For that matter rationalism and
skepticism are readily endenizened in the classical period, with
Pyrrho, Sextus Empiricus, Lucretius. So I abandoned a thesis
that was neither original nor, as I decided, significantly true,
concluding that rational and non-rational expressions are found
at any time, though in different shapes and percentages. I realized, too, that one must draw distinctions between the intelligentsia and the populace, for what prevails in one quarter may
not prevail in another, nor do attitudes obtaining in intellectual
circles inevitably sift down to the vulgar, as it is sometimes
alleged. For example, aristocratic libertinism in the Restoration
never inveigled the people and was itself counteracted by the
revival of official morality in the early eighteenth century.

While I was thus floundering about, however, one stubborn
fact remained before me. A rationalistic, anti-religious spirit
does dominate the intelligentsia today. This spirit manifests
itself in the premises and procedures of hard and soft sciences
alike; it has insinuated itself into the humanities; it has given
contemporary society its technological tone or drift. Despite
crannies of reaction or resistance, its power operates even among
the masses, though to be sure I am speaking only of the developed countries. The very difficulty I am about to discuss, the
perplexity experienced but not always recognized by modern
critics when they seek to interpret traditional literature, shows
that a new world has indeed been born. Whether it is a world
presided over by officious but benign Prosperos, or just Calibans
slouching toward their destiny, is a question beyond my ability
or desire to resolve.

My purpose in this chapter is to illustrate and define the

beliefs and principles to be traced in this study. At the same time, I shall glance at a few of the misreadings of older works perpetrated by modern critics: for surely some of these commentators are as naive as Miranda, genuinely unaware that the intellectual island they inhabit is still relatively new and, measured against the continent of human history, small. I should like to look at John Donne and *Job*. The first is often taken as a gloomy herald of the brave new world, while *Job* promotes those beliefs that it found most odious.

¤

Most studies of seventeenth-century intellectual history sooner or later mention Donne's famous remark in *The First Anniversary* (1611):

> And new Philosophy calls all in doubt,
> The Element of fire is quite put out;
> The Sun is lost; and th'earth, and no mans wit
> Can well direct him where to looke for it.
> And freely men confesse that this world's spent,
> When in the Planets, and the Firmament
> They seeke so many new; they see that this
> Is crumbled out againe to his Atomies.
> 'Tis all in peeces, all cohaerence gone;
> All just supply, and all Relation:

What, precisely, is Donne saying? We are usually told that Donne, an inhabitant of the traditional, tidy, divinely sanctioned universe, is dismayed by the naturalistic and skeptical implications of the new science. These caused him "distress and confusion," or were "profoundly upsetting" to him; he is "appalled at the destruction of order"; or he is lamenting that the cosmos now has been deprived of meaning; he is describing the "malaise" ushered in with the ascendance of revolutionary

[11]

Copernicanism.[1] Is he, then, some Jacobean Yeats, lamenting in
his quaint language: "Things fall apart; the centre cannot hold"?
In truth Donne's poem, though an elegy, does not elegize the
desuetude of an established religious view, but rather the death
of an individual. Of course it has a wider theme: man's lapse
from innocence and his mounting depravity. The earlier part of
the poem culminating in this celebrated passage expounds a perfectly orthodox view of the degeneracy of man and his world as
a consequence of the Fall and Original Sin. The doubt and apparent disorder caused by the new philosophy is but another symptom of man's intellectual corruption. Most commentators cease
quoting the passage where I have left off, but it is a trifle odd to
stop at a colon. The poem continues:

> Prince, Subject, Father, Sonne, are things forgot,
> For every man alone thinkes he hath got
> To be a Phoenix, and that then can bee
> None of that kinde, of which he is, but hee.

In other words: "Every man thinks he has come to be a Phoenix
(preferring private judgment to authority) and that then comparison ceases, for there is nothing of the same kind with which
to compare himself. There is nothing left to reverence."[2] Donne
is not expressing belief in the new philosophy; he is not saying
that we should be distressed, or fear it, because it *may* be true.
The new philosophy is only the bad fruit of our degeneracy,
and if we are disturbed by it, that is because it has contributed
to social and ethical anarchy, to rampant individualism, to a

---

[1]See: Basil Willey, *The Seventeenth Century Background* (1934; rpt. New
York: Doubleday, no date), 15; Baumer, *Religion and the Rise of Scepticism*,
92; Marjorie Hope Nicolson, *Mountain Gloom and Mountain Glory* (1959;
rpt. New York: W. W. Norton, 1963), 271 (and cf. her *Breaking of the Circle*
[1960; rpt. New York and London: Columbia Univ. Press, 1962] 120–22); Peter
Gay, *The Enlightenment*, I, 314; Alan G.R. Smith, *Science and Society in the
Sixteenth and Seventeenth Centuries* (London: Harcourt Brace Jovanovich,
1972), 161.

[2]Herbert J.C. Grierson's gloss in his *Poems of John Donne* (Oxford: Oxford
Univ. Press, 1912), II, 190. All quotations of Donne are from this edition.

denial of the holy. The theme is very like that of Ulysses's signal speech in *Troilus and Cressida*, I, iii, with the new philosophy as merely a new eruption of chaos. When in *The Second Anniversary* Donne returns to the new science, he contemptuously contrasts the trivial knowledge it affords with the intuitive understanding conferred on us in the afterlife:

> Thou look'st through spectacles; small things seem great
> Below; But up unto the watch-towre get,
> And see all things despoyl'd of fallacies:
> Thou shalt not peepe through lattices of eyes,
> Nor heare through Labyrinths of eares, nor learne
> By circuit, or collections to discerne.
> In heaven thou straight know'st all, concerning it,
> And what concernes it not, shalt straight forget.

"It was not of religion he doubted but of science, of human knowledge with its uncertainties, its shifting theories, its concern about the unimportant." Thus states Grierson, Donne's first scholarly editor, many years since.[3]

Grierson was of an older generation, and nimble-witted critics now have discerned in the passage from *The First Anniversary* a premonition that the new world of science and skepticism is displacing the old, ordered world of faith. Where Grierson sees contempt, they find fear and confusion. But the fear and confusion they find is their own, and to foist it on Donne they must blink the transparent irony of his famous passage. Donne issues a lament, not for the old way passing, but for the old way continuing: that is to say, for man's inveterate drift into egotism and blasphemy. In the olden times we threw up towers of Babel or, like Job's friends, tried to ensnare God in human concepts; now we toy with a new philosophy. I am not saying, of course, that Donne failed to see the new science as potentially destructive; I am arguing that he saw it as trumpery, just another instance of man's "vain imaginings," and that it did not cause in him or, so far as one can tell from the poem, in anyone else

---

[3]Ibid., xxviii.

a crisis of faith. For Donne, the brave new world of science and naturalism is not an intellectual threat, though it may be a threat of the sort that Voegelin, Bredvold, and Aldous Huxley see. It is the latest specimen of man's pride of intellect, when he denies his dependency on God and tries to create a world evacuated of the transcendent and the holy. Donne wrestled with God but not, I think, with belief in God.

◻

To emancipate man from the tyranny of Jehovah, who is but a projection of man's own fears and the hugger-muggery of superstition: this was the prime motive of the rationalists. This is the stimulus behind their attacks on priestcraft, the Bible, belief in Providence or the daemonic and miraculous in life. It is this that actuated Voltaire to scribble on his letters his motto or slogan, *Écrasez l'Infâme*, Crush out the Infamy (i.e., the Christian church). Of all the stories in the Judaeo-Christian tradition, none more offends against these views than the *Book of Job*. Conventional preachers interpret it to mean that we should submit to God's providence, but this is too jejune a gloss, for the concept of providence is intertwined with that of justice, and it is precisely the apparent injustice of the world that Job questions and that God, presumably, fails to answer. Victorian Idealists such as Josiah Royce assure us that God is in fact one with Job, that Job's sufferings are God's, and that this suffering is required for God's perfection. But this account, though more sophisticated than the conventional preacher's, is hardly less evasive, and in any event it slights the text, which clearly affirms that God is *not* Job but terrifyingly *other* than Job. Modern, secular humanists such as John Ciardi cynically repudiate God's reply to Job: "[Job] had asked for justice, and he had been answered with Size." Modern, liberal theologians see the message as simply "obeisance before an arbitrary and heartless Cosmic Power."[4] Archibald MacLeish updates it in *J. B.* as a humanist

---

[4]John Ciardi, "The Birth of a Classic," reprinted in *The Voice out of the Whirlwind: The Book of Job*, ed. Ralph E. Hone (New York: Chandler, 1960), 278; Henry P. Van Dusen, "J. B. and Job," reprinted in ibid., 296.

manifesto: Job in effect *forgives* God in the end; except for human love, God himself would not exist. But all of these views, from the conventionally pious to the conventionally humanistic, distort or disdain the text, and finally are no more persuasive — certainly no more consoling — than the sardonic hermeneutics of Thomas Hobbes, who finds in *Job* that the right by which God rules us is not his love, but his power, that obedience to his power is our highest worship, not love or gratitude, and hence that God has "justified the Affliction by arguments drawn from his Power."[5]

The skeptical modern humanist or intellectual descendant of Voltaire might well accept the rigor of Hobbes's logic but reject his authoritarian conclusions, as if to say, "God may be so, but *I* at least shall not worship him." The modern religious man, however, will be troubled by Hobbes's logic, and he may also wonder why, if that is the gist of *Job*, the book has haunted man's mind so long and so relentlessly. Hobbes's error lies in his verb *justify*, for God is not striving to justify himself in that work, or to furnish us with a theodicy or an intellectually comprehensible scheme. Rather, he exhibits to Job something of his ineffability, mystery, and power. Even before God appeared out of the whirlwind "Job already knew that God was big." This is Ciardi's complaint. But there are different ways of knowing things and different sorts of bigness. Job's friends have a theoretical knowledge of God's ways, and they are by no means fatuous arguers; in Lamb's fine phrase, they are superficially omniscient. But neither they nor Job have an adequate understanding of Yahweh, for they fail to grasp fully his transcendence and majesty. Thus the theme of *Job* is by its very nature incommunicable in satisfactory conceptual terms. No work better exemplifies MacLeish's own famous aphorism: "A poem should not mean / But be."

As critics and readers, however, we have an itch to analyse, and the commentary by Rudolf Otto is the best to my mind. For Otto, God's reply to Job out of the whirlwind is one of "the most remarkable [passages] in the history of religion." The poet has

---

[5]*Leviathan,*. Ch. 31.

affirmed, not just God's power and wisdom, but his mystery and awesomeness. But why does the writer so dilate on the ostrich, the wild ass, the behemoth and the leviathan? Some of these are *big*, to be sure, and so far one agrees with Ciardi. But they are also ungainly, inutile, weird; we can neither ride them with comfort, control them with security, nor eat them with gratification. Indeed, we can have nothing to do with them, for they were not made for us, and to inquire into their existence were vain. They show forth not only God's power but his great fecundity, and teach us that the being and mind of God are beyond mensuration; he is the *wholly other*. Moreover, Job feels an inward calmness and peace after the theophany; Hobbes's tyrant-god might well have struck him dumb or dead. In addition to God's power and incomprehensibility the passage conveys "an *intrinsic value* in the incomprehensible — a value inexpressible, positive, and 'fascinating.'"[6] God may show himself to man in diverse forms. To Job he has shown himself in his numinous or daemonic form, and so has convinced Job that he is not only *big* but ineffable, not only powerful but wondrous, and that we are totally dependent upon him. This is not "justification" in the usual sense, but neither is it brow-beating or bullying; such a view is inadequate to the power of the text; it would be like calling *Lear* "a study in filial ingratitude."

In theme, the *Book of Job* resembles Donne's *First Anniversary*, and both have been distorted in similar ways by those who cannot or will not abide their non-rational implications. For the author of *Job*, as for Donne, man is important and complicated, but he is finally limited and weak compared with divinity, spinning out theories, like Job's "comforters" and Donne's new philosophers, to drape over his radical incomprehension, his physical and intellectual frailty. Job wishes, in Donne's vein, to be a phoenix in his heart, "preferring private judgment to authority." Yet for many modern interpreters *Job* is, in its "true" or esoteric significance, skeptical and humanistic, while Donne,

---

[6]Rudolf Otto, *The Idea of the Holy*, tr. John W. Harvey (1923; rpt. London: Oxford Univ. Press, 1958), 80 (italics Harvey's).

prescient of Matthew Arnold or Yeats, is the threnodist of a decaying faith.

◻

However *Job* be interpreted, it is surely the *locus classicus* for the experience of the holy. Rudolf Otto, a theologian, has provided the classic modern study in his *Idea of the Holy* (1917), but it is a subject that has intrigued psychologists such as Carl Jung, sociologists such as Emile Durkheim, and literary men such as Arthur Machen, John Crowe Ransom, and C. S. Lewis. Because the experience so stubbornly resists discursive treatment, I thought it best to begin with an actual example in *Job*. I should like now to define three terms central to this book: the numinous, the daemonic, and the holy.

"Numinous" derives from the Latin *Numen* or Divine Presence. It is not perhaps an elegant coinage, but it seems indispensable, since a numinous experience is quite different in kind, not merely in intensity, from the more mundane order. It is a theophany, but one invested with a sense of fear and awe, of utter dependence and even subjugation. This fear or dread is not like natural fear, for it is imbued with the weird, the eerie, the uncanny. But like natural fear, it can assume a major or a minor form. Still, it remains distinctive. For example, our shudder at a well-told ghost story, though less urgent than our natural fear in a burning building, remains nevertheless different in kind: it is a minor numinous feeling. So intensity is not essential to the numinous itself, although the most striking instances, like Job's, will naturally be intense. At its strongest, it shows the Numen as a *mysterium tremendum*: it is a Presence uniting mystery and transcendence with energy, vitality, force. Above all, it is *wholly other*, for the creature must be awed by the great distance between him and the Numen. Yet he also feels a fascination, a captivating ravishment: despite his fear and awe, the creature is irresistably drawn toward the Numen, as the source of his being. Finally, the creature must feel an humility, an unworthiness or even sinfulness, not because he has transgressed any particular moral law, but because of a natural recognition of his insufficiency and, compared with the divine, profaneness. However, the Numen itself may be non-moral, at least in the more primitive stages of religious consciousness. This numinous feeling, Otto contends, is a priori; it is a primal instinct, feeling, or need. Of course to say it is a priori is not to say it is innate: not everyone *has* such a feeling, just as not everyone responds to music; but every normal human has the capacity to have it. It obtains not only in primitive societies but in the rituals and observances of the most refined religions. Even in secularized societies it is ventilated in the occult, ghost and horror stories, political and sexual fanaticisms.

Despite the dread and sense of profaneness, a numinous experience can be rapturous and pure; as such it is the stuff of mysticism. It can also adopt horrible and daemonic forms. The word *daemon* or *demon* has several meanings pertinent to this study. Commonly today it means "fiend" or "devil," and even in this sense it retains something of the weird and uncanny. The Greek *daimon* is something rather, but not altogether, different: it is neither god nor anti-god, but a kind of pre-god, "the numen," Otto says, "at a lower stage." It was of course a sort of conscience or spiritual guide for Socrates, but Otto identifies as the most authentic form of these daemons "those strange deities of ancient Arabia, which are properly nothing but wandering demonstrative pronouns," having no specific shape or mythology, but nonetheless felt as mighty forces. *Daemon* can be applied to the human character, too. In this sense, as John Crowe Ransom puts it, "each demon stood for the secret, or ineffable, or transcendental individuality of some individual and private person," and it makes for that person's inexhaustible and unpredictable variety. The personal daemon is analogous to the numen as wholly other: "A demon is the embodiment of variety and freedom who resists determination."[7] The daemonic, either in its

[7]John Crowe Ransom, *God Without Thunder* (New York: Harcourt, Brace, 1930), 287, 291. Differing from Otto, however, Ransom thinks even the New Testament has diluted the numinous too much; but he is a good complement in that he shrewdly applies Otto's thesis to modern expressions of Christianity.

personal or transcendental sense, is mysterious, energetic, non-rational, non-moral. Otto suggests that at an early stage of religious consciousness the daemonic may be closely joined with the numinous as expressing the Numen's horrendousness and ethically ambiguous vitality. In the creature it is the "Dionysiac" or frenzied element, as contrasted with the rational, orderly, "Apollonian" side. When alluding to actual fiends or devils, or to their possession of human beings, I shall use *demon, demonic*. In all other instances, in consideration of clarity and etymology, I shall use *daemon, daemonic*.

The numinous feeling presupposes the existence of the holy or sacred, but the holy is different: the holy refers to the Numen as it begins to acquire moral attributes. The Old Testament Yahweh often seems wayward and arbitrary, a true *deus absconditus* who enforces his will by his arcane power, who is neither complaisant nor to be approached, who is not to be judged by human principles; hence we hear much of the "wrath of God." But even in the Pentateuch the Numen begins to be rationalized and moralized; this tendency winds through the prophets and is reified in the gospels. This moralizing is not, Otto argues, bad, but a normal and healthy development of the numinous experience, which always remains its basis. By the time of *Job*, there is a sense that a distinct *value* is to be attached to the Numen, and the New Testament elucidates still more the love and goodness of Yahweh. But Otto observes that the elements of awe and dread are not abandoned in the New Testament, but supplemented. True, the fierce mountain-god of Moses is now newly shown in the Son, but Christ's Kingdom remains the "wholly other"; Christ in Gethsemane exhibits, not natural fear, but awe of the creature before the *mysterium tremendum*; the drama of the crucifixion and resurrection preserves all the elements of the Old Testament numinous. Pentecost shows the daemonic in both its transcendental and personal forms. Otto believes that some later modes of Christianity, enfeebled by Aristotle and the schoolmen, have carried the rationalizing too far, and that attempts to theologize, or petrify in conceptions, the Numen can dessicate or trivialize the religious experience, sundering it

[19]

from its true foundation in the numinous itself. We must recognize, he says, the inevitably non-rational ground of religious feeling. At the same time, we have been given reason and should use it. This we have done as we evolved profound ethical notions out of the numinous experience: "Strongly excited feeling of the numen, that runs to [daemonic] frenzy, untempered by the more rational elements of religious experience — that is everywhere the very essence of Fanaticism." Since it is easier to dramatize these states through myth and narrative than through discursive prose, some references to contemporary fiction may be helpful. Mary Renault's novel *The King Must Die* gives several instances of primitive daemonic and pre-moral, or only vaguely moral, numinous experience, as does Arthur Machen's grimly beautiful *Hill of Dreams*. C. S. Lewis's *Till We Have Faces* shows the emergence in an individual personality of the moral from the non-moral numinous; in effect, we are shown a sense of the holy flowering from what had been only a sense of the daemonic.

☐

This feeling or sentiment does not, of course, prove God, though if it be a priori, as Otto argues, it might indeed be offered in *evidence*. (The psychologists, no doubt, can contrive other explanations of its existence.) I am only asserting here that it *does* exist, as witnessed by myths, religions, literature and art, individual testimony. The new world of the *philosophes* evicts the sentiment as superstitious and absurd, and for this reason I am nearly persuaded, with Peter Gay, that the Enlightenment does not constitute a new religion; such feeling shrivels beneath — or perhaps merely eludes? — its luminous glare. That the sentiment will erupt anyway, however, is superbly illustrated by the Festival of Liberty and Reason celebrated in the Cathedral of Notre Dame on 10 November 1793 (or the twentieth Brumaire, Year II, as the new cultists would have it). A Greek temple was erected in the cathedral and decorated with busts of the famous *philosophes* and their alleged precursors.

The ceremony was garnished with liturgy and hymns, and Notre Dame itself was soon rebaptized by the Constitutional Convention as the Temple of Reason. Now it may well be that this was no new religion but a pitiable parody of the old. Yet its attempt is patent to accommodate the desire for the Holy, and examples might easily be multiplied from the secularized societies of our own age.

Many modern thinkers, not least Jung, Ransom, Lewis, have deplored the decline, or perhaps one should say the frustration, of a sense of the numinous in our time. Even sociologists partial to agnosticism such as Durkheim and Max Weber have noted with concern the "rationalization" of society; i.e., the bureaucratizing, impersonalizing, disenchanting forces operating in all of the "advanced" communities. At the same time, whig theories of progressivism have come increasingly under attack — most notably in the area of science by Thomas S. Kuhn. It used complacently to be thought that the sentiment described by Otto was merely a survival of primitive animism, when man naively ascribed consciousness and divinity to all objects.[8] But even from a rationalist perspective the matter is not so simply decided. Animism can *itself* be viewed as an early attempt to conceptualize experiences and perceptions lying deep within the soul. Animism, then, may be an awkward attempt to understand the numinous, rather than the numinous being a relic or vestige of animism. One might note, too, that Otto's psychological conjectures have been supported by Jung, who postulates three stages in the human perception of God: at first good and evil are undifferentiated (this is like Otto's primitive, non-moral Numen); next, a benevolent God and a retributive Demon or Anti-god are increasingly separated. Indeed, such distance now lies between them that the secular mind, even the modern Christian, can scarcely entertain the traditional image of the Divine Father as at once loving and protecting, yet also awe-

[8]For a recent example of this argument, see Wayne Shumaker, *The Occult Sciences in the Renaissance* (Berkeley: Univ. of California Press, 1972), 225 and passim.

some, full of authority, exacting obedience.[9] Jung envisages a
third stage when good and evil would somehow be reconciled,
but of course he is constrained to admit that there are so far no
cultural manifestations of such a stage. A recent book argues
persuasively for the ambivalence of deities in ancient Eastern
and classical religions, and it traces the "twinning" or "splitting
off" from the Godhead of evil principles. *Job* shows the incipience of this "twinning": in Jungian terms, Satan is God's
shadow, his dark side, his destructive power (like the Destroying Angel in *Exodus*). Not yet the fallen archangel, he is intimate with God; but he is also God's opponent and, perhaps, his
rival.[10] The holy and the daemonic are ineluctably if enigmatically linked: *Sine Diabolo nullus Deus.*

"The new philosophy calls all in doubt," wrote Donne in
1611. But then we have always had new philosophies and brave
new worlds. Sometimes the new is supernaturalism opposing
naturalism (as primitive Christianity against Greek rationalism
or the civil religion of Rome); in the eighteenth century it was
supernaturalism against skepticism; in the nineteenth it was
"natural supernaturalism" against positivism.[11] There are
moments when one is tempted to agree with Sir Thomas
Browne: "opinions doe find after certain revolutions, men and
mindes like those that first begot them. . . . There have beene
many *Diogenes*, and as many *Timons*, though but few of that
name; men are lived over againe, the world is now as it was in
ages past." "Man is a great deep," says St. Augustine, "whose
very hairs you have numbered, O Lord, nor are they lost in your
sight; and yet it were easier to number the hairs of his head
then the affections and movements of his heart." I have taken
this as the motto of my book, asserting as it does the transcen-

[9]See Harry Blamires, *The Christian Mind* (1963; rpt. Ann Arbor: Servant
Books, 1978), 136–38.

[10]See Jeffrey Burton Russell, *The Devil: Perceptions of Evil from Antiquity
to Primitive Christianity* (Ithaca: Cornell Univ. Press, 1977). See also R. S.
Kluger, *Satan in the Old Testament*, tr. H. Nagel (Evanston, Ill: Northwestern
Univ. Press, 1967).

[11]See M. H. Abrams, *Natural Supernaturalism* (New York: Norton, 1971).

dence yet nearness of God, and the baffling intricacy of man: the daemonic, that is, in its divine and human shapes. Some of the writers featured here are orthodox, others heterodox, in their beliefs; some are masterly, others slip-shod, in their art. But most of them are close to Augustine in this, and even the more distant, I think — Hume, say, or Blake — might concede, however regretfully, the truth of his view of man.

CHAPTER II

High Doctrines of the Holy: The Supposed Fideism of Sir Thomas Browne, Dryden, and Pascal

We destroy arguments and every proud obstacle to the knowledge of God, and take every thought captive to obey Christ.

II *Corinthians*

I perceive every man's own reason is his best Oedipus.

Sir Thomas Browne

DONNE'S CONTEMPTUOUS DISMISSAL of the new philosophy had behind it the authority of a strong character, but less robust souls craved a more methodical attack. The defenders of religion can be classed as follows. There were the Deists, who attempted to ground religion on reason. At best a shivery compromise with rationalism, Deism failed to flourish and was moribund by the middle of the eighteenth century. Opposing the Deists were Fideists, for whom, despairing altogether of reason, supernatural revelation and dogma were the foundations of faith. But Fideism is a radical position, as close to skepticism as Deism to rationalism. Declared heretical long before the seventeenth century by the Roman church, Fideism too often keeps company with fanaticism or wanton, intellectual self-indulgence. Serious religious thinkers have always been wary of it, for every Fideist may be a clandestine skeptic, and to abandon reason entirely seems a drastic course. Finally, there was the *via media* or middle way, much trod by moderates who tried to poise the claims of reason against those of revelation. This group included many Anglicans, some Puritans, the Christian Platonists, most seventeenth-century scientists. But the unpleasant name for a moderate is "trimmer": one who may incline to one side or another as interest, rather than principle, prompts. And our intellectual history suggests that the middle road of pragmatism or prudence does not unfailingly lead to wisdom. There are, then, dangers lurking in all three postures even as there are dangers in such positions as agnosticism, nihilism, or indifference.

Browne, Dryden, and Pascal have all been charged with Fideism,[1] and to be sure they all affirm a high doctrine of the holy in defiance of the claims of rationalism. But *Fideism* is an oily term. To a rationalist all believers, finally, are Fideists, whether they overtly disdain reason or, like the trimmer, twist it to support an illogical belief in Deity. Then too, few admit to being Fideists, and anyone who employs argument in defense of religion considers himself rational. Many reputable philosophers and theologians have thought that reason properly includes the intuition and conscience, and if that be so, *Fideism* becomes a particularly gauzy and hazardous term. Pascal, for example, asserts: "The heart has its reasons, of which reason knows nothing"; or again: "It is the heart, not reason, which experiences God. This then is faith: God perceived by the heart and not by reason." Wrenched from the context of Pascal's thought and rendered into modern English, these remarks may seem fideistic. But by "heart" Pascal does not mean just the emotions: he is referring to intuitive elements of knowing, which are contrasted, not with "reason" in general, but with discursive, abstract, analytical reason. Like Aristophanes in *The Clouds*, Pascal opposes a more expansive definition of reason to a narrower one; and he is on the same side as Aristophanes. A neosophist or positivist may pooh-pooh the intuitions as epistemologically inane, but others will respond that nothing is more irrational than to dismiss such immediate and vivid experiences as empty, that one is truly rational in recognizing them as informative if ambivalent pieces of evidence.

---

[1]See, e.g., such standard works as Louis I. Bredvold, *The Intellectual Milieu of John Dryden* (Ann Arbor: Univ. of Michigan Press, 1934) and Franklin L. Baumer, *Religion and the Rise of Scepticism* (1960).

The line between the Fideist and the more orthodox middle-of-the-roader is exceeding fine, so fine that the precisian might expel "Fideist" from the language as superfluous. Indeed the more closely one peers at a supposed Fideist, if he is a substantial thinker, the more inutile that label is apt to seem. Thus a highly respected authority, in a book on Swift, casually classes Dryden as a Fideist, but a few years later, in a book on Dryden, insists that he is not.[2]

It remains, nevertheless, that Browne, Dryden, and Pascal are routinely labeled Fideists. All wrote on religion in the middle part of the seventeenth century; all were influenced, if obscurely, by Montaigne and skeptical traditions; all were very familiar with the new philosophy; all were soldiers who even now are marshaled against the forces of materialism and positivism.[3] None of them, I shall argue, is a convicted Fideist, but they do tend to promote the non-rational and numinous elements of religion and to defend these against the rationalists and forerunners of the Enlightenment. In such writers, then, we can observe the earlier maneuvers in a war as yet unresolved.

⌗

A heavier charge than Fideism has been brought against Sir Thomas Browne: frivolousness. We are told that his style was more important than his substance, the latter being dismissed as "wanton ingenuity of thought," or "wonder-mongering," or "lacking in solid content, and [verging] into the pure emotionalism of music." He is always compared unfavorably with Pascal. His religion is irrational, irresponsible, puerile, merely aesthetic and recreative, altogether unphilosophical. He is "content

[2]See: Phillip Harth, *Swift and Anglican Rationalism* (Chicago: Univ. of Chicago Press, 1961), 22, and *Contexts of Dryden's Thought* (Chicago: Univ. of Chicago Press, 1968), 97–106.

[3]For example, the conservative neo-humanists Paul Elmer More and Prosser Hall Frye wrote long, polemical essays on Browne and Pascal; Bredvold, in the study mentioned above, clearly identifies himself with Dryden's Toryism; T. S. Eliot has written sympathetically of Pascal and Dryden.

to play among the fragments of the medieval system."[4] As one might expect in the case of such an apparently whimsical person, a phalanx of critics have sought, in vain, his pigeon-hole. F. L. Huntley asserts that Browne's skepticism "leads to fideism," but some pages later decides that he "subscribed to the universal laws of human reason." James N. Wise finds that in Browne "reason becomes transmuted into faith" — a conclusion that, despite the impressive verb, does not seem very helpful; and on the same page Wise speaks, a shade esoterically, of Browne's "flexibility of fideism." In the hands of his commentators he appears a veritable Proteus or shape-shifter, and it is no wonder that they exhibit, both individually and collectively, a marked flexibility of interpretation.[5]

Of all English writers in the century, Browne is one of the best at evoking, in thought and style, a sense of wonder and the transcendent. Such writers are often unsystematic, and so they are often pounced on as irresponsible. Latterly Browne's reputation as a thinker has been rising, even as those aspects of religion that he prized are again pressing into favor. But his mysticism continues either to be derided as merely epicurean or defended, feebly enough, as "artistic."[6] Browne is certainly eclectic, possibly inconsistent, often unclear. Yet I take him to be a serious thinker, however disheveled or opaque his theology,

---

[4]See: Edmund Gosse, *Sir Thomas Browne* (New York: Macmillan, 1905), 192; P. H. Frye, *Visions & Chimeras* (1929; rpt. New York: Biblo and Tannen, 1966), 193–94; P. E. More, *Shelburne Essays*, VI (New York: G. P. Putnam's, 1909), 173; Dewey Kiper Ziegler, *In Divided and Distinguished Worlds* (Cambridge, Mass: Harvard Univ. Printing Office, 1943), 90. Phillip Harth, in the same work where he retracts his charge of Fideism against Dryden, makes it against Browne; see *Contexts of Dryden's Thought*, 103–104.

[5]See: Frank L. Huntley, *Sir Thomas Browne* (Cambridge, Eng.: Cambridge Univ. Press, 1962), 182, 240; James N. Wise, *Sir Thomas Browne's "Religio Medici" and Two Seventeenth-Century Critics* (Columbia: Univ. of Missouri Press, 1973), 28. For sensible, general discussions of Browne see: William P. Dunn, *Sir Thomas Browne: A Study in Religious Philosophy* (Minneapolis: Univ. of Minn. Press, 1950) and Joan Bennett, *Sir Thomas Browne* (Cambridge, Eng.: Cambridge Univ. Press, 1962).

[6]See Ziegler, 49, and Wise, 30.

[27]

however extravagant or playful his style. Since I shall rest most of my argument on the *Religio Medici* (1642, 1643), it will be well to remember that this was a youthful work, a personal statement of faith not originally intended for publication. It has a loose, associationist structure that makes precise paraphrase risky, but of all his works it is the most pertinent to this study. I should like to examine his most developed remarks on the nature of man, human reason, God, and the creation.

A clear supernaturalist, Browne subscribes to the traditional understanding of the chain of being or, as he terms it, the "manifest Scale of creatures, rising not disorderly, or in confusion, but with a comely method and proportion" from the lowest of creation through man and the angels to God (*Religio Medici*, Part I, Section 33).[7] Man occupies a middle place, partly in the corporeal, partly in the spiritual realm; he is thus "that great and true *Amphibium*, whose nature is disposed to live not onely like other creatures in divers elements, but in divided and distinguished worlds" (I, 34). God made the universe not for us but for his own glory, and the angels are incomparably above us (I, 35). Browne stresses the inscrutability of God's creation, and especially of man. Unlike Hobbes, he affirms the immateriality of spirit, and unlike Descartes, he can pinpoint no organ of the reason or the soul: "Thus we are men, and we know not how; there is something in us, that can be without us, and will be after us" (I, 36). Man and his destiny are enigmatic: "There is therefore a secret glome or bottome of our dayes. . . . wee are not onely ignorant in Antipathies and occult qualities, our ends are as obscure as our beginnings; the line of our dayes is drawne by night, and the various effects therein by a pencill that is invisible" (I, 43). So fragile, weak, and dependent are we on God that

---

[7]All quotations from Browne are from *The Prose of Sir Thomas Browne*, ed. Norman Endicott (New York: Doubleday, 1967). Specific references to chapters or sections are provided in the text. Most of the people taken up in this study professed belief in some version of the chain of being, a concept thoroughly studied by Arthur O. Lovejoy, *The Great Chain of Being* (1936; rpt. N.Y.: Harper and Row, 1960). Another important, contemporary expression of the idea is in *Paradise Lost*, V, 470–90.

we should be happy that we can die but once (I, 44). That very dependence makes atheists absurd: "For to desire there were no God, were plainly to unwish their own being; which must needs be annihilated in the substraction of that essence, which substantially supporteth them, and restrains them from regression into nothing" (*Pseudodoxia Epidemica,* Book I, Chapter 10). We are corrupt within, and always in the presence of the Devil and God (*Religio,* II, 10). Yet we are also made in the image of God and capable of true happiness (II, 11). In short, man is a mystery and a paradox, a "Noble Animal, splendid in ashes, and pompous in the grave, solemnizing Nativities and Deaths with equal lustre, not omitting Ceremonies of bravery, in the infamy of his nature" (*Hydriotaphia,* 5).

This noble animal or amphibium particularly intrigues Browne when it is dreaming, and on that subject there is a notable contrast between him and his contemporary Hobbes. There are those, Hobbes observes in *Leviathan,* who have trouble distinguishing logically between the waking and the dream state. But:

> For my part, when I consider, that in Dreames, I do not often, nor constantly think of the same Persons, Places, Objects, and Actions that I do waking; nor remember so long a trayne of coherent thoughts, Dreaming, as at other times; And because waking I often observe the absurdity of Dreames, but never dream of the absurdities of my waking Thoughts; I am well satisfied, that being awake, I know I dreame not; though when I dreame, I think my selfe awake (*Leviathan,* Ch. 2).

For Browne, however, the relation between waking life and dreams is analogous to that between earthly and heavenly life. Nocturnal phantasms are as delusive as daily conceptions, and, if anything, the night is more real: "we are somewhat more than our selves in our sleepes, and the slumber of the body seems to bee but the waking of the soule. It is the ligation of sense, but the liberty of reason, and our waking conceptions doe not match the fancies of our sleepes" (*Religio,* II, 11). Browne the supernaturalist is distinctly more skeptical of the reality of waking

life than the materialist Hobbes. But he is not licentiously preferring reverie to reality. As the conclusion of the section shows,
sleep is like death in disentangling us from the bonds of our
animal nature and releasing reason from its prison, the passionate body. Browne's view of sleep is not whimsical but wholly
consistent with his view of man. It is in that sense rational,
though there is an implicit appeal to a skepticism more
ingrained than any in Hobbes.

Browne is notorious for his love of mystery and paradox, his
pursuing his reason to an *O altitudo*. He regrets that "there be
not impossibilities enough in Religion for an active faith," and
he rejoices that he did not live in the days of the miracles,
because then it would be too easy to believe (I, 9). "Since I was
of understanding to know we know nothing," he says, "my reason hath beene more pliable to the will of faith" (I, 10). On these
and many kindred passages will the Fideist-hunter gleefully fasten. But ever since Paul, Christians have been told to "take
every thought captive to obey Christ," and though that passage
be recalcitrant to exegesis, it has commonly been construed to
mean that through will we should subordinate our reason to our
faith. In truth Browne seldom deprecates reason. The *Pseudodoxia Epidemica*, published a few years after *Religio Medici*,
applies reason to superstitious or fanciful beliefs. Do the two
books represent, as some critics contend, two sides of that
amphibian Browne: his credulous mediaeval, and modern scientific, mind? Has there been an intellectual emancipation of
mankind, as Buckle suggested in 1857 in his whig *History of
Civilisation*, in the eight years between the two books? In fact,
they are more alike than different. The *Pseudodoxia* is less an
exercise in the Baconian method than a compendium of antiquarian lore. At the outset of the *Religio* Browne tells us he will
use "setled judgement" and "manly reason" to resolve his religious doubts: "for I perceive every mans owne reason is his best
Oedipus, and will . . . find a way to loose bonds wherewith the
subtilties of errour have enchained our more flexible and tender
judgements" (I, 6). He admits that he delights in philosophical
paradoxes, but that in religious matters "I love to keepe the road,

and though not in an implicite, yet an humble faith, follow the great wheele of the Church" (I, 6). Unlike the true Fideist, he recognizes natural religion: there are God's two books of scripture and nature, the second being a "universall and publik Manuscript. . . . those that never saw him in the one, have discovered him in the other" (I, 16). Thus reason, unassisted by revelation, can bring a knowledge of God. He believes that faith, reason, and passion may each rule harmoniously in their proper spheres (I, 19). Just as he uses reason to explode superstition in *Pseudodoxia,* so here he will sometimes use science to support religion (e.g., I, 48).

The two books are the product of the same mind, and that a dexterous but coherent one. Far from being hostile to the new philosophy, Browne is much less contemptuous than Donne: "if any affirm the earth doth move, and will not beleeve with us, it standeth still; because he hath probable reasons for it, and I no infallible sense nor reason against it, I will not quarrell with his assertion." "But," the passage immediately continues, "if like Zeno he shall walk about, and yet deny there is any motion in nature," why then Browne will disbelieve him on rational, empirical grounds (*Pseudodoxia,* I, 5). There is reason, skepticism, and faith in both books, and though Browne will not *quarrel* with the new philosophy, neither will he positively believe. That there is motion, common sense affirms. Whether the earth or the sun move, is a matter to which religious belief — for Browne anyway — is indifferent. Like Donne, then, he recognizes the limits of reason: a rational and indeed a necessary recognition given his view of man. Like Donne, too, he seems curiously blasé about the Copernican revolution. Since one finds similarly casual attitudes in, say, Milton and Cotton Mather, I should like again to argue, in passing, that the impact of that new theory on the seventeenth-century mind has been magnified out of proper proportion by the typical historian of ideas, who trots it out wearisomely, unimaginatively, to explain the intellectual perturbations of the last three centuries. After all, the connections between scientific and religious belief are at best tenuous and obscure. Copernicanism, in point of fact, with its harmonious mathematics, is as compatible with traditional theology as Ptolemy's scheme, while the Ptolemaic astronomy, although it centered Earth, saw our world as sublunary or mutable — low-down in the cosmic hierarchy — and so lends itself as readily to an uncheerful as to an optimistic view of human nature.

The attitudes I have been sketching are not distinctively Fideistic; they are conventional, and I shall be noting many variations on them throughout this book. Although Browne does not deride reason, he is ever aware of that "creature-consciousness," to use Otto's phrase, and that sense of limitation so central to the numinous experience. It may indeed be paradoxical that God should be close to his creation in exhibiting a "perpetuall and waking providence" (*Religio*, I, 43), but yet that there should be an "infinite and incomprehensible distance betwixt the Creator and the creature" (I, 54). But Browne has not contrived the paradox; it is found in Christianity and, according to Otto, in the fundamental religious experience itself. "God hath not made a creature that can comprehend him, 'tis the priviledge of his own nature; *I am that I am*, was his owne definition unto *Moses*; and 'twas a short one, to confound mortalities, that durst question God, or aske him what hee was" (I, 11). Man is a *mortality*, defined by his most insuperable limit, whom God, in defining himself, rebukes for intellectual arrogance. So he had rebuked Job, though there his reply was much longer. Browne's idea of the holy is far from naive and closely related to his style, so often accused of superfluous paradox and vagary.

Here is Browne on predestination:

> and therefore that terrible terme *Predestination*, which hath troubled so many weake heads to conceive, and the wisest to explaine, is in respect to God no prescious determination of our estates to come, but a definitive blast of his will already fulfilled, and at the instant that he first decreed it; for to his eternitie, which is indivisible, and altogether, the last Trumpe is already sounded, the reprobates in the flame, and the blessed in *Abrahams* bosome (*Religio*, I, 11).

Predestination, for Otto, is one of the most telling examples of an arid and unsavoury doctrine that, however, finds a true source in the numinous experience. We are right to feel powerless and subjugated, but have the theologians been right to conceptualize that feeling as they have done? Have they not, in fact, made God appear a "precious determiner," and then, urged by theological protocol, tried to justify the nasty deity they themselves have manufactured? Browne is no such theologian, but tries to reproduce in language the original experience of the *mysterium tremendum*. God's omniscience, conceptualized hideously as a precious determination, is here reinvigorated as "a definitive blast of his will already fulfilled." Browne's critics will say that he has written fine poetry, perhaps, but no serious analysis of predestination. Browne's point, I think, is that a "serious" analysis is vain.

Here is Browne on the spirit of God:

> I am sure there is a common Spirit that playes within us, yet makes no part of us; and that is the Spirit of God, the fire and scintillation of that noble and mighty Essence, which is the life and radicall heat of spirits, and those essences that know not the vertue of the Sunne; a fire quite contrary to the fire of Hell: This is that gentle heate that brooded on the waters, and in six dayes hatched the world; this is that irradiation that dispells the mists of Hell, the clouds of horrour, feare, sorrow, despaire; and preserves the region of the mind in serenity: whosoever feeles not the warme gale and gentle ventilation of this Spirit, (though I feele his pulse) I dare not say he lives; for truely without this, to mee there is no heat under the Tropick; nor any light, though I dwelt in the body of the Sunne (*Religio*, I, 32).

Again, this is no discursive analysis. Human weakness and fear is thrown against the wonder, power, and transcendence of the divine, though, like Augustine, Browne manages to suggest the intimate relation of the two. *Essences, virtue, hatched*, have, beyond their usual connotations, those of alchemy and occul-

[33]

tism. The passage quoted is a part of a sentence, and its rhythms carry us gently from that common spirit that is in us, but no part of us, through a celebration of its vital and sustaining power, to a meditation on our need of the holy. In the earlier passage Browne has properly stressed the *tremendum;* here, as properly, he luxuriates in the *mysterium.* But it is a justifiable luxury. Neither passage is analytic or conceptual, but why should they be? God's foreknowledge, conceptualized, can become monstrous. The spirit of God, conceptualized, can become flattened out as pantheism or vitalism or humanitarianism. If Browne is "wonder-mongering," he is doing so with a purpose: to revive or retrieve a pre-conceptual religious sense. In a way, then, it is true that style is more important than content in Browne; but content can be something other than concepts, and style something more than their garniture.

Sir Kenelm Digby, one of Browne's first critics and a Cartesian rationalist, complained of his "aeryness."[8] So commentators have always had trouble with him, and the numinous and mystical themes, strong in *Religio Medici,* are even more prevalent in some of his later works. One thinks, for example, of his account at the end of *Hydriotaphia* of "Christian annihilation, extasis, exolution, liquefaction, transformation, the kisse of the Spouse, gustation of God, and ingression into the divine shadow." Light was a central image of the divine in the passage quoted earlier from *Religio Medici.* But in *The Garden of Cyrus,* a phantasmagoria of occult and mystical numerology, it gives way to the more profound image of shade:

> Light that makes things seen, makes some things invisible.
> . . . The greatest mystery of Religion is expressed by adumbration, and in the noblest part of Jewish Types, we finde the Cherubims shadowing the Mercy-seat: Life it self is but the shadow of death, and souls departed but the shadows of the living: All things fall under this name. The Sunne it self is

---

[8]See Wise, 63.

but the dark *simulacrum*, and light but the shadow of God (Ch. 4).

One is reminded of his earlier celebration of sleep. Otto has remarked, and Browne instinctively knew, that the numinous is most forcibly conveyed through the imagery of darkness. The clouds of Sinai are more terrible than the burning bush.

Browne's paradoxical and exuberant style reminds us that there is a transcendent realm beyond the stretch of rationalism or the concepts of theology. Rebutting Digby's rationalist criticism of *Religio Medici*, Coleridge astutely notes: "Sir K. Digby's observations are those of a pedant in his own system & opinion. He ought to have considered *Religio Medici* in a dramatic & not in a metaphysical View — as a sweet Exhibition of character & passion, & not as an Expression or Investigation of positive Truth."[9] But even Coleridge, in his "sweet Exhibition" clause, is too depreciatory. And I believe that Browne does express truths, though not, it may be, of the "positive" or discursive variety. The sometimes melancholy, sometimes bustling rhythms of his sentences, the haunting phrases ("There is . . . a secret glome or bottome of our dayes"), the manifold meanings bound up in one word ("the infamy" — i.e., the depravity and the obscurity — "of our nature"), the vividness ("definitive blast of his will"): these are surely the signs of an expressive style. But it is a style aimed at producing in us sentiments of contemplative piety or wonder, and to that end it has subordinated the claims of discursive clarity and precision. The *O altitudos* are not adscititious flights of reverie but inducements to a sense of the numinous. Dramatic, Coleridge's word, is the essential trait of this style.

Browne was not a Fideist: he used, sometimes extolled, reason and believed that religious truths could be drawn from the book of nature as well as from revelation. Those who call him irre-

---

[9]Roberta Florence Brinkley, ed., *Coleridge on the Seventeenth Century* (Durham: Duke Univ. Press, 1955), 438.

sponsible misunderstand him still more grossly; even the modern unsympathetic critics are measuring him, after all, by the standards of Kenelm Digby. It is tempting to see him as a transitional figure between the mediaeval and modern world, but that is finally too facile. Like Donne he is confident in his beliefs, though less belligerent. Like intelligent but pious people in any age, he endeavored to balance his religious intuitions against the proper claims of reason and common sense. He is not a theologian when he writes on religious matters, but a devotional poet.

⛶

John Dryden's *Religio Laici, or A Layman's Faith* (1682) was published forty years after Browne's precocious sally, and between them had intervened another *Religio Laici* (1645) by the deistic Lord Herbert of Cherbury, a *Religio Stoici* (1665), and even a *Religio Clerici* (1681), these titles having been adopted, no doubt, to convey a tone of diffidence and humility. Whether Sir Kenelm Digby would have found Dryden more satisfactory than Browne is unknown, but he could scarcely have charged him with airiness. In some introductory remarks to *Religio Medici* Browne had conceded that: "There are many things delivered Rhetorically, many expressions . . . meerely Tropicall . . . many things to be taken in a soft and flexible sense, and not to be called unto the rigid test of reason." But Dryden, in his own preface, spurns the "Florid, Elevated and Figurative" style for one that is plain, natural, yet majestic. "A Man is to be cheated into Passion," he tells us, "but to be reason'd into Truth."[10]

Dryden, then, is not a devotional but a discursive poet. Yet he too has been declared a Fideist and, more recently and

---

[10]All quotations from Dryden are from *The Poems of John Dryden*, ed. James Kinsley, 4 vols. (Oxford: Clarendon Press, 1958).

[36]

absurdly, a Deist.[11] It seems to me that he is as candid an advocate of the middle way, in *Religio Laici*, as one could ever find,
and just as clearly a non-fideistic convert to Roman Catholicism
in his *Hind and the Panther* (1687). In both poems there is, to
be sure, a skeptical strain. In the Preface to *Religio Laici* he is
decidedly less confident about natural religion than Browne,
who, as we have seen, recognized a "universal and public manuscript" in which anyone might read of God. Instead, Dryden
argues that the "Principles of Natural Worship, are onely the
faint remnants or dying flames of reveal'd Religion in the Posterity of *Noah*." These principles are the "remote effects of Revelation," not the discoveries of autonomous reason. He decides:

> They who wou'd prove Religion by Reason, do but weaken
> the cause which they endeavour to support: 'tis to take away
> the Pillars from our Faith, and to prop it onely with a twig.
> . . . Let us be content at last, to know God, by his own Meth-
> ods; at least so much of him, as he is pleas'd to reveal to us,
> in the sacred Scriptures; to apprehend them to be the word of
> God, is all our Reason has to do; for all beyond it is the work
> of Faith, which is the Seal of Heaven impress'd upon our
> humane understanding.

But he is quite prepared in his preface to marshal reason against
the asperity of the Athanasian creed.

At the outset, Dryden's clear and stately metaphors limn the
relation between faith and reason:

> Dim, as the borrow'd beams of Moon and Stars
> To *lonely, weary, wandring* Travellers,
> Is *Reason* to the *Soul*: And as on high

---

[11]Bredvold, *Intellectual Milieu*, argues for Dryden's Fideism, and this interpretation is reiterated routinely in many standard texts; see, e.g., *Eighteenth-
Century English Literature*, ed. Tillotson, Fussell, Waingrow (New York: Harcourt, Brace and World, 1969), 150. But Bredvold, on this and other matters,
has been greatly challenged; see especially Thomas H. Fujimura, "Dryden's
Religio Laici: An Anglican Poem," *PMLA* 76 (1961), 205–17, and Harth, *Contexts of Dryden's Thought* passim. For the implausible charge of Deism, see
William Empson, *Essays in Criticism* 25 (1975), 74–100.

Those rowling Fires *discover* but the Sky
Not light us *here;* So *Reason's* glimmering Ray
Was lent, not to *assure* our *doubtfull* way,
But *guide* us upward to a *better Day.*
And as those nightly Tapers disappear
When Day's bright Lord ascends our Hemisphere;
So pale grows *Reason* at *Religions* sight;
So *dyes,* and so *dissolves* in *Supernatural Light.*

(1–11)

Dryden is thus maneuvering between the Deists, who would demonstrate religion by reason, and the Fideists, who would scorn even its feeble service. It is a conventional view, one shared, for example, by Dante, whom the natural reason of Virgil can guide to, but not into, heaven. So reason can show us the way to truth, not truth itself. The rest of the poem employs rational arguments to show the limits of reason and to indicate the proper form of belief. Dryden contends that the pagan philosophers and contemporary Deists have an inadequate understanding of the holy; he enumerates the marks of authenticity that reason should find in the scriptures; he propounds a reasonable conjecture concerning God's judgment of the pagans and heathens; he animadverts logically on the authoritarianism of the Roman Church and the capricious irrationality and subjectivism of the Protestant sects. The scriptures, he affirms, are clear in all matters touching our salvation, and on ambiguous points we can resort to the Patristic writings and early traditions. We must each of us use our reason in determining our faith: "For *MY* Salvation must its Doom receive / Not from what OTHERS, but what *I* believe" (302–303). Out of context these lines may seem to trench on Fideism. In context they have quite contrary implications: our salvation depends on our individual reason, and of course on God's grace, directing us to true faith. When Dryden examines irrational religious individualism at the term of the poem, he condemns it, much as Swift was to do in *A Tale of a Tub.* Although it is human nature for every man to "make *himself* a Creed," Dryden sees this as a venture in futility or fanaticism, and worse, a source of political disorder. Thus reason is our cynosure. It is precisely the error of the sectarians — to whom, Dryden says sarcastically, the *"Spirit* gave the *Doctoral Degree"* — that they would do without it. As a sometime member of the Royal Society of scientists and the author of a poem celebrating the Baconian method ("To Dr. Charleton"), Dryden was no disdainer of reason.

Dryden's high doctrine of the holy impels his dissection of the pagan philosophers and Deists. The pagans, for all their ingenuity, failed because *"finite Reason* [cannot] reach *Infinity"* (40). The Deists, complacently enough, believe that they have solved everything by the self-evident principles of reason or natural religion. But in reality those very principles have a divine source:

> These Truths are not the product of thy Mind,
> But dropt from Heaven, and of a Nobler kind.
> *Reveal'd Religion* first inform'd thy Sight,
> And *Reason* saw not, till *Faith* sprung the Light.
> Hence all thy *Natural Worship* takes the *Source:*
> 'Tis *Revelation* what thou thinkst *Discourse.*
>
> (66–71)

How else, asks Dryden, does one explain the Deists' knowing so much more by supposedly naked reason than the wise pagans? Having imbibed the truths of revelation, they foolishly take pride in their discursive reason. But even with the unacknowledged benefactions of scripture, their few principles fail adequately to comprehend sin and the need for remorse and expiation. Dryden works up his case against these audacious simplifiers with a passionate irony, which is finally ventilated in this rebuke: "Darst thou, poor Worm, offend *Infinity*? / And must the Terms of Peace be given by *Thee*?" (93–4). Again we are reminded of God's answer to Job[12] — and to Moses, as Browne interprets that episode.

[12]See Martin Price, *To the Palace of Wisdom* (New York: Doubleday, 1964), 67.

The Deists ignore that creature-consciousness and self-abasement essential to the numinous feeling; or in more conventional theological terms, they resemble Pelagians who depreciate grace and exaggerate the ability of human reason to achieve salvation. Dryden goes on to argue the necessity of Christ's redemption: no lesser sacrifice will satisfy. Reason shows us that we are sick; heaven, through Christ and scripture, provides the cure. Thus Dryden, true to the opening of his poem, uses reason to show us the need of revelation, and, consistent with his opinion in his preface, he argues that the truths of rationalism are in fact the "remnants" or "dying flames" of revelation. But his strong rebuke, never sliding into falsetto, logically precedes the rational proofs that Dryden offers in behalf of scripture and tradition. The ideas of salvation and redemption — concepts quite incomprehensible and even idiotic to the non-religious or rationalist sensibility — are fundamental to any numinous or transcendental faith. But one cannot be convinced through reason of the need for redemption. Dryden must first shock us into a sense of the vastness between our corrupt and finite nature and that of the deity: "For what cou'd *Fathom* GOD were *more* than *He*," and we, mere mortalities as Browne calls us, cannot hold that hope. The style of *Religio Laici* — note how joyously Dryden plies his capitals and italics, extreme even for his time — is greatly different from *Religio Medici*, as are its immediate purpose and *modus operandi*. But both strive to impart an awe and humility in respect of the holy, and both employ reason and rhetoric to that end.

Dryden's tactics against the Deists are perspicacious and prophetic. Few modern rationalists would agree with more than one, at most, of the self-evident principles of natural religion enounced by Lord Herbert in the middle of the seventeenth century: that there is a supreme power, that it ought to be worshipped, that the best worship is the good ordering of our faculties, that we should repent our sins, that there are rewards and punishments after this life.[13] A modern skeptic might not say

[13]Herbert, *Religio Laici:* "scilicet 1. Esse aliquod Supremum Numen. 2. Numen illud coli debere. 3. Virtutem cum pietate conjunctam optimani esse

with Dryden that the Deists were indirectly relying on revelation, but, browsing through Herbert's list, he would certainly agree that they were taking truths for self-evident that are really the conclusions of faith. Dryden is alleging that the Deists are living on a religious capital or depositum accumulated over centuries of belief. His point is proved, I think, by the growing skepticism of the Deists themselves as the next century elapsed, and by the scorn the modern positivist would have for Lord Herbert's self-evident principles. Thus I rather disagree with some modern scholars who assume that Dryden's poem is only preaching to the converted. Of course a twentieth-century rationalist would just ignore his promulgation of the holy, but a seventeenth-century Deist, if he were truly concerned for consistency, might not have been able to shrug off Dryden's arguments so easily. Dryden's high doctrine of the holy causes him to doubt natural theology more than Browne. Still, in his argument about the "remote effects of revelation," he allows that natural religion may embody *some* truths, though these are not sufficient, and though the pagans and Deists misconceive the source of these truths. In opposing Athanasius, Dryden suggests that he believes in a natural law; i.e., that elements of morality *can* be recognized by reason unassisted by revelation; elsewhere indeed he affirms that moral ideas are "In-born in Mankind."[14] And natural law, as St. Paul possibly suggests (it is a difficult passage), affords hope of salvation outside of revelation.[15]

When all these matters are considered together, the opinion of Dryden's early editor Sir Walter Scott seems clearly erroneous; that when Dryden wrote *Religio Laici* he "was sceptical concerning revealed religion." A modern editor has argued that

---

rationem Cultus Divini. 4. Resipiscendum esse a peccatis. 5. Dari Proemium vel Poenam post hanc vitam." See Basil Willey, *Seventeenth Century Background*, Ch. 7.

[14]Dryden, *Poems*, II, 791 (Dedication to *Examen Poeticum*).

[15]*Romans* ii. 14–15. The passage was habitually cited by latitudinarians who wished to argue that the virtuous pagans might be saved. It is susceptible of a reverse interpretation, however. See D. P. Walker, *The Ancient Theology* (London: Duckworth, 1972), Introduction.

that poem promotes "explicit anti-rationalism," a position Dryden abandoned for "fideism" five years later in *The Hind and the Panther.*[16] The distinction between anti-rationalism and Fideism eludes me, but neither term is applicable to either poem. Certainly Dryden defends Roman Catholicism in the later poem, while in the earlier he had objurgated it in favor of the Anglican *via media.* But there is no essential difference between these two poems regarding the nature of the holy, revelation, or reason. The God of *The Hind and the Panther* is mysterious and transcendent: his "throne is darkness in th'abyss of light, / A blaze of glory that forbids the sight" (I, 66–67). Revelation is indispensable, and like Browne and St. Paul Dryden urges that faith compel reason (I, 85). The sun-and-moon imagery of the opening of *Religio Laici* reappears early in this poem, and is similarly used to show the subordination of reason to faith (I, 89–90). There are other verbal echoes, probably intentional: e.g., "Let reason then at Her own quarry fly, / But how can finite grasp infinity?" (I, 104–105). Reason, along with the capacity for mercy, is precisely what discriminates man from the beasts, and intellectual liberty is of all freedoms the most precious: odd opinions for an anti-rationalist. Of course Dryden grants that man has misused his knowledge and lapsed into sin and discord — his view of man is very like that of Donne as well as Browne — but there is no suggestion that reason is incompetent in its proper sphere. *The Hind and the Panther,* like *Religio Laici,* is indeed highly argumentative and crammed with discursive logic. It is more emphatic on Church authority and rather less keen on individual reason, but we must remember that *both* Anglicanism and Roman Catholicism, compared with Deism and Fideism, are versions of the middle way. On that broad path Dryden has only moved more to the rightward margin.

The Pindaric ode and elegy on Anne Killigrew, published a year before *The Hind and the Panther,* is a less discursive but very animated treatment of the holy. In the first stanza Dryden

---

[16]Dryden, *Poems,* IV, 1933.

evokes the serene majesty of the divine creation as he contemplates its harmonious but intricate hierarchy and apostrophizes Killigrew's departing soul:

> Whether, adopted to some Neighbouring Star,
> Thou rol'st above us, in thy wand'ring Race,
>   Or, in Procession fixt and regular,
>   Mov'd with the Heavens Majestick Pace;
>   Or, call'd to more Superiour Bliss,
> Thou tread'st, with Seraphims, the vast Abyss.
>
> (6–11)

The concluding stanza celebrates the apocalypse, with the saintly Killigrew leading the blessed into heaven. It is Dryden's most splendid description of holy triumph and power, and it shows that he could play as nimbly at Browne's own game when he wished. Note the vigor of the meter, appropriately smoothing out in the last half, the vividness of the imagery, the cosmic sweep:

> When in mid-Aire, the Golden Trump shall sound,
>   To raise the Nations under ground;
>   When in the Valley of *Jehosaphat*,
> The Judging God shall close the Book of Fate;
>   And there the last Assizes keep,
>   For those who Wake, and those who Sleep;
>   When ratling Bones together fly,
> From the four Corners of the Skie,
> When Sinews o're the Skeletons are spread,
> Those cloath'd with Flesh, and Life inspires the Dead:
> The Sacred Poets first shall hear the Sound,
>   And formost from the Tomb shall bound:
> For they are cover'd with the lightest Ground
> And Streight, with in-born Vigour, on the Wing,
> Like mounting Larkes, to the New Morning sing.
> There *Thou*, Sweet Saint, before the Quire shalt go,
> As Harbinger of Heav'n, the Way to show,
> The Way which thou so well hast learn'd below.

[43]

Dryden's religious poems were written more than two generations after Donne's *First Anniversary*, more than a generation after *Religio Medici*, when the century was already superannuated. Yet there is no sign in any of them of that crisis of faith which, we are often told, was the central intellectual event of that age. Donne's intemperance, Browne's extravagance, may cloak inner doubts, though I find this conjecture wholly implausible. Dryden shows everywhere a cocksureness and zest for disputation that would be very unusual in a disinterested skeptic or tranquil Fideist. Like Browne he expounds a high doctrine of the holy in a calculatedly dramatic style. But he is primarily a Christian dialectician, and like his kindred in any age he opposes those who would rationalize or fanaticize the faith.

¤

... I look in all directions and see nothing but darkness. Nature offers me nothing that does not beget doubt and anxiety. If I saw there nothing to indicate a Divinity, I would draw a negative conclusion; if I saw everywhere the marks of a Creator, I would repose undisturbed in faith. But seeing too much to deny and too little to assure me, I am in a pitiful state, a state in which I have time and again wished that if Nature is sustained by a God she would reveal Him unequivocally; that if the signs which she now gives are misleading she would suppress them altogether. ... As it is, in my present state, ignorant of what I am and of what I ought to do, I know neither my condition nor my duty. My heart longs to know where is the true good, so that I may follow it; I could never buy eternity at too great a cost (*Pensées*, fragment no. 13).[17]

[17]All quotations are from Blaise Pascal, *Pensées, Notes on Religion and Other Subjects*, ed. Louis Lafuma, tr. John Warrington (London: Dent, 1960). The reader should note that the fragments of the *Pensées* are numbered differently in editions other than Lafuma's, though his arrangement is now generally accepted.

Here is the quintessential Pascal: the personal accent and undaunted self-scrutiny, the penetration of routine religious formulas, the compulsions of the heart, and in the last phrase, perhaps less alluring, the implicit commercial metaphors. That Pascal remains so well known is due partly to the modern urgency of his style, so different from the leisurely quaintness of Browne, the assured dialectics of Dryden, and partly to his acknowledgment of the moral ambiguity of the universe, so similar to that of the Existentialists. We are told that Pascal, like Browne, stands at a turning point between the old faith and the new science, but if Browne played among mediaeval fragments, Pascal is in his dilaceration of spirit the true modern man. He believes only because he is desperate; he turns to the irrational and "abdicates life in favor of death"; he is, *au fond*, not only a skeptic but a nihilist like Sade; indeed Sade is merely a "Pascal without God." "The ever-lasting silence of these infinite spaces terrifies me," Pascal confesses. Even granting that the new philosophy caused no great doubt in Donne or Browne, surely Pascal, some half-century later, suffers a cosmic anxiety.[18]

But Pascal can also be considered one of the last great apologists for Christianity, whose despair is no modern *angst*, but the spiritual dark night of the mystic, whose expatiation on the terror of infinite space is not a personal cry, but an attempt to dramatize the anxiety of the skeptic or atheist. The fragmentary state of the *Pensées* (chiefly written between late 1656 and 1658) makes interpretation particularly hazardous. Pascal, to judge from his finished writings, was a methodical thinker, and the *Pensées* were not intended to remain thus fractured. Some of

---

[18]See Lester G. Crocker, *Nature and Culture: Ethical Thought in the French Enlightenment* (Baltimore: Johns Hopkins Press, 1963), 340–44, who expresses some of these views, and quotes other modern scholars saying similar things. These attitudes were given classical embodiment in Sainte-Beuve's famous essay on Pascal. A recent example is in John Barker, *Strange Contrarieties: Pascal in England During the Age of Reason* (Montreal: McGill, 1975), 102; he calls the "infinite spaces" passage an expression of "personal anxiety," and notes that early, pious editors found it embarrassing and expelled it from their edition.

them clearly express points of view whose futility Pascal was planning to elucidate. Thus even the famous thirteenth fragment, often taken as the lament of the proto-modern intellectual in an absurd universe, may have been intended to mimic the unspeakable hopelessness of the infidel. Some advance has been made in organizing the fragments, but no scholarly consensus has been, or is apt to be, reached. Hence we shall probably never know which fragments express Pascal's own views exactly.[19]

Predominant themes, however, do run through the *Pensées;* but before remarking them it will be helpful to glance at some of the influences operating in Pascal's mind and character. Epictetus the stoic rationalist and Montaigne the genial Fideist were among his favorite writers, but they are extremities between which, like Dryden, Pascal attempts to steer. From Montaigne, nevertheless, he absorbed that skepticism of human nature and social custom which makes him so strangely like Hobbes. His sharp distinction between thought and matter brings him close to Descartes, though the Cartesian god, remote equally from the physical and the moral realms, could have no meaning for Pascal. It is the god without thunder, that god of the philosophers which Pascal ceaselessly contemns. His most inveterate foes, of course, were the Jesuits, against whom, as a Jansenist, Pascal expended much energy fulminating. No doubt the Jesuits were not so lax in doctrine and discipline as the Jansenists delighted to think; nor were the Jansenists so fanatical and heterodox as some moderns, often smugly, assume. But the Jansenists did promote that Augustinian Christianity seen in Donne, stressing man's fallen nature, the corruption (but not impotence) of reason, man's dependency on God. To them the Jesuits seemed tainted with Pelagianism; they were purveyors of "easy grace." Thus the Jesuits were in a general way like Dryden's Deists, and from Pascal's perspective they have much in common with the later *philosophes.*

Pascal had a strong sense of the holy, a sense in which he

---

[19]See Lafuma, vii–xi, for an account of the textual problems. For a further account, and a hypothetical reconstruction of the order of the *Pensées,* see Jean

found the Jesuits deficient; and in 1654 he underwent a spiritual conversion and mystical ecstasy of no little moment. He wrote a strange account of this — called the "Memorial" — which he wore in the lining of his clothes for the rest of his life. It begins:

>Feu
>Dieu d'Abraham, Dieu d'Isaac, Dieu de Jacob.
>   non des philosophes et des savants.
>   Certitude, certitude; sentiment, joie, paix.
>   Dieu de Jésus-Christ.

Two years later Pascal began work on the *Pensées*, which were intended to be an exhaustive apologia for Christianity; and such fragments as this show the close connection between his mystical experience and his understanding of the holy:

> The God of the Christians is not a God who is simply the author of mathematical truths or of the order of the elements. ... But the God of Abraham, the God of Isaac, the God of Jacob, the God of the Christians, is a God of love and consolation; He is a God who fills the heart and soul of those whom He possesses; He is a God who makes them feel a profound sense of their wretchedness and of His infinite mercy ... who renders them incapable of any end other than Himself (no. 17).

But there is a paradox lurking deep within the holy that Pascal never leaves go: "Appearances indicate neither total exclusion nor manifest presence of the godhead, but the presence of a God who hides Himself" (no. 17). Or again: "There is enough light for those who desire only to see, and enough obscurity for those who have the opposite disposition" (no. 309). God cannot be demonstrated through nature, for, as scripture says, he is hidden: *Vere tu es Deus absconditus* (*Isaiah* xlv. 15). The New Testament says we can know God only through Christ: *Nemo novit Patrem nisi Filius, et cui voluerit Filius revelare* (*Mat-*

Mesnard, *Pascal: His Life and Works* (New York: Philosophical Library, 1952), 135–66.

thew xi. 27). Those who use nature to prove God are in fact appealing to a belief already established:

> for it is certain that those in whose hearts there resides a living faith see at once that all existence is nothing else than the work of the God whom they adore. But those in whom this light is extinguished, and in whom it is proposed to rekindle it, persons devoid of faith and grace, who investigate with all the light at their disposal everything they see in nature that might lead them to such knowledge, find only darkness and obscurity (no. 49).

Some years later Dryden would urge that natural religion owes its insights to the "dying flames" of revelation. Similarly Pascal says that arguments from design, the harmony of nature, and so forth, will operate only on those already illuminated spiritually. Pascal approaches the matter from a different angle, but his primary perception, even his imagery, anticipates Dryden: rational proofs of Deity assume what can be known only from revelation.

Like Browne, Pascal is struck with the enigma and paradox of man. But Browne's "splendid animal" is Pascal's "thinking reed," and there is a world of difference between those phrases. It is man's fragility, not his splendor, that haunts Pascal. Like Job, whom he often refers to, he wonders why he exists: "Who has set me down here? By whose order and direction have this place and this time been allotted me?" (no. 116). If man for Browne was an amphibium, for Pascal he is a chimera, a contradiction, a prodigy or monster:

> Judge of all things, yet an imbecile earthworm; depositary of truth, yet a sewer of uncertainty and error; pride and refuse of the universe. . . . Know then, proud man, what a paradox you are to yourself. Humble yourself, helpless reason; be silent, foolish nature; understand that man is infinitely beyond the comprehension of man, and learn from your Master your true condition, of which you are ignorant. Listen to God (no. 246).

Sir *Thomas Browne, Dryden, and Pascal*

Pascal's dualistic view of human nature is sufficiently conventional, but he dilates with unusual vigor on man's depravity and wretchedness, a condition actually aggravated — not, as Browne would say, complemented — by his capacity for greatness. While Browne is often entranced by the puzzles and mysteries of the world, Pascal lays stress on its sterility. Our pleasures give no enduring satisfaction (no. 11); we are forever seeking distractions to take us out of boredom and prevent us from reflecting on our nothingness and dependency (no. 160); never satisfied with the present, we are continually escaping into the past or the future: "Thus we never live, but only hope to live" (no. 84); and if ever we attain the pleasures we seek, we contrive still others to keep us in perpetual agitation and expectancy (no. 143). This restlessness shows "that there was once in man a true happiness of which there now remain to him only the imprint and empty trace, which he tries in vain to fill with the whole of his environment, seeking from absent things the succour he does not obtain from those that are present" (no. 300). Compared with Pascal's spare urgency, Browne does seem vacantly eloquent at times, and Pascal would doubtless have viewed his *O altitudos*, not as a means of engendering wonder, but as a diversion, no more contemptible than any other, from the torpor of life and *horror vacui*.

Man nevertheless, wretched and flimsy as he is, has reason. Nature can easily destroy him, yet in knowing that he dies, he rises superior to his destroyer; therefore his essential dignity lies in thought (nos. 217, 391). To be sure, this reason or thought is frail enough: it is vacillating, less certain even than custom or habit (no. 7); it is easily deceived by the senses (no. 82). Yet it is man's distinctive quality and must not be ignored: "Men despise religion; they hate it and fear it may be true. To overcome that difficulty we must begin by showing that religion is not contrary to reason; it is worthy of veneration, make it respected" (no. 35). He who would defend religion, however, cannot appeal to the senses or nature, for their witness is deceptive and equivocal; nor can he address the discursive intellect, for that is vague and doubtful; and anyway, intellectual proofs of God make little impression, are quickly forgotten (no. 381). Only two avenues remain open: the supernatural, and human nature. It is clear from the *Pensées* that Pascal proposed to place much weight on supernatural evidences, especially the biblical prophecies and miracles. But the average modern reader will find him strongest in his argument from the human heart. Of all subjects, this excites most frequently his aphoristic vein: "The heart has its reasons, of which reason knows nothing" (no. 224); "It is the heart, not reason, which experiences God" (no. 225); "The heart has its own order; the intellect has its own, which is by way of principle and demonstration. ... Jesus Christ and St Paul employ the method of charity, not of intellect; for they sought to humble men's pride, not to instruct. St Augustine likewise" (no. 575). The heart is not merely emotionalism or sentimental self-indulgence; it is a part of the order of charity or spiritual illumination, as distinguished from the order of the discursive intellect. The following passage contains his most detailed account of the heart and must be quoted entire:

> We know truth, not only with the reason but also with the heart. It is in this latter way that we recognize first principles, and it is in vain that reason, which has no part therein, tries to impugn them. The sceptics, who have no other purpose, labour ineffectively. We know that we are not dreaming; and however impossible it may be for us to prove as much by reason, this very inability demonstrates the weakness of our reason, but not, as is affirmed, the uncertainty of all our knowledge. For the knowledge of first principles — for example space, time, motion, and number — [is] as sure as any of those procured for us by reason. And it is upon this knowledge of the heart and instinct that reason must rely and base all its arguments. (We know intuitively that there are three dimensions in space and that numbers are infinite, and reason goes on to show that there are no two square numbers one of which is double the other. Principles are known by intuition, propositions are inferred, all with certainty but in different ways.) And it is as useless and absurd for reason to seek from

[50]

the heart proofs of her first principles as it would be for the
heart to demand from reason an intuition of all demonstrated
propositions before accepting them.

This inability ought then to serve only to humble reason,
which would like to be judge of all, but not impugn our certainty, as if reason alone were capable of instructing us.
Would to God, on the contrary, that we never needed it, that
we knew everything instinctively and by intuition! But
nature has withheld from us this boon. She has indeed given
us but very little of such knowledge; all the rest can be
acquired only by ratiocination.

Those, therefore, to whom God has granted religion
through intuition are most fortunate and very rightly convinced. But to those who have it not we can impart it only by
reasoning, waiting upon God to grant them spiritual insight,
without which faith is only human and useless for salvation
(no. 214).

Hobbes and Browne, we will recollect, discriminated between
the dreaming and waking state. Hobbes, appealing to principles
of coherence and continuity, is confident that reason can keep
the two distinct. Browne contends that the sleeping state
actually frees the reason from the hindrances of sense and our
animal nature; the slumber of the body is the waking of the
soul. Pascal is no less certain than Hobbes that we can distinguish, but we do so by intuition, not demonstration. Browne's
opinion would probably have seemed to him too skeptical, and
Hobbes's argument just otiose. We know intuitively, even as we
grasp other first principles. Discursive reason pertains to another
order, and Pascal might say that Hobbes was confounding the
two. Hobbes's rational demonstration, like rational demonstrations of God, presupposes things already held intuitively. But
Pascal does admit that we know many matters through
ratiocination.

The fragment poses another problem. Pascal draws the analogy between religious intuition and mathematical intuition. But
we have already seen that for Pascal the Christian God is not

[51]

merely the author of mathematical truths—the philosophers' god—but the God of individuals, of Abraham, Isaac, and Jacob. Every intelligent person can be convinced of mathematical truths, but that is not so with religious truths. For God must grant these truths through spiritual grace or insight, call it what one will. Hence the analogy, like all such, is faulty: we can all agree, perhaps, that numbers are infinite, but not that God exists. Thus even to the heart of man God may, if he choose, remain hidden; it is he who must incline the heart to begin with. God, finally, is the *mysterium tremendum:* we *can* apprehend him through the heart, but only when moved by love and grace; we can see his evidences in nature, but only when he is already active within us. And as scriptures tell us that the fear of the Lord is the beginning of wisdom, so for Pascal true knowledge of God comes from the numinous experience, a poignant sense of his transcendence and our creatureliness:

> True conversion consists in annihilating ourselves before that universal Being whom we have so often provoked and who might justly destroy us at any moment; in recognizing that we can do nothing without Him, and have deserved nothing but His displeasure. It consists in knowing that there is an invincible opposition between us and God, and that without a mediator there can be no communion with Him (no. 728).

At the end of no. 214 Pascal says that it is possible to impart religion through reasoning even to those devoid of spiritual insight, but that such faith is vain until it is actuated by that insight. Rational arguments can be used, in other words, to *prepare* man to receive spiritual understanding, though these arguments in themselves will not produce wisdom. Of such arguments, the most famous or notorious of Pascal's is the wager. To paraphrase it briefly: we cannot truly be neutral in religious matters, for we conduct our life either assuming God's existence or not; in effect, there are no true agnostics, for such are practical atheists. If we bet on God and Christianity, if we assume their existence and truth, we may win a stake of infinite value, no matter how slender the likelihood of their existing or being

true. But if we bet against God, we may still lose the world, and shall certainly lose eternity. Therefore the sportsman will opt for the greater stake, despite the longer odds. Now this argument has disgusted many people, and there is indubitably something distasteful and eudaemonistic about it. Pascal has been defended here on the grounds that he is appealing to libertines and gamesters, not saints; but then Christ, who preached to disreputable people, did not cast his message so. Nevertheless, Christ did sometimes appeal to self-interest, as in his admonitions about hell. Then, too, it is to be considered that Pascal may have been arguing, not as a gamester, but as a mathematician concerned with the calculus of probabilities, and that the disagreeable side of wagering was not foremost in his mind. His argument has been compared with the more "respectable" arguments from probability excogitated by theologians such as Bishop Butler and Cardinal Newman, or, in a variant but recognizable form, by William James in *The Will to Believe*.

But the wager is best compared, I think, to Kierkegaard's leap of faith. Too often Pascal's argument has been prized loose of its context and merely sketched, even as I have just done. But let me try to make amends. The argument occurs in a lengthy fragment (no. 343) headed *"Infinity. Nothingness."* Long before he gets round to the wager, Pascal meditates on the infinity and arcanum of God, which he contrasts with our creatureliness. Having impressed on us the transcendence of the holy (we remember that that is the necessary prerequisite to true conversion), Pascal develops the argument of the wager. After this, the person hypothetically addressed remonstrates: Very well, but I am *forced* to wager one way or the other; I'm not free; yet I am so constructed that I cannot believe. Pascal responds: that may be true, but if so, your inability to believe is the result of your passions. "Try therefore to convince yourself, not by piling up proofs of God, but by subduing your passions." He then advises the unbeliever to practice spiritual exercises *as if* he believed: true belief will follow in due course. Pascal concludes by assuring us that this chain of arguments has been made "by a man who has knelt, both before and after its delivery, in prayer to that Being, infinite and without parts, before whom he submits all that is his." At least three factors are often overlooked when the wager is considered: it is made along with the suggestion, frequently proposed by religious writers, that one should *act* as though one believed; it is made while at the same time the true problem is identified as emotional, compared with which all intellectual proofs are of limited use; finally, it presupposes a numinous view of the Deity. It is an argument that makes sense only in relation to a God wholly other and, to the unsanctified soul, wholly obscure; and in a dimension where, in Dryden's phrase, the finite cannot hope to reach infinity. Just as Dryden's arguments in *Religio Laici* follow his affirmation of God's transcendence, so the argument of the wager assumes recognition of the numinous. It is no more an autonomous or rational proof of God than the argument from design in nature, and it will fail with unreligious persons. Voltaire's response, which I shall examine shortly, shows this to be true. The argument may be of some use to those who are wavering, but it is to be seen, finally, not as a logical proposition, but a metaphor for the ineludibility of choice.

For Pascal, then, reason is indeed ancillary. God is not the abstract Cartesian deity or the complaisant, elderly gentleman of the Pelagians and Jesuits. He is, as Pascal says in the "Memorial" and the *Pensées*, the God of Abraham and Isaac and Jacob, the wrestling, inscrutable, apparently arbitrary God, illuminating some hearts, leaving others dark; remote from his creation, not as the deistic divine clockmaker is remote, but by virtue of his transcendence. As the "Memorial" shows us, and the *Pensées* everywhere proclaim, knowledge of God is rooted in experience, an experience full of turmoil and incertitude, the seemingly incongruous mixture of hope, awe, fear, and fascination characteristic of the numinous. Of the three writers studied here, Pascal is mentally the most subtle and spry, the most aware of the limits of reason. But there is nothing in him of that *ataraxy*, that genial tranquillity and resignation found in the true skeptical Fideist such as Montaigne, whose motto, *Je suspends*, contrasts so glaringly with Pascal's restlessness. Few thinkers indeed have made more of an Oedipus of their reason, unquiet and curious, humbled finally before the absconding God.

◻

Voltaire has been called the spirit of the Enlightenment, and though I am skeptical of such hypostatized spirits, it is certainly true that he was one of the most ardent rebels against the sacred. In Pascal he properly saw his ideological enemy, and in 1734 he added to his *Lettres philosophiques* a polemical commentary on the *Pensées*. It would be hard to find a sharper conflict between two volatile, inquisitive, but otherwise contrary sensibilities. For this reason, and because the rivalry between Pascal and Voltaire has been resuscitated in the pages of modern criticism, I should like to glance at some of Voltaire's animadversions. Pascal and Voltaire represent, after all, two perennial dispositions of the human spirit, and Voltaire was wiser than some of his intellectual descendants in recognizing that there could be no dialogue — at best a grudging respect, and often not that — between the two parties.

Voltaire says that he grants Pascal's genius, but deplores his exorbitant pessimism: as for Voltaire, he will side with "le parti de l'humanité contre ce misantrope sublime" (Introduction).[20] He excludes from the start the metaphysical dimension so fundamental to Pascal, asserting that Christianity teaches only simplicity, humanity, charity, the last term being used in a humanitarian sense very different from Pascal's; Christianity is, in other words, no more than an ethical scheme. The enigmatic and paradoxical nature of man, so intriguing to Pascal, is mere mystery-mongering to Voltaire. Man is simply a being with his own place in nature, above the animals, with whom he shares physical traits, below other beings whom he may somewhat resemble intellectually; to be sure he is a confection of good and

[20]All quotations are from the *Lettres philosophiques*, ed. Gustave Lanson, vol. 2 (Paris: Édouard Cornély, 1909).

evil, of passions that move him to action, and of reason that governs those actions. Were he perfect, man would be a god, but "ces prétendues contrariétés que vous [Pascal] appellez contradictions, sont les ingrédiens nécessaires qui entrent dans le composé de l'homme, qui est ce qu'il doit être" (paragraph 3). Like Browne and Pascal, Voltaire sees man as a mixture occupying a middle place on the chain of being, but there is nothing here of Browne's rhapsodic wonder or Pascal's stringent religious scrutiny. Man, after all, is "what he should be"; he has his moods, but that is no great mystery (4). As for Pascal's morbid notion that man's condition is like that of a slave in chains condemned to death: well, man is like the animals and plants, born to live a certain while, to procreate, to die; why dwell on the wretchedness and brevity of life when we might instead luxuriate in its felicity and duration (28)? Pascal laments that we live in the future, not the present, and seek endless diversion. But what is so bad about that? Did we not think ahead, we should never do anything, never have hope; man is born for action and derives satisfaction from his achievements (22–24). Thus Voltaire quite misses or represses Pascal's point that we do *not* find permanent satisfactions in this world, and so are condemned to ceaseless restlessness. He cannot understand why Pascal dwells on the obscurity of religious truth: after all, there is light too (18). As for the wager, it is "un peu indécent & puérile," inappropriate to the subject; and anyway, if God is so severe a judge, it were better *not* to believe in him (5). Reason is not, as Pascal cynically alleges, so often self-deceived; it may indeed sometimes be so "en fait de goût, [mais] non en fait de science" (48). We cannot know all things, of course, but we can know the things useful and relevant to our condition (54).

Pascal would probably have seen in all this a lightly secularized version of Pelagianism and Jesuitism. Voltaire projects himself in this piece as a common-sensical man of the world, optimistic, well-adjusted, immune from cosmic shivers or morbid and metaphysical hauntings, cheerfully spurning all gratuitous mystification. His god is not one that is apt to give trouble; indeed, it has been variously described as "remote, nebulous,

[56]

inscrutable, do-nothing" and as "beyond good and evil."[21] There is something of the fatuous Pangloss in this commentary, and it would be well to remember that we are not dealing at present with Voltaire at the height of his powers. *Candide* is not complacent. But there is much in this commentary that is representative enough. Voltaire attacks Pascal from a similar vantage on several occasions in his long life, and many of the other *philosophes* joined in the assault. Unlike conventional supernaturalists, Pascal fortifies his position by examining the human condition. Since this is what the Enlightenment philosophers prided themselves on doing too, it is no wonder they found him an elusive but imperative target.

Religious fanaticism and persecution was still very much alive when Voltaire wrote: one can understand his attitude and admire his courage. Less intrepid are some of the modern scholars and *soi-disant* champions of Voltaire, who feel that they too must give Pascal a kick to evince, I suppose, their fealty to the master. Some, for example, have taken up seriously Voltaire's notion that one can account for Pascal's thought by seeing it as the consequence of his illnesses, neurotic personality, and so forth.[22] Not only is this too easy a way to discredit an opponent, but it is also a dangerous game. Such critics are apt to be the same sort who will reprove the "facile optimism" of *An Essay on Man*, never minding that Pope was as wretched physically as Pascal. Or here is a scholar commenting with supposed objectivity on Voltaire's critique of Pascal: "In every case Voltaire pointed out the practical reasons for man's discontent, refusing to spend time on the so-called spiritual implications of Pascal's thought."[23] There is no hint that Voltaire's "practical reasons" might also be subjected to that sneering qualifier, *so-called;* and

---

[21]See: Crocker, *Nature and Culture,* 347; Norman L. Torrey, *The Spirit of Voltaire* (1938; rpt. New York: Russell & Russell, 1968), 244.

[22]See, e.g., Clement C.J. Webb, *Pascal's Philosophy of Religion* (Oxford: Clarendon Press, 1929), 39; Mina Waterman, *Voltaire, Pascal and Human Destiny* (New York: King's Crown Press, 1942), 17. And see Mesnard, 179–86, for a good dissection of these sorts of tactics.

[23]Waterman, 35.

Voltaire's cavalier dismissal of Pascal's metaphysical scheme, making it easier for him to ridicule the rest of Pascal's thought, is softened into a refusal to spend (i.e., waste) time on it. Even Theodore Besterman, the most highly regarded of authorities on Voltaire, perpetrates such caricatures as this: Voltaire thought "rightly, that Pascal represented all the things which to him were anathema: party spirit, dogmatism, intolerance, instinctive pessimism, obscurantism."[24] It would have been more accurate, and as just to Voltaire, to have put it thus: Pascal represented belief, odious to Voltaire, in the holy and transcendent, in man as corrupt, paradoxical and finite, in the ultimate mystery of existence. After all, Voltaire just as surely had the party spirit — his "party of humanity" was a very exclusive coterie indeed, and had its own fond dogmas. To call Pascal obscurantist betrays some slight failing of academic impartiality and correctitude. Again, Besterman speaks, a trifle hieratically, of Voltaire's "annihilating" Pascal with his arguments; he several times resorts to this drastic verb. But though Voltaire was a witty and indefatigable ax-grinder, a disinterested observer will not find that he had such total powers as this. Most annoying of all, Besterman chooses to conclude his magnum opus and life's work with a grotesquely lopsided comparison of Voltaire with Pascal, in which the latter is caricatured as a superstitious, twisted, misanthrope and fanatic. He quotes with approval Voltaire's self-serving remark that while Pascal "teaches men to hate themselves, I would sooner teach them to love one another."[25] Even a critic with a less crusading spirit thus concludes his comparison of Voltaire and Pascal: "Voltaire will always remain the hero of the intellectually curious; while those whose greatest need is

---

[24]Theodore Besterman, *Voltaire* (New York: Harcourt, Brace & World, 1969), 172. Two pages later Besterman refers to Pascal's "sloppy thinking" when Pascal asserts that God would be *too* manifest if there were but one religion. One is free to think differently from Pascal, perhaps even to call his argument on this point a rationalizing; but his opinion is consistent with his conception of the "hidden God." There is no sloppy thinking evident here, at least not in Pascal.

[25]Besterman, 541.

consolation will continue to seek it in the direction indicated by Pascal."[26] *Either* Pascal or Voltaire might be a hero to the intellectually curious, and to imply that Pascal will be a consolation to the incurious shows a smugness and condescension — and an inability to read Pascal — that can only be pitied. One might as well say that *Hamlet* is consoling because in the end the murder is avenged and divine justice thereby vindicated.

I wish to decry a tendency in whig scholars to label Browne, Dryden, and Pascal Fideists, and hence to dismiss them more easily as reactionaries trying to slink away from the skeptical implications of the new philosophy. Another contention I should like to question is that the rise of the new science threw intellectuals into a state of crisis with traditionary views becoming more enervated and paranoiac. Finally, I find very silly this championing of Voltaire at the expense of Pascal. Voltaire's genius and courage speaks for itself; it took no less courage for Pascal to explode the respectable and officially sanctioned proofs of Deity. This talk of his consoling the incurious is deceptive: it gives a show of fair-mindedness behind which lies the supercilious smirk. After all, a scholar partial to skepticism will be just as apt to find consolation in Voltaire — while at the same time posing as an independent thinker charitably tolerant (howsoever secretly contemptuous) of the needs of his weaker brothers. Such a position entails a twofold duplicity.

Browne, Dryden, and Pascal were not systematic theologians. They were intelligent Christians alert to the new philosophy but unintimidated by it. They tried to reason out their faith in the light of their own traditions and against the contemporary varieties of skepticism and rationalism. They did in their age what St. Paul and St. Augustine, Coleridge and Newman, T. S. Eliot and Tillich, have done in theirs. On specific matters they differ, but none, I believe, compromised with rationalism, and they each anticipate later rebuttals. Browne is very like Blake in his endeavor to evoke, through extravagance of style, a pre-conceptual sense of the numinous; and his influence, or at least his

[26]Torrey, 216.

congeniality, is felt in nebulously religious romantics such as Wordsworth and Byron. Dryden's espousal of the *via media* has been emulated by many, and his ridicule of fanaticism greatly resembles Swift's, despite the Dean's scorn for the ex-poet-laureate. But ultimately his religious career foreshadows the *Apologia pro Vita Sua.* Pascal appealed to Pope in certain moods, to Edward Young and, more profoundly, to Samuel Johnson. There is something of him even in *Clarissa,* and his kinship with existentialism is clear, however eager he would be to disclaim paternity. But whatever their disagreements, they are all clearly of a different party from Voltaire's.

CHAPTER III

The Witch of Endor and the Gadarene Swine: The Debate over Witchcraft and Miracles in the Seventeenth and Eighteenth Centuries

For the Sadducees say that there is no resurrection, neither angel nor spirit; but the Pharisees confess both.

The Acts of the Apostles

Your recent indifference to cosmical ideas is actually puzzling to me. Of course, we know that there is no life after death . . . but about us stretches an illimitable expanse of space . . . wherein we are as nothing. . . . What I cannot comprehend, is how your *imagination* can fail to react to these mysterious abysses; how you can escape the burning curiosity of a child at a nearly-closed door through whose crevice come sounds of strange and unearthly wonder, and fragments of sights that suggest unthinkable things. How, after these terrible glimpses, you can still remain indifferent to ultramundane hints. . . .

H. P. LOVECRAFT

ON 13–14 MARCH, 1664/65, at Bury St. Edmunds, Suffolk, Rose Cullender and Amy Duny were tried and convicted for bewitching several children. The judge was Sir Matthew Hale, renowned for his learning and his moderation. The evidence was of a sort familiar to students of the New England trials: hysterical fits, unaccountable afflictions such as lameness, untoward events such as the vomiting of pins and nails, the appearance of some specters and a great toad that, when cast into the fire, exploded with a preternatural flash and sharp report. A contemporary account mentions the testimony of one "Dr. *Brown* of Norwich, a Person of great knowledge," who believed that the children were bewitched and cited some fresh stories of

[61]

witches in Denmark, a place that, like Lapland, had long been a notorious resort for such people. The account continues:

> ... his Opinion was, That the Devil in such cases did work upon the Bodies of Men and Women, upon a Natural Foundation. ... for he conceived, that these swouning Fits were Natural ... but only heightned to a great excess by the subtilty of the Devil, co-operating with the Malice of these which we term Witches, at whose Instance he doth these Villanies.[1]

Less than half an hour after the verdicts were returned, the children were relieved of their distress. Duny and Cullender were hanged without confessing anything.

Sir Thomas Browne has been much censured for his testimony. "[T]his was a Case of Blood, and surely the King's Subjects ought not to lose their Lives upon the Credit of Books from *Denmark*," sneers Francis Hutchinson, a skeptic of witchcraft, early in the eighteenth century; and two hundred years later Edmund Gosse condemns it as "the most culpable and the most stupid action of his life." More recent scholars are prone to minimize Browne's influence on the jury, and hence his culpability, if not his stupidity.[2] But Browne's testimony is consonant with his own written opinion, and indeed with that of most educated opinion of his time. More than twenty years before, Browne had professed belief in spirits, arguing from the chain of being, and in the possibility of copulation between spirits and mortals. He also suggested that the denial of spirits and witches is tantamount to infidelity and atheism. Of course the devil is subtle,

---

[1] *A Tryal of Witches ... Taken by a Person then Attending the Court* (1682), 41–42. For a fuller account of the trial see C. L'Estrange Ewen, *Witchcraft and Demonianism* (London: Heath Cranton, 1933), 347–52.

[2] Francis Hutchinson, *An Historical Essay Concerning Witchcraft* (1720), 151; Edmund Gosse, *Sir Thomas Browne*, 147–50 for entire account. See also: Ewen, *Witchcraft*, 135; Keith Thomas, *Religion and the Decline of Magic* (London: Weidenfeld and Nicolson, 1971), 441. W. P. Dunn, *Sir Thomas Browne*, 26–33, argues persuasively that Browne had an insignificant role in the affair. See also Joan Bennet, *Sir Thomas Browne*, 11–16, 75–76.

Browne tells us; he can sometimes truly possess men, but at other times possess them through the spirit of melancholy or delusion. The witch's magic is often merely applied science, but that makes it no less devilish, and anyway the demon may deceive witches into thinking it magic, even as he deceives them into believing that their spells and conjurations have intrinsic power. He plays these tricks to promote superstition. Even more insidiously he can encourage disbelief in himself and so plunge men into atheism. The devil is wily and circumspect and the father of lies; he can seduce us into superstition or skepticism, and he often operates through natural causes, even through physical or psychological maladies.[3]

So it was not "stupid," not at least in the jejune sense of the word, for Browne to have testified as he did. To be sure, he might have asked himself whether, in that particular case, the devil might not be tricking us into hanging innocent people — especially since there was evidence available at the time pointing to the fraudulence of the accusations. It is all very well to pursue the Oedipus of one's reason in a book; it is another thing to pursue it in an arena of fatality. Still, Browne no doubt considered himself pious, but open-minded and empirical. Is it not reasonable that one should recognize the natural causes of things but also be alert to demonic influence where the evidence suggests it and resist any theories debouching into skepticism? As a scholar has recently noted: "The two great sources of knowledge for the eighteenth century, revelation and reason based on experience, both argued for the reality of witchcraft."[4] Browne's opinion was moderate, reasonable, and would be shared by other moderate, reasonable men for more than a century.

On the matter of miracles, Browne was very cautious. Like most of his fellow Anglicans, indeed like most Protestants, he

---

[3]See *Religio Medici* I, 30, 31, 37; cf. *Pseudodoxia Epidemica*, I, 10, 11.

[4]Herbert Leventhal, *In the Shadow of the Enlightenment: Occultism and Renaissance Science in Eighteenth-Century America* (New York: New York University Press, 1976), 94.

believed that the biblical miracles were genuine — they had been required to establish Christianity — but that the age of miracles had ceased long since. For this he is grateful:

> I blesse my selfe, and am thankefull that I lived not in the dayes of miracles, that I never saw Christ nor his Disciples; I would not have beene one of those Israelites that Passed the Red Sea, nor one of Christs Patients, on whom he wrought his wonders; then had my faithe beene thrust upon me, nor should I enjoy that greater blessing pronounced to all that believe and saw not. (*Religio Medici*, I, 9).

But Pascal would probably have scented in Browne a spiritual arrogance. Miracles were not only necessary for the establishment of Christianity, but they are still necessary "to convince the entire man, in both body and soul" (*Pensées*, no. 884). The New Testament miracles, especially the exorcisms, are integral to Christ's mission: "For Jesus Christ opposed the devil, and destroyed his power over hearts, of which exorcism is symbolic, in order to establish the kingdom of God" (no. 898). Miracles are a sign of Christ's Messiahship (no. 883) and one means of distinguishing true from false religions (no. 907); the existence of fraudulent miracles, far from discrediting the miraculous, shows that there must be authentic ones to account for people believing the false (no. 477). But of course miracles give no more certitude than the evidences of natural religion or reason. Browne need not have worried about living in Christ's time, in other words, for miracles can always be explained away. On the other hand, the best of us are weak, and like to have all the evidence we can.

Now I suppose that Pascal must be reckoned the more consistent of these two thinkers, though Browne is more representative of English belief. Lynn Thorndike, abandoning the imperturbability of an encyclopedist, smartly rebukes those who, like Browne, believed in contemporary witchcraft but not in contemporary miracles: "This was not logical. It was a delusion, an aberration, a wrong-headedness that was almost sinful and criminal."[5] He means, of course, that they ought not to have believed in either. But Browne's belief in the contemporary demonic, and Pascal's in the contemporary miraculous, proceed from the same source: they both wished to affirm an enchanted world in opposition to the dead mechanism, the world of mere extension and movement, ushered in by the new philosophy. Moreover, it was not "illogical" for Browne to think that the New Testament miracles, performed to evince Christ's divinity, had fulfilled their purpose, but that the malevolent angels might still be at large to plague mankind. It may be he yielded too much to that "god of the philosophers" who will not be so indiscreet as to intervene in his creation. But Browne's was an intelligent position and gives a show of plausibility. Clear miracles were not rife in seventeenth-century England, but bewitchings and possessions still happened from time to time; so it was reasonable for someone opposed to skepticism to look to witchcraft and demonic possession, rather than the miraculous, for witness of a supernatural world. The debate on witchcraft reached its zenith in the Restoration, while the debate on miracles had to wait till the eighteenth century. The reasons for this delay are several. Since most Englishmen agreed that the age of miracles was done, the miraculous was not so urgent an issue as witchcraft, where lives yet hung in the balance and laws were in the books. But at the same time it was more hazardous to attack the authenticity of biblical miracles than the reality of witchcraft, for the Bible clearly affirms them, as it does not so irrefragably recognize witchcraft. Then too, after belief in contemporary bewitchings and possessions had been undermined, it was less risky for the skeptics to go after the scriptural narratives.

In this chapter I shall examine in some detail the debates concerning witchcraft, possession, miracles. These are inextricably mingled, but since the arguments over witchcraft laid the foun-

[5]Lynn Thorndike, *A History of Magic and Experimental Science* (New York and London: Columbia University Press, 1923–1958), VIII (1958), 586–87.

dation for the arguments over miracles, I shall consider that matter first. I shall also have some things to say about the attitudes of the participants in these debates and about the way in which the debates developed. I have argued in the previous chapter that those who held to high doctrines of the holy were not, as they are often represented, reactionary Fideists, but sophisticated men well aware of the intellectual currents of their time. I shall make similar arguments about the believers in witchcraft. Like Browne they were interested in the new philosophy and admitted some of its claims. They considered themselves undogmatic and open-minded, and in fact they were usually more tolerant than the mass of their countrymen of other forms of belief like Roman Catholicism. Their opponents were not for the most part pioneers of humanitarianism or the Enlightenment; some of them were occultists, and many of them showed a strident bigotry against the Roman faith. Moreover, the rise of science and rationalism did not cause, as some whiggish scholars contend, "an abrupt change of heart." It is clear, in fact, that throughout the eighteenth century "the supernatural was a matter for discussion; the question of belief or nonbelief was a real and lively issue."[6] The evidence suggests that Rose Cullender and Amy Duny were innocent of the charge of witchcraft. But it is also clear to me that Christianity postulates a diabolic, as well as a human, source of evil, and that the general experience of mankind buttresses the supernatural theory. The debate examined here is one important phase in the controversy, yet continuing, between those who credit that theory, and those who do not.

☐

The Renaissance, not the Middle Ages, saw the efflorescence of witchcraft as a social problem and subject of theological dis-

---

[6]The first quotation is from K. M. Briggs, *Pale Hecate's Team* (New York: The Humanities Press, 1962), 15; the second is from Patricia Meyer Spacks, *The Insistence of Horror* (Cambridge, Mass.: Harvard Univ. Press, 1962), 28.

course. In England it was not a felony punishable by death until 1542, when Parliament made it so, and under Henry VIII and Elizabeth — such was the turbulence of the times — it was often mixed up with treason. Under James I some fifty witches were executed; the most notable trial was that of the Pendle Forest coven in 1612. Under James, too, the most famous of the witchcraft statutes was passed, and this was not to be definitively replaced until 1736, when a new law was enacted implicitly denying the reality of witchcraft. There was but little activity under Charles I, though the Pendle Forest affair was raked up again and some seventeen people condemned but reprieved by Charles in 1633–1634. During the interregnum the "witchfinder general" Matthew Hopkins instigated persecutions in the mid 1640s, and scores of people were hanged. Persecutions and executions continued through the 50s, 60s, and 70s, but considerably diminished, the most newsworthy trial of the period being that of Duny and Cullender.

The earliest discussions of witchcraft were Continental. The *Malleus Maleficarum*, or Hammer of Witches (c. 1486) was the most influential credulous work, and its Dominican authors drew support and prestige from St. Thomas Aquinas, who had argued that it was heretical to deny witchcraft, and from a 1484 bull on the subject by Innocent VIII.[7] But books such as Johann Weyer's *De Praestigiis Daemonum* (1563) and Friedrich von

---

[7]See Henry Charles Lea, *Materials Toward a History of Witchcraft*, ed. A. C. Howland, 3 vols. (1939; rpt. New York: Thomas Yoseloff, 1957), 214–15. On the Continental and pre-Restoration English works generally, see Lea, Briggs, *Pale Hecate's Team*, and Wayne Shumaker, *The Occult Sciences in the Renaissance*. It is not my purpose to enter into the considerable and often controversial body of modern studies of witchcraft. A reasonably objective survey of that material can be found in Norman Cohn, *Europe's Inner Demons* (New York: Basic Books, 1975), Ch. 6, and in Elliot Rose, *A Razor for a Goat* (Toronto: Univ. of Toronto, 1962). Keith Thomas's *Religion and the Decline of Magic* approaches the subject from a useful, sociological point of view, but in a future edition he should correct the intimation that it was Saul, rather than Samuel, whom the witch of Endor invoked (589). Montague Summers's *History of Witchcraft* and *Demonology* (1926; rpt. New York: University Books, 1956) is a lively, theologically credulous study; it is not without value.

Spee's *Cautio Criminalis* (1631) had clear, even heterodox, skeptical strains. This skepticism was given a very muscular expression in Reginald Scot's *Discoverie of Witchcraft* (1584), a book which King James, who had written a less skeptical but not wholly credulous *Daemonologie* in 1597, is supposed to have ordered burnt on his ascension to the English throne. Scot's imposing work was reissued several times, once in 1665 just as the Restoration controversy was getting under way, and it provided the later skeptics with much ammunition. Scot is highly praised by most modern writers for his courage, humanitarianism, and foresight; his book is a "noble work, full of learning, humane feeling"; it is a "brilliant beacon in the prevailing fog of ignorance and superstition." Only the pious Montague Summers demurs, for whom Scot was "naturally sceptical . . . utterly without imagination, a very dull, narrow, and ineffective little soul."[8] But I daresay few scholars have more than glanced at the work, in which vast quantities of paper are given over to expositions of legerdemain, ponderous ridicule of charms and spells, routine but windy diatribes against popery. Few books so historically important are so dated. But mixed in with all the rubbish are the very arguments, or most of them, that the Restoration skeptics would use: the witches supposedly condemned under the Mosaic law were cozeners, poisoners, diviners, sleight-of-hand magicians, and their contemporary counterparts are similarly plain frauds; Christ worked miracles, but now miracles are ceased; the witches' "night-riding," transformations, devilish pacts, and Sabbats are just dreams; their confessions are elicited by torture or spring from melancholy and madness; the authors of the *Malleus Maleficarum* and similar works are fabulists and liars.

Scot's two most important points are these: that the Bible does not support belief in witchcraft, and that belief in diabolic

---

[8]Montague Summers, *The Geography of Witchcraft* (1927; rpt. Evanston and New York: University Books, 1958), 128. The other quotations are from E. Cobham Brewer, *A Dictionary of Miracles* (London, 1884), 315, and Ewen, *Witchcraft*, 10.

power derogates from God's omnipotence. To argue the first position, he explains such events as Nebuchadnezzar's beastly transformation (*Daniel*, iv. 30) as allegorical, and he subjects the story of the witch of Endor (I *Samuel*, xxviii) to very close scrutiny. The witch's "familiar spirit" is a translation of the Hebrew '*ôbh*, which means "bottle" and implies ventriloquism. Samuel could *not* have been raised from the dead — "it was an illusion or cosenage practised by the Witch" — because the righteous remain with God. Nor could it have been the devil that appeared, for the specter "admonishes" Saul, and the devil would perform no such genial service. Therefore, the witch either used ventiloquism or had a confederate hidden in a closet. In respect of God's omnipotence, Scot argues that to believe that the witch or devil can cause thunder, tempests, and so forth is not only intrinsically ridiculous — after all, we should still have *weather* even if all the devils were dead! — but it is also injurious to God's omnipotence and slides into the old, heretical dualism. Such beliefs may also be a sort of idolatry, for they attribute "to a witch, such divine power, as duly and only appertaineth unto God." Satan has no real power. God, not Satan, sent Job's punishments, and though the gospels tell us that Satan could transport Christ through the air, he may have been given a special dispensation from God so that scripture might be fulfilled; or we may view the whole affair as a vision. Scot also notes, and this is much to his credit, that the witchcraft laws operate chiefly against poor, friendless, ignorant females, and he urges that their severity be abated.

Structurally, Scot's book is a shambles. His biblical interpretations are often strained, his theological arguments, as we shall see, inconclusive. There is a further anomaly, or so it may seem to a modern reader. Toward the end of his book Scot professes his belief in the natural magic of Renaissance occultism. He recognizes "sympathies" and "antipathies" in nature, and by such means accounts for the well-known fact that the corpse of a murdered man will bleed in the presence of his murderer. But this is not really so singular. Scot's book is clearly influenced by Weyer — or Wierus, to use the more familiar Latin form — and

[69]

Wierus was a physician and pupil of the renowned Renaissance occultist Agrippa. The ligature between skepticism and occultism — the science of its day — is natural enough; but we shall continue to find it in many of the Restoration skeptics, when it had become distinctly antiquated. Whether this persistence points to some innate disposition in the skeptics, or rather to the influence of Scot is hard to say. Certainly it seems wrong of Summers to call Scot ineffective, for his book was reprinted well into the seventeenth century. *The Discoverie of Witchcraft* is indeed dull and very reductive in its explanations, yet its author must have had courage and a sense of charity. It remains one of the most original and substantial of the early English attacks. Between Scot and the middle of the seventeenth century little of interest was written on either side. The attitudes in Robert Burton's *Anatomy of Melancholy* (1621) are representative of educated opinion: that devils can work miracles, stop rivers, turn back the stars in their courses, and so forth, are "poetical fictions." But the devil does exist as God's avenger; he can influence us mentally and physically; he can work through melancholy and operate in our imagination; he is a chief cause of enthusiasm and superstition.[9]

But the controversy became very animated from the middle to the end of the century. Persecution had been rekindled in the 1640s and, after something of a lull in the 1650s, it was again accelerated in the 1660s; and of course the unpleasantness at Salem, vividly reported back to the mother country, sustained interest in the 1690s. On the intellectual plane, it was surely the rise of rationalism that precipitated the debate. In my opinion the publication of Hobbes's *Leviathan* in 1651, specifically, incited a catena of attacks and defenses that was to run for more

---

[9]The most pertinent portions of the *Anatomy of Melancholy* are: Part I, Section 2, Member 1, Subsection 1–3; Part III, Section 4, Member 1, Subsection 1–2, and Member 2, Subsection 6. There were other skeptics besides Scot, most notably George Gifford in *A Dialogue Concerning Witches and Witchcraftes* (1583) and Francis Bacon in *Sylva Sylvarum*, but they are less elaborate, generally more cautious, and seem to have had little influence.

than half a century. The cautelous Hobbes is remarkably candid on witches, demons, possessions, and apparitions, all of which he remands to the realm of madness or of dream. Departing from Scot, however, he sees the witch's trade as "neerer to a new Religion, than to a Craft," and he quite lacks Scot's human-itarian tone: "as for Witches, I think not that their witchcraft is any reall power; but yet that they are justly punished, for the false beliefe they have, that they can do such mischiefe, joyned with their purpose to do it if they can." Devils and witches can-not work miracles, and the demoniacs of the Bible were suffer-ing from natural causes: "That there were many Daemoniaques in the Primitive Church, and few Mad-men, and other such sin-gular diseases; whereas in these times we hear of, and see many Mad-men, and few Daemoniaques, proceeds not from the Change of Nature; but of Names." It is true that Christ spoke to the "demons" in his exorcisms, but then he rebuked the winds, too; such language is figurative. Christ really knew bet-ter, but his purpose on earth was not to teach us the lowly pre-cepts of natural philosophy or science. Like Scot, Hobbes sug-gests that Christ's temptations were visionary, and there is no dissemblance in his rationalizing of biblical miracles. Demons are imaginary; they are invoked by the authorities to keep man in awe, fear, and subjection (*Leviathan*, Chs. 2, 8, 37, 45). Polit-ically, Hobbes is more conservative than Scot, although he is a shade more outspoken in his skepticism of the supernatural. The age, nevertheless, thrust on him a certain coyness, and he will occasionally disparage the Sadducees or materialists; but such subterfuge could not deflect criticism, howsoever it soft-ened the blows.

In less than two years Henry More concocted *An Antidote against Atheisme* (1653), clearly aimed at Hobbes. More was one of the ablest, clearest, and most concise of the Cambridge Platonists, and he was no fond fanatic. His parents had been Cal-vinists, but he could never swallow, as he puts it himself, that hard doctrine. In another book published in 1656, he attacks irrationality and enthusiasm and warns us against those for whom "the Wind cannot be more than ordinarily high, but

[71]

they are prone to imagine the Devil raised it."[10] The *Antidote*, then, breathes in part a very modern air. More recognizes and admires much in the new philosophy, but he notes, like Browne a decade earlier, that "the Tempter would take advantage where hee may, to carry men captive out of one darke prison into another, out of *Superstition* into *Atheisme* it self." Avoiding appeals to scripture, dogma, or theology, he presents a form of the ontological proof of God with extraordinary lucidity and sophistication. Having offered this *mental* proof, he looks to empirical evidence. First he stresses, as so many have done before and since, the order and regularity of the universe. Then he examines another kind of empirical evidence: the unaccountable and miraculous events that show God's special providence and a spiritual world. Some of these tales may be false, he knows, and he carefully establishes three criteria to apply to miraculous narratives: Does the narrator have any self-interest in the story's being believed? Were there many eye-witnesses? Does the miraculous event leave "any sensible *effect*" behind? He then retails with vivacious credulity stories of charms, Lapland witches selling winds to sailors, raising of storms by magic, demoniacs foretelling the future, the Pied Piper (a tale irrefutably proved by the ancient records), familiar spirits, the sabbat, transformations. These events, he concludes, cannot be wholly explained by imagination; for atheists so to argue shows in them an even greater credulity and fondness for simple explanations.

It is not strictly accurate, though it has been recently affirmed, that "almost half" of the *Antidote* is concerned with the miraculous; one-fourth is closer to the truth.[11] Still, the proportion is noteworthy, and the book is an interesting early example of the close connection seen between belief in witch and miracle narratives, and in religion. It is curious, too, that

[10]Henry More, *Enthusiasmus Triumphatus* (1656): Augustan Reprint Society facsimile of 1662 edn. (Los Angeles: Univ. of California Press, 1966), 11.

[11]M. V. De Porte asserts this of the *Antidote* in his preface to the facsimile edn. of More's *Enthusiasmus* (note 10, above), viii. The *Antidote* (1653 ed.) consists of 164 pages in the body, and 24 prefatory pages; the miraculous portion runs from pp. 105–51.

More makes no serious attempt to apply his three criteria of truth to his own stories, which are hustled on and off his stage pell-mell and will not stay for verification. Among them are interspersed intemperate and even defamatory remarks, such as his calling the moderately skeptical Wierus an "industrious *Advocate of Witches*." More's short book is quite readable, but it presents to the modern mind a quaint inconsistency. The first and longer section shows the author to be a delicate and sedulous philosopher with an up-to-date and even compassionate understanding of the skeptical propensities of his audience; his treatment of innate ideas and the ontological proof is sensitive and deft. In the second, miraculous part he becomes a credulous wonder-monger peremptorily disdaining as atheist any who would doubt his tales. But of course More considered himself a modern and reasonable man emancipated from superstition and enthusiasm. For him, the miraculous section of his book constitutes empirical evidence supplementing the philosophical arguments in the first part.

A fellow Cambridge Platonist, but intellectual enemy of More's, was Thomas Vaughan, brother of the poet Henry Vaughan and an Anglican priest. Vaughan was an occultist of sorts and a mystic, whose cabbalistic jargon and avid transcendentalism greatly irritated More. *Magic* is a good word for Vaughan; he defined it, one year before *Leviathan*, as "nothing else but the wisdom of The Creator revealed and planted in the creature." But the higher wisdom of ceremonial magic has been misconstrued and debased by "the common man" into the vulgarities of black magic; it is the difference between theurgy and goetia. He traces the noble tradition of magic from the Egyptian and Chaldean antiquity and observes: "I will not deny but in the shades and ivie of this wildernesse, there are some birds of night, owles and bats, of a different feather from our phoenix; I mean some conjurers whose dark indirect affection to the name of magic, made them invent traditions more prodigious than their practices." Lucifer has tried to nullify God's creation, but he and his confederates "are expelled from Light to Darknesse, and thus rebellion is as the sin of witchcraft—a witch is a rebel in physicks, and a rebell is a witch in politicks: the one acts against nature, the other against order, the rule of it; but both are in league with the devil, as the first father of discord and sorcerie."[12]

Such was this heterodox priest, neither routine skeptic nor regular believer. Essentially he is on the side of Scot and Hobbes with respect to black magic: it is either fraud or superstition. But he embraces much more than Scot a belief in natural magic that verges, so far as one can tell from the thickets of his style, on authentic mysticism. Theurgy or white magic enables the mage to communicate with the elementals or good spirits. By this means, rather than by More's innate ideas or the rites and sacraments of the Church, one can penetrate the ultimate arcana. Like More, Vaughan considered himself a modern — indeed, a kind of prophet. In fact he is one of the last of the Renaissance occultists. Yet he scorned Aristotle — More admired him — and was keenly interested in Descartes, whom More detested. Such is the complexity of the intellectual patterns of the seventeenth century.

To the lavish, 1665 edition of Scot's *Discoverie* there is attached an anonymous addendum that has been represented by some scholars as credulous and therefore contradictory of Scot's thesis; it is an attempt, some suggest, to vindicate the Cullender-Duny trial. It is true that the author disagrees with Scot on the witch of Endor: she did indeed raise Samuel's *"Sydereal Spirit."* But the author is actually an occultist like Vaughan, and in the main he only elaborates on the natural magic endorsed by Scot himself. For example, though he does not ridicule charms and spells as Scot does, neither does he place any credence in their *words*. They are the ritual side of a more profound theurgical understanding of the nature of things. He shares Scot's disgust

---

[12]*The Magical Writings of Thomas Vaughan*, ed. A. E. Waite (London, 1888), 87, 90, 117, 24. See Charles Williams, *Witchcraft* (London: Faber and Faber, 1941), Ch.10, for an illuminating discussion of Vaughan and his ilk. Williams's book, by the way, is a pleasant contrast with the mechanical skepticism of most modern studies and the effervescent credulity of writers such as Summers.

[74]

for vulgar witchcraft. In general, Restoration occultism found common ground with Hobbesian skepticism concerning witchcraft, possessions, and the like, though Hobbes seems much more modern to the twentieth-century mind.[13] The other major Restoration skeptics are closer to Hobbes than to Vaughan, though at least one of them shares Vaughan's Cartesianism, and another his belief, rather attenuated, in natural magic. It is to this group that I should like to turn now.

⊓

John Webster and Francis Hutchinson were the most indefatigable and original English skeptics of witchcraft; to their names, however, we must add that of Balthazar Bekker, a Dutch Cartesian whose voluminous work was highly controversial on the Continent and in England as well. There are, in addition, some earlier attacks that deserve brief mention. In 1656 an obscure but pugnacious person named Thomas Ady wrote *A Candle in the Dark*. There are signs of eccentricity in this production: it is formally dedicated to God, and there are several fragmentary prefaces of a feverish and esoteric nature that may remind the modern reader of *A Tale of a Tub*. Clearly inspired by Scot, Ady contemplates the present state of witch beliefs and laments that *"England* hath shamefully fallen from the Truth which they [the Elizabethans] began to receive." He accepts the validity of prophetic dreams, biblical miracles (other than possessions),

---

[13]Nevertheless, books employing cabbalistic language might go in any direction. The eccentric geologist John Beaumont's *Historical, Physiological and Theological Treatise of Spirits . . . and other Magical Practices* (1705) is very credulous, citing Cotton Mather, Glanvill, and attacking the skeptic Bekker. Jacques Daillon's *Treatise of Spirits* (1723) turns out to be euhemerist, and provides skeptical interpretations of the story of the witch of Endor, the New Testament possessions. Daniel Defoe's pseudonymous *System of Magick* (1727) follows Vaughan in arguing that the earliest magicians were sages, and that magic has now been degraded to hocus-pocus. But in his other books on the subject, which I shall take up later, he expresses conventional, moderate attitudes very far removed from Vaughan's. On the connection between Renaissance occultism and modern intellectual strains, see S. A. McKnight, "Understanding Modernity," *The Intercollegiate Review*, 14 (1979), 107–17.

even astrology, but otherwise presents a redaction of Scot, following his explanations of the witch of Endor, Satan in *Job* and the gospel Temptations; possibly influenced by Hobbes, he interprets the biblical possessions psychologically. Like Scot, he strikes an humanitarian note: we should stop hanging poor, aged, lame, helpless people as witches. It is for this reason, no doubt, that the modern skeptical authority, C. L'Estrange Ewen, calls him an "advanced" thinker. But this is to take a partial view. Ady is virulently anti-Catholic. Since witches are idolaters, the *true* witches are Mahometans and Papists: "Therefore," he says, emending the Mosaic law against permitting a witch to live, "it were a good Law in *England*, if duly kept That no Jesuite, or Popish Priest should be suffered to live." Advanced thinking in the 1650s could do better than this. Henry More's book against enthusiasm appeared the same year as Ady's, and if it is more credulous of witchcraft, it is also more tolerant of Roman Catholicism. Still, Ady is a very lively pugilist, and without eclipsing Scot's work, he made available those arguments in a more portable form.

In 1669 two books appeared on the subject. One of them, *A True Interpretation of the Witch of Endor* by Lodowick Muggleton, has been called an "extended elaboration" on Scot's interpretation, a signal contribution to the skeptical side, a work "entirely rationalistic."[14] One might not guess from these remarks that it is a crudely printed, nearly illiterate pamphlet by a fanatic whose objections to the story of Endor are theological, not rationalistic: neither God nor any prophet or witch ever raised spirits from the dead *without bodies*. The book is thus really a symptom of Muggleton's obsession with physical resurrection, without which, he believed, the soul must be mortal. He does pose, in a tortuous way, psychological or materialistic explanations: Samuel was Saul's conscience, Satan in *Job* was Job's troubled soul, Satan in the gospel Temptations was a real man. He thus exhibits the internalizing tendencies of seven-

---

[14]See Jackson I. Cope, *Joseph Glanvill, Anglican Apologist* (St. Louis: Washington Univ. Press, 1956), 98.

teenth-century, radical Protestantism, tendencies that were later to issue in agnostic humanism and nineteenth-century Idealism. But Muggleton never questions the existence of the devil or hell in eternity (temporally there is "no other Satan but what is in man"), and I rather think he would have had little love for the twentieth-century academics who include him among the harbingers of the Enlightenment. The other book is in fact much more in Scot's tradition, an eighty-page pamphlet, as crudely printed as Muggleton's, *The Question of Witchcraft Debated.* The author, one John Wagstaffe, presents Scot's arguments still more concisely than Ady, and there is even more of an animus against priestcraft, possibly encouraged by Hobbes: the priests have imposed the foolish belief in magic on the people in order to keep them in subjection or exploit their goods.

In 1677 John Webster, a non-conformist influenced by the mysticism of Jacob Behmen, published the first exhaustive skeptical treatment of the subject after Scot: *The Displaying of Supposed Witchcraft.* The title continues, informatively: "Wherein is affirmed that there are many sorts of Deceivers and Imposters, and Divers persons under a passive *Delusion* of *Melancholy* and *Fancy.* But that there is a *Corporal League* made betwixt the Devil and the Witch . . . is utterly denied and disproved." Webster praises Wierus, Scot and Wagstaffe; but he feels that he must amplify their arguments because contemporary defenders of the belief like Casaubon and Glanvill "have afresh espoused so bad a cause, and . . . have newly furbished up the old Weapons . . . of the Popish Sink and Dunghills, and put them into a new dress." Webster shows the same anti-papist sentiment as the other skeptics, ridicules Glanvill's ghost and witch stories as incredible and ludicrous, attacks Casaubon as "a sworn Witchmonger, even to the credulity of the filthiest and most impossible of their actions." Webster's gravamen, like Scot's, is that "to ascribe to the Devil the efficiency of those operations we do not clearly understand, is to allow him a kind of Omnipotency, and both to rob God and Nature of that which belongeth unto them." The Bible does not proscribe "true" witchcraft, but only frauds, poisoners, and the like, though the translation of the

Authorized Version, which Webster straitly censures, sometimes gives a false impression. The witch of Endor used ventriloquism; the biblical possessions, the prologue to *Job*, should be taken figuratively.

But Webster has some new weaponry. Responding to the argument from consensus or the experience of mankind, employed by More, Casaubon, and Glanvill, Webster dares to say that such consensus may be addlepated, and he cites as an example Christ's persecution by the conforming Jews. More than the other skeptics he appeals to natural philosophy: science has explained, and will continue to explain, many phenomena that now seem diabolic or miraculous. Here at last, the twentieth-century reader will exclaim, is a *modern* argument; and he will be right. Again reacting to More, Casaubon, Glanvill, Webster repudiates indignantly the notion that atheism or Sadduceeism is implied by a denial of witchcraft; these beliefs are not interconnected. Nowhere does scripture mention humans making a formal pact with the devil, copulating with him, being transformed by him into a beast, having imps, and so on, all of which are of the essence of alleged witchcraft. Adopting More's criteria for evaluating miraculous stories, Webster turns them against More and argues that no truly convincing, verifiable account of such things is available: even testimonies of several or many apparently honest people may be vitiated by interest, credulity, envy, and so forth. I do not know whether Webster has ever been given credit for anticipating Hume's famous arguments against miracles, but virtually everything Hume has to say on this point is here. One must observe, however, that Webster establishes conditions which make it impossible to accept *anything* on testimony: witnesses, he says, must be perfectly sound in their sensory organs and in judgment, and they must be free of superstitious notions, with Webster presumably the one to adjudicate what is superstitious. He also contends that tales of apparitions do not prove the existence of spirits, for that would be a *petitio principii:* first we must be shown that the apparitions *were* spirits.

Webster's book intelligently renews old arguments and offers some others. He has a scientific bias absent in the earlier skeptics, and he questions with real courage some of the canons of the other side: that consensus and the antiquity of beliefs assures their truth, that atheism and denial of witchcraft are connected, that ghost stories really prove anything, that scripture supports any notion of witchcraft in its more highly evolved theological definition, with pacts, transformations, and the like. At the same time he advances an intricate and dubious theory about angelic bodies, professes belief in astral spirits and "effluvia," and can lapse into the cabbalistic jargon of Vaughan. There is the same potpourri of "modern" and quaint beliefs as in More's *Antidote,* though the particular beliefs are different. A century and a half later Coleridge praised Webster's "excellent good sense" and "sound judgment," and he also noted that skeptics of Webster's age had to explain everything by deliberate imposture or deceit, while the later discovery of "self-magnetism" provides a third explanation.[15] The early skeptics were additionally hampered by the need to reconcile disbelief in witchcraft with faith in the scriptures. *Job,* even the temptations of Christ, may be seen as figurative and visionary, but the Mosaic laws (*Exodus* xxii. 18; *Leviticus* xix. 26; *Deuteronomy* xviii. 10, 11), the dramatic narrative of the witch of Endor, the demonic possessions of the New Testament (especially the Gadarene swine): these often hurried them into contorted and sophistical exegesis.

From 1691 to 1693 Balthazar Bekker, a Dutch divine and admirer of Descartes, published an even more elaborate and intrepid criticism than Webster's: *De Betoverde Weereld,* in four volumes. It was translated into German in 1693 and into French the next year, causing generally a great hullabaloo in Europe. Bekker was deposed from the ministry and died in Amsterdam in 1698. The first volume, very poorly printed, appeared in English in 1695 as *The World Bewitch'd,* but though the title page bears the hopeful legend, "Vol. I," the rest

[15]See copy of Webster in British Library, shelf no. C 126, front cover verso and pp. 69–70. There are notes by other hands in this copy, but Coleridge's are signed or initialed; one is dated 27 Oct. 1819.

was not forthcoming. The first volume contains, indeed, what would have been the most appetizing part of the entire work for English Protestants: an historical survey tracing most of the beliefs about demons to the pagans and the papists. Bekker rehearses the old arguments, often more gracefully and with more erudition. Bekker was a pioneer in the comparative study of religions, and he descants on heathen and Catholic theology with more sophistication than Scot or Webster. He is sometimes more moderate than they were: for example, demonic possessions in the Bible were diseases, but then they were very dangerous, incurable diseases, and so Christ's cures remain miraculous. Beneath his commentary, too, there slinks a furtive Cartesianism. Spirits and demons may exist, but there is no evidence in scripture that mortals can traffic with them: Christ's temptations were visionary, the Mosaic laws were against cozeners and idolaters, the witch of Endor was an evil person, but nothing more. Nor is such unholy communion proved by empirical evidence. He serves up a rational explanation for one of Glanvill's most celebrated stories of the preternatural, the Drummer of Tedworth, and he ridicules as credulous those who, like More, feed us tales of the Pied Piper. All these matters can be accounted for by natural causes or human deception.

In March 1711/12 one Jane Wenham was tried for witchcraft, condemned, but royally reprieved; this was probably the last time in England that the death sentence was imposed for witchcraft. It also occasioned a pamphlet war in which several incondite denunciations of witches were wrought by a local clergyman, Francis Bragge, and published by the notorious printer Curll. These works regurgitate standard arguments and were met by skeptical pamphlets of similar, deplorable quality. The most ambitious result was a two-volume *Compleat History of Magick, Sorcery, and Witchcraft* (1715–1716), published anonymously but later claimed by an obscure and unsuccessful physician, Richard Boulton. This, too, was published by Curll, and is nothing more than a venture in sensational journalism. In all this material even the antiquary will find little to flutter his pulse, but it did serve the useful purpose of vexing Francis

Hutchinson, future Bishop of Down, who as a consequence wrote the last important skeptical study, *An Historical Essay Concerning Witchcraft* (1718; reissued with additional matter, 1720). Since the Restoration, Hutchinson complains, books favoring the witch belief have continued to appear; these, alas, "are read with great Eagerness, and are continually levening the Minds of the Youth, who delight in such Subjects." Although Hutchinson spends much time on scripture and rehearses arguments from Scot, Webster, and Bekker, he was the first to compile statistics on the witch trials, and he shows an awareness of the psychological and social dimensions of witch-belief beyond anything in the other skeptics. Hutchinson will not deny the abstract possibility of witchcraft, and he attaches to his study two sermons against Sadduceeism, one affirming the reality and importance of Christ's miracles, the other the existence of good and evil angels in the chain of being. But he notes that witchcraft is most rampant in superstitious Catholic countries or where laws and customs sanction such beliefs: this is prima facie suspicious. He further notes that outbreaks of witchcraft are often preceded by the circulation of credulous books like those by the Mathers, and that persecution typically ceases when wealthy people begin to be charged. He slyly observes that Cotton Mather's account of the disturbances at Salem enhanced his own reputation and power, as well as that of his illustrious family. There is no quaint occultism in Hutchinson, but hard statistics and skeptical insinuations. Of all the skeptics, only Hutchinson much conforms to the whig stereotype: a moderate humanitarian imbued with eighteenth-century common sense. While earlier skeptics tried to reduce everything to fraud, Hutchinson perceives the important element of self-deception and hysteria, and so works up an explanation that has since been questioned, though sometimes very shrewdly, by only a few revisionists.[16]

[16]For example, in his excellent *Witchcraft at Salem* (New York: George Braziller, 1969) Chadwick Hansen argues that there *were* witches there: i.e., people deliberately and quite sanely endeavoring to work witchcraft.

With Hutchinson, then, we have truly entered into the modern world. Thomas Gordon's short essay "Of Witchcraft," written for the popular press at about this time, is as up-to-date as one could wish. Priests fostered belief in witchcraft because only priests could cure it. But they were assisted by our natural credulity: we have a "wondering Quality" that delights in such mysteries. We have wrought great cruelties in indulging this pleasure, but "an old Woman may be miserable now, and not be hanged for it." Reiterating a point going back to Scot, Gordon says he will be "so much a heretick as to believe, that God Almighty, and not the Devil, governs the World." But Gordon had no fears of being hunted out as a heretic, and Oliver Goldsmith imperturbably appropriates both his opinions and his language thirty years later. By Scot's age Goldsmith might have been considered a heretic; by modern standards he is only a plagiarist.[17]

The skeptical attitude tends to prevail in Restoration poetry and drama. The grand exception to this, of course, is Milton, whose Satan can corrupt the human imagination, assume various shapes, raise storms. The temptation of Christ in *Paradise Regained* is no mere vision. Milton also exploits witch-beliefs for poetic purposes, as when, in *Paradise Lost*, he describes the "Night-Hag," Hecate, goddess of witches, "riding through the Air . . . / Lur'd with the smell of infant blood, to dance / With *Lapland* Witches" (II, 662–666). But at the same time Samuel Butler ridicules magic and witch beliefs in his satiric *Hudibras*: the "*Feats of Witches*" and the "*Lapland Hag*" are derisory, and he singles out Glanvill's tale of the Drummer of Tedworth for special mockery. All this is part of his anti-Puritan satire, but it is to be noted that the foremost Puritan writer of the time, aside from Milton, seems deliberately colorless when dealing with

---

[17]See Thomas Gordon, *The Humourist*, 3d ed. (1724), 74–77, and cf. Oliver Goldsmith, *The Bee*, 8 (24 Nov. 1759). In another essay in *The Humourist*, "Of Ghosts and Apparitions," Gordon recounts some stories that are probably parodies of Glanvill's spectral narratives.

demonic materials.[18] In *The Lancashire Witches* (1681) Thomas Shadwell endows his witches with supernatural powers; in his prefatory remarks, however, he says that he would rather have given everything a natural explanation, but that he might then have been accused of atheism. The desire for sensationalism, one suspects, was his true motive. Nevertheless, in the play the sane, sensible people are either skeptics or neutral, while those who support witch belief, and who accuse the sane ones of being Hobbists, are papists, dunces and knaves. The fact that the dunces are right about the witches, according to the action of the play, is not something that the spectator is to reflect on. At about the same time William Mountfort can give the Faustus story, which had been dramatized with some gravity by Marlowe, a wholly farcical treatment: after the wretched magician has been rent to pieces at the end of the play, we are told by the stage directions that "Faustus *Limbs come together, a Dance, and Song.*"

Addison, writing around the time of the Wenham affair, is coy and equivocal on the subject (*Spectator*, nos. 110, 117). His unsuccessful play *The Drummer* (1716) was inspired by Glanvill's Drummer of Tedworth, but the story is greatly altered. Natural explanations are given for everything, and supposed poltergeists and conjurers are exploited for comedy. But Addison, ever bold in pursuit of moderation, attacks Sadduceeism too—in the silly, cowardly, hypocritical, and unprincipled freethinker Tinsel. Allan Ramsay's pastoral drama, *The Gentle*

---

[18]It is evident in John Bunyan's spiritual autobiography, *Grace Abounding* (1666), that he views the devil as a real entity capable of speaking in the minds of tempted Christians; but Satan figures there as little more than an evil conscience. *The Pilgrim's Progress* (1678, 1684) contains no striking depictions of demonism, despite some apocalyptic passages; and although his rather wearisome *Holy War* (1682) is true to the traditions of the witch tales in representing Diabolus as a black man or Negro, the devil operates there politically, as it were, rather than spiritually or psychologically, and his characterization is insipid. The evil portrayed in *The Life and Death of Mr. Badman* (1680) is altogether mundane. At the opposite extremity are the witches and demons of the Restoration heroic drama and opera; these I have considered too exotic and factitious to be pertinent here.

Shepherd (1725), presents an entirely benevolent "witch" in Mause, who, however, is feared and given supernatural powers by the ignorant peasantry "Because by education I was taught / To speak and act aboon their common thought." Compared with Shadwell's play, the tone of *The Gentle Shepherd* is very mild. On the one hand Ramsay's "witch" is infinitely more intellectual, philosophical, and sympathetic than Shadwell's; but his portrayal of the credulous peasants is softer, too, as though their fatuities were beneath ridicule. Of course there are no supernatural phenomena in the play. From these works of Addison and Ramsay, as from Gordon's essay, one gets the feeling that the debate is over. Yet in half a century explicit supernaturalism would revive in the Gothic novels, and the "wondering quality" to which Gordon condescends would be once again engaged.

¤

Those who defended belief in witchcraft—I shall call them *apologists*, for short—were usually skeptics of Renaissance magic; in fact they were often partisans, though not always zealous partisans, of the new philosophy. Meric Casaubon, for example, was the son of the great humanist and scholar Isaac Casaubon, whose linguistic and textual studies helped to discredit the authority of the hermetic writers so revered by Agrippa and other Renaissance occultists. Like More, Meric was a Calvinist by background, an Anglican by choice, and he wrote a skeptical *Treatise Concerning Enthusiasme* in 1655, a year before More's shorter work on the same subject. "Let others admire Witches and Magicians ... I honour and admire a good Physician much more," he says, and the book shows a very modern insight into psychological and physical problems. But in 1668 he published *Of Credulity and Incredulity*; to this essay he added an important section in 1670, and the whole was reissued posthumously in 1672 as *A Treatise Proving Spirits, Witches, and Supernatural Operations, By Pregnant Instances and Evidences*. Casaubon argues from consensus, common

[84]

sense, empirical evidence, scripture, and he attacks Wagstaffe among others. Some of his arguments we have seen in Browne and More; others are found in Glanvill and will be examined then. What I should like to stress about Casaubon is his attitude toward the new philosophy. He recognizes, even salutes, the advances of Baconian science; but he also fears that the method, so intensely devoted to *things*, may come to slight spiritual matters. In the 1670 additon to *Of Credulity and Incredulity* he observes:

> Now this, the not believing the real existence of incorporeal essences, whether through dulness or coarseness of brain; or long accustomance to earthly objects, and contemplation of nature, and natural causes, where no ground, or foundation is laid to sanctifie such enquiries . . . is the most immediate, and intrinsick . . . cause of Atheism, or *Incredulity, in things divine.*

Casaubon is admonishing against an habitual prejudice, animated by the scientific method, in favor of rationalism and skepticism. Repeatedly he draws the connection between materialism or Sadduceeism, and the questioning of miracles and witchcraft. To be skeptical is to be arrogant; it is to deny revelation, reason, consensus. Such skepticism is also unprogressive: had Columbus not believed in the existence of a great continent ere he experienced it, *"America* might have been unknown to this day." A modern reader would be quite wrong in seeing an inconsistency between Casaubon's earlier book on enthusiasm and this one on witchcraft. The first attacked one error, superstition; the other attacks the opposite error, skepticism. Casaubon, like Browne and More, pursues the middle way. A modern reader is also apt to share Webster's indignation at Casaubon's linking skepticism of witchcraft with irreligion, and perhaps he *should* share it. But the connection Casaubon sees between science and the skeptical sensibility is not to be blinked. Had he beheld Hume, or our present positivists, he would have felt vindicated.

Joseph Glanvill is easily the most substantial, influential, and interesting of the Restoration apologists. Like More and Casaubon he had a Calvinist background, but he became an Anglican and was all his life a vigorous promoter of the new philosophy and its empirical method. His first book, *The Vanity of Dogmatizing* (1661), is a Baconian attack on the Peripatetic philosophy and the mediaeval schoolmen; his *Plus Ultra* (1668) is a complementary work extolling the new science; and his *Philosophia Pia* (1671) asserts the compatability of science and Christianity. He is always a latitudinarian, somewhat mistrustful of the miraculous, and a critic—long before Hume—of the laws of causation. If there are modern elements in More and Casaubon, then Glanvill must be reckoned a thorough modern. Yet *as* such he questioned narrow-mindedness and dogmatism, and he found these unpleasant qualities most at work in the rationalists and skeptics. And so this lively and *au courant* person is remembered today, when he is remembered at all, for his colorfully titled *Sadducismus Triumphatus: Or, A Full and Plain Evidence, concerning Witches and Apparitions.* The modern horror-story writer, constructing a list of terrible or weird tomes on the black arts to evoke a shudder, inevitably includes Glanvill; and even a reputable scholar is capable of calling the book a "chamber of horrors." But Montague Summers, for all of his crotchets, is much more just to Glanvill when he describes him as "undoubtedly the most able as he is the fairest-minded English writer upon Witchcraft in the seventeenth century."[19] First published in 1666 under the blander *Philosophical Considerations Touching Witches and Witchcraft,* the book went through innumerable and confusing revisions, amplifications, retitlings. It appeared in 1668 as *A Blow at Modern Sadducism,* and it was not till 1681 that it was new baptized with the familiar Latin title, possibly supplied by his friend More; Glanvill had died the year before. More continued to make additions,

---

[19]Summers, *Geography of Witchcraft,* 163. E. A. Baker, *History of the English Novel,* vol. 5 (London: Witherby, 1934) 208, calls Glanvill's book a "chamber of horrors." Glanvill is included in a list of "shuddery" books by, e.g., H. P. Lovecraft in his short story, "The Festival."

and the edition of 1689, two years after More's own death, is the most complete. The book was reprinted regularly well into the eighteenth century, and its quaint title and flamboyant illustrations, including a bold frontispiece showing the witch of Endor conjuring up Samuel, do give it a macabre air.

The 1689 edition is prefaced with a prolix, polemical letter by More in which he castigates Scot, Ady, and, above all, Webster, whom he styles a "sworn Advocate of the Witches, who thus madly and boldly, against all sense and reason, against all antiquity, all Interpreters, and against the inspired Scripture it self, will have no *Samuel*" in the story of Endor. Souls *can* appear to whomsoever they will, as Christ's own example shows. More dissects scrupulously the story of Endor to prove that the rationalistic explanations of ventiloquism or a confederate in a closet are gross misreadings of the account. He defends the standard translation of "witch," "wizzard," enchanter," from the Old Testament Hebrew, arguing that these truly capture the sense of the words, which signify more than cozener, poisoner, or the like. He notes, too, that the capital punishment enjoined by Moses would be too severe if these people were only cheats. He complains, justly, that Webster vulgarizes and trivializes the beliefs of the opposition. He says, for example, that Webster portrays the witch-pact with the devil "as if it were no League or Covenant, unless some Lawyer drew the Instrument, and engrossed it in Vellum or thick Parchment, and there were so many Witnesses with the Hand and Seal of the Party." Webster, it is true, resorts to literalism and *reductio ad absurdum:* hoary weapons of the debater, but tactics which a sober Platonist such as More would highly resent.

The *Sadducismus Triumphatus* itself is divided into two parts; the first takes up the theoretical possibility of witchcraft, the second musters evidence for the real existence of witches. Glanvill explicitly links Scot with Hobbes and the denial of witches with atheism. Materialism is simple-minded, dogmatic, implausible. There are many things we cannot understand, but it is reasonable to believe in spirits because of the chain of being, human experience, and consensus. Those who would explain away all preternatural phenomena by imagination or delusion are too reductive, too cynical about human testimony. To believe that evil spirits may harm us is no more to deny God's omnipotence or providence than to recognize that natural evils can harm us. If the soul can be separated from the body, as Christians believe, why cannot it be conveyed through the air, or even inhabit another body? Glanvill attacks Descartes, whom earlier he had admired, as a sophistical thinker at once affirming the existence of spirits but denying that they are anywhere in the world. Cartesianism is thus a skulking Hobbism, and Glanvill had no need of Bekker's example to perceive its implications. Fundamental to Christianity is the distinction of soul from body, spirit from matter; but they are interconnected. A witch cannot work miracles, but she can do strange things through a compact with an evil spirit. It is the spirit that really performs the wonders, and he may work them directly, or indirectly through natural causes. These compacts can be vulgarly misunderstood, and skeptics such as Webster, in ridiculing copulation between the devil and the witch, prove nothing more than "if a Man should define an Angel to be a Creature in the shape of a Boy with Wings, and then prove there is no such Being." Assuredly we may be deceived or deluded, but we must examine the evidence impartially. This the skeptics fail to do; they ignore some evidence; they try to make the Bible say what *they* wish it to. Scripture itself distinguishes between physical disease and demonic possession, and episodes like that of the Gadarene swine particularly resist rationalist exposition. Besides, if all these were merely diseases, Christ has imposed on us. Hobbes may say that Christ spoke according to the beliefs of his age and had no wish to waste time teaching natural philosophy. But there *were* materialists in those days—the Sadducees—who denied supernatural phenomena; Christ clearly dissociates himself from them. And into what contortions are the skeptics thrust when they face that "grand Instance of Confederacy with Evil Spirits," the tale of the witch of Endor! Scot and Webster are "not interpreting a Story, but making one."

Glanvill then turns to contemporary stories, beginning with

[88]

his most celebrated, the demon drummer of Tedworth. This is a classic, poltergeist narrative, though the person supposedly responsible for the disturbances, a rascally drummer, was still alive, and so presumably commanding a spirit to work them. The phenomena included: untoward sounds and lights, horrid smells, the hurling of boards and chairs and raising of beds, spectral manifestations such as spots of blood and an apparition with "a great Body with two red and glaring Eyes." Glanvill personally investigates, and he experiences some of the less spectacular, but still inexplicable, manifestations. He notes that the party thus persecuted, John Mompesson, had no motive for any deception, was not of melancholy humor, could not have profited from it in any way, but indeed was greatly incommoded. Glanvill's other stories involve horrible apparitions, appearances of the devil, sabbats, witching dolls. They are more contemporary and much more circumstantial than those in More or Casaubon, and they are usually followed by a commentary analysing the nature of the phenomena, the numbers and characters of the witnesses. These narratives have little of the drama and spiritual horror of the later ghost story, but their profusion, contemporaneousness, and detail give the book a cumulative power much greater than the earlier compendiums. We do not have here a retelling of Pliny's tale of the haunted house, old even in Pliny's time I suspect, or the fable of the Pied Piper; we are told instead of John Mompesson of Tedworth, who in 1661 made the mistake of throwing a vagrant drummer into jail.

Glanvill, and More in his dilatations of *Sadducismus Triumphatus*, apply conscientiously to the stories the criteria that More had himself devised, but failed to employ, in his own *Antidote*. Far from being a "chamber of horrors," the book is among the first to provide the data later sought so assiduously by the Society for Psychical Research. If the narratives are matter-of-fact, that is what Glanvill wished them to be. The biblical exegesis is also logical. So long as the skeptics had to conciliate scripture, so long would they be on the defensive. It is indeed arguable that Scot and Webster are ignoring important connotations when they interpret the Mosaic laws against witchcraft as merely regulations about prestigiators. And as for the witch of Endor, no professor of literature today would tolerate from his students an interpretation so wildly untextual, so "inventive," as theirs. Finally, in his theoretical discussion of the possibility of witchcraft, Glanvill has all the advantages over the skeptics, since he can always appeal to the circumscriptions of our reason, the perils of intellectual pride, and so on. At least until that skeptical sensibility feared by Casaubon had become intrenched, Glanvill's views would seem the more enlightened, the more open-minded, the more plausible.

On theology and scripture, Casaubon and Glanvill said pretty much everything that the Restoration apologists were prepared to say. But more stories could always be heaped up, and the 1680s and 1690s saw a spate of witch and ghost anthologies usually patterned after Glanvill's. To read such stories for mere delight was still considered shamefully sybaritic, and so the anthologists represent themselves — sincerely enough, no doubt — as foes of Hobbism. The title alone is instructive of Richard Bovet's *Pandaemonium, or the Devil's Cloyster, Being a further Blow to Modern Sadducism* (1684); it is dedicated to Henry More. A year later appeared George Sinclair's *Satan's Invisible World Discovered*, which inveighs against Cartesianism and the *"Saducean Principle."* Richard Baxter's popular collection, *The Certainty of the World of Spirits Fully Evinced* (1691), features those stories that show "God's arbitrary sovereign power." These storytellers, in the main, exhibit greater narrative ability, if less theological sophistication, than Glanvill; their tales are often quite contemporary, circumstantial, vivid, and some of Sinclair's were reworked by Sir Walter Scott and R. L. Stevenson. The vigorous market for such material is shown by *The Kingdom of Darkness; or, The History of Daemons, Spectres, Witches, Apparitions,* compiled by the hack Nathaniel Crouch writing under the pseudonym of Robert Burton. First published in 1688, it reappeared several times, once as late as 1728. According to the *Dictionary of National Biography* this is one of Crouch's "original publications," and no one seems to have noticed in his own time or since that it is a protracted plagiarism of the miraculous portions of More's *Antidote* (and possibly other works), given a more peppery title. Arguments against Hobbism other than the Casaubon-Glanvill sort can be found, but they are generally quaint. The anti-rationalist Thomas Tryon defends madness as a source of truth in his *Treatise of Dreams and Visions* (1689); it is a *"Waking Dream"* in which the "Soul is unchain'd, or set at liberty from the dark Confinements of the groser *Senses* and *Reason*." This recalls Sir Thomas Browne on sleep, mentioned in the previous chapter, but I daresay would be even too airy for Browne. Richard Burthogge's *Essay upon Reason, and the Nature of Spirits* (1694) assaults Hobbes with a new weapon, Lockean epistemology, which he tries cumbrously to join with Platonism; it is dedicated to Locke. Like Tryon's, the book is a curious fiasco: an arid and abstruse exposition of Locke united to a collection of classical and contemporary ghost stories recounted with a credulity equal to More's in his *Antidote*.

Daniel Defoe's several books on diabolism and ghosts, published pseudonymously in the 1720s, are clearly aimed at an audience more interested in narratives than theological disputation, and their tone is sometimes ironical, sometimes jocose, often equivocal. In *The Political History of the Devil* (1726) he affirms the actual existence of his subject, but is doubtful about such things as demonic pacts — anyway, the devil won't keep a bargain, as we all know. Defoe is reluctant to discuss the witch of Endor "because there are so many Scruples and Objections against that Story." Like Scot a century and a half before, he dilates on legerdemain, with a knowledge of which, modern sorcerers do not *need* to sell their souls for supernatural powers. But he defends the biblical possessions as authentic and denies that the devil is constrained in hell. Not only does Satan have a vast empire in the air, but he may well exercise power "in all the habitable parts of the *Solar System;* nay, of all the other *Solar Systems*." Defoe presents a number of well-told if unlocalized supernatural stories, but his tone is very different from Glanvill's, as when he remarks of a witch: "The Stories of her bewitching several People . . . are so formidable and extravagant, that I care not to put any ones Faith to the stretch about them, tho' publish'd by Authority, and testified by abundance of Witnesses." He is a timid controversialist, too, in his *Essay on the History and Reality of Apparitions* (1727): "Mr. *Glanville* and his Antagonists, the *Hobbists* and *Sadduces* of those Times" have exhausted that side of the matter. Many supernatural experiences proceed in fact from our consciences: "nor is it the least Testimony of an invisible World," he remarks with a sly reference to Glanvill, "that there is such a Drummer as that in the Soul." But he believes in guardian angels and thinks that it was such a benevolent spirit that addressed Saul at Endor; it could not have been the true soul of Samuel, however, for that would give too much power to witchcraft; Defoe doubts, in fact, whether any human spirits are ever allowed to return to earth. In this volume, too, he tells a number of good tales, and though he never gives names, dates, or places, they are usually contemporary and very circumstantial.

The difference in temper between Defoe and the Restoration writers is conspicuous. No skeptic like Scot or Webster, he is essentially orthodox.[20] But he is much less keen as an apologist than Glanvill. His chief interest is in the stories, and he tells them well; but, unlike Bovet or Sinclair, he dispenses with a polemical frame. In other words, we are well on our way to the modern ghost-story anthology. Defoe, indeed, is often considered the author of the first modern ghost story, for the celebrated *Apparition of Mrs. Veal* (1706), though published anonymously, is surely his. The technique of this early story is very much indebted to Glanvill. The story is supposedly based on fact; it is sober and circumstantial. We are assured as to the character of the witness: like John Mompesson of Tedworth, she was

[20]See Rodney M. Baine, *Daniel Defoe and the Supernatural* (Athens: Univ. of Georgia Press, 1968), 5. See Baine passim for a thorough analysis of Defoe's supernatural books, but from a different perspective from mine. For a good discussion of the background and attribution of "Mrs. Veal," which I shall mention shortly, see Baine, 73–108, and also *Accounts of the Apparition of Mrs. Veal*, introduced by Manuel Schonhorn (Los Angeles: Univ. of California Press, 1965).

not naturally melancholy, but indeed cheerful and known for her honesty. Defoe analyzes the validity of the story: the ghost gave information that the witness could not otherwise have known. As in Glanvill, the story is offered as evidence of a spiritual world. But Defoe shows an artistry beyond Glanvill in his setting the scene and disposing of the material, and he is especially shrewd in waiting till the most effective moment to reveal that the visitor is an apparition.

Very different, too, from the Restoration apologists was Dom Augustin Calmet, O.S.B., who in the 1740s wrote some essays in French that were given a sumptuous edition in English: *Dissertations upon the Apparitions of Angels, Daemons, and Ghosts, And concerning the Vampires of Hungary, Bohemia, Moravia, and Silesia* (1759). Calmet was at that time an elderly but famous biblical exegete, and he is rightly considered by Montague Summers to "smack of heterodoxy."[21] Calmet vehemently disclaims any intention "to promote superstition, or to furnish entertainment for the fond credulity of visionary minds." His gloss on Endor shows how far we have come from More or Glanvill: "whether Samuel was really raised up or not, whether his soul, or only a shadow, or even nothing at all appeared to the woman, it is still certain that Saul and his attendants, with the generality of the Hebrews, believed the thing to be possible." As a model of the discretionary style, this is unsurpassable. Note too that it is now practicable for a commentator to recognize supernaturalism, or at least a supernatural attitude, in the Bible without perforce sharing it. Calmet's views are as different from Scot's as from Glanvill's. For Calmet most tales of ghosts and devils are "gross impositions"; lycanthropy is but a delusion; witches only *think* they fly to the sabbat; vampires can generally be accounted for by natural causes (trances, and so forth). Of course Calmet does not embrace materialism, but neither is he defensive about his skepticism of witchcraft; he is not intimidated by charges of Sadduceeism, nor does it appear

[21]Montague Summers, *The Vampire: His Kith and Kin* (1928; rpt. New York: University Books, 1960), 174.

that there *were* any such charges. His essays are important in the history of anthropology and folklore. But like Defoe he is also a good storyteller, and that is the reason, I suspect, that most Englishmen bought the handsome translation of his essays. The polemical frames of Glanvill and Sinclair, rickety in Defoe, are wholly abandoned by Calmet, who in fact exerts himself to counteract credulity.

Thus the apologists of witchcraft turn their attention increasingly to the stories and away from scriptural or philosophical disquisition. Those who continued to write on that side of the matter tend to be perfunctory and unimaginative. Thus Philip Doddridge, in his *Lectures on ... Pneumatology, Ethics, and Divinity* (published posthumously, 1763), cites Bekker, Hutchinson, and other skeptics, and concedes that many biblical passages can be read figuratively. Still, scriptures affirm demonic possessions; witch pacts are mostly due to a "disordered imagination," but the stories about them have a continuity that gives one pause; ventriloquism fails to explain *everything* in the tale of Endor. All this is very sensible, very familiar, very jejune. The only thing new that Doddridge says was forced on him by the abolition of the witchcraft statute in 1736: "a contract with *Satan*, considered merely in this view, is not by human laws to be made penal."

It will be appropriate to conclude this section with John Wesley, who in his journals is a good index of the temper of the times. His defense of witchcraft is well known: "the giving up of witchcraft is, in effect, giving up the Bible." He says in 1776:

> I cannot give up to all the Deists ... the existence of witchcraft till I give up the credit of all history, sacred and profane. And at the present time I have not only as strong, but stronger proofs of this, from eye and ear witnesses, than I have of murder; so that I cannot rationally doubt of one any more than the other.

Here, in germ, are the essential arguments: scripture, consensus, experience. Like Casaubon and Glanvill, Wesley reproves the narrow-mindedness of the modern infidel, who speaks "so dogmatically against what not only the whole world, heathen and Christian, believed in past ages, but thousands, learned as well as unlearned, firmly believe at this day." Like Glanvill, he investigates some matters firsthand. In 1746 he met a woman "whom Satan had bound in an uncommon manner for several years"; in 1770 he saw a case of convulsive fits that had persevered ten years, which, together with some other curious symptoms, lead him to suspect witchcraft; he gives a fascinating and elaborate account of diabolic possession and exorcism, Methodist style, in 1663; his eldest brother had even quizzed John Mompesson's son, who staunchly affirmed the truth of the demon drummer of Tedworth. Yet even Wesley is tempted by doubt. He reads Glanvill and, after reading him, remarks: "I wish the facts had had a more judicious relater — one who would not have given a fair pretence for denying the whole by his awkward manner of accounting for some of the circumstances." And he sticks at some of Glanvill's explanations: "Indeed, supposing the facts true, I wonder a man of sense should attempt to account for them at all." He reads Baxter's *Certainty of the World of Spirits*, but is troubled: "How hard is it to keep the middle way; not to believe too little or too much!"[22]

The middle way between enthusiasm or superstition and skepticism: such was the position claimed by the Restoration apologists. But was it still the middle way a century later? It would be considered the moderate view so long as three conditions prevailed: respect for scripture as a significant authority, respect for historical consensus, a disposition to believe, rather than to deride, supernatural stories.

The "initial fallacy" contributing to belief in witchcraft, declares a modern authority, was "rigid adherence to the letter of the scriptures."[23] If only it were so simple! The Bible obvi-

---

[22]*The Journal of the Rev. John Wesley, A. M.*, ed. Nehemiah Curnock, 8 vols. (London: Robert Culley and Charles H. Kelly, 1909–1916): V, 265; VI, 109; V, 374–75; III, 250–51; V, 32–35; V, 266; III, 537; V, 311; V, 103. For other accounts of apparitions, see: IV, 148–49, 166; V, 178, 224, 487; VI, 212–13.

[23]Ewen, *Witchcraft*, 25.

ously affirms a spiritual world, and most modern commentators would go at least so far as Calmet and allow that its authors believed in witchcraft as something more than legerdemain, or even poisoning. Christ, who could correct erroneous theology when he wished (e.g., *John* ix), never contradicts the principle of demonianism, even encourages it; it is integral to his understanding of his mission, and the exorcisms of the gospels lead naturally to the final triumph in *Revelation*.[24] Whatever our own persuasions, I think we might agree that the apologists were more reasonable, more textually responsible, in exegesis than their opponents. The skeptics indeed, ransacking the story of Endor for evidences of ventriloquism or closet-confederates, were in a manner the literalists of the age. The apologists, like the Fathers and the scholastic theologians, recognized the legitimacy of figurative interpretation. But they did wish to preserve the Bible as a consequential document, and so resisted attempts to explain things away (e.g., devils are diseases) or to read things in (the witch of Endor threw her voice). They wished to keep alive a sense of wonder and reverence, an awareness of the spiritual world, and also of evil. Belief in the devil is not only supported by scripture, but compels us to acknowledge that evil will not be overcome by reason, education, conditioning, or whatever the nostrum *à la mode* may be. It can of course collapse into dualism, as Scot and the Restoration skeptics charged. But the apologists gave the orthodox response: God permits the devil to act, just as he permits natural evils. Now everyone recognizes the existence of natural evils, and the seventeenth-century skeptics, at least, professed belief in a benignant deity. So upon them was thrust the *onus probandi*: why is natural evil reconcilable with such a deity, but not demonic evil? Much more than literalism is bound up in this controversy. The rationalist repudiates the "diabolic hypothesis." Scripture affirms it, in letter and in spirit. The modern rationalist, with a care for

---

[24]See Roy Yates, "Jesus and the Demonic in the Synoptic Gospels," *Irish Theological Quarterly*, 44 (1977), 39–57, and G. B. Caird, *Principalities and Powers* (London: Clarendon Press, 1956).

consistency, will repudiate scripture as well; the seventeenth-century rationalist could not, or dared not.

But the Restoration skeptics *did* help to undermine the super-naturalist disposition to which the apologists appealed. Writers such as Scot and Hobbes established the groundwork for incre-dulity, and the three most important later skeptics built on it in rather different ways. Webster develops the notion that science and medicine will gradatim explain more and more things that seem supernatural or miraculous. Bekker diffuses a sly Carte-sianism, so opposed by Glanvill, that discourages any lively belief in the intrusion of the supernatural into the natural world. Hutchinson's socio-psychological examination of the witch trials and their causes evacuates them of theological or moral significance. These views clearly obtain today, and they are all found in, for example, Hume's attack on miracles. We cannot credit *any* miraculous story, he says, because the laws of creation are uniform and not to be suspended arbitrarily, even by God (Bekker); things that appear miraculous are owing to our present ignorance of natural causes (Webster); human testi-mony of the miraculous is not persuasive, for there are too many psychological factors involved (Hutchinson and Webster). Like any other thinker, Hume is operating from assumptions. For a Glanvill, they would exemplify the vanity of dogmatizing. For a Gibbon, they are merely canonical.

Many forces fostered the decline of witch beliefs. The social tensions generated in the Renaissance began to relax; human insecurity retreated with the ascendance of technology, the fruit of the Baconian method; Pelagianism and Benevolism, sunny theories of human nature generally, began to prevail. (One of the objections that Glanvill tries to rebut is that diabolic pacts are "too base" for human beings to consider: here, of course, a modern, contemplating Buchenwald and the "Gulag Archipel-ago," might grant him the last laugh.) But among the intellec-tuals, at any rate, the decline of belief can be traced in large measure to that emergent, skeptical sensibility so alarming to Casaubon, which drew sustenance from the attitudes of men such as Webster, Bekker, and Hutchinson. Without lingering

[97]

over its abracadabras, one ought also to mention the anti-Peri-
patetic Logic of Petrus Ramus, which caused such agitation from
the latter sixteenth century forward. Though in a sense revolutionary, it was espoused by Calvinists and other conservative
theologians because it bestowed a new respectability on the kind
of belief resting on testimony and revelation. Ramism declined
precipitously in the eighteenth century as the Lockean epistemology seeped through the age. Its obsolescence was due, in
part, to the same causes as the decline of witch belief; and since
Ramism defended types of knowledge derided by the Enlightenment, its own decay may well have fertilized the bourgeoning skeptical consensus.

And yet, obstinately, that "wondering quality" fails to atro-
phy. The Glanvillean anthologies proliferate, and out of Glanvill, Defoe, theologically reticent, contrives the modern ghost
story. Calmet, a pious man, is intrigued by the lore of demonology and vampirism, though it provides no nutriment for his
faith. The wondering quality persists, but something else is van-
ishing. Browne, we recall, rejoiced to live in an age without miracles, for otherwise belief were too easy. But Wesley regrets that
Glanvill had not more ably prepared his empirical evidence for
a supernatural world. In his *Antidote* More had disdained arguing from scripture, preferring, as he thought, the more universal
testimony of experience. But the empirical arguments seem now
the most *démodé* in the apologists' arsenal. For they fetch their
power from a predilection that, in less than a century, and in
even an ardent Christian such as Wesley, has become enfeebled
and nervous.

◻

To pursue narrowly the debate over miracles would be otiose.
As I have suggested, it arose on the groundwork of the earlier
controversy, than which it was at once more and less exigent:
less, because English Protestantism believed that the age of overt
miracles was done, and there, at least, consorted with skepticism; more, because at its most belligerent the argument against

miracles struck at the heart of scriptural Christianity. But I must refine my remark about the age of miracles being done. A good part of Protestantism continued to recognize God's active and vigilant providence in the world and to urge us to see many events as truly miraculous — as signs of God's direct superintendence of his universe — which the rationalist would attribute to natural causes.[25] I should like first to survey the main lines of the controversy concerning overt miracles, especially the New Testament exorcisms, drawing such parallels as seem enlightening with the earlier debate. I shall conclude the chapter with a discussion of Defoe's *Robinson Crusoe*, one of the happiest attempts, early in the eighteenth century, to reinvigorate a sense of the miraculous in its providential form.

The chief skeptics of miracles in the early and middle eighteenth century were Thomas Woolston, Conyers Middleton, and David Hume. In a curious way, the relation between Woolston and the later skeptics is rather like that between Scot or Webster, and Hutchinson. Woolston was an eccentric Deist who in a series of discourses "on the Miracles of Our Saviour" (1728–1729) denied the literal reality of the New Testament miracles on several grounds. Since we cannot know exactly what were the diseases Christ healed, we cannot affirm that they were miraculous: "Faith and Imagination" may have had much to do with them. In respect of some of them, such as Christ's curing blindness with dirt and spittle, there is clearly no miracle, for "our *Surgeons*, with their Ointments and Washings" can do as much. Other more dramatic miracles Woolston simply denies: of the healing of the paralytic on the roof, "no Tale more

---

[25]Representative of conventional belief is Bishop William Fleetwood's "Essay upon Miracles" (1701): Christ worked overt miracles "to procure Attention and Belief"; in addition, there are non-scriptural miracles, and examples of personal providence, which may enforce no doctrine, but do show God's mercy: "God has more Ends to serve by Miracles, than the Confirmation of the Truth of a Religion" (*A Compleat Collection of . . . Sermons* [1737], 29, 149, 160–65). Personal providence was thus affirmed by educated Anglicans as well as by Calvinists, Puritans, and so forth. For a miscellany of remarks on miracles, see John Evelyn, *Diary*, 16 September 1685.

monstrously romantick can be told"; of Christ's curing palsy, "The literal Sense of it is so encumber'd with romantick Circumstances, as are enough to turn a Man's Heart against Christianity it self." Such accounts as the raising of Lazarus proceed from "Fable and Forgery," and are replete with absurdities: e.g., was Lazarus deaf, that Christ had to summon him, as we are informed, with a loud voice? In his sixth and last discourse, Woolston tackles Christ's own resurrection, relying on the old rabbinical argument that zealots absconded with the body.

Partly because of these discourses, Woolston was presently to be convicted of blasphemy, though he tries to cover his skepticism with frequent flights into allegory, and indeed lays on such an inspissated patina of mystical and cabbalistic jargon that one wonders if he can be properly pigeon-holed — as he commonly is in standard texts — a Deist. Professing himself a sound Christian, he argues that the spiritual, mystical, or allegorical interpretations of the miracles are much more edifying than the "carnal" interpretations, which in fact do disservice to God and Christ and encourage "downright *Antichristianism*." Hence, although it may appear that Christianity rests on fraud, the corporal resurrection of Jesus, yet it is his spiritual resurrection that is the glory and vindication of Christianity. Woolston, like Webster, presents to us an odd mixture. He is deistic in his rationalistic solutions, his sense that belief in literal miracles derogates from Christianity. But he is also like Muggleton, Gerrard Winstanley, and the other spiritual allegorizers of seventeenth-century, radical Protestantism. There is as well a mystical strain recalling Vaughan, which along with everything else makes Woolston very difficult to class in modern terms.

Bishop Richard Smalbroke's response to Woolston is the most representative and elaborate: *A Vindication of the Miracles of our Blessed Saviour* (2 portly volumes, 1729, 1731). The only lively thing about this largely unreadable performance is the epigraph on its title page, from *Luke* xxii. 48: "But Jesus said unto him, Judas, Betrayest thou the Son of Man with a Kiss?" The point is that Woolston professed to be an orthodox Christian and repeatedly cited the patristic writers as precedent for his allegorizing. But Smalbroke properly rejoins that the mystical or allegorical glosses of the Fathers presuppose as a foundation "the *Reality* of the *Facts* that are thus *Allegorized*." Further, one can make no allegorical sense out of such episodes as the Gadarene swine, although they make plenty of literal sense; and even if some of Christ's cures could be approximated by modern medicine, his were immediate and enduring, so that the manner of the cures remains miraculous. Like the Restoration apologists, Smalbroke charges Woolston with granting too much power to the imagination, and he complains significantly of Woolston's reducing devils and hell "to merely *Mystical* and *Cabalistical* Notions . . . to deprive them of all *literal* and real Existence." Pascal, echoing St. Augustine, summarizes Smalbroke's lengthy thesis in a sentence: "Two errors: 1, To take everything literally; 2, To take everything spiritually" (*Pensées*, no. 486).

There were other attacks on Woolston, most notably Bishop Thomas Sherlock's *Tryal of Witnesses of the Resurrection of Jesus* (1729). Like the Restoration apologists, Sherlock defends the credibility of human testimony: many people saw the risen Christ at different times, and after his resurrection he imparted to his disciples effective powers. Anyway, to filch and hide a corpse would have been, under the circumstances, no easy matter; it is a more incredible explanation than the received one. Many years later Sherlock was rebutted by "a Moral Philosopher" in *The Resurrection of Jesus Considered* (1743?). This philosopher argues that an uncommon story ought to have more than common proof—different criteria apply. He remarks discrepancies in the gospel versions of the resurrection. We should scrutinize every miraculous account before we embrace it in defiance of the maxim that nature is unvarying. Recalling Webster's argument against testimony, and anticipating Hume's (whose essay on miracles had already been written but not yet published), he concludes: "Positive and presumptive Evidence, is of no Weight against the Reason and Nature of Things. Such Evidence should be rejected, rather than the Nature of Things should be reason'd against to support such Evidence." In other words, *no* miraculous account can muster sufficient testimony to prompt us to disbelieve in a tidy, clockwork cosmos. Like Woolston, and the early skeptics of witchcraft, he defends his position as the truly religious one: belief in miracles is "as contrary to the Attributes of God, as to the Nature of Things." Even belief in biblical miracles "is destructive to the moral Character of the Deity." Christ's chief purpose was to teach us virtue and morality, and for this he required no supernatural assistance. This "moral philosopher" remains anonymous, and understandably so. The implicit Cartesianism that had ruined Bekker's career flourishes triumphant here.

Twenty years after Woolston, a freethinker with Hobbesian tendencies, Conyers Middleton, published *A Free Inquiry into the Miraculous Powers Which are supposed to have subsisted in the Christian Church* (1749). In this book, and in his *Vindication of the Free Inquiry* (1751), he denies that he is questioning the scriptural miracles. But he does oppose, not only the popish belief in continuing miracles (this is obviously superstition) but also the respectable Anglican position, enounced by Bishop Tillotson and many others, that miracles continued in the primitive church through the third century, but ceased in the fourth when the church was established in the secular world. To delimit the age of miracles, he says, is not so easy: "where then are we to stop? and to what period must we confine ourselves?" Once we venture beyond the scripture miracles, we weaken the foundations of Christianity, for all the other miracles are as explicable, by superstition and fraud, as the mediaeval ones; and the church fathers were as grossly credulous as the schoolmen. Like Woolston but in a different way Middleton tries to shield his orthodoxy even as he assails miracles. But since he explains the post-scriptural miracles by fraud or rationalization (e.g., demoniacs were epileptics, possession can be counterfeited by ventriloquism), Middleton is asking us implicitly, "to what period must we confine ourselves" when we profess belief in miracles? Like the witchcraft skeptics, Middleton challenges the arguments from testimony and consensus; in fact he cites witchcraft as an example of something often witnessed to, "yet the incredibility of the thing prevailed and was found at last too strong for all this force of human testimony: so that the belief of witches is now utterly extinct."

In his defense of his book, the *Vindication*, Middleton again claims that he is not dismantling scriptural authority, but wishes rather to dissolve "a chain of pretended Miracles which at this very day enslaves and ties down the whole Christian Church to certain doctrines and practices, which tend to debase the simplicity of the Gospel, and to give a superstitious turn to the piety and devotion of it's professors." But this sentence nearly gives the game away. If supervening miracles are to be disbelieved because they debase scripture, what are we to say of scripture miracles? The way had already been opened by the witchcraft skeptics and clandestine writers such as the "moral philosopher" to view even those episodes as "contrary to the Attributes of God." The gospel miracles, the later overt miracles, even the providential miracles that some profess still to see: do not all of these stand or fall together? Like Hume, he argues that the intrinsic credibility of the facts themselves must overwhelm the supposed credibility of the witnesses. Middleton does not explicitly pose the question, but he no less assuredly raises it: is it not a pious evasion to exempt the biblical witnesses from this maxim? Toward the end of his *Vindication*, citing the multitudinous resurrections reported in early church times, he notes that the pagan writers omit to mention these events, and so invites us subtly to recall that the pagans were also silent about Christ's resurrection. Middleton is more devious than Woolston, but his arguments are more incisive. Hume was quite correct to view this attack as superior to his own, and to him Gibbon is greatly indebted. If Woolston reminds us of Webster, Middleton may be compared with some justice to both Bekker and Hutchinson. Like them he is more Cartesian than cabbalistic, and his skepticism, however stealthy, is quite modern.

Hume's essay on miracles, published in 1748, will be dealt with in a later chapter; it is brief and in substance adds little or nothing to earlier arguments. But its gumption and rhetorical ingenuity whipped the controversy to a tempest. As a literary review remarked a few years later, Hume's piece, though "thrown out carelessly," soon became considered "the touchstone of wit and subtility"; hence every ambitious gentleman "of sacred function" must have at Hume.[26] Some of the reverend gentlemen were more sapient than others, if truth be told (not surprising in an age when few were called but many were chosen), and I shall attempt to recapitulate the most forcible assaults. At bottom, Hume's argument is a *petitio principii*, or circular reasoning: we cannot admit testimony for miracles because miracles violate the laws of nature, and these cannot be violated. That God might intervene in his creation is an opinion not inconsistent, but indeed quite consonant, with a reasonable philosophy. It is after all arrogant to assign limits to God, and he may wish to work miracles for many reasons: to confirm the validity of his messengers, to enforce a doctrine, to remind us of his providence and power. Hume may be himself inconsistent in arguing against miracles, since elsewhere he throws doubt on the inevitability of cause and effect; is nature regular or not? We believe many things on human testimony and consensus, which after all are a part of our experience and an important means of acquiring knowledge. It is arrogant to prefer private to collective experience, and the latter supports belief in miracles. Hume exaggerates man's love of novelty when explaining human credulity; or he fails to consider that such love of novelty may have been implanted in us by God to lead us to him. Hume also exaggerates the ignorance and barbarity of primitive Christian times: after all, Christianity had to make its way against skeptical, even Sadduceean Jews, who would not be gullible concerning its miracles. The early witnesses to Christ's miracles do not seem to have been enthusiasts or melancholiacs, and no self-interest actuated them; quite the contrary. Christ's miracles meet one of Hume's criteria: they were performed in a public manner. Hume fails to define "experience" clearly or to tell us *how many* witnesses are requisite to prove a miracle; he says the witnesses must be "educated," by which he may mean

[26]*The Critical Review*, 14 (1762), 81.

"skeptical." But courts of law require only that witnesses be honest, and if Hume is equating education with skepticism, this is another circular argument. Hume's distinction between what is "contrary to experience" (unusual) and "not conformable to experience" (miraculous) is specious, since we only know the laws of nature from experience, which on Hume's own admission is limited, and so have no indubitable criterion to sort out what is contradictory from what is non-conformable. The fact that some miracles are frauds does not prove that they all are, but may even suggest (following Pascal's logic) the reverse.[27]

Hume's opponents, like the Restoration apologists, see themselves as open-minded and undogmatic; *they* are the resilient ones. Many of them argued strenuously that belief in miracles is far from degrading to God, that (reversing Middleton's reasoning) if miracles once occurred, it is logical to believe in a continuing providence; and this remark on the episode of the Gadarene swine reminds us of More and Glanvill on the witch of Endor:

> We must either admit the agency of evil spirits in this case, or entirely reject the accounts that are given of the Gadarene daemoniacs, as unworthy Christ; which would be to overthrow the credit of three Evangelists . . . and with theirs, that of the whole Gospel, while, at the same time, it would have the appearance of an unreasonable attack upon the faith of all history.

All excellent arguments; yet John Wesley, for whom Hume was "the most insolent despiser of truth and virtue that ever appeared in the world," thus laments in 1781: "The doctrine of

---

[27]These arguments are culled from the following sources: William Adams, *An Essay on Mr. Hume's Essay on Miracles* (1752); John Leland, *A View of the Principal Deistical Writers . . . in England,* 3 vols. (1754, 1755, 1756); George Campbell, *Dissertation on Miracles* (1762); Richard Price, *Four Dissertations* (1768); James Beattie, *An Essay on the Nature and Immutability of Truth* (1771); Hugh Farmer, *A Dissertation on Miracles* (1771). Campbell's is probably the best and most comprehensive rebuttal.

a particular providence is absolutely out of fashion in England —
and any but a particular providence is no providence at all."[28]

There is another kind of defense of scriptural miracles, and
of the ambiguities of the Bible in general, which ought to be
mentioned, appealing as it does to the non-rational and the
numinous. In the later seventeenth century Thomas Burnet
finds an edifying pleasure in magnificent and amazing objects
of nature. They remind us of God's greatness, and "whatsoever
hath but the Shadow and Appearance of INFINITE, as all
Things have that are too big for our Comprehension, they fill
and over-bear the Mind with their Excess, and cast it into a
pleasing kind of Stupor and Admiration." As early as 1661, at
the very dawn of the Royal Society, no less a scientist than Robert Boyle extols the obscurity of the Bible: it becomes not "the
Majesty of God to suffer himself to be fetter'd to Humane Laws
of Method . . . devis'd onely for our own Narrow and Low Conceptions"; a "Complication of . . . Rhetorick and Mystery" is a
more effective religious teacher than rational discourse. In 1678
the Cambridge Platonist Ralph Cudworth rebuts Hobbes's opinion that belief in witches, possessions, and miracles is encouraged by civil magistrates to keep men in subjection. On the contrary, these beliefs stimulate an authentic religious fear; terror
often awakens in us a true sense of God, but atheists can never
understand this.[29]

As they move into the next century, such strategies are often
employed. The accomplished Hebraist, Bishop Robert Lowth,
lauds "the expressive brevity and simplicity of . . . 'And God
said, Let there be light, and there was light.' The more words
you would accumulate upon this thought, the more you would

[28]Wesley, *Journal*, V, 458; VI, 326. John Fell, *Daemoniacs* (1779), 396, thus
comments on the Gadarene swine. For discussions of personal providence see
Philip Doddridge, *Lectures on . . . Pneumatology* (1763), 222–23; Richard
Price, *Four Dissertations* (1768), 70–71.

[29]Thomas Burnet, *Sacred Theory of the Earth*, 6th ed., 2 vols. (1726), I, 188;
Robert Boyle, *Some Considerations Touching the Style of the H. Scriptures*
(1663 ed.), 38, 53–54; Ralph Cudworth, *The True Intellectual System of the
Universe*, 2 vols. (1743 ed.), II, 654–61.

detract from the sublimity of it: for the understanding quickly comprehends the Divine power from the effect, and perhaps most completely, when it is not attempted to be explained." Against the Deists and Hume, Lowth even praises biblical anthropomorphism: we are so ignorant we can never "attain to a simple and pure idea" of divine nature; there is always a mingling of human and divine in our conceptions of the godhead, and this mingling can render the notion of God even more sublime and majestic; it produces a conception intellectually obscure, but grand and magnificent. In such apologetics, the line between aesthetics and theology is often indistinct; it becomes even more so in Anthony Blackwall's discussion of the New Testament miracles. The man possessed with Legion, he says, is described in so lively a way

> that the attentive reader has all that glorious scene of wonder and astonishment full in his eye and mind. . . . Who is not shocked with horror and trembling at the first appearance of the raging Demoniac. . . . Then with what religious awe, reverence and tenderness of devotion do we view the mild Saviour of human race commanding the infernal Legion to quit their possession of the miserable sufferer!

Such undulant writing seems now theological discourse, now literary criticism; but it provides a new defense of the episode of the Gadarene swine. In a similar vein Blackwall examines the raising of Lazarus, stressing the qualities of suspense, surprise, and amazement; and so with Christ's healing the leper and calming the waves. St. Paul is often obscure, some charge. Rightly so, responds Blackwall, since Paul is struggling to express "the magnificence and infinite glories of [religious] mystery."[30] What Woolston derided a few years later as "monstrously romantick" Blackwall extols as kindling religious awe. Was Lazarus hard of hearing that Christ must needs speak in a

---

[30]Robert Lowth, *Lectures on the Sacred Poetry of the Hebrews* (1753), tr. from Latin G. Gregory (1787), 2 vols., I, 350, 361–62; Anthony Blackwall, *The Sacred Classics Defended and Illustrated* (1725), 250–54, 277–78, 365.

[107]

loud voice? The answer to Woolston's raillery is implicit in Blackwall. Christ speaks in a loud voice to show his victory over the powers of death.

In 1769 James Usher, a schoolmaster and adult convert to Roman Catholicism, published a greatly expanded edition of a remarkable treatise: *Coli: or, a Discourse on Taste*. There he praises enthusiasm and the religious sublime, a "mixture of terror, curiosity, and exultation. ... In the sublime we feel ourselves alarmed, our motions are suspended, and we remain for some time until the emotion wears off, wrapped in silence and inquisitive horror." The constituents of the sublime are obscurity, irregularity, terror and awe — "appearances of disorder." All these are associated with "the idea of invisible immense power." Moderns, he says, despise these emotions as superstitious, but "The truth is, the impression of this obscure presence ... is beyond the range of the philosophy of the ideas of sense." Terror and awe are essential parts of the religious experience, and even superstitious dread is more fundamental than all the conclusions of reason. Burke's important *Philosophical Enquiry into ... the Sublime and Beautiful* (1757) had appeared some years before, and it may be that Usher thence draws his inspiration. But of all discursive writers in eighteenth-century England he most fully expounds the numinous; the religious sublime, adumbrated by Boyle, Cudworth, and Burnet, is here given its first elaborate exposition.[31]

To value the drama of the Gadarene swine for its sublimity is quite different, however, from urging its literal acceptance in the interests of scriptural and historical authority. The latter is a philosophical argument, whether or not one approves it. The former is psychological and, a Woolston might contend, aesthetically self-indulgent, hedonistic. Boyle and Cudworth, Lowth, Blackwall and Usher, were all striving to conserve a nonrational element in the religious experience. They esteemed

---

[31]J[ames] U[sher], *Clio: or, a Discourse on Taste* (1769), 101, 103, 107–109, 116, 237–40. The standard authority on this subject is Samuel Monk, *The Sublime* (1935; rpt. Ann Arbor: Univ. of Michigan Press, 1960).

that disorder, unpredictability, latency, dread of an "obscure presence" which the skeptics and Deists highly resented. For the rationalists, these were ignominious relics of mediaevalism, but they were relics that had fed the flames of fanaticism and religious war in the Renaissance and seventeenth century; one understands their hostility and contempt. But just as the apologists of witch belief, in the eighteenth century, abandoned theology for spectral narrative, so the defenders of scripture and miracles wander further and further into the precincts of aesthetics and psychology. Whether they are seen as retreating from reason or enlarging the compass of theology depends on the perspective of the viewer.

⊓

I have sought in this perambulation to note the most striking features of two related controversies, accenting the virtues of the side usually slighted nowadays without, I hope, calumniating the other. More courage, it must be owned, was required of the skeptics; but the prevailing assumption is simply fallacious that the skeptics were scientific progressives and the apologists were slaves of reaction and hebetude. Because the rest of this book will be largely concerned with literature, I wished also to note that both debates deviate from theology and philosophy into more purely literary paths as the eighteenth century wears on. Daniel Defoe is an important figure in both controversies. His early ghost story, his pseudonymous "non-fiction" books on demonology and magic in the 1720s, lie significantly between the more polemical Glanvillean anthologies of the Restoration and the immodestly sensational appeals of the Gothic novel. In his better-known fiction, especially *Robinson Crusoe* (1719) and *A Journal of the Plague Year* (1722), he dramatizes a providential world, and though he eschews the overtly miraculous, his use of omens, visions, coincidence, strongly suggests a watching, not a watchmaker, Deity much involved in his creation. The novel, it is often said, is the product of the modern, secular world-view. And so in Defoe, the titular father of that form, critics frequently remark a "profound secularization of . . . out-look" characteristic of his, and future, time. This portrait of Defoe as the first modern sensibility is often overdrawn, but he was assuredly a contemporary man inquisitive about all those things contemporary men should be: economics, education, politics, finance. The conservative providentialism of his major novels is thus particularly interesting.[32]

Defoe would certainly have agreed with John Wesley that "any but a particular providence is no providence at all." Not only is a personal or special providence affirmed by *Robinson Crusoe*, but the presiding Deity of this novel exhibits that rough and arbitrary interventionism so odious to the skeptic. Disobeying his parents and repudiating his proper place in society, Crusoe insists on going to sea. Now the sea has long been an emblem of fortune: whimsical, unstable, treacherous. The ship of fools was a prominent theme in Renaissance painting; in *The Tempest* fools are delivered from the sea of fortune to the providential island of Prospero, where they are instructed, through suffering, in the divine plan; the deteriorate apprentice is sent off to sea in Hogarth's *Industry and Idleness*, for he has given himself over to fortune rather than studying the signs of providence. Several people advise Crusoe to remain on land, and providence speaks through the terrifying storms and other misfortunes that he encounters on his first expeditions; but Crusoe is driven as if daemonically:

> my ill Fate push'd me on now with an Obstinacy that nothing could resist; and tho' I had several times loud Calls from my Reason . . . to go home, yet I had no Power to do it. I know not what to call this, nor will I urge, that it is a secret over-

---

[32]On Defoe's secularized outlook, see Ian Watt, *The Rise of the Novel* (1957; rpt. Berkeley: Univ. of California Press, 1964), 82. For discussions of religious themes in Defoe, see: Baine, *Daniel Defoe*, G. A. Starr, *Defoe and Spiritual Autobiography* (Princeton, N.J.: Princeton Univ. Press, 1965), Maximilian E. Novak, *Defoe and the Nature of Man* (Oxford: Oxford Univ. Press, 1963), J. Paul Hunter, *The Reluctant Pilgrim* (Baltimore: Johns Hopkins Univ. Press, 1966).

ruling Decree that hurries us on to be the Instruments of our own Destruction, even tho' it be before us, and that we rush upon it with our Eyes open (14).[33]

Crusoe is compared with Jonah, who flouted God's will; he suffers his father's curse for his "original sin" of disobeying his parents. The entire first sixth of the novel, before Crusoe is cast onto his island, is charged with images of storm, fog, disorientation, sinister and inhuman perils. Even his final "deliverance" on the island is accounted "dreadful" (47).

The fear and suffering continue on the island: it is "horrid" (63), an *"Island of Despair"* (70), a "Prison" (96); but God's mercy is there too. Seeing some ears of English barley strangely sprout, Crusoe reflects for the first time on providence: "I began to suspect, that God had miraculously caus'd this Grain to grow without any Help of Seed sown, and that it was so directed purely for my Sustenance, on that wild miserable Place" (78). Discovering presently that there was a natural cause, Crusoe's belief in its miraculous and providential nature begins to abate; he is as yet too immature in his religion to see that God's providence can operate through natural or second causes. More rigorous methods are required, and so Crusoe suffers through an earthquake and is then afflicted with a great illness, which occasions his first prayer, though it is more properly but an exclamation to the Lord. After this comes a "terrible Dream":

I thought, that I was sitting on the Ground on the Outside of my Wall, where I sat when the Storm blew after the Earthquake, and that I saw a Man descend from a great black Cloud, in a bright Flame of Fire, and light upon the Ground: He was all over bright as a Flame, so that I could but just bear to look towards him; his Countenance was most inexpressibly dreadful, impossible for Words to describe; when he stepp'd upon the Ground with his Feet, I thought the Earth trembl'd,

[33]All quotations and references are from: *The Life and Strange Surprizing Adventures of Robinson Crusoe,* ed. J. Donald Crowley (London: Oxford Univ. Press, 1972).

[111]

just as it had done before in the Earthquake, and all the Air look'd, to my Apprehension, as if it had been fill'd with Flashes of Fire.

He was no sooner landed upon the Earth, but he moved forward towards me, with a long Spear or Weapon in his Hand, to kill me; and when he came to a rising Ground, at some Distance, he spoke to me, or I heard a Voice so terrible, that it is impossible to express the Terror of it; all that I can say, I understood, was this, *Seeing all these Things have not brought thee to Repentance, now thou shalt die:* At which Words, I thought he lifted up the Spear that was in his Hand, to kill me.

No one, that shall ever read this Account, will expect that I should be able to describe the Horrors of my Soul at this terrible Vision, I mean, that even while it was a Dream, I even dreamed of those Horrors; nor is it any more possible to describe the Impression that remain'd upon my Mind when I awak'd and found it was but a Dream (87–88).

This is the most extraordinary recreation of a numinous experience that I know of in the early eighteenth century. The self-abasement and dread is superbly evoked; the images of black cloud and flashing fire unite the two most potent signs of deity, darkness and light. The "Man" is the avenging angel, or God in his daemonic epiphany, dreadful of countenance, terrible of voice, armed to kill. He is like the angel seen by Joshua, "a man . . . with his sword drawn in his hand" (*Joshua* v. 13), but more menacing, more, perhaps, like the Yahweh who assaulted Moses: "And it came to pass by the way . . . that the Lord met him, and sought to kill him" (*Exodus* iv. 24). But it is all splendidly wrought up and just circumstantial enough to persuade; more details might have made it seem silly or "allegorical." Note finally the relaxed and repetitive, somewhat disordered, syntax of the last paragraph, conveying vividly the state of a man just waking from a dream that he knows to be more than a dream.

This, surely, is the climax of the religious theme in the novel.

[112]

That Crusoe has a new religious perspective is seen in his recognizing God's miraculous providence even in such natural events as the growth of grain (132). His spiritual progress is not unhindered, and he is often terrified, especially when he notices that footprint, the *single* footprint, that he imagines for awhile to be the devil's; but like a religious hermit or desert father he strives to establish a religious life. No longer driven daemonically, he learns to await, and hearken to, the subtle proddings of providence, behind which are supernatural agencies:

> Let no Man despise the secret Hints and Notices of Danger, which sometimes are given him, when he may think there is no Possibility of its being real. That such Hints and Notices are given us, I believe few that have made any Observations of things, can deny; that they are certain Discoveries of an invisible World, and a Converse of Spirits, we cannot doubt; and if the Tendency of them seems to be to warn us of Danger, why should we not suppose they are from some friendly Agent, whether supreme, or inferior, and subordinate is not the Question; and that they are given for our Good (250)?

This is precisely the argument propounded eight years later in Defoe's *History of Apparitions*. Like Job, Crusoe does sometimes "invade the Soveraignty of *Providence,* and as it were arraign the Justice of so arbitrary a Disposition of Things, that should hide that Light from some, and reveal it to others," but he submits to the inscrutable mystery (210). He has difficulty, too, in explaining to Friday why God does not abolish the devil straightway and prevent further evil — Reginald Scot would have applauded Friday's natural good sense. But, untutored in theology as he was, Crusoe's difficulty only points up the more the need for divine revelation to complement "meer Notions of Nature" (218–19).

There are many dimensions to *Robinson Crusoe,* of course, but those critics, from Defoe's contemporary Charles Gildon to Ian Watt, who depreciate the importance of the religious theme, or disdain it as meretricious, are unpersuasive. The theme, after all, occupies a great bit of the text and occasions much of Defoe's most vigorous writing. Watt objects that "if Crusoe's original sin was filial disobedience . . . it is certain that no real retribution follows, since he does very well out of it."[34] To be sure Crusoe winds up wealthy. He himself compares his end with that of Job (284), and both he and Job may be reckoned examples of God's mysterious providence. But no one says that Job did not suffer. After all, Crusoe's twenty-eight years of terror and loneliness, however punctuated with mundane triumphs, may strike some readers as "real" retribution. Anyway, it is not just filial disobedience with which Crusoe is to be charged. He has a religious delinquency or obtuseness at the start of the novel; unable to read the signs of providence, he is, as Defoe puts it elsewhere, a practical atheist. He is in a manner possessed, compelled by irresistable fatality until, assailed by the visionary exorcist, he becomes aware of the "secret Hints" of providence. There is no overt supernaturalism here; God works through natural causes in maturing the barley and communicating with Crusoe through his dreams. Crusoe's possession is daemoniac, not demonic; that is to say, it is psychologically represented, and there is no devil patrolling the island *in propria persona*. Still, God does manifest himself — through vision, through prophetic dreams, through chastisement and succor, and it is precisely the point of the novel that Crusoe must learn to *see* natural events as miraculous. Elsewhere, as I have noted, Defoe suggests that our consciences, our innermost thoughts, are the "drummers" that most truly evince a supernatural world. Upon such principles *Robinson Crusoe* is constructed. Compared to Prospero's island, Crusoe's is pretty barren; but like the fools in *The Tempest*, he is brought there "by providence divine." The universe of *Robinson Crusoe* is certainly not Cartesian, nor is it secular in the modern acceptation of that word, notwithstanding its internalized supernaturalism.

Otto has observed that the desire for the numinous, when

---

[34]Watt, 80.

1. Henry Fuseli, *Witch of Endor* (1777)

unappeased by authentic religion, will seek satisfaction in such alternatives as the ghost story. One of the modern masters of that genre, H. P. Lovecraft, reproaches those whose imaginations are not actuated by "strange and unearthly wonder . . . terrible glimpses . . . ultramundane hints." Yet Lovecraft was a true rationalist and sturdy despiser of religion. The "secret hints" of Defoe relate to individual salvation; Lovecraft's "ultramundane hints" are chastely aesthetic. The first conception is religious, the second truly secular. In this instance the demarcations are clear, but at other times they can be elusive. An Anthony Black-wall, a Robert Lowth: are they recognizing a non-rational religious quality sadly neglected by empirical apologists such as Glanvill, or are they themselves symptomatic of the subjugation of theology by aesthetics? The stories of the witch of Endor and the Gadarene swine are vivid and imaginatively told. Henry Fuseli's representation of the first, executed in 1777, seizes on the most emotional moment, when Saul, having received Samuel's dire prediction, "fell straightway all along on the earth, and was sore afraid." The witch's hierophantic gestures, mediating, as it were, between the supernatural and the natural worlds, are a fine touch; but it is all rather histrionic. As a sense of the holy and the daemonic decays, the more such stories will be valued for their psychological power instead of their theological import. If ever that sense be wholly lapsed, they will be exhumed only in the researches of the cultural anthropologist.

CHAPTER IV

Propping with a Twig:
Rationalism and Daemonianism
in Pope and Swift

The fear of the Lord is the beginning of wisdom: and the knowledge of
the holy is understanding.

Proverbs

Irony: A mode of speech in which the meaning is contrary to the
words: as, *Bolingbroke was a holy man.*

Dr. Johnson's Dictionary

IN THE PRECEDING CHAPTERS I have tried to pick a
bit at some lax assumptions. I have argued that the Restoration
"Fideists," though skeptical of reason, made much use of it in
their religious writings, that the believers in witchcraft considered themselves empiricists and moderates, that some of the
skeptics were occultists and, far from being tolerant, were often
disagreeable zealots. Browne, Dryden, and Pascal, the believers
in witchcraft and miracles, should all be seen, against their age,
as reasonable travelers of the middle way. But I have also
allowed that the skeptics did indeed lay the groundwork for
what we loosely call the "modern world view." This rationalism, with respect to the holy at least, is quite pronounced in
Pope and Swift. I must not be misunderstood at the outset. Both
Pope and Swift thought of themselves as sufficiently orthodox
Christians, and it is not for me to correct them. But the perspective of Browne or Defoe is not theirs. When they write about
the experience of the holy, they are not in my judgment felic-
itous. Pope relies too heavily on rationalism, Dryden's "twig."
Swift is perfunctory on such matters and, depending on how

[117]

one reads Part IV of *Gulliver's Travels*, seems also very drawn to rationalism.

On the daemonic, however, they excel. For this apparent discrepancy there are several possible explanations. I have noted earlier a trend away from theological and toward aesthetic treatments of the holy and the daemonic. Both Pope and Swift show this tendency, but since they are chiefly satirists rather than philosophers or apologists, they are naturally specialists in the daemonic. Then too, the numinous experience at its most primitive is characterized by daemonic dread: Crusoe's "terrible dream" is a good example. Out of this fear emerges, at any rate in the higher religions, a more exalted and finally ethical sense of the holy; it is thus that the "fear of the Lord" leads to wisdom. Now rationalism and skepticism can corrode a sense of the holy, but the sense of the daemonic, more firmly impressed in human nature, is less easily effaced. Swift and Pope are strongly scored by rationalism, but the deeper intuition has endured.

Until recently, Pope's *Essay on Man* (1733–34) has been considered a work of rationalism. Paul Elmer More, in a fine phrase, speaks of Pope's being swept "into the shallows of the deistic evasion." Yvor Winters dismisses the poem as "inept deism," and he asserts that its intellectual flimsiness was not imposed on Pope by his age, but was rather the effect of his own theological asthenia. Winters then deplores Pope's influence on religious thought: "had he possessed as sharp a mind as Samuel Johnson the history of the age might easily have been greatly different from what it was." Modern scholars fully conversant with the deistic texts have not scrupled to class his poem among them.[1] *An Essay on Man* is addressed to Lord Bolingbroke, a friend whom Pope excessively revered and whose ideas he partly absorbed. It used commonly to be thought that the poem

[1]P. E. More, *With the Wits (Shelburne Essays, 10th Series)* (Boston and New York: Houghton Mifflin, 1919), 119; Yvor Winters, *In Defense of Reason* (Denver: Alan Swallow, 1943), 488. See also: Norman Sykes, *From Sheldon to Secker: Aspects of English Church History, 1660–1768* (Cambridge, Eng.: Cambridge Univ. Press, 1959), 160; Roland N. Stromberg, *Religious Liberalism in Eighteenth-Century England* (London: Oxford Univ. Press, 1954), 82–83.

expresses Bolingbroke's genteel Deism, from which, however, Pope retreated when the poem was attacked; and Bolingbroke himself says that he stimulated the work, though at the same time he seems regretful that Pope failed to embroider his ideas with sufficient assiduity.[2] But Bolingbroke's own thought is quite eclectic, and Pope's debt to it is nugatory. Most recent critics, those anyway who discard the deistic interpretation, either stress the orthodoxy of the poem and praise its coherence or despise it as a hotch-potch of empty paradoxes and fatuities that no one could now take seriously.[3]

A central problem is that the word *Deist*, like *Fideist*, is annoyingly slippery. Generally it signifies a thinker who minimizes the supernatural, the mysterious, the dogmatic, in reli-

[2]On the influence of Bolingbroke on Pope, see R. K. Root, *The Poetical Career of Alexander Pope* (Princeton, N.J.: Princeton Univ. Press, 1938), 167–68. For Bolingbroke's own remarks, see his letter to Swift printed in *The Correspondence of Alexander Pope*, ed. George Sherburn (Oxford: Clarendon Press, 1956), III, 214. On his thought more generally, see Isaac Kramnick, *Bolingbroke and His Circle* (Cambridge, Mass.: Harvard Univ. Press, 1968), and Jeffrey Hart, *Viscount Bolingbroke: Tory Humanist* (London: Routledge and Kegan Paul, 1965).

[3]So vast is the criticism of *An Essay on Man* that one can only cite representative views. It is generally considered an ungainly and inconsistent mélange by: Hoxie Neale Fairchild, *Religious Trends in English Poetry* (New York: Columbia Univ. Press, 1939), I, 501–508; and John Laird, *Philosophical Excursions into English Literature* (Cambridge, Eng.: Cambridge Univ. Press, 1946), 39–48. It is seen as a conscious and somewhat successful compromise between orthodoxy and rationalistic or pre-Romantic tendencies by: Chester Chapin, "Alexander Pope, Erasmian Catholic," *Eighteenth-Century Studies*, 6 (1973), 411–30; F. B. Thornton, *Alexander Pope: Catholic Poet* (New York: Pellegrini & Cudahy, 1952); G. Wilson Knight, *The Poetry of Pope* (London: Routledge and Kegan Paul, 1965). Probably the most exuberant yet sophisticated vindication of the orthodoxy and excellence of the poem is by Maynard Mack in the introduction to the Twickenham edition of *An Essay on Man* (London and New Haven: Methuen and Yale, 1950, 1951). All quotations from Pope, by the way, are from the Twickenham edition. Its most suave dismissal issues from the hands of F. R. Leavis: "No one, I imagine, willingly reads through the *Essay on Man* (Pope piquing himself on philosophical or theological profundity and acumen is intolerable . . .)," *Essential Articles for the Study of Alexander Pope* (Hamden, Conn.: Archon Books, 1964), 20.

gion. Yet at this time many Anglicans, such as Archbishop Tillotson and Samuel Clarke, occupied positions close to
rationalism, whereas a number of Deists allowed far wider scope
to the supernatural than ever their modern congener, the Uni-
tarian, would tolerate. In the first half of the eighteenth century, then, there is a "singular resemblance between Christians
and deists."[4] For example, Sir Richard Blackmore's *Creation*
(1712) is an interminable poem against the Deists, but it argues
almost entirely from natural religion: the universe is harmonious, relatively perfect, points to a divine Designer. Blackmore
omits to mention Christ and touches but briefly on the afterlife;
and though he parades his orthodoxy in his preface, the poem
is no more explicitly Christian than *An Essay on Man.* Natural
religion lies at the heart of a much more significant attack on
Deism, Bishop Joseph Butler's *Analogy of Religion* (1736). The
first section of his book is wholly given over to it, and shares
much with Pope's poem. The second part, "Of Revealed Religion," does go beyond Pope, but Butler concedes that even revelation is often very obscure. The episcopal apologist is indeed
much closer to Pope than to Dryden. For Dryden reason is the
mere twig inadequately propping the faith, or the dying flame
of the light of revelation. Butler reverses Dryden and indulging
a theological hysteron-proteron, regards revelation as an adjunct
or supplement of natural religion.

On the other side there is Anthony Ashley Cooper, the third
Earl of Shaftesbury, who seems the exact opposite of someone
such as Pascal. He emphasizes the benevolent and social qualities of humankind and discommends "the height of devout
Extasy and Contemplation" as inane distractions from our
duties. The doctrine of rewards and punishments is repudiated
as a base appeal; we should delight in doing good for its own
sake. Shaftesbury is nothing if not fastidious; he calls himself a
Theist rather than Deist, speaks — some would say insipidly —

---

[4]Sir Leslie Stephen, *History of English Thought in the Eighteenth Century*
(3d ed., 1902; rpt. New York: Peter Smith, 1949), I, 158. The more recent studies of Sykes and Stromberg (note 1, above) substantiate this view.

of the "Friendship" between God and man, and is given to such pronouncements as: "To *philosophize* . . . is but to carry *Good-Breeding* a step higher." Yet like Blackmore and Butler he praises the order, harmony, and perfection of the universe, which surely evince a God; and from the injustice at work in the world, he infers an afterlife. All this he says in his highly influential *Characteristicks of Men, Manners, Opinions, Times* (1711), a work that will strike a modern reader as gauzy and insufferably genteel. Much less influential, viewed indeed with horror and detestation by the orthodox, was William Wollaston's *Religion of Nature Delineated*, clandestinely printed in 1722. Yet Wollaston demonstrates God using the argument from design and the first mover; he believes in a particular providence; in the probability of a future state (because the virtuous suffer on earth); in the immateriality and immortality of the soul. Like Butler later, he claims that he is not trying to undermine revelation, but pave the way for it. Now it may be that Wollaston is not wholly candid, but even discounting some of his more pious reassurances, his resemblance to Blackmore or Butler is remarkable. Such was the religious welter when *An Essay on Man* came forth into the world.

⌑

Such it was, indeed, when Pope came into the world, or at least as he was shaping his religious opinions. I will not say with one critic, who is apparently a telepathist, that Pope "lacked any firm spiritual centre."[5] Yet to judge from his remarks in his correspondence and conversation, Pope pursued Paul's ideal of being all things to all men rather too nimbly. He does genuinely admire Bolingbroke, chiefly for his easy-going tolerance and freedom from dogmatism. Yet for Bolingbroke's opposite number, the volcanic and abusive Christian apologist William Warburton, he has equal praise, and considers him, at most half-jocosely, as one who understands *An Essay on Man* better than

[5]Fairchild, I, 492.

himself. He can be flippant about religion, theological or meta-physical writings, his own Roman Catholicism. He is opposed to bigotry, intolerance, and in the main professes belief in a God that is benevolent and forgiving. But at the same time he refuses to abandon his Catholicism, opposes free thinking, identifies himself sometimes with Erasmus, whose open-mindedness he esteems, sometimes with Pascal, whose ardor he admires; he believes in an afterlife and a particular providence.[6] At fourteen he read the Protestant and Catholic sides and "found my self a Papist and a Protestant by turns, according to the last book I read." Even the death-bed was apparently no great coagulant of faith: on being asked if a priest should be sent for, he replied, "I do not suppose that is essential, but it will be right, and I heartily thank you for putting me in mind of it."[7] Two final curiosities may be set down. Pope was going to include an "address to our Saviour" in *An Essay on Man*, but on showing it to Berkeley, was advised to withdraw it. On the earliest extant manuscript of the poem, Pope wrote, for his eyes alone it seems, "Thy will be done, in Earth as it is in Heaven."[8] One could not say that Pope exhibits more inconsistency over a lifetime than most of us, but he is clearly mercurial and perhaps a trifle too eager to conciliate at once a Bolingbroke and a Warburton.

The relaxed latitudinarianism of the early eighteenth century, the genial blurring of lines, suited Pope's own temperament. The God of *An Essay on Man* is more akin to that of the philosophers than to that of Abraham, Isaac, and Jacob. There

[6]For praise of Bolingbroke, see: Pope, *Correspondence*, IV, 6; Joseph Spence, *Observations, Anecdotes, and Characters of Books and Men*, ed. J. M. Osborn (Oxford: Clarendon Press, 1966), I, nos. 270, 273, 274, 282. On Warburton: *Corresp.*, IV, 288; Spence, I, no. 509. Flippant on religion: *Corresp.*, I, 114–15, 310–11, 342; Spence, I, nos. 114, 303, 304. Opposed to bigotry, for benevolence: *Corresp.*, I, 126–28, 151, 209, 220, 331, 454, 498–99; II, 172; III, 81; IV, 7. Belief in afterlife, providence, attraction to Pascal, Erasmus: *Corresp.*, I, 128, 190, 454; III, 81, 144, 155; IV, 207, 416; Spence, I, nos. 352, 654.

[7]*Corresp.*, I, 453–54; Spence, I, no. 655 (some mss. have "look right" for "be right": see II, 73–75).

[8]See Mack, introduction to Twickenham ed., xxiii–xxiv.

is, one feels, a sense of *embarrassment* when Pope touches on the holy. And yet, compared with even an officially orthodox poem like Blackmore's, there is more liveliness and awe in Pope's conception of God, and this difference is not only owing to Pope's superiority as a poet. Pope in *An Essay on Man*, I think, is drawn two ways. On the one side he wishes to fabricate a *theodicy*, a coherent, rational account of Deity; on the other he is attracted by a *Job*-like sense of God's ineffability and grandeur. A tension is thus established in the poem, but I do not know whether it is a sign of health or disease. It is almost as though Pope were aiming, not consciously of course, at a synthesis of Bolingbroke and Warburton; but what if such synthesis is not feasible or can be achieved only by a sort of theological legerdemain?

Before studying the poem more systematically, I should like to look at a specific example of what I take to be Pope's indecisiveness or equivocation. In I, 99–112, he draws our attention to "the poor Indian, whose untutor'd mind / Sees God in clouds, or hears him in the wind." Pope clearly prefers the Indian's sense of divinity, primitive though it be, to the sophisticated intellectual's in the ensuing passage who presumes in his pride to judge God (and in II, 110, Pope also speaks seriously of seeing God in the storm and wind). But his admiration is not undiluted, for he stresses at the end of the passage the naive theology of the Indian, who thinks "admitted to that equal sky, / His faithful dog shall bear him company." In IV, 177–78, the Indian reappears, this time in a distinctly unflattering context. Here Pope is ridiculing the foolish, prideful man who, placing happiness in externals and material things, is thus dismissed: "Go, like the Indian, in another life / Expect thy dog, thy bottle, and thy wife." In the first passage the Indian is praised for his humility but pitied for his innocence; in the second the Indian is the *reductio ad absurdum* of those ignorant of true happiness. The Indian appears yet again in Pope's conversation, when he scoffs at the notion — a notion, by the way, that a Christian such as Dr. Johnson willingly entertained — that we shall enjoy "the company of our friends here when in the other world." This,

[123]

says Pope, is but "too like the Indians thinking that they shall have their dogs and their horses there."[9] A sophisticated Christian, trying to conceive of heaven, wants to avoid crude materialism, but he also wants a heaven sufficiently human to be desirable, it being a worthless conception otherwise. Pope swings between a somewhat sentimental attitude toward the Indian and a skeptical raillery. A more balanced perspective might see in the Indian's belief a rudimentary articulation of a genuine religious insight; but this perspective is sought in vain from Pope.

Critics hostile to *An Essay on Man* have amused themselves by noting that Pope altered its sixth line, in which he defines creation, from "A mighty maze of walks without a plan" to "A mighty Maze! but not without a Plan." Pope, we are told, was unable to make up his mind even on this most fundamental of questions. This is sportive criticism. The first version, through a figure of speech, puts greater stress on the obscurity of the divine plan, but the two versions need not be viewed as contradictory; that is mere captious pedantry.[10] That Pope should have revised the line to emphasize the rationality of the universe is significant, however, and in the rest of the first epistle he alternates between stressing the intelligibility, and the enigma, of God. Very early, for example, he employs the rhetorical questioning, found in *Job* and Dryden's *Religio Laici*, to remind us of our insignificance and impotence (31–34); but presently we are reassured that all is for the best and "Man's as perfect as he ought" (70). Instead of Pascal or Dryden or *Job*, then, we are given Voltaire's *response* to Pascal: man is "ce qu'il doit être." In 86–90 we are offered something like the Christian God, omnipotent and omniscient, and again in 121–22 Pope recalls *Job* as he rebukes the cynics: "Snatch from his hand the balance and the rod, / Re-judge his justice, be the GOD of GOD!" But again this ejaculation is wedged into a theodicy like the youthful Vol-

---

[9]Spence, I, no. 575.

[10]For an example of ridicule, see Fairchild, I, 494; but cf. William Empson, *Seven Types of Ambiguity* (1930; rpt: New York: New Directions, n.d.), 204.

taire's, stressing man's relative perfection and the universal order and harmony that are witness to God's benevolence. The last third of the epistle describes eloquently the chain of being and the spirit of God pervading it. Pope's is the conventional conception of a scale of sensual (i.e., merely appetitive and sensory) entities ascending upward to the partly mental (man, angel, God). But Pope features, more than Browne, say, the elements of *system* and *mutual dependency*. All the possible positions on the chain are occupied and though man is still far from the Deity, God is nevertheless made to seem an intrinsic part of the scale. Line 238, describing the chain, read originally: "Ethereal Essence, Spirit, Substance, Man," but was altered to "Natures aethereal, human, angel, man." The first version suggests the traditional, Renaissance hierarchy of value, the second gives a repetitive jumble (what is the difference between "human" and "man"?); the Renaissance discontinuities and gaps are blurred. Pope then reaches his climax:

> All are but parts of one stupendous whole,
> Whose body Nature is, and God the soul;
> That chang'd thro' all, and yet in all the same,
> Great in the earth, as in th' aethereal frame,
> Warms in the sun, refreshes in the breeze,
> Glows in the stars, and blossoms in the trees,
> Lives thro' all life, extends thro' all extent,
> Spreads undivided, operates unspent,
> Breathes in our soul, informs our mortal part,
> As full, as perfect, in a hair as heart;
> As full, as perfect, in vile Man that mourns,
> As the rapt Seraph that adores and burns;
> To him no high, no low, no great, no small;
> He fills, he bounds, connects, and equals all.
>
> (I,267–80)

Now Pope is no pantheist, as he has often been charged. But his account of the spirit of God is notably different from Browne's, discussed in Chapter II. Both are developing the idea of a "world-spirit" found in neo-Platonism and not incompatible

[125]

with the Christian Spirit of God. Browne asserts more clearly than Pope that God is not to be identified with nature (Browne says that the "spirit plays within us, yet makes no part of us," Pope, more equivocally, that "changed through all, [it is] yet in all the same"). Browne emphasizes the creative aspects of the spirit and its direct influence on the individual, Pope, more abstractly, its all-pervading vitalism and general tidying up. Browne recognizes human weakness and divine transcendence and mystery, Pope stresses divine immanence, mutual dependency, the reasonable order of it all. And of course Browne's occult and alchemical imagery is stripped away. Pope's passage owns an Apollonian majesty admirably conveyed through the balanced couplets, but has little if any numinous feeling.

The second epistle opens with the justly celebrated passage on human nature, obviously inspired by Pascal's *Pensées*, especially no. 246:

> Plac'd on this isthmus of a middle state,
> A being darkly wise, and rudely great:
> With too much knowledge for the Sceptic side,
> With too much weakness for the Stoic's pride,
> He hangs between; in doubt to act, or rest,
> In doubt to deem himself a God, or Beast;
> In doubt his Mind or Body to prefer,
> Born but to die, and reas'ning but to err;
> Alike his ignorance, his reason such,
> Whether he thinks too little, or too much:
> Chaos of Thought and Passion, all confus'd;
> Still by himself abus'd, or disabus'd;
> Created half to rise, and half to fall;
> Great lord of all things, yet a prey to all;
> Sole judge of Truth, in endless Error hurl'd:
> The glory, jest, and riddle of the world!
>
> (II, 3–18)

Pope's reading of Pascal went back a long way, and he had written a similar passage in prose in a letter of 1713.[11] It is a theo-

---

[11]*Corresp.*, I, 185–86.

logical obbligato, as I have noted in an earlier chapter, and there can be no doubt that Pope gives it superb and sincere expression. The following verse paragraphs (19–52) are consistent with the Renaissance pessimism of Donne and Browne and Pascal. But in this epistle, as in the first, Pope retreats from this view of man as mystery and paradox. He proceeds to provide a mechanical and rationalistic exposition of human nature quite out of character with the Pascalian opening. It is true that he returns to a Pascalian theme at the end: we seek relief in a variety of distractions that are largely dictated by mere custom and opinion. But whereas Pascal sees man as pathetic, even tragic, in his vain flight from a sense of his nothingness, Pope sees the distractions as, on the whole, comforting and consoling. He is not, in fact, adopting Pascal's views at all, but Voltaire's defense of distractions *against* Pascal, though Pope has not quite the blustery pragmatism of that muscular *philosophe*.

There is a similar dilution of Pascal in the third epistle. No doubt recollecting Pascal's definition of man as a thinking reed, Pope calls him nature's "only thinking thing" (78). But for Pascal this is man's tragic glory: we *know* we shall die, and hence we triumph over the imbecile universe. Pope transforms the idea into a consolation: we know we shall die but, thank heavens, do not know when. To vindicate God's benevolence, Pope stresses, not our knowledge of the fact of death, but our ignorance of its date: a most lenitive readjustment! He mentions the elements of the numinous experience, but only in their most debased and superstitious form:

> She [Superstition], 'midst the light'ning's blaze, and
>   thunder's sound,
> When rock'd the mountains, and when groan'd the
>   ground,
> She taught the weak to bend, the proud to pray,
> To Pow'r unseen, and mightier far than they:
> She, from the rending earth and bursting skies,
> Saw Gods descend, and fiends infernal rise:
> Here fix'd the dreadful, there the blest abodes;
> Fear made her Devils, and weak Hope her Gods;

> Gods partial, changeful, passionate, unjust,
> Whose attributes were Rage, Revenge, or Lust;
>
> (III, 249–58)

And he draws to his conclusion in a clearly latitudinarian vein:

> For Modes of Faith, let graceless zealots fight;
> He can't be wrong whose life is in the right:
> In Faith and Hope the world will disagree,
> But all Mankind's concern is Charity.
>
> (III, 305–308)

The last line recalls *Religio Laici*, 449–50: "For points obscure are of small use to learn; / But common quiet is mankind's concern." But Dryden's are set in a lucid, theological context: the fundamental Christian beliefs are evident, he is saying, so we should not squabble over the minor issues. But in Pope the point is typically equivocal. Dryden talks about personal salvation; Pope says a man can't be "wrong whose life is in the right." Pope never troubles himself to define "right" and "wrong," but he is in effect remanding religion to ethics; and the "charity" is more like Voltaire's than Pascal's: it is humanitarian, not spiritual. Note, finally, the several connotations of "graceless." "Without divine grace"? Perhaps. One senses, rather, that the zealots are graceless in that they are boorishly, ungenteelly, concerned with matters of doctrine or faith; they are people, in other words, sadly deficient in Shaftesbury's polite taste and philosophical good breeding.

The fourth and last epistle, on happiness, has been compared with George Herbert's "The Pulley," which it is claimed "contains in miniature the theme that Pope works out, in somewhat different terms, in this epistle."[12] But the comparison reveals a distinct difference between Pope's notion of the holy and that of Herbert, a traditional seventeenth-century Anglican. In "The Pulley" man is given everything except "rest," so that his restlessness will prevent him from delighting exclusively in God's

---

[12]Mack's observation in the Twickenham ed., 128n.

creation but force him to turn to God himself. Although Pope dilates on the vanity of human wishes, he does so to show that we must seek happiness in "virtue" (310), which as the passages following suggest is a kind of benevolence; we should take pleasure in doing good for our fellow man. To be sure, we are led from social love to love of God (340). This is the route, however, of natural religion: Pope's ideal man is "Slave to no sect, who takes no private road, / But looks thro' Nature, up to Nature's God" (331–32). Pope does, it is true, trot out an argument for immortality (341–52) — an argument also used by latitudinarians and Deists; he even slips in Pascal's wager very unobtrusively (315–16). But his main theme is Shaftesburian benevolence; in Herbert it is salvation. The God in Pope is the God of nature, not wholly immanent, but not very transcendent either, who in an ever-widening circle of love incites us to enlarge and universalize our benevolence. Pope gives us a nearly secular humanitarianism, round which now and again weave the traceries of a vaporous Christianity. The *deus absconditus* of Pascal, the transcendent deity of Herbert and Dryden and Browne, dwindles to an affable schoolmaster instructing us in love of our fellow man.

The earliest hostile commentaries fasten on Pope's conception of God: he is not self-sufficient enough, he is too bound to his creation, too lacking in free will; similarly Pope's view of man was censured as too optimistic, too perfectionist.[13] Yet orthodox defenders of the poem such as William Warburton contend that Pope gives "a sublime description of the Omniscience of God, and the miserable Blindness and Presumption of Man." Warburton justifies such passages as the "modes of faith" by saying

---

[13]The remarks in J. P. Crousaz's two attacks on the poem are representative, and on these particular points they have some validity despite Crousaz's working with inaccurate translations of Pope; see his *An Examination of Mr. Pope's Essay on Man*, tr. Elizabeth Carter (London, 1739), 33, and his *A Commentary on Mr. Pope's Principles of Morality, or Essay on Man*, tr. Samuel Johnson (London, 1742), 13–14. Crousaz perceptively observes that Pope in Epistle III spends more time on the rise of superstition than on the rise of religion; see *Examination*, 159–60.

[129]

that Pope was confining himself deliberately to natural religion. But upon Warburton and Pope's other apologists has been devolved the task of explaining evil, to imp out Pope's own account, which is dexterous enough, no doubt, but perhaps a bit too breezy.[14] This disagreement among the contemporary critics persists among the modern, with some seeing only insipid Deism, some inane confusion, some an agile exposition of orthodox Christianity. Bolingbroke had doubts about the poem, possibly because Pope stressed the non-rational elements, the holy, too much for his taste. A modern humanist, recalling Ciardi's strictures on *Job*, dislikes the same passages because they put him in mind of Big Brother.[15] The poem is orthodox enough, measured against the gossamer apologetics of Pope's day; there is more of the holy in it than in Blackmore and Butler. But it is all leavened with a good bit of Bolingbroke and Shaftesbury. *An Essay on Man* is a congeries of moods, all finely executed but spasmodic and unharmonized. Pope's view of the holy, like his view of the "poor Indian," is shifty, and even the exquisite couplets cannot constrain Job or Pascal to sit down companionably with Voltaire or Bolingbroke; fire and water are generally immiscible. One may indeed wish, with Yvor Winters, that Pope had been, theologically, "as sharp" as Samuel Johnson, yet I cannot persuade myself that he could have written a different poem or that a different poem would have attained to a similar hegemony. *Religio Laici*, after all, had united reason and revelation as ably as they *can* be; at least Dryden avoided Pope's discrepancies of tone, and his style was not yet outmoded. But the theological groundwork of the holy, as I have tried to show in the previous chapter, had greatly deteriorated by the first third of the eighteenth century. One concludes that Pope fed

[14]Elizabeth Carter, for example, in her translation of Crousaz, *Examination*, 84–88, finds it necessary to relate the story of Adam and Eve, since Pope omitted it. And see Gilbert Wakefield, *Observations on Pope* (1796), 186, for an orthodox but anti-Warburtonian censure of the "modes of faith" passage.

[15]James Reeves, *The Reputation and Writings of Alexander Pope* (New York: Barnes and Noble, 1976), 217.

his rather upper-class, certainly genteel, audience the poem it craved.

¤

Like other writers at this time, Pope is very successful when he refrains from theology and, instead, dramatizes the daemonic. Even in *An Essay on Man* he had been able to portray "Superstition" with vivacity, and the earlier *Eloisa to Abelard* (1717) is one of the finest delineations of the daemonic character in the eighteenth century. Of course Eloisa is not literally possessed of a fiend, though she speaks figuratively of fiends and demons possessing her several times; but she is in the grip of daemonic passion. The poem itself embodies vividly the more traditional attitudes in *An Essay on Man*: belief in Pascalian dualism, in an awesome Deity, in, implicitly, the chain of being. But here these are not diluted or contravened by rationalism.

Eloisa is torn between the "Idea" or image of God and that of her mutilated lover Abelard; the two are indeed "mix'd" in her heart (12), but also incompatible (25). As she recollects her experience of falling in love with Abelard, she descends, in a figurative way, the chain of being from the mental into the sensual: on first meeting Abelard she thought him "of Angelick kind," skilled in the teaching of holy truths. She continues:

> From lips like those what precept fail'd to move?
> Too soon they taught me 'twas no sin to love.
> Back thro' the paths of pleasing sense I ran,
> Nor wish'd an Angel whom I lov'd a Man.
> Dim and remote the joys of saints I see,
> Nor envy them, that heav'n I lose for thee.
>
> (68–73)

Having run "back through the paths of pleasing sense," having preferred man to angel, and erotic man at that, she perceives but does not regret the chasm between her passion and saintly happiness. She goes on immediately to contemn marriage and "all laws but those which love has made!" True love, she says, dis-

[131]

dains "human ties," and after running along in this vein for awhile she thus apostrophizes illicit love:

> Oh happy state! when souls each other draw,
> When love is liberty, and nature law:
> All then is full, possessing and possest,
> No craving Void left aking in the breast:
> Ev'n thought meets thought ere from the lips it part,
> And each warm wish springs mutual from the heart.
> This sure is bliss (if bliss on earth there be)
> And once the lot of *Abelard* and me.
>
> (91–98)

A romantic or modern might salute this passage as profound, but there is less to it than first appears. Some years later in *An Essay on Man* Pope repeated a line from this passage in III, 208: "When love was liberty, and nature law." But *is* significantly becomes *was*, for Pope is describing mankind in the golden age. Eloisa wishes not only to descend the chain of being into pure feeling or sensuality but also to return to a paradisal state of infantile hedonism. This is something of an obsession with her. When Abelard establishes his monastery, she sees it as a restoration of paradise in the wilderness of fallen nature (134), even as, implicitly, Christ restored a paradise; like Christ's, Abelard's eyes shoot forth a "reconciling ray, / And gleams of glory" (145–46). The blameless vestal or nun can enjoy another Eden (217), but Eloisa dreams only of "unholy joy" (224). She then seeks paradise in her sleep. For Browne, as we have seen, sleep released the soul from sense and made it more amenable to holy influences. For Eloisa it is quite the reverse: "Then conscience sleeps, and leaving nature free, / All my loose soul unbounded springs to thee [Abelard]" (227–28). She has an erotic dream generated by "provoking Daemons," but it is fugitive and frustrating. As her imagined blameless nun dies away in visions of eternal day, so Eloisa wakes "to all the griefs I left behind" (248). She asks on one occasion that the mutilated Abelard give all he has and let her *dream* the rest. Eloisa's quest is visionary, futile, hideously frustrating, not just because Abelard has been castrated, but because the passion itself is ungovernable and self-destructive. She cannot truly or permanently descend the chain of being or retreat to a narcissistic golden age. There is no liberation there, and she knows it, confessing candidly that she is "the slave of love and man" (178). Against all this, her celebration of the lovers' "happy state" is surely ironic and for Eloisa an exercise in self-deception. That state is no more real than her erotic dream, and as Robert Burton told us long ago in the *Anatomy of Melancholy* (III, 4, 1, 2) the dreams of nuns often come from the devil.

Eloisa views God and Abelard as "rivals" for her heart, and she acknowledges that one or the other must triumph. She longs sometimes for mystic union with God, but Abelard's image obsesses and pursues her, rising in the grove, before the altar, stealing "between my God and me." She hears his voice in every hymn and invites him to oppose and blot out the image of God (269–88). Swinging endlessly between desire for God and Abelard, relapsing down the chain of being and vainly solacing herself with hopes of an erotic paradise, Eloisa seems truly possessed, and she experiences intellectual as well as emotional confusion. Christian example tells us to love the sinner but hate the sin: but since her sin *is* love, she asks how she can "love th'offender, yet detest th'offence?" (192). She has no understanding of Pascal's order of charity and cannot distinguish religious from erotic love.

There are two ceremonies in the poem. In the first (107–18) Eloisa assumes the veil of a nun in the presence of Abelard; they are both "victims," and Eloisa's eyes are fixed on her lover instead of the cross. "Heav'n scarce believ'd the conquest it survey'd," she says, and the reader may well add: No wonder! In the second ceremony, toward the end of the poem (321–36) she imagines her death and Abelard administering the last rites; he stands before her in his sacred vestments and presents the cross. This, it has been argued, is a resolution: now Abelard is priest *and* lover, and he is one with the cross; Eloisa can lawfully behold both. But the context, tone, and imagery of the passage militate against such a view. Even as she foresees her death, she lapses into erotic imagery ("Suck my last breath, and catch my flying soul!"), and yet again in 331–32. When she imagines Abelard entering into heaven, the saints embrace him "with a love like mine" (342). Considering her confusion over types of love, and the insistent erotic imagery, this line is indeed equivocal. Eloisa is obsessed, befuddled, unstable to the last. Her loves for God and Abelard are jangling and irreconcilable. From such an impasse she endeavors to escape through dreams, through visions of paradise and of death. But death cannot resolve the conflicting passions, however surely it will end them. Pope imbues the second ceremony with even more eroticism than the first, and he omits a supernatural part of the legend that dramatizes the union of the lovers after death, thus accenting the futility of the passion.[16]

Three questions have most bothered the critics: whether there is a resolution, whether we are to sympathize with Eloisa, whether we are to admire or condemn the obvious artificiality of the poem.[17] I shall return presently and briefly to the problem of the resolution. The next two questions may be answered

[16]See Dom Augustin Calmet, *Dissertations upon the Apparitions of Angels, Daemons, and Ghosts* (1759), 238: "We are told, that after the death of the famous Abelard ... Eloisa, his wife, dying not long after and being buried ... in the same grove, Abelard stretched out his arms and received her into his bosom. ... But this fact is by no means certain, or even probable."

[17]One can include only representative views. Arguing for a resolution are: Aubrey Williams, *Poetry and Prose of Alexander Pope* (Boston: Houghton Mifflin, 1969), xxxi, and Brenden OHehir, "Virtue and Passion: The Dialectics of *Eloisa to Abelard*," in *Essential Articles*, 333–52. Sympathizing with Eloisa, or seeing Pope on her side, are: E. Audra, *L'Influence Française dans l'Oeuvre de Pope* (Paris: Librairie Ancienne Honoré Champion, 1931); Ronald Paulson in *English Satire* (Los Angeles: Univ. of California Press, 1972), 55–106; David B. Morris in *Modern Language Quarterly*, 34 (1973), 247–71. Those who object to the artifice of the poem include: E. Sitwell, *Alexander Pope* (1930; rpt. Harmondsmith: Penquin, 1948); Reuben A. Brower, *Alexander Pope: the Poetry of Allusion* (Oxford: Clarendon Press, 1959). But Bonamy Dobrée praises the sincere emotion in the poem in *Alexander Pope* (1951; rpt. London: Oxford Univ. Press, 1966). These interpretations are wittily dismantled by D. W. Robertson, Jr., in his *Abelard and Heloise* (New York: Dial Press, 1972), Ch. 11; to his reading I am much in debt.

together. There is much to sympathize with in Eloisa's case, but then we must remember that the story is narrated from her perspective. She finds her surroundings gloomy, and to be sure the rugged rocks, caverns, grottos, streams, graves, and dying gales were all to secure a prominent place in the later "graveyard" poems and Gothic novels. But their source is Milton's *Il Penseroso* (1645), where their gloominess is rather pleasant. Milton's "pensive Nun," rapt in divine meditation, is thus gently addressed: "There held in holy passion still, / Forget thyself to Marble" (41–42). Conversely Eloisa, being in no *holy* passion, exclaims: "I have not yet forgot myself to stone" (24). For Milton's nun, the surroundings encourage contemplation and even religious ecstasy. The speaker in that poem, musing in an ancient cloister, reflects:

> There let the pealing Organ blow
> To the full voic'd Choir below,
> In Service high and Anthems clear,
> As may with sweetness, through mine ear,
> Dissolve me into ecstasies,
> And bring all Heav'n before mine eyes.
>
> (161–66)

For Eloisa, endeavoring at prayer, it is rather different:

> When from the Censer clouds of fragrance roll,
> And swelling organs lift the rising soul;
> One thought of thee puts all the pomp to flight,
> Priests, Tapers, Temples, swim before my sight:
> In seas of flame my plunging soul is drown'd,
> While Altars blaze, and Angels tremble round.
>
> (271–76)

The settings are similar, but the first induces a desire for the numinous, while the second (never mind the latent pun in the second line) yields a daemonic lubriciousness. The scenery itself is not intrinsically horrible; at one time it assisted even Eloisa in her meditations (161). It is her passion that makes it so, and makes her seem more pitiable than she really is.

[135]

Pope's rhetoric and artifice, the studied antitheses of his couplets, the very extremity and sharp vacillation, the passion and derangement of Eloisa, are intended to counteract any sentimental admiration. She is neither very sympathetic nor, I believe, disgusting, but rather, pathetic. Her will and her reason have been largely corroded by daemonic obsession. We are sorry for her; we do not wish to be like her. For some critics the poem is a glorification of romantic love. They cite passages from Pope's letters that suggest he was in a state of infatuation himself.[18] They cite the last line of the poem — "He best can paint 'em, who shall feel 'em most" — to show that Pope is pouring into it his own ardent emotions. But the letters are clever and a shade factitious: Pope was something of a *poseur*, after all. And the concluding line is a no less witty adaptation of Horace, *Ars Poetica*, 102–103: "Si vis me flere, dolendum est primum ipsi tibi." Finally, Pope is writing an Ovidian epistle, a form that more often ridicules than adulates romantic love.

There is a sophisticated variation on the romantic reading of *Eloisa to Abelard*. This argues that human and divine love are synthesized at the end; each is incomplete without the other. This interpretation is as gratifying to the Marxian or Hegelian critic as the other is to the sentimentalist. But both try to impose on the text later and possibly flimsier philosophies. The God of this poem is indeed hidden, but there is no suggestion that he is like the tyrant god of Superstition described in *An Essay on Man*: "partial, changeful, passionate, unjust, / Whose attributes were Rage, Revenge, or Lust." The only god dealing out revenge in the poem is Cupid (81–82). Eloisa is something of a female Dr. Faustus. Like him, she complains of fiends tearing her from God (288); her will, like his, seems paralyzed. God remains hidden to both because neither can truly turn to him. Death and damnation conclude Faustus's sufferings; death only can end Eloisa's. Of course there is no literal damnation in Pope's poem: Eloisa's sin is less willful and grave, and in any event the Ovidian epistle is supposed to arouse emotions of pathos, not fear or

[18]See especially *Corresp.*, I, 338, but cf. I, 364–65, 367, 389–90.

horror. But the forces in conflict, at bottom, are good and evil, charity and cupidity, agapé and eros: not here, not in *Dr. Faustus*, not, say, in the *Book of Revelation*, are they joined in holy matrimony. Hence the theatricality and artifice of the poem. Critics out of sympathy with the *Book of Revelation* often sympathize with Faustus and Eloisa, but when that happens, ideology has triumphed over style. We are to remain detached witnesses of the destructiveness of daemonic passion, and the stylistic barriers help to keep us on the right side.

☐

Pope's two mock epics are also mock daemonics, though this element is more peripheral and less serious in *The Rape of the Lock* than in *The Dunciad*. The sylphs and gnomes in the enlarged version of the *Lock* are elemental spirits, and such spirits had frequently inhabited the hypotheses of Renaissance occultism. Pope derived them more specifically from seventeenth-century Rosicrucianism and most specifically from the Abbé de Montfaucon de Villars' discursive novel, *Le Comte de Gabalis* (1670). In Pope the sylphs had been coquettes in life and are now denizens of the air; the gnomes had been more splenetic, melancholy women and so are of the earth. Of course Pope's attitude is facetious: the sylphs are the ludicrous counterparts of the gods and goddesses of the classical epic. Lord Chesterfield's sentiments, expressed in 1748, would no doubt have matched his own:

> I stumbled, the other day, at a bookseller's, upon Comte de Gabalis . . . which I had formerly read. I read it over again and with fresh astonishment. Most of the extravagances are . . . in the unintelligible jargon which the Cabalists and Rosicrucians deal in to this day. Their number is, I believe, much lessened, but there are still some; and I myself have known two, who studied and firmly believed that mystical nonsense. What extravagancy is not man capable of entertaining, when once his shackled reason is led in triumph by fancy and prejudice!

[137]

It should be noted that *Le Comte de Gabalis* is far from wholly serious, and that it insinuates an eroticism not alien to *The Rape of the Lock*.

The daemonic element appears in Canto IV, after Belinda's lock has been successfully severed. The gnome Umbriel, "a dusky melancholy Spright, / As ever sully'd the fair face of Light," descends into the Cave of Spleen, or Belinda's unconscious mind. Like Eloisa's convent, the cave is decorated with grottos, haunted shades, visions of fiends, specters, tombs, lakes, angels. Much of this phantasmagoria is hyperbolized, perhaps only slightly, from the scenic extravagances of early eighteenth-century opera and pantomime — sources to which Pope will return in *The Dunciad*. Here abides the "wayward Queen" of the Spleen, or melancholy. Umbriel, contending that Belinda has disdained this goddess, urges her to exert her power. This she does, providing him with a bag containing sighs, sobs, passions, fainting fears, soft sorrows, melting griefs, flowing tears. Exploding the bag over Belinda's head, he causes her to lose self-control, common sense, good humor: qualities that hitherto have kept reason and passion in harmony. Belinda, like Eloisa, descends downward on the chain of being from airy coquette to heavy gnome, prudish and, denying her proper nature, Amazonian in her rage and self-obsession.

The Cave of Spleen resembles Eloisa's convent, and the psychology underlying the passage is also similar to that of the other poem. The enlarged and completed version of the *Lock* was published the same year as *Eloisa*, and they have in common: a ghastly, even nightmarish landscape, erotic imagery, a vivid account of the enraging and libidinous effects of melancholy on a frustrated sensibility. The moral of the *Lock* is that Belinda should seek self-fulfillment in the situation where providence has placed her, or to put it less grandiosely, she should accept reality; that, I take it, is the point of *Eloisa* as well, though no officious Clarissa is there to platitudinize it. Without trying to make the daemonic a central theme in the *Lock*, I would mention Pope's own comment on his poem: "People who would rather it were let alone laugh at it, and seem heartily merry, at the same time that they are uneasy. 'Tis a sort of writing very like tickling." It is not odd that Henry Fuseli, a master of the daemonic and macabre, should have selected the Cave of Spleen as the subject for one of his most applauded paintings.

♯

The Dunciad (Books I–III: 1728, 1729; IV: 1742) was hardly grasped by the educated contemporary reader, and since then its commentators have too often emulated the dull critic in the poem itself, who plans to "explain a thing 'till all men doubt it, / And write about it . . . and about it." But *The Dunciad* performs three tasks relevant to this study: it repudiates a Deism sometimes attributed to *An Essay on Man* by petulant critics; it presents, in a whimsical manner, a magical and daemonic world more electrifying than any in *Eloisa* or the *Lock*; it incarnates (though that is hardly the right word) in the goddess Dulness an actual but Satanic *mysterium tremendum*. Pope shows the apocalyptic triumph of this deity, a Last Judgment, and the advent of what may be termed the New Pandaemonium.

Pope was vexed by the attacks on *An Essay on Man*, and was almost pathetically grateful to Warburton for vindicating his orthodoxy. If such a pungent apologist could blink the nebulosities of that poem, surely it might survive any inquisition! But he wished to set the record straight himself, and while theology is not the prime purpose of *The Dunciad*, Pope does take a fling at Deism wherever he can. In Book IV he introduces a "gloomy Clerk" — either a Deist or a very rationalistic Christian apologist like Samuel Clarke — who is sworn foe to religious mystery and implicit faith. This doctrinaire personage exclaims:

> Let others creep by timid steps, and slow,
> On plain Experience lay foundations low,
> By common sense to common knowledge bred,
> And last, to Nature's Cause thro' Nature led.
> All-seeing in thy [i.e., Dulness's] mists, we want no guide,
> Mother of Arrogance, and Source of Pride!

[139]

We nobly take the high Priori Road,
And reason downward, till we doubt of God:
Make Nature still incroach upon his plan;
And shove him off as far as e'er we can:
Thrust some Mechanic Cause into his place;
Or bind in Matter, or diffuse in Space.
Or at one bound o'er-leaping all his laws,
Make God Man's Image, Man the final Cause,
Find Virtue local, all Relation scorn,
See all in SELF, and but for self be born;
Of nought so certain as our *Reason* still,
Of nought so doubtful as of *Soul* and *Will*.
Oh hide the God still more! and make us see
Such as Lucretius drew, a God like Thee:
Wrapt up in Self, a God without a Thought,
Regardless of our merit or default.

(IV, 465–86)

This is Pope's definitive *analytical* objection to Deism or free thought. But it is a notably different rebuttal from Dryden's or Pascal's. The freethinkers he singles out for ridicule are those who "take the high Priori road," i.e., who commence with abstract theoretical conceptions and "reason downward" till they either doubt God or fabricate one that is remote from creation, shrunk to a mechanical cause, emptied of personality through being identified entirely with matter, or entirely etherealized. Such deities have dwindled into mere human images and projections, and those often of the most prideful sort. The clerk hopes that Dulness might go even farther than these and produce a god altogether at the other end of the chain of being, without intellect or thought, unconcerned with human merit or default, the authentic Voltairean deity *beyond* good and evil, the last word in *dei absconditi*.

Now this is so far very satisfactory. Pope wishes to preserve a moral and tremendous deity vitally involved in his creation. But Pope opposes only one sort of rationalist here, the a priorist. This category might include Hobbists and Cartesians; and apologists such as Glanvill and Pascal had anticipated Pope's objections. Yet the other sort of rationalist is more insidious: the natural religionist who pursues the a posteriori road, who reasons from experience to God, bypassing revelation. Pascal and Dryden had attacked this sort as well by stressing the limits of reason and natural theology. But Pope aims at the easier target, the a priorists, and even seems to exculpate the other type at the beginning of the passage. The a priorist is an easier target because he is less empirical and more dogmatic, and because his method leads more ineluctably to a denial of the need for revelation. Pope's tactics, I think, are evasive. He would scorn the rationalist without actually disowning the very rationalism most often imputed to *An Essay on Man*. One might argue that at least Pope is faithful to the principles of that poem, which does follow the a posteriori road. But two difficulties spring up here. First, the strictures laid by Pope on the a priorists can also be applied to the other method. Natural theologians such as Shaftesbury or Blackmore could also "shove God off" and reduce him to the merely mechanical, to the impersonal, and so on. Second, the distinction between those two methods, if truth be told, is not always plain. In *An Essay on Man*, Pope worked from assumed, theoretical conceptions that, as we shall see in a later chapter, were not inexpugnable: the chain of being is one of them, of course. Yet he also claimed there to "trace" God in our own world and to reason from what we (empirically) *know*. There is something dilapidated and slipshod about the theology underlying both *An Essay on Man* and *The Dunciad*.

There is nothing slipshod, however, in Pope's evocation of a daemonic universe. The surrealistic, nightmarish, often animistic world of *The Dunciad* is Belinda's unconscious mind writ large. Here, too, infernal goddesses — Cloacina as well as Dulness herself — influence mortals and are to be propitiated. Here too all the phantasmagoria of opera extravaganza and mime, grotesquely vitalized, are summoned forth: sorcerers, gorgons, dragons, fiends, wizards, all commingled in a chaotic panorama or daemonic farce; a magician-chef-priest, for example, in a Satanic parody of the Mass, transforms beeves to jelly, hares to larks, and so on. By 1728, when the first version of *The Dunciad* appeared, J.- B. S. Chardin had finished his macabre painting *The Ray* or *The Skate*, through which is infused the same weird, monstrous energy, the same uncanny animism of the mundane or hideous.[19] The goddess Dulness does not represent only stupidity, of course, but arrogance, lack of a sense of proportion, and under her malign rule the arts and sciences decay into selfish and trivial pursuits. The effect of Dulness indeed, like that of the daemonic in *Eloisa* and *Lock*, is to cause a general sliding down the chain of being from the truly rational to the fragmented, the sensual, and the selfish. In sleep, for example, Dulness imparts raptures that "high the seat of Sense o'erflow, / Which only heads refin'd from Reason know." As with Eloisa's "raptures of unholy joy," these visions include "the Fool's Paradise ... / The air-built Castle, and the golden Dream, / The Maid's romantic wish" (III, 9–11). Music declines into its elemental chaos, noise (II, 235–68); the student's language degenerates, is perverted, winds up "the Echo of a Sound" (IV, 322). The wizard or high-priest of Dulness, a jocular version of Circe, administers a potion that obliterates intellectual and moral principles in mortals, who, however: "never to escape / Their Infamy, still keep the human shape" (IV, 527–28). Thus it is the nature of the daemonic to alter inwardly rather than outwardly. To the extent that *The Dunciad* has any coherent plan, it would seem to be this: the collapse of all that distinguishes man as a reasoning animal into nonsense and bestiality.

The goddess Dulness is portrayed as a vortex, a daemonic Negativity who pulls in three types of worshippers: the first, impelled by attraction, fall into her center; the second, moving within the sphere of her attraction but swayed by contrary motions as well, revolve planet-like round her center; the third,

---

[19]The electricity of the cat is obvious, but one should also note the ghastly personification of the ray itself as a monstrous human, a Caliban, a Dagon. The *philosophe* Diderot considered the painting "disgusting": "I cannot make head or tail out of this magical stuff" (quoted in A. Schönberger and H. Soehner, *The Rococo Age* [New York and London: McGraw-Hill and Thames and Hudson, 1960], 95).

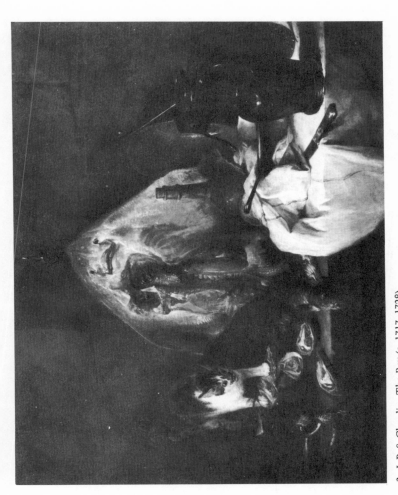

2. J.-B. S. Chardin, *The Ray* (c. 1717–1728)

even less under her influence, sometimes move far away from her, sometimes approach her, much in the fashion of comets (IV, 73–90: but see also the Pope-Warburton notes on this passage). Evil has traditionally been viewed as the absence of good, and so Dulness is a mindless but powerful non-entity consisting *essentially* of her worshippers. One thinks of Dante's Satan, immobile, without volition, in the center of hell and hemmed round with fog, but gnawing mechanically the three worst sinners in the world and encircled by others, by gradations less evil as they are removed from that infernal core. Despite this vacuity, Dulness is a daemonic-numinous presence. The daughter of chaos and eternal night, she shines in clouded majesty (I, 45). "Her ample presence fills up all the place; / A veil of fogs dilates her awful face: / Great in her charms!" (I, 261–63). What is more ominous, her field of attraction is dilating: "As what a Dutchman plumps into the lakes / One circle first, and then a second makes; / What Dulness dropt among her sons imprest / Like motion from one circle to the rest" (II, 405–408). So Pope had described the ever-expanding circle of love in *An Essay on Man:* "Self-love but serves the virtuous mind to wake, / As the small pebble stirs the peaceful lake; / The centre mov'd, a circle strait succeeds, / Another still, and still another spreads" till there is universal love (IV, 363–72). Dulness's gravitational pull parodies the enlarging, unifying love of God. At the end of the poem her yawn, the "Yawn of Gods," infectiously communicates itself to the nation, to all civilization, annihilating art, philosphy, religion, morality, science, drawing everything down the chain of being to the merely sensual, and thence into nothingness:

> Lo! thy dread Empire, *Chaos!* is restor'd;
> Light dies before thy uncreating word:
> Thy hand, great Anarch! lets the curtain fall;
> And Universal Darkness buries All.

Here is the negation of all that Dryden celebrated so vividly at the end of the Killigrew ode. There the revivifying power of the judging God is displayed as he articulates the bones and calls them to life. On that "new morning" the sacred poets will be the first to mount to heaven, to lead the choir in hymning God's praise. In Pope, "all the Nations [are] summon'd to the Throne," but the judge is Dulness. Chaos and anarchy reestablish their empire, the word is inarticulate, and eternal night shuts down. The spread of Dulness compels the astringence of human intellect and its retreat into fragmentation and solipsism.

Now each of us must decide for himself how solemnly to take *The Dunciad*. It is certainly an attack, peevish enough, on personal enemies and rival poets, and one might well conclude with an indignant critic that the duces "were pilloried for the greater glory of Alexander Pope."[20] It is also possible to see in it a fine threnody on the moldering classical-humanist-Christian civilization: those tremors sensed by Donne more than a century ago in *The First Anniversary* are now recorded more nicely, more ominously, by Pope, who shares Donne's Christian humanism but not his confidence, who is sounding the alarm where Donne breathed defiance. Assuredly Pope had serious motives in this poem. He spent, or squandered, much of his finest writing on it; the apocalyptic fourth book was his favorite of all his works, and his favorite couplet is in Book III (87–88), lines describing death-like coldness and inactivity. The many allusions to *Paradise Lost* impart a truly daemonic quality to the poem.[21] Still, we must not forget that it presents a farcical, not an authentic, apocalypse. Nor should we forget that its message, if we take it seriously, is quite incompatible with the optimism of *An Essay on Man*. Viewed as a lively and grandiloquent admonition, on the other hand, or as a lavish and masterly indulgence of a mood, it is not incompatible. And it is a romantic error to imagine that the daemonic can never be pictured effectively when the tongue sneaks, even partly, into the cheek.

---

[20]Reeves, 255

[21]See William Kinsley, "Physico-Demonology in Pope's 'Dunciad,'" *Modern Language Review*, 70 (1975), 20–31. A fresh scientific analogy for the vortex-like Dulness, he shrewdly suggests, might be the black holes of modern astronomy.

As a portraitist of the daemonic, Pope is superb, whether he is drawing on the individual or the cosmic scale. As a dialectician or theologian he is rather weak, though really not so bad when it is recalled that he is an amateur and that his age had no surplusage of keen theologians. But I will insist that *An Essay on Man* is less sophisticated than *Religio Laici*. Dryden's position, or Pascal's, can degenerate into Fideism, it is true. But solely on empirical grounds the natural religion favored by Pope and Bolingbroke is very dubious. If man is "as perfect as he ought," and if the principles of reasonable religion are self-evident, then surely there should be more religious questions on which reasonable men may agree than in fact there are. An inspection of reality suggests that the natural religionists are wrong either about the self-evident quality of the principles, or about the perfection of man, or both. Dryden and Pascal understood that the rational proofs of God, the self-evident principles of natural religion, were in truth the lingering attitudes of Christianity, sundered from their dogmatic and theological bases, but retaining some intellectual and emotional force. That is why Dryden called reason a twig; more indirectly perhaps, that is why Pascal called man a thinking *reed*. The test, after all, is this, that a Christian can still accept the arguments of *Religio Laici* and the insights of the *Pensées*. But an up-to-date rationalist will probably scorn the ratiocination of *An Essay on Man*, a poem, finely wrought as it is, that constructs too much on too little. On Pope, as on Shaftesbury, there has settled a gauziness of thought from which the more sapient theologians and poets of the previous century had been quite free; but then none of them limned a Dulness or an Eloisa.

□

Swift's Christianity, like Pope's, has been called into question. If Pope in his personal religious views seems too unbraced, Swift's personality strikes some people as too prickly, and his attitude toward his church, they say, is that of a bureaucrat or politician instead of a priest. Swift was wholly cynical, they may go on to allege, but like a good Pyrrhonist he supported Christianity as an anodyne for the *mobile vulgus*. But this is the telepathic school of criticism, which I mistrust. In such works as his "Letter to a Young Gentleman, Lately Entered into Holy Orders," his "Thoughts on Religion," his "Mr. Collins's Discourse of Free-Thinking," his sermons, especially the "Trinity Sermon," Swift clearly affirms divine revelation and the fundamental tenets of Christianity, and he ridicules the insipid dilutions of Deism and latitudinarianism. Implicit in the "Argument against Abolishing Christianity" is surely the notion that authentic Christianity is the ideal, and he attacks not only Deism there but also that nominal Christianity to which Swift himself, some say, was attached. There is of course an official quality to all of these that will render them suspect to the telepathists. And it is true that his better known and more imaginative works seldom touch on the holy or expound religion in any very direct or forcible way. Then, too, his assaults on religious fanaticism and enthusiasm have been taken, from their first appearance, as sure manifestations of a skeptical mentality.[22]

Swift's most ambiguous satire is, I suppose, Part IV of *Gulliver's Travels* (1726), and I am going to suggest that in a curious way it is rather like *An Essay on Man*. Here Gulliver is placed on the "isthmus of a middle state" between the languidly rational Houyhnhnms and the bestial Yahoos. But of course there is none of that paradoxical grandeur so fascinating to Pope. The Yahoos are the "flesh," less intellectual even than Caliban, who can at least dream of beauty. Yet the European Yahoos, the civ-

[22]Arguing for the compatibility of Swift's writings and orthodox Christianity are: T. O. Wedel, "On the Philosophical Background of *Gulliver's Travels*," *Studies in Philology*, 23 (1926), 434–50; Louis A. Landa, "Jonathan Swift," *English Institute Essays 1946* (New York: Columbia Univ. Press, 1947), 20–40; Roland Frye, "Swift's Yahoo and the Christian Symbols for Sin," *Journal of the History of Ideas*, 15 (1954), 201–17; Martin Kallich, *The Other End of the Egg: Religious Satire in "Gulliver's Travels"* (Bridgeport, Conn.: Univ. of Bridgeport Press, 1970); Ronald Paulson, *Theme and Structure in Swift's "Tale of a Tub"* (New Haven: Yale Univ. Press, 1960).

ilized ones, have degraded themselves even below their less sociable cousins, yielding to malice and perversion unknown to the lower reaches of the chain of being. And Gulliver makes himself ridiculous, striving vainly to identify himself with the lofty horses, imitating their least significant attributes, their voice and gait, like any crack-brained convert. He remains nevertheless a true Yahoo, as he himself must own when he is lasciviously assaulted by a female Yahoo in heat. For Swift man is not Browne's "splendid animal"; he is just an animal, or worse than one. All this seems quite clear, quite consistent with Judaeo-Christian conceptions, however repugnant it may have been to the likes of Shaftesbury. One may recognize the satiric hyperbole yet still feel the bite.

The Houyhnhnms are the problem. Of course they contrast favorably with the Yahoos. Like the angels on the upper half of the chain of being they have an intuitive understanding of truth and lack even a word for "lie"; their society is peaceful, harmonious, healthy. But they labor under minor deficiencies, being rather unimaginative, stodgily conventional, somewhat snobbish, finical. Their rationalism, more significantly, is so gelid that it may call to mind the pagan Stoic, the Deist, or even, in its most extreme form, the mad intellectual or utilitarian of Swift's "Modest Proposal." As incarnations of anything holy they are not very appetizing. They show no particular respect to their parents, as Moses enjoins; they have no need for revelation or Christ; they practice an aesthetically fussy eugenics; the only deity mentioned is some "first Mother" (Ch. 9). We know that Swift hated rationalists: the "Voyage to Laputa" takes very much the same view toward them as Donne in *The First Anniversary*. We can also surmise, not wildly, that he would have been unenthusiastic about a religion of Magna Mater. Is he then satirizing Deism in the Houyhnhnms? If so, there is no explicit norm in Part IV; if not, the norm remains at best equivocal.

As part of his argument for seeing the horses as Deists, one critic mentions that they "are incapable of an *O altitudo*; they have no sense of the sublime mystery, no special reverence for

... matters religious."[23] In other words, they are insensible to the numinous. But then Swift does not delight in *O altitudos* either, and often derides those who do; so this may be a virtue in the Houyhnhnms and not a sign of Deistic angularity. Frankly I cannot bring myself to see them as satiric, though certainly Swift can have a bit of fun with them. If they are unappealing as embodiments of the holy, yet it must be confessed that few such embodiments are entirely successful. Numerous are those who are unattracted by Milton's God or Dante's Beatrice. If the horses seem languid and self-sufficient, it must be remembered that they are not human; they are a race that has never experienced a fall and so has no need of a redeemer. Swift's contemporary Edward Young explored this idea, as have such modern apologists as C. S. Lewis. Finally, if the Houyhnhnms can be compared to the fiendish intellectual of "A Modest Proposal," they can also be compared to the precisian Jonathan Swift who advocates an academy to regulate the English language and dissipate malodorous slang. The Houyhnhnms will forever elude facile interpretation, reflecting as they do the psychic complexity of their creator.

What is clear about Part IV, though, is that Gulliver imitates, pedestrianly if you will, the superficial traits of the horses, and that at the end, denying his human nature, he retreats to the stables and rails like Timon of Athens, that great misanthrope from whom Swift dissociates himself in his famous letter to Pope, 29 September, 1725. Gulliver may also be sequestering himself from the holy: the language in the last paragraph of Chapter 11, with its reference to the bread and the cup, reminds us of the Eucharist, that ritual where we recognize our common humanity and seek union with the divine. The language is also reminiscent of the prophet Nathan's parable of charity, where a poor man permitted a lamb to eat his meat and drink "of his own cup" (II *Samuel*, xii. 3). Uncharitable, prideful, reclusive, lacking self-knowledge, Gulliver is an enthusiast, a puerile convert to Houyhnhnmism. However we may take the horses,

[23]Kallich, 76–77.

[149]

their effect on Gulliver is disastrous; he has lost a sense of his place on the chain of being, of his very nature.

Despite a vastly different tone, there are notable similarities between Part IV and *An Essay on Man*. Both attack pride and mock at man who would aspire beyond his nature. Both see in human nature a union, or it may be a jarring together, of the sensual and mental planes of the scale of being. Both are vague or equivocal in their representation of the ideal and have been arraigned as Deistic. Epistle IV of Pope's poem promulgates a nearly pagan Stoicism; so, taken in one way, does Part IV of *Gulliver's Travels*. And there is a final contrast, Pope showing at the end of his work the widening circle of love, Swift the contraction of pride and hate. If the Houyhnhnms were intended as ideals — and I think they were — they are as indeterminate as the Deity of *An Essay on Man*. But if the holy did not catch Swift's imagination, the daemonic did.

◻

In 1704, early in his career, Swift published in one volume three related satires: *A Tale of a Tub*, *A Battel between the Antient and Modern Books in St. James's Library*, and *A Discourse Concerning the Mechanical Operation of the Spirit*. Although widely understood to be his — they exercised a deleterious effect on his advancement — Swift never acknowledged this satiric trilogy, as I shall call them. *The Dunciad* came many years later, toward the end of Pope's career, but all the satires have much in common: the protean complexity of structure, kaleidoscopically shifting themes, grotesque conceptions, and noisome imagery; all satirize contemporary degradations and perversions of knowledge. Swift's persona, the alleged author of the satires, complicates things still more. Since he is seldom, though occasionally, to be identified with Swift himself, everything he says must be taken *cum grano salis*. Generally the persona is intended to be a hack writer infatuated with all things contemporary; but he sometimes seems to be a scientist, sometimes an historian, a Rosicrucian, a latitudinarian, an enthusiast or dissenter, a Cartesian, sometimes, perhaps, Sir Thomas Browne. The assiduous critic can find still other possibilities. Thus, like Dryden's Zimri, he is "everything by starts and nothing long," or like Pope's Dulness he is a non-entity assuming a variety of forms and guises to conceal his essential vacuity—nothingness is, by the way, a subject on which he delights to enlarge. The trilogy itself, governed by the vagaries of the persona, is highly irregular, with many digressions, lacunae, and so on.

In his facetious but usually candid "Apology," prefixed to the trilogy in 1710 to rebut hostile criticism, Swift claims to be exposing "gross Corruptions in Religion and Learning . . . Fanaticism and Superstition."[24] In fact he is chiefly satirizing three things: modern self-sufficiency and egotism in intellectual matters; inordinate love of mystery and restless pursuit of novelty, with the concomitant empty verbalism and pretentious pedantry; enthusiasm and insanity, or the subdual of reason by rampant and anarchistic imagination and subjectivity. But these are all connected, and the first two may well culminate in the third. To exemplify abuses in learning, Swift presents an array of fatuous modern philosophers, poets, criticasters, and scholars; for religion there are the fanatical and fundamentalist Christian sects, Roman Catholicism, occultism, Gnosticism, various species of idolatry and demonism. Swift moves freely among all these groups, which share a compulsive egoism and grant willingly the exactions of the libido.

The narrative portions of the *Tale*, the story of the three brothers, describe allegorically the deterioration of the Christian Church, first through the excesses of Peter (Roman Catholicism), who appends gratuitous decorations to the coats (the doctrine and faith of Christianity) that had been left them by their father (Christ), and then through the reforming zeal of Jack (Calvinism), who rends the coats in trying to remove Peter's embellishments. Jack is poised against Martin (standing for

---

[24] *A Tale of a Tub*, ed. A. C. Guthkelch and D. Nichol Smith (Oxford: Clarendon Press, 1958), 4–5. All quotations from the trilogy are from this edition, but passages entirely italicized in the original have been romanized.

Luther, but more generally for the Anglican *via media*), who renovates his coat without destroying the essential fabric. The narrative parts are interrupted by digressions that satirize abuses in learning. There are numerous thematic connections between the digressive and narrative parts: irresponsible scholars and critics misinterpret and mutilate their texts just as the brothers misconstrue their father's will (the New Testament) in order to warrant their fashionable alterations of the coats; the critics, of whom the hack author-persona is himself one, and the brothers consider themselves emancipated from tradition (the hack refuses to observe the inane custom of putting a preface only at the beginning of a work; the brothers will not submit to the clear intention of their father's will); all save Martin are flighty neophiles and indulge their wayward imaginations at the expense of their reason. In tracing the decline of Peter and Jack, Swift suggests that the difference is often subtle between folly or self-indulgence and actual lunacy. The brothers begin to go wrong through idolatry. The demonic Tailor-God, described in Section II, demands worship of dress, which is the real or spiritual essence of man. Therefore the brothers make many changes in the coats to conciliate fashion; they wish, in short, to suit themselves, and they do so through rationalization and a certain amount of self-deception. But by Section IV Peter has obviously gone mad, his alterations are no longer mere embellishments, and his brothers see the folly of trying to humor him. By Section VI Jack has himself gone mad in his fanatical rage and zeal. Jack is the founder of the sect of Aeolists, described at length in Section VIII. For the Aeolists, wind is the primary element; arguing syllogistically, they contend: "Words are but Wind; and Learning is nothing but Words; Ergo, Learning is nothing but Wind." Thus like Falstaff on honor they reduce discourse to inanity, a mere vibration of the vocal chords. As in *The Dunciad*, noise — belching here — usurps the place of rational converse. Dryden, whose views in *Religio Laici* are very like Swift's in the *Tale*, also describes the type: "he was gifted most that loudest bawl'd." Section IX, the heart of the satire, concerns madness, and here the hack author cynically argues that it is relative to current fads, and to one's position in society, whether one's actions are declared insane or not. In what critics commonly regard as the climax of the *Tale*, the hack persona lauds self-deception, contentment with the surfaces of things; for not only does it require effort to see within, but what we see, says the hack, is disgusting. Far better is "the sublime and refined Point of Felicity, called, *the Possession of being well deceived; The Serene Peaceful State of being a Fool among Knaves.*"

To Swift himself F. R. Leavis and others have imputed this extravagant cynicism: we are all ignorant, says Swift, and we are all mad, though some of us, favored by fortune, have escaped Bedlam.[25] But this imputation commits the first fallacy of literary criticism: it disregards the speaker in the work. Not that Swift's persona is always silly or wrong; often, even in Section IX, he seems to speak with Swift's voice, as here: "when a Man's Fancy gets *astride* on his Reason, when Imagination is at Cuffs with the Senses, and common Understanding, as well as common Sense, is Kickt out of Doors; the first Proselyte he makes is Himself." But elsewhere he is not to be trusted. When he remarks, to discourage us from probing beneath the surface of things: "Last Week I saw a Woman *flay'd*, and you will hardly believe, how much it alter'd her Person for the worse," he is but offering us another surface, not an inner or spiritual reality; for he himself is an adherent of the Tailor idolatry, which levels everything down to the material and physiological. In C. S. Lewis's allegory, *The Pilgrim's Regress*, a tempter called the Zeitgeist gives the central character X-ray vision so that he can see that our insides are merely an unwholesome collection of slimy sacks and red tubes. But the skeptical Zeitgeist is not showing him our real or spiritual nature, only another "outside." Lewis's character is not, finally, deceived by the Zeitgeist, and so shows more acuteness than some of Swift's commentators. The hack persona is, at last, only a bewildered Sadducee.

[25]See, e.g., F. R. Leavis, *The Common Pursuit* (London: Chatto and Windus, 1965), 73–87; A. L. Rowse, *Jonathan Swift: Major Prophet* (London: Thames and Hudson, 1975), 31–36.

Then too we must not forget Martin, who embodies a sane but uncynical perspective and contrasts with Jack at the end (XI), who has degenerated to a stupid, literal-minded convert very much like Gulliver — except that he is more expert in imitating an ass than Gulliver a horse. Finally, we should note that Swift never exhibits that tranquillity and resignation, that *ataraxy*, so characteristic of the veritable skeptic. All of these points, well considered, suggest that we must not associate Swift with the persona in Section IX. One of Swift's themes, indeed, is the *ease* with which Peter and Jack slide from rationalizing self-indulgence into lunacy. To grasp that theme it is necessary to see a difference, however exiguous, between the two states. But the persona is not one to make fine distinctions.

The Battel of the Books is shorter and less confusing. The satire centers on corruptions in learning, and the corresponding deity set up for worship is the goddess Criticism. Described in monstrous and grotesque imagery, she is clearly intended to parallel the Tailor god in the *Tale*. Among her daughters is the goddess Dulness, but one might rather compare the mother herself to Pope's Dulness or, diminutively, to the goddess of Spleen in *The Rape of the Lock*. Like the others, she turns everything topsy-turvy and animates the lower elements of human nature; she can change her shape at will; she sheds malign influence over the land. The inset fable of the spider and the bee is delightfully expressive of Swift's own principles. The spider represents the modern spirit in its narcissism, its restless pursuit of the novel and worthless, its rampaging subjectivity. The bee is an image, conventional enough, of the equilibrium, breadth, and sanity of traditionalism; Robert Burton's "Democritus to the Reader," in his *Anatomy of Melancholy*, gives a similar view of the bee. It poses the basic question:

Which is the nobler Being of the two, That which by a lazy Contemplation of four Inches round; by an over-weening Pride, which feeding and engendering on it self, turns all into Excrement and Venom; producing nothing at last, but Fly-bane and a Cobweb: Or That, which, by an universal Range, with long Search, much Study, true Judgment, and Distinction of Things, brings home Honey and Wax.

The hack in the *Tale* often brags of disdaining such wearisome procedures as long search or much study would impose; nor is he very interested in a true distinction of things. For this reason, again, he is to be mistrusted.

Religious themes reappear in *The Mechanical Operation of the Spirit*, and the persona, who had approximated lucidity in the *Battel*, relapses into his amiable unreliability. So again we must try to sort out Swift's voice from the general cacophony. For example, the persona ridicules the conception of a devil, which is merely the opposite of everything the fanatics imagine in a god, and he goes on to mock even the notion of personal providence: "Who, that sees a little paultry Mortal [a preacher], droning, and dreaming, and drivelling to a Multitude, can think it agreeable to common good Sense, that either Heaven or Hell should be put to the Trouble of Influence or Inspection upon what he is about?" Of this passage an eminent scholar and recent biographer of Swift remarks: "How much of people's religious hopes (and illusions) is left after that?" He suggests that Swift had no strong belief in religion except as an opiate for the ignorant *canaille*, and he alleges, to bolster that point, that the great Swift scholar Herbert Davis once told him that he saw "in the margin of a book, in Swift's hand, against a reference to the Nicene Creed, *Confessio digna barbaris.* . . ."[26] One can only surmise what prompted Swift to write that disparaging comment, if indeed it is his; its existence is supported more by gossip than documentation. But in the passage disputed here, Swift is only sacrificing providence and the devil to his more immediate purpose: a deflation of human self-importance. We must not be as literal-minded as the dull critics Swift pillories. Cannot one believe in a devil yet satirize the malefactor who pleads at the bench that the devil made him do everything? Cannot one believe in providence yet smile at the pious motorist who prays for an opportune parking place? To interpret thus is to miss half

[26]Rowse, 31–32.

of Swift's humor, for he is not only ridiculing religious fanaticism by reducing it to the merely biological, but he is also ridiculing those materialists that find biological explanations for everything satisfactory. Swift has told us persistently that he is satirizing abuses of religious thought, not the thought itself; but critics, as persistently, disregard him: the dull ones because the satire is too intricate for them, the sophisticated ones because they are always trying to "see through" the satire to some underlying and congenial nihilism. To be sure, Swift's subject in the trilogy is the *corruptio optimi pessima*, and it requires "true judgment and distinction of things" to follow him.

Two demonic deities preside in the trilogy: the idol of the Tailor-god, and the goddess of Criticism. Both are allegorical contrivances, sufficiently hideous, but more grotesque, even bizarre, than terrifying. The idol is in "the Posture of a *Persian* Emperor, sitting on a *Superficies*, with his Legs interwoven under him," and the rest of the description, implying human sacrifice, brings to mind the obsecrations performed before a Baal or Moloch. Swift aptly unites the degraded numinous awe of the Canaanite deities with the tyranny of the oriental despot. The goddess of Criticism, partly assembled, I think, from Spenser's monster of Errour and Milton's Sin, is shown gnawing on half-devoured volumes and flanked by her father and husband, Ignorance, and her mother, Pride; present also are her sister, Opinion, and her children, Noise, Impudence, Dulness, and so on. "The Goddess herself had Claws like a Cat: Her Head, and Ears, and Voice, resembled those of an *Ass*; Her Teeth fallen out before; Her Eyes turned inward, as if she lookt only upon herself. . . ." The allegory of this description needs no gloss, but one might enlarge a bit on the reference to the ass. One level of meaning is obvious; contemporary title pages of *The Dunciad* feature an ass laden with books. In addition, societies, whether pagan or Christian, have traditionally accused heretics and dissenters, whether pagan or Christian, of worshipping the ass; this is a charge ingeminated with astonishing regularity from the earliest times. Thus both of Swift's deities are associated with barbaric, eldritch rites, vain in themselves, perhaps, but potentially disruptive of society; both express pride, self-sufficiency,

mindlessness. As a motto or epigraph for the *Tale*, Swift chose
a passage of jargon slyly attributed on his title page to Irenaeus:
"Basima eacabasa eanaa irraurista, diarba da caeotaba fobor
camelanthi." This is indeed found in Irenaeus's *Adversus
Haereses*, but it is his example of a nonsense initiation ritual
employed by the Gnostics; the language means nothing — or
anything — one wants it to. From the Christian point of view, of
course, the Gnostics are authentic demonists, worshipping as
their lord the serpent of the Old Testament and despising Jehovah, who wrought the intrinsically evil material world. But in
a wider sense all of the sectaries jumbled together in the trilogy — the cabbalists and Cartesians, the Rosicrucians and Aeolists, the numerologists and materialists — are daemonic in their
zestful subjectivity and self-deception.[27]

Pope and Swift were satirists of chaos. Dulness is hailed at the
end of *The Dunciad* as the "great Anarch." At the end of the
Tale Jack, ingenious in his enthusiasm, has "introduced a new
Deity, who hath since met with a vast Number of Worshippers;
by some called *Babel*, by others, *Chaos*." A new deity, perhaps,
but an old terror. There is the witch in Apuleius, who could
cause even the light of the stars to be swallowed up in ancient
chaos ("quae . . . istam lucem mundi sideralis . . . in vetustum
chaos submergere novit"). Dryden's devilish Achitophel engenders a son, "a shapeless lump, like Anarchy." Pope, it may be,
works up the numinousness more than Swift: his Dulness has
an horrendous and memorable majesty quite unapparent in the
allegorical descriptions of the Tailor idol and Criticism; but
Swift's was an older, more farcical style, and it has its own effect.
It is even arguable that Swift's trilogy, despite the sinuosities of
its persona, is more comprehensible today than *The Dunciad*.
At least it never, like that poem, sinks beneath a load of proper
names, many of them obscure even two centuries ago; and the
writing is vigorous and colorful. Certainly that critic was very

---

[27]On Gnosticism in Swift see Paulson, *Theme and Structure*, 87–144; on
Swift's use of occultism more generally, see Guthkelch-Smith ed. of *Tale*,
appendix F; on the cultural significance of the ass through the ages, see Norman Cohn, *Europe's Inner Demons* (New York: Basic Books, 1975).

wide of the mark who considered that the *Tale* addressed a subject no longer of interest and was undertaken "in a lost cause."[28] In the galimatias of governmental bureaucracy, the continuing religious and political fanaticisms, the faddish "intellectual" movements, the projects of the academy — or the capitulation of Webster's Third Edition to the god of Babel — Swift would have found much to fertilize his wit. In another more depressing sense, of course, such satires as his are always written in a lost cause; hence their perennial value.

Around 1760 William Hogarth finished a striking picture, *Enthusiasm Delineated*, which he later revised, toned down, and published in 1762 as *Credulity, Superstition, and Fanaticism*. In theme and technique both versions, but particularly the first, have much in common with Swift and Pope. Here, for example, is the *noise:* the bawling from pulpit and lectern to the right and in the center, the baying dog at center, the old Jew at the left exclaiming over a picture of Abraham sacrificing Isaac. Here is the furtive sexuality. Here is the idolatry, which is a satire on transubstantiation as well, a belief at which Pope and Swift also take a fling. The popish and Protestant fanaticisms are joined, even as Peter and Jack, fully demented, renew their friendship in the *Tale:* "For, the Phrenzy and the Spleen of both, having the same Foundation, we may look upon them as two Pair of Compasses, equally extended, and the fixed Foot of each, remaining in the same Center; which, tho' moving contrary Ways at first, will be sure to encounter somewhere or other in the Circumference." Here is the chaos, the mindless and mechanical movement, the grotesquerie.[29]

---

[28]Miriam K. Starkman, *Swift's Satire on Learning in "A Tale of a Tub"* (Princeton, N.J.: Princeton Univ. Press, 1950), 3.

[29]Added to the revised engraving were several books: Glanvill on witches, King James's *Demonology*, Wesley's sermons. Removed were some sexual innuendoes and the obscene satire on transubstantiation in the background. A witch replaces the decrepit puppet-god suspended in the upper middle of the picture and supported by two putti. The figure was intended to be a parody of Raphael's god, but, uncannily, it might well be a representation of Blake's Urizen. Horace Walpole praised the picture highly, it haunted Keats's dreams, it is severely discommended by Montague Summers.

3. William Hogarth, *Enthusiasm Delineated* (c. 1760)

Here also is the satiric distancing. For Pope and Swift, unlike some of the writers figuring later in this book, are not trying to entice us *into* their daemonic world. We are the sane onlookers peering through the rear window at all the freakishness, like the pipe-smoking, imperturbable Mahometan in Hogarth. Both Pope and Swift were friends of Bolingbroke, and while I have defended their orthodoxy, I do think they shared with him a certain fidgetiness in respect of the holy. The daemonic they could represent, but it is never with them the beginning of wisdom; and as we read them we are not to be vicarious participants but admonished spectators. Off the record Pope somewhat admired *Robinson Crusoe*, but on the record, in *The Dunciad*, he pillories Defoe in the same line with the ranting, seventeenth-century puritan polemicist William Prynne. The "terrible dreams" of Eloisa, the visions of Pope's dunces and Swift's fanatics, are never, as they were for Crusoe, intimations of the divine; and indeed Crusoe himself, with some slight coarsening of his character, might easily be slipped into Swift's trilogy. One of the original motives behind Hogarth's picture may not be apparent to the casual viewer. It was to caricature earlier and inept expressions of the sacred.

CHAPTER V

Terror and Awe in Mid-Century Poetry: Watts, Akenside, Thomson, Young

And mount Sinai was altogether on a smoke, because the Lord descended upon it in fire; and the smoke thereof ascended as the smoke of a furnace, and the whole mount quaked greatly.

Exodus

The heavens declare the glory of God; and the firmament sheweth his handywork.

Psalms

IN THE PREFACE (1709) to his *Horae Lyricae* Isaac Watts claims for the province of poetry "the scenes of religion in their proper figures of majesty, sweetness, and terror! . . . the inimitable love and passions of a dying God; the awful glories of the last tribunal; the grand decisive sentence, from which there is no appeal; and the consequent transports or horrors of the two eternal worlds." As a catalogue of those scenes omitted from *An Essay on Man*, this is admirable, although a few of them are to be found in the pejorative passage on Superstition. But what Pope was later sedulously to exclude, Watts actively seeks. He believes that Christianity is especially suited to poetic treatment, an opinion he bolsters with many biblical quotations. These quotations, it is true, are drawn chiefly from the Old Testament, and particularly from the *Psalms* and *Job*. But Watts's God is the God of Thunder, whose traits are power, majesty, and "transcendent eminence above all things." Job's melancholy reflections on the grave appeal to Watts, as does his terror and self-abasement. A discursive and rational promoting of religion is effective with some people, he concedes, but others "are

[161]

best frighted from sin and ruin by terror, threatening, and amazement; their fear is the properest passion to which we can address ourselves, and begin the divine work."[1] He inveighs against Deism and praises that often inventive and always earnest critic John Dennis, whose *Grounds of Criticism in Poetry*, published five years earlier, may well have influenced him. Dennis had argued there that "Enthusiastick Terror" is superbly induced by such religious images as "Gods, Daemons, Hell, Spirits and Souls of Men, Miracles, Prodigies, Enchantments, Witchcrafts, Thunder, Tempests" and, most animating of all, "the Wrath and Vengeance of an angry God"; these fetch their power from our sense of comparative ignorance and weakness. In a still earlier essay, *The Usefulness of the Stage*, he had urged that such terrors fortify religious feeling.[2]

Dryden, we recall, had declined to "cheat us into passion" in *Religio Laici*, and neither Pope nor Swift saw in religious fear anything but fanaticism. Dennis is in fact one of the earliest writers to employ *enthusiasm* in a more genial way; after all, Hogarth was still using it contemptuously more than fifty years later. But I have noted in Chapter III an aptitude, evident even in the Restoration, to vindicate non-rational elements of scripture as inspiring religious awe; and we have seen spiritual terror applied to Crusoe to "begin the divine work." At the very vestibule of the eighteenth century, then, pious critics such as Watts and Dennis — neither of them nincompoops, by the way — were deliberately forging an aesthetics of the numinous, and this precisely at the moment, as we have been informed by many literary historians, when the numinous sense was withering and lapsing into desuetude.

Of course that sense *may* have been withering; certainly it is atrophied in Pope and Swift. It is when things start to fall away that men become self-conscious about them. My point, how-

---

[1] Preface to *Horae Lyricae* in *The British Poets* (Chiswick, 1882), XLV, 33–46. All quotations from Watts are from this edition.

[2] John Dennis, *The Critical Works*, ed. Edward Niles Hooker, 2 vols. (Baltimore: Johns Hopkins Press, 1939, 1943), I, 361–62; 183.

ever, is that this sense is never annihilated or very long suppressed. It flourished in the Renaissance and again in Romanticism, nor does it lie wholly inert during the interregnum of rationalism that allegedly lies between. The poets taken up in this chapter have been viewed from many perspectives: as pre-Romantics or harbingers of the glories of *The Prelude*; as reactionaries rebelling against the school of Pope and seeking solace and inspiration in Shakespeare and Milton; as the first bards of the Newtonian science; as votaries of the cult of the sublime, or of melancholy, or of the graveyard.[3] I neither dispute the partial truth of these views nor wholly subscribe to any one of them. I see these poets as attempting to preserve in their verse some elements of the holy and the daemonic, and this despite the fact that two of them were charged with Deism — I have already remarked the flaccidity of that label. I am not concerned with fixing a *terminus a quo* for romanticism or *ad quem* for rationalism. At least two of the poets, Thomson and Young, were immensely popular in their own time, an odd phenomenon if in truth they were great reactionaries or pioneers. Pope encouraged all of them but Watts, and so did not regard them as cantankerous inferiors but worthy if distinctive colleagues. I believe they were catering for a need, however, which *An Essay on Man* was unable to satisfy and which a *Robinson Crusoe* could not meet in a respectable enough way. The grandiloquence of their blank verse, the sumptuousness of some of their editions, gained them readier entrance to polite homes than popularly written novels tinged with Calvinism. They continued to

[3]Some classic studies are: R. D. Havens, *The Influence of Milton on English Poetry* (Cambridge, Mass.: Harvard Univ. Press, 1922); Eleanor M. Sickels, *The Gloomy Egoist: Moods and Themes of Melancholy from Gray to Keats* (New York: Columbia Univ. Press, 1932); Patricia Meyer Spacks, *The Insistence of Horror: Aspects of the Supernatural in Eighteenth Century Poetry* (Cambridge, Mass.: Harvard Univ. Press, 1962). See also: Samuel H. Monk, *The Sublime* (1935; rpt. Ann Arbor: Univ. of Michigan, 1960); Amy Reed, *The Background of Gray's Elegy: a Study in the Taste for Melancholy Poetry, 1700–1751* (New York: Columbia Univ. Press, 1924); Marjorie Hope Nicolson, *Newton Demands the Muse* (Princeton, N.J.: Princeton Univ. Press, 1946).

be popular, at least Thomson and Young, well into the nineteenth century, and perhaps have ceased to be read widely only
because later writers have more ably or relevantly fulfilled their
purpose. Of the authors examined in detail in this book, these
have been the least enduring. Yet I find a true vein in all of
them and believe that they might, without certain humiliation,
be set next to most twentieth-century poets. In giving them
some time, I do not consider myself a mere antiquarian.

◻

Isaac Watts was a dissenting preacher, a philosopher sufficiently
deep to earn the esteem of Samuel Johnson, and the capital
hymn-writer of the early eighteenth century. He was dissatis-
fied not only with the secular nature of much poetry but also
with the insipidity of much religious verse; in his preface he
disparages the standard but unimaginative metrical translations
of the psalms and yearns for a Christian poetry as arousing as
the classical. His own poetry, especially the collection *Horae
Lyricae*, is professedly an attempt to infuse new vigor into devotional verse. It is not to everyone's taste, and Samuel Johnson
put his finger on its greatest defect, repetitiveness. As we consider Watts's poems, or those of any of the other poets in this
chapter for that matter, we might recall Johnson's shrewd
remarks in his *Life of Waller:*

> From poetry the reader justly expects, and from good poetry
> always obtains, the enlargement of his comprehension and
> elevation of his fancy; but this is rarely to be hoped by Chris-
> tians from metrical devotion. Whatever is great, desireable, or
> tremendous, is comprised in the name of the Supreme Being.
> Omnipotence cannot be exalted; Infinity cannot be amplified;
> Perfection cannot be improved. . . . The ideas of Christian
> Theology are too simple for eloquence, too sacred for fiction,
> and too majestick for ornament; to recommend them by
> tropes and figures, is to magnify by a concave mirror the
> sidereal hemisphere.

[164]

Watts himself was quite alert to this difficulty. The opening poem of his collection, "Worshipping with Fear," affirms the dangers of describing or even praising the Deity, whose frown brings destruction and "humble awe." Not by mortal thought, not even by considering God's works, can we achieve any true comprehension: "So much akin to nothing we, / And thou the' Eternal All." But if "perfection cannot be improved," the pious and pedestrian jog-trot of Sternhold and Hopkins could.

For Watts, God is truly the *mysterium tremendum.* He transcends nature and natural theology, though he is not so utterly withdrawn as Pascal's:

> Far in the Heavens my God retires,
> My God, the mark of my desires,
>   And hides his lovely face;
> When he descends within my view,
> He charms my reason to pursue,
> But leaves it tired and fainting in the' unequal chase.
> ("The Incomprehensible")

In "God Glorious, and Sinners Saved" Watts concedes that "Part of thy name divinely stands / On all thy creatures writ," but he insists that only through faith can we begin to understand God and his plan, "where vengeance and compassion join." Even that understanding is not intellectual or discursive, but issues in "reverend awe" and adoration. God leaves his footsteps in his creation, but is most to be found in the heart, and so we must seek him at home ("Address to the Deity"). Like Pope, Watts sees the spirit of God running immutable through a perpetually changing universe. But his God is at once more and less vivid than Pope's: more, because he is frankly anthropomorphized, and his *glance* "rules the bright worlds, and moves their frame"; less, because he is finally transcendent, and though we are made in his image, yet we are but *shadows* of his face ("The Creator and Creatures"). Mysterious in his nature, he is also mysterious in his ways. For his actions "Not Gabriel asks the reason why, / Nor God the reason gives; / Nor dares the favourite angel pry / Between the folded leaves" ("God's Dominion and Decrees").

[165]

The next poem, "Divine Judgments," expatiates on the rigors of
nature. There is the polar world, where "God has a thousand
terrors in his name" such as frost and icestorms: "Sublime on
Winter's rugged wings / He rides in arms along the sky, / And
scatters fate on swains and kings; / And flocks and herds, and
nations die." There is also parching drought and disease, the
"flashes of a wrathful eye." Hail, whirlwinds, hurricanes sweep
away forests and fields and drown millions: "Earthquakes, that
in midnight sleep / Turn cities into heaps, and make our beds
our graves." There is no theodicy in this poem, nothing of
Pope's "partial evil is universal good." "Be thou my God," says
Watts, "and the whole world is mine." But far from rationalizing them, he avidly stresses the cruel and arbitrary ways of
nature.

The majesty, as well as the mystery, of God is dramatized in
such poems as "The Law Given at Sinai," where God parts the
Red Sea, drowns Pharoah's army, and here is descending to the
holy mountain:

> His chariot was a pitchy cloud,
> The wheels beset with burning gems,
> The winds in harness with the flames
> Flew o'er the' etherial road;
> Down through his magazines he pass'd
> Of hail and ice, and fleecy snow,
> Swift roll'd the triumph, and as fast
> Did hail, and ice, in melted rivers flow.

As God descends, despair and death seize the Jewish remnant.
Even

> Moses the spreading terror feels,
> No more the man of God conceals
> His shivering and surprise:
> Yet, with recovering mind, commands
> Silence, and deep attention, through the Hebrew bands.
> Hark! from the centre of the flame,
> All arm'd and feather'd with the same,

> Majestic sounds break through the smoky cloud:
>   Sent from the All-creating tongue,
>   A flight of cherubs guard the words along,
> And bear their fiery law to the retreating crowd.

Watts's "Day of Judgment" is rather hackneyed, but the same theme is well urged in "To the Memory of the Rev. Mr. Thomas Gouge." The Christ of the Last Day is very like the Sinaitic Jehovah: he is the "man whose awful voice / Could well proclaim the fiery law, / Kindle the flames that Moses saw, / . . . All Sinai's thunder on his tongue." Christ's fiery arrows pursue the fugitive atheist, striking him through:

> The marble heart groans with an inward wound:
>   Blaspheming souls of harden'd steel
> Shriek out, amaz'd at the new pangs they feel,
>   And dread the echoes of the sound.
>   The lofty wretch, arm'd and array'd
> In gaudy pride, sinks down his impious head,
> Plunges in dark despair, and mingles with the dead.

Both "The Law Given at Sinai" and "Gouge" attempt to excite religious terror. At the Last Judgment Christ comes in a golden cloud, whereas Jehovah had appeared in a pitchy cloud at Sinai, but otherwise Christ is much more like the Mosaic God of thunder than he is the Galilean of the gospels. Of course Sinai and the Last Judgment are manifestations of the same triune God, and there is much in the Apocalypse to warrant Watts's imagery in the second poem. There is nevertheless a remarkable difference between his treatment of the theme, and Dryden's in the Killigrew ode; in the latter we have only the jubilation of rebirth, in the former the dread of judgment. The imagery of both Dryden and Watts derives from the Bible (in Dryden's case, of course, from *Ezekiel*), yet in both it has a freshness as well as propriety. God's melting his own hail and ice as he descends on Sinai; his manifestation as a flame encompassed with smoke, whose words are armed and feathered with fire: these decorations do not perhaps escape Johnson's general cen-

[167]

sure of religious tropes and figures, but they evince more than a mediocre talent. Like Dryden too, Watts exploits, often with adroitness, the metrical variety of the pindaric ode to engage the emotions of his readers.

Watts can also evoke the daemonic or nightmarish side, as in his "Hurry of the Spirits, in a Fever and Nervous Disorders." Here he describes a terrifying hallucination in which his soul, a "worthless chip of floating cork," is caught in a raging storm at sea, tossed from wave to wave, apparently annihilated, then seized by the wind and "hurried many a league / Over the rising hills of roaring brine, / Through airy wilds unknown, with dreadful speed." Deposited near a tranquil coast, he begins to hope, but just then is snatched back into the waves, "Helpless, amidst the bluster of the winds / Beyond the ken of shore." There are religious implications in all of this, of course, of the sort that Cowper was to unfold more boldly years later in his "Castaway". But Watts confines himself almost entirely to the psychological experience, fastening to the end only a brief and unpretentious moral. The inchoate, erratic, interminable qualities of a nightmare are finely captured, and not least that hideous sense of advancing hope abruptly intercepted. There is no attempt to *distance* the reader here, as I have argued there is in Pope's *Eloisa*.

Watts is the first person mentioned in this study to attempt *affective* literature, by which I mean literature that aims at reproducing in the reader the emotion actually delineated in the piece itself. Swift and Pope deliberately avoid doing that, though there are occasional moments in Browne and possibly Pascal where such a purpose is intended. Not that there is mysticism in these poems, and certainly not the "erotic mysticism" that some critics have thought to find.[4] *Enthusiastic piety* would be an apter phrase than mysticism, and while some pietists are erotic, I cannot imagine anyone less tinged with it than Watts. There is nowadays an iconoclasm that reduces divine love to an illusory projection of the "real" or human variety. But for Watts

[4]See, e.g., Sickels, 18

the human was but a shadow of the divine love, and the divine love was sharply tempered with fear and awe.

⌑

Although they were nearly contemporary, two poets more dissimilar than Watts and Mark Akenside would be hard to find. Of humble birth and raised in the dissenting faith, the adult Akenside was surely ashamed of both. When only twenty-two he published his best known work, *The Pleasures of Imagination* (1744, 1772), inspired by the series of *Spectators* (nos. 411–421) written by Addison on that subject thirty years before. Although Pope apparently browsed through the poem in manuscript and urged the respectable printer Dodsley to undertake it, it was assaulted by that indefatigable apologist of *An Essay on Man*, Warburton, who discerned in Akenside a disciple of Shaftesbury and a closet Deist. The poem does in fact owe as much to the loose Platonism of Shaftesbury as to the psychology and aesthetics of Addison. It was popular in its time, but never achieved the preeminence of Thomson's and Young's poems, and the modern reader is apt to find it as unappealing as Shaftesbury's own work. There is the same indistinctness, or perhaps one should say, elusiveness, of thought, and where Shaftesbury is frothily genteel, Akenside is frigidly pompous or pleonastically exuberant. He is, ostensibly, concerned with what appeals to our aesthetic sense and with the mechanism of that appeal. But since with Shaftesbury he believes that beauty is truth, and that a true understanding of the former will yield insight into the ultimate nature of things, he devotes considerable attention to the Deity and his, or its, relation to man and the creation. But even measured against other works in a genre notorious for its structural inadequacies — the long didactic poem in Miltonic blank verse — *The Pleasures of Imagination* is a daunting maze, it is not easy to say whether with or without a plan. Johnson admired Akenside's talent but confessed he could not get through the poem.

To complicate things more, Akenside, as a respite perhaps

from his quotidian labors as a physician, incessantly revised his youthful poem, and died in the midst of an altogether new section in 1770 at the age of forty-nine. Critics have never agreed on which is the superior performance, some seeing the revision as more restrained and pruned of purple superfluities, while others consider it to be more turgid, labyrinthine, and flat. The debate is now purely academic, I suppose, with modern critics tending to prefer the revision as exhibiting more of an interest in the fanciful, in the supernatural, and in orthodox religion.[5] Nevertheless, I should like to glance briefly at some of Akenside's major themes and their alterations in revision. Like Pope, Akenside wished very much to be intellectually fashionable, yet he does somewhat heighten the elements of the holy and the mysterious in his second version. At the same time, however, he prescinds one of the more spectacularly imaginative episodes in the original, though some passages from it survive. It is not a safe generalization, therefore, to say that the second version lays greater stress on the supernatural. In both versions, and in the differences between them, we see an uneasy compromise with rationalism very like that in *An Essay on Man*, but even more haphazard and shifty.

In both versions Akenside's conception of God is explicitly Platonic. Before the material creation, he says, there existed:

> ... the Almighty One: then, deep-retir'd
> In his unfathom'd essence, view'd the forms,
> The forms eternal of created things;
> The radiant sun, the moon's nocturnal lamp,
> The mountains, woods and streams, the rolling globe,
> And Wisdom's mien celestial. From the first
> Of days, on them his love divine he fix'd,
> His admiration: till in time complete
> What he admir'd and lov'd, his vital smile

---

[5]See Jeffrey Hart, "Akenside's Revision of *The Pleasures of Imagination*," *PMLA*, 74 (1959), 67; Spacks, *Insistence of Horror*, 75–6.

> Unfolded into being. Hence the breath
> Of life informing each organic frame. . . .
> (1st version, I, 64–74).[6]

Watts had said "Far in the Heavens my God retires," but Akenside's deity has the reclusiveness of the philosopher. It is even more abstract than Pope's, though the "vital smile" suggests Shaftesburian benevolence, and there is more proximity between the Almighty One and the creation than a staunch Deist would permit. In the revised passage (I, 106–116) the substance is little changed. "Almighty One," however, gives way to "Great Spirit," which is a trifle less grimly Platonic. But "whom his works adore" replaces "then deep-retir'd," and while we are continuing to move away from Platonism here, our destination seems to be natural religion. "Vital smile" becomes "vital power," which represents some slight triumph over insipidity. In another passage, Akenside even more clearly heightens his conception of the Deity. In the first version, the divine Mind is described in a most subdued, neutral, and abstract manner (I, 473–86). In the revised passage, "Mind" becomes "God most high"; the impersonal pronoun is suitably masculinized; and he adds to the passage an apostrophe to the creative "Father" who quickens all things and surveys delightedly the multitude of forms wrought out of chaos, whether they be "the gloomy fires / Of storm or earthquake" or the "purest light / Of summer" (I, 553–79 for entire section). On the whole, the alterations and additions contribute color, personality, and energy to Akenside's presentment of the holy.

The second version also supplies a more elaborate account of the chain of being, though an abbreviated description is found in the first as well:

> The same paternal hand,
> From the mute shell-fish gasping on the shore,

---

[6]All quotations from either version of *The Pleasures of Imagination* are from the *Poetical Works of Akenside*, ed. Alexander Dyce (Aldine Series, 1845).

> To men, to angels, to celestial minds,
> Will ever lead the generations on
> Through higher scenes of being: while, supplied
> From day to day by his enlivening breath,
> Inferior orders in succession rise
> To fill the void below. As flame ascends,
> As vapours to the earth in showers return,
> As the pois'd ocean toward the attracting moon
> Swells, and the ever-listening planets charm'd
> By the sun's call their onward pace incline,
> So all things which have life aspire to God,
> Exhaustless fount of intellectual day!
> Centre of souls!
>
> (II, 257–71)

Like Browne and Pope, Akenside sees the spirit of God as pervading and enlivening creation: this is no deistic Divine Watchmaker. But where Browne drew on the old sciences of alchemy and occultism for some of his imagery, Akenside injects Newtonianism into his references to the attracting moon, the planets moving to the sun's call, God as the center of souls. We find the Newtonianism in Pope, too, not so much in *An Essay on Man* as in *The Dunciad*, where the "attractive" goddess of Dulness, vortiginous center of fools, might but for derangement of chronology have been an obscene parody of Akenside's God. There are also some hints of evolution here, but they are very obscurely introduced. We are told that God will "lead the generations on / Through higher scenes of being," and that the lower orders will "in succession rise / To fill the void below": this suggests an ontological movement within the chain of being quite absent in Browne and actually denied, I believe, by Pope. But Akenside's examples do not ably illustrate an evolutionary theme. Flame assuredly ascends, but is it transformed into something higher? Water, vaporized, ascends, but is returned to earth in its original form. The oceans and planets respond to gravity, but are not intrinsically changed. In this passage Akenside has thrown together a traditional vitalism ("enlivening breath")

[172]

seen in Browne and Pope, a vaguely evolutionary scheme, and the harmonious if mechanical Newtonian world-view; he has thrown them together, but not joined them. Still, the passage itself, and the contrast with Browne, is most interesting. Neither Browne nor Akenside was a Deist, but Browne's conception is as thoroughly Renaissance as Akenside's, however inexpert, is eighteenth-century. Akenside also recedes a bit from his Shaftesburian optimism in the second version, recognizing that man is "restless" as well as happy (I, 213) and that he is the "slave of hunger and the prey of death" (II, 110). But the Pascalian echoes are feebler here than in Pope, and no more agreeable with the dominant theme.

Akenside was aware of the aesthetics of terror and, as an enlightened Platonist, highly disapproved. In both versions he assures us that he will sing a "cheerful song" and eschew superstition, which is sometimes but erroneously conjoined with religion; therefore he will not "bid the jealous thunderer fire the heavens, / Or shapes infernal rend the groaning earth" (2nd version, I, 387–88). The passage on Superstition in *An Essay on Man* probably inspired Akenside: both mention thunder, rending earth, and shapes or fiends infernal; certainly Akenside's attitude is the same. But in both versions he attaches to this abjuration an account of the groundless fears provoked by superstition. In the first version it is colorless and perfunctory; in the second it is considerably decorated:

> . . . though at length
> Haply she [Superstition] plunge him into cloister'd cells
> And mansions unrelenting as the grave,
> But void of quiet, there to watch the hours
> Of midnight; there, amid the screaming owl's
> Dire song, with spectres or with guilty shades
> To talk of pangs and everlasting woe;
> Yet be ye not dismay'd.
>
> (I, 465–72)

And so Akenside *does* indulge the mood of terror after all — surreptitiously, even hypocritically it may be. It is the philosopher amusing himself with a factitious shudder. The ironic detachment scented in Pope's passage is not so strong here, and if Akenside is wandering from his principles, at least he has been able to express with some vivacity a non-rational theme. But even as he enhanced a passage like this, he struck out from the revision a very exceptional episode to which I shall now turn.

In the second book of the first version, Akenside undertakes to explain why in a benevolent universe we should endure violent emotions. Departing uncharacteristically from his reflective and didactic tone, he contrives "an allegorical vision" in which are exemplified "sorrow, pity, terror, and indignation." He tells the story of one Harmodius, old and wise, who as a youth was much given to solitary musing and rumination. When a friend of his, the young, innocent, and virginal Parthenia unaccountably dies, Harmodius is plunged into despair. "Impatient," he exclaims against creation, but suddenly "celestial day / Burst through the shadowy void." A purple cloud slowly descends and, floating amongst the trees, opens. Straightway "a more than human form / Emerging lean'd majestic o'er my head, / And instant thunder shook the conscious grove." This "godlike presence," garbed in classical attire and named the Genius of mankind, exhibits "displeasure, temper'd with a mild concern," and in a *Job*-like harangue rebukes Harmodius with a series of indignant questions: "Dost thou aspire to judge between the Lord / Of Nature and his works? to lift thy voice / Against the sovereign order he decreed, / All good and lovely? to blaspheme the bands / Of tenderness innate and social love, / Holiest of things!" And so on. Harmodius is naturally "abash'd and silent . . . aw'd / Before his presence." But the Genius, perhaps feeling that his discourse had somewhat failed in its effect, shows Harmodius a vision of the "primeval seat / Of man." After another windy exposition of the harmony and benevolence of the universe (which includes the first version of the passage on the chain of being), the vision unfolds.

Adam is never named and Eve never mentioned, but Harmodius is shown a primal man to whom the "Sire Omnipotent"

[174]

dispatches two divine creatures, Virtue, who is to instruct him in the good, and Beauty or Pleasure, named Euphrosyné after one of the classical graces. Unfortunately the man finds Euphrosyné more appealing than the sublime but matronly Virtue. Alarmed at this disturbing if as yet innocent predilection, Virtue and her partner report back to the Father. The Father is nothing alarmed, however, for he sees it as a natural development. Still, he decides to send Virtue back accompanied, not by Pleasure this time, but by "the son of Nemesis . . . / The fiend abhorr'd!" who will teach the man a lesson. Harmodius then sees this creature:

> A vast gigantic spectre, striding on
> Thro' murmuring thunders and a waste of clouds,
> With dreadful action. Black as night his brow
> Relentless frowns involv'd. His savage limbs
> With sharp impatience violent he writh'd,
> As through compulsive anguish; and his hand,
> Arm'd with a scorpion lash, full oft he rais'd
> In madness to his bosom; while his eyes
> Rain'd bitter tears, and bellowing loud he shook
> The void with horror.
>
> (II, 507–16)

The man is of course terrified, but Virtue comes to his assistance, repels the fiend, and gives him a lecture. The man having thus learned fortitude and disdain of slothful joy, Euphrosyné is safely restored to him; he is now a virtuous stoic and can rise superior to "the outrage of external things." The "grisly phantom" may return, but man can face it, seconded as he now is by Virtue and, in the exercising that virtue, pleasure.

The entire episode, absurd as it may sound in paraphrase, is quite interesting. The "allegorical vision" in fact consists of two visions: the story of Harmodius and, set into that, of primeval man. In the framing story Harmodius is awed into submission; in the inset story the man is terrified into virtue. So the episode as a whole frankly exploits the aesthetics of terror and awe. The inset story implicitly supports Watts's view that some are

brough̄t to a sense of religious duty only through fear. Harmodius, being a more sensitive soul, is more gently treated: Jehovah
spoke to Job out of a whirlwind, but Harmodius is rebuked out
of a purple cloud by a Genius of humanity who shows *mild*
concern. The rhetorical questions of this creature may be modeled on *Job*, but their substance is pure Shaftesbury. The inset
story combines *Genesis* with the classical tale of the young Hercules, who had to choose between Virtue and Pleasure — the
Hercules episode was a favorite of Renaissance painters and well
known.[7] But both stories are sentimentalized. Since Euphrosyné
is herself virtuous, the man can have *both* Virtue and Pleasure.
Like the serpent in *Genesis* and Satan in *Job*, Nemesis is sent
down to afflict and tempt man — to tempt him to despair, here.
But there is no real sin; man only betrays an indecorous preference for Euphrosyné. Nor is there any real triumph over
temptation: the man is frightened, appeals to Virtue, who repels
the specter and then simply *tells* him that as a consequence he
has matured in self-mastery. The whole episode was supposed
to explain why we have violent emotions in a benevolent universe. We have violent emotions because there are natural and
moral evils in the world that rightly excite our indignation,
pity, and so forth. But if we ask why there are moral and natural
evils in a benevolent universe, we shall not be satisfied by
Akenside. Parthenia's premature death, which opened the
vision, has been long forgot by the end, its impact muffled in
Shaftesburian gauze.

Yet the vision shows some imagination in its idea, some
sprightliness in its execution. It is probably the only part of
Akenside's poem that might interest the non-pedantic modern
reader. Why then did Akenside cancel it? He may have thought
it unsuccessful; certainly it is obscurely developed and, viewed
unsympathetically, absurd enough. He may have judged it

[7]For a contemporary account of Hercules' choice, see Joseph Spence, *Poly-
metis* (London, 1747), who even supplies a poem of his own on the subject, pp.
155–62.

[176]

inconsistent in tone and theme with the poem as a whole; certainly it is that. Pope had been wise to refrain from mythologizing in *An Essay on Man;* it is a device ill suited to the rationalistic theodicy of that poem and Akenside's. The redoubtable but divinely sent instructor Nemesis goes quite against Akenside's formal disavowal of the aesthetics of terror. Since the story is an unorthodox version of *Genesis*, his eliminating it might have been part of his progress toward more traditional views, as Jeffrey Hart has argued. Nevertheless, Akenside does at least probe, however gingerly, some Dionysian matter in this episode, and in Nemesis he is willing to give the divine a daemonic form. The most optimistic parts of the episode—the insistence on God's benignity, the affirmation of universal harmony, and so on—are retained in the revision. But we do not find there the pitiful death of Parthenia or the scourge of the son of Nemesis.

□

Like Akenside, James Thomson had a Calvinist background to which his conscious thought, at least, is very little indebted. Their long, Miltonic poems were both charged with Deism, and the poems are indeed rather spasmodic anthologies of traditional and modish views. Both poets revised indefatigably, the motive in Thomson's case being to necessitate new editions, for he was ever impecunious. The first of *The Seasons* to appear was *Winter* in 1726; it was essentially a descriptive-meditative poem like Milton's *Il Penseroso*, and only a little more than 400 lines (by the final revision it was more than 1000). *Summer* followed in 1727, *Spring* in 1728, and *Autumn* in 1730. After innumerable revisions, the ultimate *Seasons* appeared in 1746 and was to remain very popular for more than a century. Nature and Nature's God is its gravamen, but Thomson soon found the subject confining, and he departs from it more and more in the later seasons and in the amplifications and embellishments. Not only is the major theme thus diluted by a flood of heterogeneous material, but the expression of the theme itself is often sapped

[177]

in the revisal.[8] For example, in the first version of *Summer*, 160–75, Thomson describes God in terms reminiscent of Watts: "How shall I then attempt to sing of Him, / Who Light Himself, in uncreated Light / Invested Deep, dwells awfully retir'd / From Mortal Eye, or Angel's purer Ken." But praising God a year later in the first *Spring*, Thomson more nearly anticipates the dull Platonising of Akenside: "Hail, Mighty Being! Universal Soul / Of Heaven and Earth! Essential Presence, hail!" Even in *Spring* he will sometimes evoke the more traditional God: "The tempest blows His Wrath, / Roots up the Forest, and o'erturns the Main. / . . . / The Thunder is His Voice; and the red Flash / His speedy Sword of Justice." But all these lines were expelled from the revisal.

The older view of God, a relic of Thomson's Calvinist heritage, becomes less and less distinct as *The Seasons* passes through its multifarious transformations; and one suspects that this was not so much a matter of evolving personal convictions as an attempt to conciliate those intellectual fashions to which *An Essay on Man* was also appealing. It is now customary to deride the philosophy of the poem as a paltry and disorganized Deism, and those who wish to put up any defense at all for Thomson argue that he is to be valued for his descriptions of nature, of which his actual ideas are merely the dispensable underpinnings.[9] It is also the fashion now to see Thomson as a Newtonian who reduces "the mysterious and dangerous cosmos to manageable order."[10] This is not very exciting. Even one of his few admiring, twentieth-century critics, John Beresford, has

---

[8]On Thomson's revisions, and *The Seasons* generally, see: Patricia Meyer Spacks, *The Varied God: A Critical Study of Thomson's "The Seasons"* (Berkeley and Los Angeles: Univ. of California Press, 1959); Alan Dugald McKillop, *The Background of Thomson's Seasons* (Minneapolis: Univ. of Minnesota Press, 1942); Ralph Cohen, *The Art of Discrimination* (Berkeley: Univ. of California Press, 1964) and *The Unfolding of the Seasons* (Baltimore: Johns Hopkins Univ. Press, 1970).

[9]Comments of this sort are quoted or cited by McKillop, 6–7, and Spacks, *Varied God*, 9.

[10]Hugh l'Anson Fausset, quoted with approval in Spacks, *Varied God*, 184.

to concede that Wordsworth shows us more of the mysterious
and divine in nature. But Thomson, he says, offers something
different to the sensitive reader, who "will find, when he has
finished any one of the four parts of the year, a sense of peace
come upon him."[11] Yet I will contend that Thomson's philosophy is more than dilapidated Deism and that his descriptions
can no more be sundered from it than they can in any respectable poet — I do consider Thomson respectable. I *am* sorry that
Thomson retreats from his original, more vigorous conception
of the holy. In his only published criticism, a preface to the
second edition of *Winter* (1726), Thomson had sounded very
like Watts in *his* preface to *Horae Lyricae:* he deplores the profane uses to which poetry has been put, praises a poem on the
Last Judgment, speaks favorably of "poetical Enthusiasm," cites
Job as a wonderful example of religious poetry. Thomson never
wholly discards these ideas, however. Even in his final version
of *The Seasons*, which I shall use from now on, there are strong
elements of the mysterious and daemonic, though these are
admittedly more pronounced in the first two parts, *Winter* and
Summer. Critics zealous to find Newtonianism in eighteenth-
century poetry will find it aplenty in Thomson, and *have* done.
But nature in *The Seasons* is as enigmatic as it is in *The Prelude*,
I think, and even more disturbing. I get very little "sense of
peace" from Thomson, and will here endeavor to show why
that is.

Spring and *Autumn* are the more bland, partly because they
were the last two written, partly because they are naturally less
strenuous, more transitional seasons. The apostrophes to nature
and the Deity do tend to be rather abstract and perfunctory. In
Autumn, however, Thomson vividly invokes "philosophic
melancholy":

> Oh bear me then to vast embowering Shades!
> To twilight Groves, and visionary Vales!

[11]John Beresford, Introducton to *The Seasons* (London: the Nonesuch Press,
1927), ix. All further quotations from *The Seasons* are from this edition.

To weeping Grottoes, and prophetic Glooms!
Where Angel-Forms athwart the solemn Dusk,
Tremendous sweep, or seem to sweep along;
And Voices more than human, thro' the Void
Deep-sounding, seize th' enthusiastic Ear.

(1028–34)

This is not, of course, that black melancholy which is charged
with sin and guilt and so often precipitates despair, madness,
and suicide. It is rather the meditative and introspective sort
that denotes a "sensitive soul" open to divine truth. *Il Penseroso*
had popularized this type, of which Thomas Warton's *Pleasures
of Melancholy* is the most gratifying eighteenth-century example. Pope's *Eloisa to Abelard* illustrates the blacker variety in an
erotic form. But the visual trappings are similar: we have in
Thomson, as in Pope, the groves, vales, grottos, glooms. What
Eloisa would escape as depressing, Thomson seeks for its inspiration; and he ably delineates that weird half-light so congenial
to presentiments and visions. But such a note is never long sustained, and Thomson follows this passage immediately with the
description of a cheerful English garden. Elsewhere in *Autumn*
he effectively portrays the superstitious awe and panic produced
by comets, and tells a gruesome story about a "benighted
Wretch" wandering lost in the dark, "Full of pale Fancies, and
Chimeras huge," who is finally seduced by a will-o'-the-wisp
into a swampy death.

In *Spring* Thomson apostrophizes a Shaftesburian "Smiling
God" who imparts to all creation "Tenderness and Joy." But this
is followed presently by a very muscular representation of
lover's melancholy (1001–1109). Like Pope's Eloisa, the disappointed suitor is obsessed: his loved one "possesses every
Thought, / Fills every Sense," and his erotic passion sweeping
his soul out of his body, he "leaves the Semblance of a Lover,
fix'd / On melancholy Site." He neglects his affairs and,
loathing society, frequents "glimmering Shades, and sympathetic Glooms / Where the dun Umbrage o'er the falling
Stream, / Romantic, hangs; there thro' the pensive Dusk /

Strays, in heart-thrilling Meditation lost, / Indulging all to
Love." When exhausted he is forced to sleep, he has nightmares
reminiscent of Watts's, but naturally in an erotic vein. He spies
"th' Enchantress of his Soul," almost achieves her, but is
straightway snatched to huge forests, desolate heaths ravaged by
night and tempest; or he struggles and drowns in a raging
stream. Caught by the "Witchcraft of ensnaring Love," he exists
in endless distraction and torment. A short passage then super-
venes on virtuous love, and with that *Spring* concludes. But it
is surely the longer, more vigorous story of daemonic eroticism
that would linger in any reader's mind; and that reader might
well wonder — for Thomson has not explained it — how such a
terrible experience is to be reconciled with the tenderness and
joy bestowed on creation by the Smiling God of Spring.

The "prophetic Glooms" of *Autumn* and the "sympathetic
Glooms" of *Spring* may be set against the "kindred Glooms" and
"cogenial Horrors" welcomed at the beginning of *Winter*.
These "glooms" are in effect numinous spots for Thomson, and
Winter naturally affords them more readily than the two
demure seasons. Winter is a "heavy Gloom oppressive o'er the
World"; it is the "Father of the Tempest . . . Wrapt in black
Glooms." It engenders philosophic or contemplative melancholy and is therefore associated with night, when the "weary
clouds, / Slow-meeting, mingle into solid Gloom." Thomson
chiefly prizes the season for the "pleasing dread" aroused by its
storms, and his descriptions try to actuate the pot-pourri of
agreeable excitement, awe, and fear found in the numinous
experience:

> Huge Uproar lords it wide. The Clouds commix'd
> With Stars swift-gliding sweep along the Sky.
> All Nature reels. Till Nature's KING, who oft
> Amid tempestuous Darkness dwells alone,
> And on the Wings of the careering Wind
> Walks dreadfully serene, commands a Calm;
> Then straight Air, Sea and Earth are hush'd at once.
>
> (195–201)

Note that God is anthropomorphized gently, but not so precisely as in Watts; he is intimately related to his creation but, since he is its commander, not to be identified with it; he dwells in dark solitude. Thomson describes *in extenso* the evils wrought by the season on dumb animal life (240–75) and tells the tale of a shepherd lost in a storm and at length dying (276–321); a story more developed and grim than that of the wretch lost in the swamp in *Autumn*. To be sure these passages are counterpoised with a plenitude of optimistic, "liberal" outbursts: "What cannot active Government perform, / New-moulding Man?" he exclaims. But the terrors of Winter cannot be obviated by any human government, no matter how industrious and active. Such a government has nothing to offer these sailors at the North Pole, described toward the end of *Winter*:

> Ill fares the Bark with trembling Wretches charg'd,
> That, tost amid the floating Fragments, moors
> Beneath the Shelter of an icy Isle,
> While Night o'erwhelms the Sea, and Horror looks
> More horrible. Can human Force endure
> Th' assembled Mischiefs that besiege them round?
> Heart-gnawing Hunger, fainting Weariness,
> The Roar of Winds and Waves, the Crush of Ice.
> . . . .
> More to embroil the Deep, Leviathan
> And his unwieldly Train, in dreadful Sport,
> Tempest the loosen'd Brine, while thro' the Gloom,
> Far from the bleak inhospitable Shore,
> Loading the Winds, is heard the hungry Howl
> Of famish'd Monsters, there awaiting Wrecks.
>   (1004–11; 1014–19)

In the next lines, it is true, Thomson appeals to the ever-waking eye of Providence and concludes that Winter is but part of a perfect whole, however evil that part may seem; it is Pope's theme in the first epistle of *An Essay on Man*, but less abstractly put. Nevertheless, like the episode of the melancholy lover at the end of *Spring*, the perishing sailors and Leviathan, the gen-

[182]

erally oppressive and disastrous effects of Winter, are apt to remain more powerfully with the reader than the closing pieties of the piece. Thomson includes far more elements incongruous with his conclusion than Pope — but they are not incongruous with this remark in his preface: "The book of Job, that noble and ancient poem . . . is crowned with a description of the grand works of Nature."

Summer we should expect to be everything *Winter* is not; but such a view would be too simple. Certainly Thomson describes aestival bustle and vitality. God is light itself, the "uncreated Light," and the Sun is his chief symbol. The prevailing images of *Winter* — dormancy, closing down, shutting up — give way to their opposites. Sleep, praised by Browne as emancipating the soul, is discommended: it leads to "total extinction," and keeps us from enjoying life and nature. The Sun and Summer animate all existence from the smallest to the greatest in the scale of being:

> Has any seen
> The mighty Chain of Beings, lessening down
> From INFINITE PERFECTION to the Brink
> Of dreary *Nothing*, desolate Abyss!
> From which astonish'd Thought, recoiling, turns?
> Till then alone let zealous Praise ascend,
> And Hymns of holy Wonder, to that POWER,
> Whose Wisdom shines as lovely on our Minds,
> As on our smiling Eyes his Servant-Sun.
>
> (333–41)

More than Browne, Pope, or Akenside, I think, Thomson appeals to the aesthetics of awe, accenting in a rather more personal or emotional manner than the others our ignorance, astonishment, and wonder.

But even by the ninth line Thomson has become restive; he wants to flee the Sun and "haste into the mid-wood Shade, / Where scarce a Sun-beam wanders thro' the Gloom." He does finally manage to escape into an "awful listening Gloom," one of the "Haunts of Meditation." In such holy places, as in

[183]

Autumn, there are "Angels, and immortal Forms," a thousand dusky shapes that arouse in the poet a "sacred Terror," a "severe Delight." So *Summer* also has its glooms and terrors, and Thomson does not show us so much the moderate, seemly Summer of Albion as the torments of the torrid zones: scorching suns, the Behemoth and elephant, life-deserted sands, the venomous snake, the tiger, the hyena. The Sun itself, earlier the image of a quickening God, becomes a relentless withering tyrant "o'er this World of Slaves." And so Thomson piles up "the Terrors of these Regions here, / Commission'd Demons oft, Angels of Wrath": whirlwinds, typhoons, and worse even than the ravages of storm, the sharks that mangle the limbs of the sailors unfortunate enough to have survived the tempest. This is no Newtonian shrinkage of the cosmos "to manageable order." It is the universe of Isaac Watts. Thomson even includes one of the children of "Nemesis Divine," the plague, which, far more hideous than Akenside's fiend, not only destroys man but pollutes all those Shaftesburian affections:

> Dependants, Friends, Relations, Love himself,
> Savag'd by Woe, forget the tender Tie,
> The sweet Engagement of the feeling Heart.
> . . . .
>
> Thus o'er the prostrate City black Despair
> Extends her raven Wing; while, to compleat
> The Scene of Desolation, stretch'd around,
> The grim Guards stand, denying all Retreat,
> And give the flying Wretch a better Death.
> (1080–82, 1087–91)

This concatenation of horrors, occupying the vast center of *Summer*, culminates in the most famous episode of the entire poem, the story of Celadon and Amelia. These two lovers, innocent and virtuous, are caught in a violent storm. Amelia has dire presentiments, eyeing "the big Gloom," but Celadon piously if tritely reassures her that though God may seem to frown, yet

[184]

his thunderbolts will never harm the upright. He has no sooner finished this recital of catechism when

> From his void Embrace,
> (Mysterious Heaven!) that moment, to the Ground,
> A blacken'd Corse, was struck the beauteous Maid.
> But who can paint the Lover, as he stood,
> Pierc'd by severe Amazement, hating Life,
> Speechless, and fix'd in all the Death of Woe!
> So faint Resemblance, on the Marble-Tomb,
> The well-dissembled Mourner stooping stands,
> For ever silent, and for ever sad.
>
> (1214–22)

The account is terse. Amelia's repulsive death follows immediately on the reassurances of Celadon, who is facile enough, but whose copybook piety would have been applauded by a good many of Thomson's readers. Her death seems to rebuke Celadon's theological presumption, even as Jehovah rebukes, but so much less gruesomely, that of Job's friends; the thunderbolt, of course, is the traditional emblem of God's wrath. Thomson makes no effort to justify her death, and so, like Akenside's Parthenia, Amelia remains mute evidence of God's apparently cruel and arbitrary power.

Now of course the tale *can* be judged sentimental, with the pathos of the lovers the central point. But the story is relatively unembellished and straightforward. The lovers are briefly introduced, and we are not asked to empathize with them. Thomson does not linger over Amelia's death with the necrophilic ardor that a lesser writer — or even a greater such as Dickens — might have indulged. The story comes at the end of a long series of natural cruelties; it is the last; it is the most shocking and intense, perhaps; but it is given with a restraint worthy an emulator of *Job*. Where Thomson may be evasive is in the passage immediately following: there *another* storm ends, and Thomson urges us to be thankful to God, who "hush'd the Thunder, and serenes the Sky." This is a sort of poetic shell-

[185]

game, with a less tragic storm substituted for Amelia's. For the end of *this* storm we can more easily thank God, because we can more easily grasp its place in the divine plan. By transference Thomson may be suggesting that Amelia's storm, too, is reconcilable with a benevolent Deity. Amelia's actual death, meanwhile, like Parthenia's, has begun to fade from our distracted minds.[12] Still, Thomson need not have included the story in the first place, nor need he have told it so effectively; and he did not later expel it, as Akenside did Parthenia's. Whether taken sentimentally or not, it is a memorable episode and most apt for poetic treatment.[13] Fuseli's illustration, done many years later in 1801, is not strictly faithful to the text. But spiritually it is accurate enough. Thomson had associated God with darkness in *Autumn* and with light in *Summer*, with the violence of the storm and the calm of its aftermath. In Fuseli the shocking contrast of light and dark enforces the ambiguous connection between the holy and the daemonic. As in his *Witch of Endor* nearly twenty-five years before, he seizes the actual moment of prostrating terror or death. In the biblical story the supernatural explicitly intrudes into the natural world; in Thomson the supernatural is left implicit, but it is very strongly suggested. In either instance the effect is the same for Fuseli, whose Amelia is the mirror-image of his Saul.

Of course I have been highlighting the numinous and daemonic qualities in *The Seasons*, but I do not consider that I have misrepresented the poem; at least I have no more done so than those who expatiate on its tidy and decorous Newtonianism. Like others in this study, Thomson was drawn in several directions. He wished to be fashionable and to be devout, to show

[12]"Celadon and Amelia" is actually an inset story, a digression in a longer account of a less fatal storm.

[13]Pope is fond of recounting in his letters the pathetic death of two lovers struck by lightening at Stanton Harcourt; see *Correspondence*, I, 480–81, 494–96. He seems strangely fascinated by the story, though not invariably solemn: "Upon the whole, I can't think these people unhappy: The greatest happiness, next to living as they would have done, was to dye as they did" (496). Lady Mary Wortley Montagu wrote a mock-elegy on them; see I, 523.

4. Henry Fuseli, *Celadon and Amelia* (1801)

the order of the universe but preserve the ineffability of God, to arouse Shaftesburian optimism and Wattsian fear. But for Thomson these were not *directions*, but manifestations of the "varied God." Thus, in the first paragraph of his "Hymn" he throws together the smiling god of tenderness and love with the dread thunderer and master of the whirlwind. It would be foolish to ransack the poem for a coherent theology. Thomson was no Dante, and he would not now have more readers had he tried to be. But he was more than a Deist; indeed, he was probably more orthodox than Pope, if we may judge them by their poems. *The Seasons* is consciously, deliberately, constructed on the aesthetics of awe and terror. Awe is the more dominant, but there is plenty of terror in the stories of lost, perishing travelers, sailors, shepherds, not to mention Celadon and Amelia. Thus his descriptions and episodes are most definitely connected with an intellectual purpose. "Gloom" is a central term. Browne had spoken enigmatically of a "secret glome or bottome of our days"; I suppose he meant our preternatural destiny. In Thomson the word denotes places, traits, and moments associated with eeriness, awe, or horror.

☐

Edward Young's *The Complaint*, more often referred to by its subtitle, *Night Thoughts*, began to appear in 1742 and was completed by 1746, the same year as the ultimate *Seasons*, and two years after *The Pleasures of Imagination*. Mid-century, then, saw the efflorescence — the cancerous tumescence, some would say — of the long, religious-descriptive-didactic poem in blank verse. Posterity has handled *Night Thoughts* even more discourteously than *The Seasons*, but it probably progressed through more editions in the century after its first publication than any other eighteenth-century English work. Young had already behind him a considerable body of verse, including a relatively youthful exercise in terror, *The Last Day* (1713), where the anticipatory agonies of the damned are shown with a personal intensity surpassing even that of Watts. The desperate wish of the expectant damned for annihilation, or for the amoral life of the beasts, is quite reminiscent of the end of Marlowe's *Dr. Faustus*, and the torments of hell are vividly retailed. That such scenes have retained force is shown by the naive reaction of a modern scholar, who accuses Young of being "morbid beyond the limits of reason and taste; he expresses the very substance of fear and of that cruelty which fear begets."[14] Young is actually quite orthodox. The slightly later *Paraphrase on Part of the Book of Job* (1719) is less successful, but perhaps only because of the inevitable comparison with the original. The heroic couplets, crammed with neo-classical parallelisms and antitheses, are inapt, and God seems like a second-class version of Homer's Zeus dictating to Pope. But Young devotes substantial passages to the Behemoth and Leviathan, and throws in material on the comet and the sun to modernize and give a more cosmic sweep to his original. *The Paraphrase* aims at awe, *The Last Day* at terror.

Night Thoughts is too long, too diffuse, too studiedly rapturous ever to recover its popularity. Boswell probably spoke for the majority of contemporary readers when he called it "a mass of the grandest and richest poetry that human genius has ever produced." George Eliot doubtless represents the modern majority: "a Juggernaut made of gold and jewels, at once magnificent and repulsive." For bluntness one cannot improve on the opinion of a leading authority in the subject, R. D. Havens, who calls it "one of the dullest and falsest poems that ever achieved fame."[15] But modern criticism of Young is contradictory. He is denounced, for example, for his melancholy and deep despair: he has a "sick soul" and professes a "shallow philosophy of pessimism"; but we are also informed that his faith is "above all . . . optimistic."[16] The style of the poem, and Young's self-image

---

[14]C. V. Wicker, *Edward Young and the Fear of Death* (Albuquerque: Univ. of New Mexico Press, 1952), 49.

[15]R. D. Havens, 149.

[16]See Wicker, 14–15, 34, 89; Isabel St. John Bliss, *Edward Young* (New York: Twayne, 1969), 124.

or persona, give as much trouble as its philosophy or length. I should therefore like to begin with a few remarks on its style, for I think many of the charges against Young reflect too obsequiously the taste of our time, a taste we are willing to suspend or adjust in behalf of "favored" poets such as Donne. An impartial reader may well feel that George Eliot's description could be applied with equal propriety to Joyce's *Ulysses*, as for that matter could Havens's two superlatives. Yet that work is as highly esteemed today, at least among academics, as Young's poem has been, and one needs a store of critical audacity to suggest that it will be nothing more than a mouldy curiosity, a subject only for antiquarian linguists and students of the quaint, a century hence.

Young's style is characterized chiefly by two qualities: its rhetorical, ejaculatory tone, and its personal intensity. For many modern critics, these point to an emotional falsity or meretriciousness. But let us indulge Young as we are prepared to indulge Donne or Joyce, and try to see the effect intended by such an apparently idiosyncratic and licentious style. In 1743, a year after the beginning of *Night Thoughts*, another very popular poem was published, *The Grave*. Its author was Robert Blair, an Evangelical, though not a dissenter, who aligned himself with Watts and the Wesleys.[17] On his title page he places that part of Job's reflections on the grave which Watts had praised and quoted in his preface to *Horae Lyricae*. *The Grave*, only 767 lines long, shares with *Night Thoughts* several traits: short, exclamatory, or questioning sentences, often very emotional in tone, a particular emphasis on the belief in immortality, a recognition of the paradoxical nature of man:

> *Death's Shafts* fly thick! Here falls the Village Swain,
> And there his pamper'd Lord! The Cup goes round;
> And who so artful as to put it by?

[17]See James A. Means, Introduction to *The Grave*, Augustan Reprint Society (Los Angeles: Univ. of California, 1973). All quotations are from this facsimile of the first edition. See also Means, "A Reading of *The Grave*," *Studies in Scottish Literature*, 12 (1975), 270–81.

'Tis long since *Death* had the Majority;
Yet strange! *the Living lay it not to Heart.*

. . . .

Oh! slipp'ry State of Things! What sudden Turns?
What strange Vicissitudes, in the first Leaf
Of Man's sad History? To-day most Happy,
And 'ere To-morrow's Sun has set, most Abject!
How scant the Space between these vast Extremes!
(447–51, 560–64)

Blair's poem extends Watts's aesthetics of terror into the graveyard, where Watts seldom intrudes, and it attempts through the
exclamatory style to induce emotional excitement and religious
feeling. It is, or endeavors to be, an *affective* poem. Funereal
caparisons are always good for a numinous shudder, and while
Blair is by no means the most exorbitant of the "graveyard
school," he aims at such horror here:

Ah! how dark
Thy long-extended Realms, and rueful Wastes!
. . . .
The sickly Taper
By glimmering thro' thy low-brow'd misty Vaults,
(Furr'd round with mouldy Damps, and ropy Slime,)
Lets fall a supernumerary Horror,
And only serves to make thy Night more irksome.
Well do I know thee by thy trusty *Yew*,
Chearless, unsocial Plant! that loves to dwell
Midst Soulls and Coffins, Epitaphs and Worms:
Where light-heel'd Ghosts, and visionary Shades,
Beneath the wan cold Moon (as Fame reports)
Embody'd, thick, perform their mystick Rounds.
(11–12, 16–26)

Because of chronology, it can hardly be determined whether
Young influenced Blair or Blair encouraged Young. But I have
digressed to Blair for several reasons. First, I wanted to show that

[191]

Young's style is not the unique product of a "sick soul." Both poems are affective — deliberately exhortatory and personal; both were praised and utilized by the Wesleys because they try to arouse religious concernment. Second, I should like to suggest that Blair is transitional between Watts and Young: *The Grave* is a poetic application of Watts's belief in the religious efficacy of fear. To criticize the style of either Young or Blair, then, because it is too self-conscious, emotional, or personal, is to commit the same fallacy as the sophomore who grumbles at Walt Whitman's egotism. (I am not saying, of course, that we must *like* the styles of Young or Whitman, or that they cannot be censured on other grounds.) In Young, however, there is actually a retreat from that religious terror which he himself essayed in *The Last Day* and which we find in Blair: "The knell, the shroud, the mattock, and the grave; / The deep damp vault, the darkness, and the worm; / These are the bugbears of a winter's eve, / The terrors of the living, not the dead" (IV, 10 – 13).[18] Thus a Victorian critic, arguing that *Night Thoughts* is "a good poetical contrast" to *The Seasons*, gets things rather reversed when he adds: "the one delighting as much to exhibit the gloomy, as the other the cheerful face of things."[19] Thomson is the more "gloomy," in several senses, while the dominant emotions of *Night Thoughts* are awe, astonishment, wonder, rapture; there is much more terror in *The Seasons*.

The strengths of this style can best be seen in a passage like this, Young's famous reflection on man and his place in the scale of creation:

How poor, how rich, how abject, how august,
How complicate, how wonderful is man!
How passing wonder HE who made him such!
Who centred in our make such strange extremes!

[18]All quotations from *Night Thoughts* are from Young's *Works*, 3 vols. (1802).
[19]James R. Boyd, introductory memoir to *Night Thoughts* (New York and Chicago: A. S. Barnes, 1870), 59.

From diff'rent natures, marvellously mixt,
Connexion exquisite of distant worlds!
Distinguish'd *link* in being's endless chain!
Midway from *Nothing* to the *Deity!*
A beam ethereal, sully'd and absorpt!
Though sully'd and dishonour'd, still divine!
Dim miniature of greatness absolute!
An heir of glory! a frail child of dust!
Helpless immortal! insect *infinite!*
A worm! a god! — I tremble at myself,
And in myself am lost. At home a stranger,
Thought wanders up and down, surpriz'd, aghast,
And wond'ring at her *own.* How reason reels!
O what a miracle to man is man,
Triumphantly distress'd! What joy, what dread!
Alternately transported and alarm'd!
What can preserve my life? or what destroy?
An angel's arm can't snatch me from the grave;
Legions of angels can't confine me there.

(I, 68–90)

Similar views we have seen in Browne and Pascal, Pope, Thomson, and Akenside. The most telling contrast is with *An Essay on Man*, where Pope adopts the Olympian or Apollonian perspective in the opening of Epistle II, quoted earlier. The chiseled antitheses brought forth and positioned with irony prepense: this, surely, is the *classical* style if that adjective, so often laxly used, has ever any meaning. How inferior then must Young seem with his plethora of exclamation points, his jangling and crude oxymora — "insect infinite" indeed! — his collapse halfway through into private and rambling monologue. But that is not the only way to view it. Young has in fact developed the germ of emotion in Thomson's account ("dreary *Nothing* . . . From which astonish'd Thought, recoiling, turns"). He tries to capture, too, the wonder in Browne, and the Dionysian sense of self-disclosure and immediacy to which the more tidy Apollonian cannot or dare not stoop. In Pope we are detached onlookers

[193]

viewing intellectually the human paradox; in Young we are invited to share the poet's own amazement. Akenside had tried to invigorate the conception by wedding it, but inharmoniously, with new *intellectual* conceptions: Newtonianism, evolution. More successfully, Young gives it freshness by treating it in a more subjective and affective manner. And I will make two further points. However inferior Young is as a poet to Pope, he is truer to my sense of Pascal: the disjointed observations, the violent antitheses — "frail child of dust" — seem closer to the *Pensées* than Pope's couplets. I also think that the Pascalian view runs more consistently through Young's gargantuan work than through Pope's poem. Halfway through *Night Thoughts*, for example, Young returns to the "child of dust" theme (IV, 299); and in the ninth and last section, contrasting immortal with mortal humanity, he writes: "The soul of man was made to walk the skies; . . . / Nor, as a stranger, does she wander there; / But wonderful herself, through wonder strays; / Contemplating *their* grandeur, finds *her own*" (IX, 1018, 1025–27). In imagery and import this complements, and is consistent with, the celebrated passage in Night I.

Young was not an inveterate reviser like Thomson and Akenside, but apparently he had no general plan in mind when he published the first of his nine parts or Nights, and there is consequently a good bit of tiresome iteration and backtracking. His central theme is human immortality, and he views his poem as a necessary supplement to the natural religion of *An Essay on Man* (I, 453–60). In general it may be safe to say that the first five nights are moral reflections on life, death, and human nature, while the last four consist of Christian apologetics;[20] but the distinction should not be pressed too hard, since much apologetic material can be found, for instance, in Night IV. It is interesting to note, though, that at least one hypothetical reconstruction of the *Pensées* observes the same progression: the edification of Christian doctrine upon an empirical study of human psychology. As an apologist Young is usually connected with

[20]Bliss, 112.

[194]

the more rationalistic Christian theologians; his sense of space, his cosmic awareness, is traced to Newton or his popularizers; and his stylistic obscurity and egocentricity has even been explained by Hume's philosophy.[21] Yet it seems to me that Pascal is an equally plausible source for all of these. Now I have noted Pascal's mistrust of natural theology, and it is true that Young makes use of natural theology from time to time, chiefly in Nights IV and VI. But even in IV he lays stress on the inadequacy of reason and the need for supernatural expiation, and his conception of God is very like the *deus absconditus* (IV, 391–98). Night VI, one of the feeblest sections of the poem, is followed by three Nights in which Pascalian themes strongly preponderate.

Night VI had tried to demonstrate immortality by analogies drawn from nature: it was the game Bishop Butler had played much more expertly. But Night VII turns for arguments to the human condition, and has some considerable power. Man seems an *alien* in this world; he entertains hopes that must be frustrated; he suffers under desires that cannot be satisfied; he has developing powers tragically intercepted by death. Beasts themselves, living from moment to moment, are better off than man. But immortality resolves the riddle, makes sense of his obstructed desires, his warring impulses, his irrepressible sense of something higher and holy. These are not the arguments of natural theology, but the reasons of the heart. We have the choice, says Young, of believing either in a Deity who has fashioned an afterlife where we shall find fulfillment or in a demonic, all-annihilating creator. If the latter is true, we face this prospect:

> A trembling world! and a devouring god!
> *Earth*, but the Shambles of Omnipotence!

[21]See: Isabel St. J. Bliss, "Young's *Night Thoughts* in Relation to Contemporary Christian Apologetics," *PMLA*, 49 (1934), 37–70; Marjorie Hope Nicolson, *Newton Demands the Muse* and *Mountain Gloom and Mountain Glory* (1959; rpt. New York: Norton, 1963); John E. Sitter, "Theodicy at Mid-century: Young, Akenside, and Hume," *Eighteenth-Century Studies*, 12 (1978), 105.

> *Heav'n's* face all stained with causeless massacres
> Of countless millions, born to feel the pang
> Of being lost.
> . . . .
> *Being,* a shadow; *consciousness,* a dream?
> A dream, how dreadful! Universal blank
> Before it, and behind! Poor man, a spark
> From non-existence struck by wrath divine.
> (VII, 946–50, 960–63)

But this is the image of God traditionally ascribed to despairing people,[22] and in its place Young offers the Old Testament God, who manifested his will in thunder and storm at Sinai, who confounded the Egyptians and Assyrians, who speaks majestically in the elements (1101–19). So Young drives on, inexorably, toward the Pascalian wager. There are two possibilities:

> All is delusion; *nature* is wrapt up,
> In tenfold night, from reason's keenest eye;
> There's no consistence, meaning, plan, or end,
> In all beneath the sun, in all above,
> (As far as man can penetrate) or heav'n
> Is an immense, inestimable prize;
> Or all is Nothing, or that prize is all.
> (1121–27)

Like Pascal, Young introduces the wager only after exhausting natural theology (though he is more sanguine than Pascal), after exploring the wretchedness of the human condition, after adumbrating a numinous and transcendent God. No more than Pascal does he offer it as an argument in the rigorous sense. Consonant with the affective nature of his poem, it is a direct and existential appeal.

Some of the *Pensées* are clearly addressed to the libertine and skeptic; similarly, Night VIII is directed to "the Man of the

---

[22]See Robert Burton, *Anatomy of Melancholy,* III, 4, 2, 6.

World," and Young's arguments, like Pascal's, have been deni-
grated as selfish.[23] But whether or not we accept that verdict, we
can observe the Pascalian strain: true love of self pursues not the
brevity, insufficiency, and destructiveness of sensual pleasure,
but piety and faith. An honest self-scrutiny shows that we were
made for another world, in which, because the alternative of
the "devouring god" is too hideous, we should actively believe;
and if we actively believe it, we should behave virtuously. In
this way do reason, virtue, and self-interest point in the same
direction. If this is selfish, it is also an inseparable concomitant
of the wager, and Christians, starting with Christ himself, have
appealed to what a puritan or rigorist might consider selfish feelings. As Dr. Johnson said in another context, nothing is too little
for so little a creature as man.

In Night IX Young returns to the themes of his earlier
poems — the Last Judgment and Job — and develops a new Pascalian theme, the sense of space. The day of wrath is described
far less luridly here, with exclamation and argument replacing
narrative and portraiture. In this way Young gains more in
sophistication and concentrated power than he loses in forego-
ing the more operose appeals to terror. It is also a treatment in
better accord with the prevailing tone of the last section: awe.
But terror is not wholly abandoned; it remains a characteristic
of that "Great God of Wonders" whose law is girded with terror
and thunder, and whose chastisments, though "rough and
gloomy," are just (445–93). The poet compares himself with Job
and yearns for a glimpse of the hidden God (1689–95). Such is
the chasm between man and Deity that we can attain no true
understanding of him. But through awe, inflamed by a contemplation of the heavens, we can approach understanding; and so
Browne's "public manuscript" gives way in Young to the "manuscript of heav'n," and a favorite topic of Watts's is newly, more
grandiloquently, raised. Now the notion that the heavens
declare the handiwork of God is at least as old as the psalmist,

---

[23]See, e.g., Wicker, 90 and passim, and for a recent variant, Sitter, 94.

and Addison expresses it with classical crispness in his ode on "The Spacious Firmament on High" (1712):

> [The] spangled Heav'ns, a Shining Frame,
> Their great Original proclaim:
> Th' unwearied Sun, from Day to Day,
> Does his Creator's Power display,
> And publishes to every Land
> The Work of an Almighty Hand.
> . . . .
> What tho' nor real Voice nor Sound
> Amid their radiant Orbs be found?
> In Reason's Ear they all rejoice,
> And utter forth a glorious Voice,
> For ever singing, as they shine,
> "The Hand that made us is Divine."
> (3–8, 19–24)

These verses are deposited in the translator's appendix to Otto's *Idea of the Holy* as a specimen of *rationalized* awe and deliberate avoidance of the numinous. Certainly, like Pope's if less brilliantly, they adopt the Olympian tone, and their serenity, designed to convey confidence, will strike many a modern ear as merely complacent or insipid, however stirring they are in Haydn's setting. I think Addison was aiming at a kind of awe, but the speaker is too unhuman, the meter too orderly and neat, and the vision too abstract. The personifications are feeble, and consciously so: the heavens may proclaim, the sun may be unwearied, the Almighty may be given a figurative hand; but there is no *real* voice or sound, only the rejoicing in *reason's* ear.

We will remember, however, that the biblical scholar Robert Lowth justified the frank anthropomorphism of scripture, and, not a decade before Lowth, Young indulges it grandly. "Who rounded in his palm these spacious orbs?" he asks, "Who bowl'd them flaming thro' the dark profound?" This is more like *Job* or, to anticipate, Blake's "Tyger." Similarly the stars and planets themselves are invested with life and sing and dance their praise with real rapture, not as in Addison's banausic orrery. Natural theology is not altogether abandoned, but it is given a new and cosmic resonance: "Say, by what name shall I presume to call / HIM I see burning in these countless suns, / As *Moses*, in the *bush?*" Young's long excursions into celestial awe are still very fine, if one has a taste for them; they have a cumulative force that cannot be represented easily in abstracts. But intellectually there is the same equivocation I have noted in Thomson and Pope, here plastered over with ostentatious antitheses and oxymora. God is called "Reveal'd — yet unreveal'd." He is the "Triune, Unutterable, Unconceived, / Absconding, yet Demonstrable GREAT GOD!" Young is Pascalian, but he is not Pascalian (if I may be permitted a similar paradox). The general plan of his poem may resemble the intended plan of the *Pensées*. The infidel's remarks in Night IV recall some of the *Pensées* that were probably to represent the position of the skeptic. There is a like emphasis on the human condition, the paradox of our nature, the reasons of the heart, the ambiguous and retreating God, the wager, the vastness of space. But in a rather different way from Pope, Young alters, and in my opinion compromises with, Pascal. God is absconding — but still demonstrable. For Pascal, Pope, and Young, man is a frail child of dust; but for Pascal his glory lies in his ability to contemplate his own death. Pope glories in the paradox itself, which makes man unique in creation; and it is his consolation that he does *not* know when death will come. For Young man's grandeur is his capacity to wonder at the heavens and to sense his true home there. There can be no doubt which of these views is the most unflinching and least sentimental; I do not pass on their relative validity. Pascal had written, "The everlasting silence of these infinite spaces terrifies me." He may have been speaking as an unbeliever and not for himself. But whichever the case, he returns often enough to cosmic solitude. Young's universe is filled with life and sound.

Terror and awe, shunned in the main by theodicies like *An Essay on Man*, appear in short, religious poems and hymns such as those by Watts, and in the longer, more "respectable" and decorated works we have been examining. None of them has held up well, and none of the poets is really a first-rate thinker — as I shall argue Hume and Johnson were. Akenside is the most rationalistic, Young the most orthodox; but in all of their poems there is that crumbling away of such settled, theological foundations as underlie, for example, *Religio Laici.* Few long religious poems have enjoyed a popularity commensurate with their length, however. *The Divine Comedy* has been the most durable, I suppose, and it is also the most coherent intellectually. Johnson's strictures on devotional verse are perceptive, and the continued decay of theology makes good modern religious poetry even less hopeful of achievement. T. S. Eliot's *Four Quartets* may last, but I can think of nothing else.[24] In view of these problems, it is remarkable how readable Thomson and Young still are, at least in moderate dosages, despite their now unfashionable sententiousness and pomp, or an occasional fiasco of phrase. The brisk demand for their poems throughout the century and well into the next, in cheap as well as lavish editions, shows that the taste for non-rational and numinous religious subjects was never dormant and obtained even at the very heart of the "Age of Reason."

[24]For an extremely intelligent discussion of this problem, see Harold L. Weatherby, *The Keen Delight: The Christian Poet in the Modern World* (Athens, Ga: Univ. of Georgia Press, 1975).

CHAPTER VI

Skeptical and Reverent Empiricism: Hume and Johnson

I have frequently had it in my Intentions to write a Supplement to *Gulliver*, containing the Ridicule of Priests. . . .

DAVID HUME

Malevolence to the clergy is seldom at a great distance from irreverence of religion. . . .

SAMUEL JOHNSON

NEARLY EXACT CONTEMPORARIES, Hume and Johnson are both vibrantly empirical, moderately skeptical, mistrustful of social and political innovation and religious enthusiasm, alert to the sophistries of self-deception. Like most exceptional thinkers, they resist the established categories. Hume's recognition of the limits of reason distinguishes him from the rationalists, whose premises, indeed, he seriously defies. Johnson's religious views, intricate and scrupulous, separate him from the apologetics, so often equivocating, aesthetic, or sentimental, to which many pious writers of the time resort. I have grumbled in previous chapters about the exaggerating of an "intellectual crisis" supposed to have occurred in the seventeenth century, but I do think that here, in the middle of the eighteenth, the deepest implications of rationalism and skepticism are clear to men of the caliber of Hume and Johnson. So very similar but turning down such disparate paths, they were in a manner competitors for the intellectual future of mankind; and I do not know that the competition has yet been resolved. "The worst speculative Sceptic ever I knew, was a much better Man than the best superstitious Devotee & Bigot," Hume writes in a let-

[201]

ter.[1] Yet Johnson defends Christopher Smart's neurotic and compulsive public praying as less mad than not to pray at all, though it cause a greater disturbance of the peace. In such *obiter dicta* the men themselves appear.

Boswell greatly admired them both, and could never reconcile himself to Hume's religious skepticism. For Carlyle they are the "two half-men of their time," Hume being characterized by "intrepid Candor and decisive scientific Clearness," while Johnson had "Reverence, Love, and devout Humility." Even more than Pascal and Voltaire, Johnson and Hume are corivals whose philosophical differences are resumed, often with no less zeal, by their scholarly partisans. Thus E. C. Mossner, Hume's most highly respected modern critic, caricatures and condescends to Johnson much as Theodore Besterman and other votaries of Voltaire have done to Pascal. Hume's arguments, we are informed, "were always rational," while Johnson's were "frequently emotional and subjective." He rehearses that hoary stereotype, long since exploded, of the Draconian Dr. Johnson, who "ruled his court with imperial authority, imposing his opinions and crushing resistance. The members were disciplined to follow the leader, and perceptively even the most independent learned to do so." He quotes Johnson's "I have not read Hume" with the implicit but clear suggestion that Johnson could not be bothered to read other views than his own. The remark, in fact, shows Johnson's humility, for it occurs during a discussion of the styles of various historians and was Johnson's confession that, since he had read none of Hume's histories, he could not judge his style. We are assured that "in sober truth" Johnson's writings do not compare with Hume's "in quality, in scope, or in influence." Turning critical telepathist, Mossner argues that Johnson's dislike of Hume was a defensive mechanism against his own reli-

[1]*The Letters*, ed. J. Y. T. Grieg (Oxford: Oxford Univ. Press, 1932), I, 154. On patterns common to the thought of Hume and Johnson see R. D. Stock, *Samuel Johnson and Neoclassical Dramatic Theory* (Lincoln: Univ. of Nebraska Press, 1973), 13–14, 90–92, and Chester Chapin, "Samuel Johnson and the Scottish Common Sense School," *The Eighteenth Century*, 20 (1979), 50–64.

gious doubts. Like another scholar I have earlier cited on Voltaire and Pascal, he concludes that Hume is to be styled the "Inquirer, philosopher or scientist," while Johnson, of course, is the "Consoler, priest or lay-preacher." "Intellectually, the age was Hume's," not Johnson's.[2]

I have already questioned the value of terms — hardly more than sobriquets — such as "the age of this" or "the spirit of that." If we are talking of what the majority of people thought, even confining ourselves to intellectuals, I rather imagine that the second half of the century should be assigned to Johnson instead of Hume — or perhaps to Boswell. If such nomenclature is to be governed by who is the most influential or progressive or what not, why then it must be recognized that the Romantics revolted as much against the arid skepticism (as they would have seen it) of Hume as against the neo-classicism of Johnson. But I shall try to avoid such terminology altogether, even as I shall try to repel the allure of egregious ax-grinding. Carlyle was right, I think, to see Hume and Johnson as embodying "the two grand Antagonisms of Europe . . . [in] their very highest concentration." Equally, Mossner is right to call Hume "the most authentic voice of the Enlightenment,"[3] assuming that there is a difference between the most authentic and the most representative. Voltaire was more representative, in my opinion, in his courage and wit, his dogmatism, flippancy, and shallowness. Though no less industrious than Voltaire, Hume is more retiring in manner and supple in thought. If to be enlightened means to be untroubled by the deepest religious instincts, even by a sense of the holy itself, it would be hard to be more enlightened than Hume. But then his skepticism also subverts Voltaire's flimsier version of the Enlightenment. Johnson loathed

[2]Ernest Campbell Mossner, *The Forgotten Hume* (New York: Columbia Univ. Press, 1943), 189–210. Johnson's "I have not read Hume" is in James Boswell, *The Life of Johnson*, ed. G. B. Hill and L. F. Powell (Oxford: Clarendon Press, 1934), II, 236, and is quoted in Mossner, 167.

[3]E. C. Mossner, *The Life of David Hume* (Austin: Univ. of Texas Press, 1954), 4.

both Hume and Voltaire, but Hume was at once his grander
antagonist and singular bedfellow.

◻

Like others I have mentioned — More and Casaubon, Thomson
and Akenside — Hume grew up in a Calvinist milieu. But where
they sought alternatives in moderate Anglicanism or modish
Deism, Hume owns that presumptively skeptical temperament
foreseen gloomily by Casaubon two generations earlier. Hume
himself says that he had abandoned religious belief as an adolescent after reading Locke and Samuel Clarke; and Norman
Kemp Smith's definitive opinion is that he was never a "skeptical inquirer" into religion: i.e., that, having early imbibed the
prejudices of skepticism, as an adult he could never quite appre-
ciate, even from a merely psychological angle, the role of religious sentiment in human experience.[4] This incapacity colors
even his best work, however subtly, and is clearly seen in his
less guarded reflections. Thus in a letter, a little ingenuously,
Hume views prayer as a sort of magic designed to influence God,
and he refuses to acknowledge that we can feel affection for a
Being whom we can neither see nor fathom.[5] Hume, then, is no
disinterested commentator, no Laodicean, on the subject of religion. He may have been a Theist: a non-combative Deist who
accepts a highly intellectualized god and is agnostic (but in
effect a skeptic) as regards supernatural revelation. But he is
even tricky about Theism, and anything beyond it is superstition. These biases he shared, of course, with many intellectuals
of his age; perhaps that is why he failed to turn them over with
the same meticulousness that he accorded other preconceptions.
I should like first to sample Hume's historical writings and mis-

[4]See Smith's remarks in his edition of the *Dialogues concerning Natural
Religion* (Indianapolis: Bobbs, Merrill, n.d.), 11–12. For excellent recent discussions of various aspects of Hume's religious thought, see the *Revue Inter-
nationale de Philosophie*, 30, nos. 115–116 (1976).

[5]*Letters*, I, 51–52.

cellaneous essays, his assumptions being more nakedly exposed
there than in his more involute books on religion.

Hume spent much time and care on a voluminous and spir-
ited *History of England* (1754–1762): through the last century
he was classed more often as a historian than a philosopher. Like
any readable history, it is imbued with a distinct perspective,
skeptical and Erastian in drift. Monks and ascetics are nearly
always seen as hypocrites seeking power, prestige, or wealth;
religion is supported by fear, deceit, superstition, or covetous-
ness; religious retreat or monasticism leads almost inevitably to
moral degeneration; the crusades were fostered by fanaticism
and greed; controversies over religious doctrine are fatuous and
trivial.[6] Hume can be generous, can give the benefit of the
doubt, when he wishes, when it serves his purposes. Thus he
can praise the Saracens, who were more learned and humane
than the Christians (II, 17), and he can even compliment the
Catholic Church — for preserving order and encouraging the arts
in barbarous times (IV, 24–25). In a way Hume is impartial, for
the Protestant reformers are as mauled at his hands as the Catholics: Wickliff was an enthusiast (III, 42); Luther was actuated
chiefly by egotism (IV, 27); the Puritans "confounded all ranks
and orders: the soldier, the merchant, the mechanic, indulging
the fervors of zeal, and guided by the illapses of the spirit,
resigned himself to an inward and superior direction" (VII, 109).
The Puritan government was a "base populace exalted above
their superiors; hypocrites exercising iniquity under the vigor
of religion" (VII, 185).

Post-mediaeval Catholicism is even more relentlessly
aspersed. On the seminaries at Douay and Rheims: "These seminaries, founded with so hostile an intention, sent over every
year a colony of priests, who maintained the catholic superstition in its full height of bigotry" (V, 182). Hume knows the

---

[6]See David Hume, *The History of England from the Invasion of Julius Cae-
sar to the Revolution in 1688* (London, n. d.), I, 86, 95, 101, 102, 185, 201, 228–
33, 235–36, 275, 301; II, 2; IV, 69, 113–14; V, 284. All references are to this
early nineteenth-century edition.

Popish Plot for the fraud it was, but cautions that the "restless and enterprising spirit of the catholic church" is a continuing threat, and that "in one sense, there is a popish plot perpetually carrying on against all states, protestant, pagan, and Mahometan" (VIII, 180). Of course Hume is not to be judged by the modern, if diffident, ideal of ecumenism. In 1570 the bull *Regnans in Excelsis* excommunciated Queen Elizabeth and encouraged her countrymen to rebel. From that moment, Roman Catholicism became treasonable in England. During the Popish Plot a century later Andrew Marvell denied that it was a religion: "nor is it to be mentioned with the civility which is . . . decent to be used." Yet John Bunyan, in Part I of *The Pilgrim's Progress*, is not so much hostile to Catholicism as contemptuous. And as I shall argue later from Johnson's example, not all Britons, two centuries after *Regnans in Excelsis*, were moved by such outworn militancy. Something more than patriotic fervor excites Hume's animosity.

Hume's discussion of Becket gives a good specimen of his rhetoric and the play of his prejudices. Becket's transformation from an ornate and sybaritic chancellor to an austere and holy archbishop was hypocritical, we are told; he "affected care to conceal" the sackcloth he wore next his skin so it would be all the more remarked. On his martyrdom Hume thus meditates:

This was the tragical end of Thomas à Becket, a prelate of the most lofty, intrepid, and inflexible spirit; who was able to cover to the world, and probably to himself, the enterprises of pride and ambition, under the disguise of sanctity and of zeal for the interests of religion: an extraordinary personage, surely, had he been allowed to remain in his first station, and had directed the vehemence of his character to the support of law and justice [this is just the point Dryden makes of his fiendish Achitophel]. . . . But no man who enters into the genius of that age can reasonably doubt of this prelate's sincerity. The spirit of superstition was so prevalent, that it infallibly caught every careless reasoner. . . . All the wretched literature of the times was engaged on that side. . . . Folly was possessed of all the schools as well as all the churches; and her votaries assumed the garb of philosophers, together with the ensigns of spiritual dignities. . . . It is indeed a mortifying reflection to those who are actuated by the love of fame . . . that the wisest legislator and most exalted genius that ever reformed or enlightened the world, can never expect such tributes of praise as are lavished on the memory of pretended saints, whose whole conduct was probably to the last degree odious or contemptible, and whose industry was intirely directed to the pursuit of objects pernicious to mankind (I, 324–25, 328).

Hume is gentler with Joan of Arc, perhaps out of gallantry, perhaps because she was the dupe at once of common superstition and her own delusions — Hume always equates mystics with fanatics.[7] Hume often speaks highly of Thomas More, but deplores his inflexibility, the "weakness and superstition" of his cause (IV, 107). Laud was "misguided," but he was probably right in trying to restore Catholic elements to the liturgy — to appease the taste of "the rude multitude" (VII, 124–26). Hume himself prefers the "naked and simple" worship of the reformed church in Scotland, which "borrowed nothing from the senses, but reposed itself intirely on the contemplation of that divine essence which discovers itself to the understanding only." That is the adoration truly "worthy of the Supreme Being, but so little suitable to human frailty" (VI, 65–66).

Measured against his time, Hume is conspicuous but not extravagant in his hatred of non-rational religious motives and ideals; indeed, he is obviously confident of an echo in most of his readers' chests. But it is not the highest praise of an historian to say that he is kindling stereotypes already impatient of release and apt to flare into bigotry, to use Hume's own favorite word.

---

[7]See, e.g., *Letters*, I, 17: "I have notic'd in the Writings of the French Mysticks, & in those of our Fanatics here, that . . . they mention a Coldness & Disertion of the Spirit." He considers his own state of depression to be "pretty parralel" with their own dark night of the soul.

Of course there is something to be said for his views. Base motives may lie behind pious exteriors, and even the best of us are palimpsests. One may also agree that the order and stability of the state must not be rent by religious turmoil and controversy. Informing his remarks on Catholicism, Puritanism, Becket and More, is an Erastianism that is by no means uncompelling. I shall insist, however, that in these passages we do not have reasoned arguments but hearty prejudices flung out partly because Hume believed them, partly because he knew that they would conciliate fashion; and while they make for lively prose, they would scarcely be tolerable in any modern historian, who has no doubt learned in graduate school to camouflage his prejudices in pseudo-scientific or sociological jargon. Hume is at once too courageous and too sneering, too candid and too snobbish, for namby-pamby modern taste, and while even we may be able to swallow such diatribe and scorn in a free-wheeling satire such as Swift's *Tale of a Tub* or Hogarth's *Enthusiasm Delineated*, we shall gag at it in "objective" history. I am not concerned to judge Hume by professional standards or shibboleths alien to his time and perhaps no more honest if truth be told, but to remark his operative prejudices. In his *History* religious worship is to be as intellectual and abstract as possible; religious controversies are always viewed from a secular stance; religious actions are always traced to selfishness, superstition, hypocrisy. Johnson spoke of Hume the historian as "an echo of Voltaire." This is not literally true, since Hume's work had been planned and substantially written before the appearance of Voltaire's *Age of Louis XIV*. However, his perspective is sufficiently representative of the Enlightenment philosophers and such historians as Gibbon.

Hume's miscellaneous essays shed further light on some of these attitudes. In the *History*, for example, Wickliff the enthusiast is considered for that very reason a fine opponent of the Roman Church, "whose chief characteristic is superstition" (III, 42). In "Of Superstition and Enthusiasm" Hume describes the two as equal but different corruptions of true religion — his outlook is very like Swift's and Hogarth's. The superstitious think poorly of themselves and so commit themselves to the care of priests; they seek the direction of forms, external disciplines, and authority. The enthusiasts, on the contrary, believe that they are peculiarly favored of God and so, disdaining mediation or guidance, immerse themselves in the inward life. Both tendencies are unhealthy and obsessive, but enthusiasm can have one good side-effect, at least, since the independence of the enthusiast may inadvertently promote civil liberty. In the main, though, the word retains for Hume the old pejorative sense it had for Swift and Hogarth, not the newer, favorable usage found in Watts or Dennis. As an aesthetician, Hume loathes religious themes, especially those addressing poignantly the holy or the daemonic. Thus in his essay on tragedy he deplores the "ghastly mythology" of "crucifixions and martyrdoms, where nothing appears but tortures, wounds, executions." In the essay on taste he prefers the genteel Addison to the low-brow and rudely picturesque Bunyan. One suspects that Addison's ode, "The Spacious Firmament on High," just suited Hume in its jocund and impersonal piety — no depressing crucifixions there; but of course he would later challenge its implied analogy of God as creator.

Except in the notorious essay on miracles, Hume seldom takes up religious matters directly in his *magnum opus*, the *Enquiry concerning Human Understanding* (1748). But the central theme of that work, the questioning of the common-sense theory of Causation, throws into doubt the whole status of belief. In Section V, for example, he suggests that the difference between our crediting a mere fiction of the imagination and actual *belief* is but one of degree, and that the two are inextricably mingled in Roman Catholicism ("that superstition") with its "mummeries," devotional exercises, images, and so on. In Section VII he flirts deistically with the notion that God need not perpetually attend on his machine, the universe; and through a persona in XI he throws doubt on providence, rewards and punishments after death, the argument from design. In VIII he insinuates that God is responsible for evil, and in II he hints that our idea of God is assembled from our own best traits, augmented without limit — a distinctly humanistic definition. But to hint or flirt or insinuate — my verbs of course — is not to commit oneself to heterodoxy; and so far as I can tell, Hume never does so commit himself in the *Enquiry*, though by innuendo and nuance he has raised up a host of perplexities. From these generalizations, however, the essay on miracles must be excluded; its irony is just a trifle too broad, and its argument is glaringly — it may be, even provocatively — unphilosophical.

"On Miracles" is actually one of Hume's earlier essays, omitted from the first version of the *Enquiry* — the *Treatise* — lest that precocious work give supererogatory offense; it found its way into the 1748 version, as Section X, some dozen years after its writing. It aroused a considerable tempest, some part of which I have inspected in an earlier chapter, and it remains the most noisy of Hume's pieces. But its final significance in the history of philosophy is now as debatable as was its thesis in Hume's time. Devotees of Hume such as Peter Gay apply to it the redoubtable epithet "deadly" and contend that it was this work above all that "troubled and threatened" Johnson.[8] But David Laird, who can praise Hume highly, considers it "one of the weakest 'demonstrations' ever perpetrated by a major philosopher on a serious issue. . . . an outrageous *petitio principii*" that is mainly interesting because it illuminates "the stubborn condition of his own mind." A. E. Taylor agrees that the argument is a *petitio principii* and, after an exhaustive study of the essay, wonders whether Hume "was really a great philosopher, or only a 'very clever man.' "[9]

---

[8]Peter Gay, *The Enlightenment*, I, 402, 407. Representative of much modern opinion is Donald Greene, *The Age of Exuberance* (New York: Random House, 1970), 111–12: "the last word was said by David Hume, whose devastating essay 'Of Miracles' (1748) went deep into the fundamental epistemological question."

[9]David Laird, *Hume's Philosophy of Human Nature* (London: Methuen, 1932), 121–22; A. E. Taylor, *Philosophical Studies* (London: Macmillan, 1934), 365. These scholars, and others with similarly unflattering views of Hume, are strangely omitted from the capacious "Bibliographical Essay" appended to Gay's *Enlightenment*.

Hume and Johnson

Hume states his thesis succinctly toward the beginning, and it is a simple one: "A miracle is a violation of the laws of nature; and as a firm and unalterable experience has established these laws, the proof against a miracle, from the very nature of the fact, is as entire as any argument from experience can possibly be imagined."[10] This is really all there is to it. Miracles by definition depart from the laws of nature, and since all our experience tells us that these laws are regular, no amount of testimony from witnesses, no matter how reliable they may seem to be, can suffice to counteract our intuition that probability lies on the other side, that it is more likely that the witnesses are wrong, deceiving or self-deceived, than that a miracle has actually occurred. Upon this argument Hume embroiders other and adventitious considerations: most miracles are in fact fraudulent or forged; they occur most frequently in primitive or barbarous countries and pander to man's irrational love of wonder; *all* religions have their miracles, but if only one religion be true, then the general validity of miracles is rendered doubtful. Now the first thing that a philosophical reader will notice is that Hume's argument is tautological, a *petitio principii* like Descartes's *Cogito, ergo sum*. Hume assumes what he is trying to "demonstrate" (Laird is quite right to put that verb in inverted commas); he bases his argument on a principle that he considers self-evident, and confuses presumption with proof. The philosophical significance of the piece would therefore seem to be slight. A reader who is already a convinced naturalist will applaud Hume's good sense and commend him for saying outright what any reasonable person must believe. A reader committed to the transcendence and ineffability of a godhead, ought to be able to dismantle Hume's apparatus easily enough. There is no reason why someone of Johnson's intellectual rigor should have been "threatened" by the essay.

[10]All quotations from the essay on miracles, *The Natural History of Religion*, and *Dialogues concerning Natural Religion*, are from *Hume on Religion*, ed. Richard Wollheim (Cleveland and New York: World Publishing Company, 1969).

A literary scholar may be more interested in the style than the argument of the piece, and he may even suspect that the speaker is not Hume himself but a persona, and that not everything he says is to be taken *au pied de la lettre*. For example, Hume opens by endorsing Archbishop Tillotson's argument against the Real Presence, despising that doctrine as "so little worthy of a serious refutation." Such arguments, he continues, will "at least *silence* the most arrogant bigotry and superstition, and free us from their impertinent solicitations." Is this, we may well ask, the language of the philosopher, or are we not still being treated with the rhetoric of the popular historian? He continues: "I flatter myself, that I have discovered an argument of a like nature, which, if just, will, with the wise and learned, be an everlasting check to all kinds of superstitious delusion, and consequently, will be useful as long as the world endures." The self-confidence or arrogance, the hyperbolical peroration, puts one in mind of Swift's mad rationalist in "A Modest Proposal": grandiose in his asseverations, imperceptive of his assumptions and inconsistencies, professing himself reasonable yet incredulous of anyone else's proposals and the motives behind them.

But of course it would be perverse to argue that a persona operates here. Hume is just being ironic, well aware, like any good skeptic, of how slightly reason is valued by mankind. Still, it is tantalizing to think of the piece as a deliberate *tour de force*. Such a sentence as this: "But it is a miracle, that a dead man should come to life; because that has never been observed in any age or country," so patently contains within it the assumption asking to be proved, that no one *has* risen from the dead, that a writer so clever as Hume must surely have tongue-in-cheek. Or again, he spends much time retailing accounts of factitious miracles, relying the while on two tacit but obvious assumptions, that the miracles he ridicules *were* fake, and that, even if they were fake, those examples perforce undermine *all* miracles. Hume imperturbably splashes his gross generalizations about, making no attempt to discuss miracles individually. He affirms dogmatically that miracles of one religion must discredit the miracles of another, but that is so only if one miracle

[212]

contradicts another on some point of doctrine, or if God works miracles for only one sect. Hume says he *might* believe an account of week-long darkness, but he has earlier said that *no* testimony of an extraordinary story could compel belief: he introduces a bit of off-hand and half-baked cosmology to explain his credulity about week-long darkness, but it is hardly convincing. Nor does he provide any principle of differentiation to show why he would believe in seven days of night but not in a case of resurrection from the dead: it is by no means self-evident that the one is less intrinsically fantastic than the other, or for that matter less susceptible of rationalistic explication. As in the *History*, Hume is perpetually cynical about the motives of those who testify to religious truths: they are either deceiving others for some ulterior purpose or are fanatics. Fundamentally, of course, the essay reposes an implicit trust in the testimony of experience for the regularity of nature, but elsewhere the *Enquiry* heaps great doubt on such testimony.

The essay on miracles is to be considered chiefly a flight of rhetoric rather than a piece of argumentation. *Vox et praeterea nihil*. Tautological formulations can of course be justified as rhetoric; such an excuse can be made, perhaps, for the famous tautology of Descartes. But distinctions between rhetoric and logic are not inutile. From the start we are seduced by a speaker — I will not go as far as to call it a persona — that engages a cynical "common sense" in the reader, the same to which the *History* appeals. And so in tracing the prevalence of miracles to that "passion of *surprise* and *wonder*" so rampant in man, Hume does not stay to inquire whether the passion for wonder may have some metaphysical source or end. When he adds "if the spirit of religion join itself to the love of wonder, there is an end of common sense," it is evident that by spirit of religion he expects us to understand "superstition, enthusiasm, bigotry," or other of his favored terms of opprobrium. When at the end of the essay he rebukes those who would defend Christianity on rational grounds as in fact weakening it, propping it with a twig, because it rests more securely on faith, Hume is *saying* precisely what Dryden had asserted years before in the Preface to *Religio*

Laici. But of course the speaker here is really giving us the wink as fellow-skeptics and men-of-the-world, inveigling us in this manner to own that Christianity not only *seems* foolish, as St. Paul boasted, but *is* foolish. Here is a parody, not an iteration, of Dryden.

No wonder the essay got people worked up. The speaker is, to my mind, deliberately outrageous and provocative, burlesquing the language of piety while at the same time imposing the veneer of logic upon a dogmatic rationalism. There is much in the essay consistent enough with Humean empiricism, yet Hume seems too sophisticated to be associated entirely with the pretentious speaker. Still, it is not always easy to assign the limits of irony. If Hume be indeed the thoroughly skeptical sensibility predicted by Casaubon, he may have become oblivious of his own assumptions. Contemporary as well as modern readers spotted the tautology, and also the inconsistency between the specific skepticism of this essay and the more diffusive skepticism of the *Enquiry*. One of Hume's ablest posthumous critics was William Paley, of whom his recent biographer observes: "in the miracle controversy it was Paley, and not Hume, who was the more authentic empiricist."[11] But Newman's remark in *A Grammar of Assent* is the most apposite:

> Philosophers of the school of Hume discard the very supposition of miracles, and scornfully refuse to hear evidence in their behalf in given instances, from their intimate experience of physical order and of the ever-recurring connexion of antecedent and consequent. Their imagination usurps the functions of reason; and they cannot bring themselves even to entertain as a hypothesis (and this is all that they are asked to do) a thought contrary to that vivid impression of which they are the victims, that the uniformity of nature, which

[11]D. L. LeMahieu, *The Mind of William Paley* (Lincoln: Univ. of Nebraska Press, 1976), 98. LeMahieu is by no means an enemy of Hume, yet he is willing to criticize him, and so inflames the wrath of the Humeans, who spring righteously to their master's defense: see E. C. Mossner's review of LeMahieu, *Studies in Burke and His Time*, 19 (1978), 172–74.

they witness hour by hour, is equivalent to a necessary, inviolable law (Part I, ch. 4).

"Their imagination usurps the functions of reason," the "impression of which they are the victims": Newman might have been describing the obsessed sectaries of *A Tale of a Tub*, or the know-it-all prating to us in "A Modest Proposal." There are resemblances, unexpected perhaps, but worth contemplating.

⌑

By the early 1750s Hume was well into two books on religion that are among the most distinctive of the eighteenth century. *The Natural History of Religion* was published in 1757 along with his shorter essays on tragedy and taste. The *Dialogues concerning Natural Religion*, at about the same time, was circulated among his friends, and on their advice Hume withheld publication, revising it desultorily over the years. Of this piece he was very fond, chaffing incessantly under his friends' prudential monitions and taking care that it should be published soon after his death, as indeed it was, in 1779. If I have seemed unduly harsh on the essay on miracles, it is because I think that it has enjoyed, in its own time and since, a notoriety far surpassing its merits. The two books on religion, however, are the finest that Enlightenment skepticism has to offer.

The *Natural History* is the slighter work. Still very readable, it is not so adventurous or intricate as the *Dialogues*, and it draws much of its inspiration from the skeptical psychology of Hobbes, who had found the origin of religion in man's fear of the unknown and his craving for security. One of Hume's central theses, that polytheism preceded monotheism, is now widely, though by no means universally, embraced, but his evidence, judged by present standards of scholarship, is not weighty. His enumeration of the natural causes of religion — fear, terror, inability to understand or control natural phenomena — and his account of the effects of religion on man — fanat-

[215]

icism, intolerance, and so forth — are too angular and dogmatic, too derivative from Hobbes, to be very exciting. One of his other arguments, that polytheism encourages humanitarian feelings more than monotheism does, cannot be sustained by any impartial study of pagan societies. As in the *History*, Roman Catholicism throws him into a state impervious to fairness or discretion. For example, arguing that Catholicism fosters pusillanimity and abasement while paganism had encouraged fortitude, he contrasts Brasidas with Bellarmine: the former, a pagan, praised the courage of noxious creatures but rightly defended himself against their depredations; the latter, a Christian, fatuously suffered their assaults (Section X). But in place of Bellarmine Hume might as aptly have mentioned St. Francis, who expresses much more sensibly the humanitarian side of Christianity. This substitution would not have violated Hume's principles, for he counts Franciscan benevolence a virtue; but since Francis had courage, it would have impaired his case against Catholicism. The Real Presence coerces Hume to narrate, as if they were philosophical arguments against it, several blasphemous tales resting on a vulgar misunderstanding of the doctrine (Section XII). In fact, they are such stories as might titillate a clever adolescent working through his iconoclastic phase. As a final complaint: Hume associates himself with Theism and on several occasions affirms his belief that the design and harmony of the cosmos irrefragably points to a divine author. But in view of his questioning of that notion in the *Dialogues*, being written at the same time, it is most uncertain *what* beliefs are endorsed by Hume. Either he is serious, and therefore probably inconsistent with the point of view urged in the *Dialogues*, or he is employing a deceptive persona cloaking his true agnosticism. Most modern scholars think that he is doing the latter, and will defend his subterfuge on the grounds that public opinion imposed it. But this is not at all clear.

But for all its faults, *The Natural History of Religion* is a gracefully written and often pungent study of human psychology. "It abounds with shrewd reflections, and just observations, upon human nature: mixed with a considerable portion of that sceptical spirit, which is so apparent in all his works, and with some insinuations, artfully couched, against the Christian religion.''[12] That is one of its first reviewers, and his summary is quite accurate. The *Natural History* lives today, not so much because of its theoretical content, but because of its exposure of religious melancholia, the restless desire of man for amazement and mystery, darkness and obscurity, the essential irrationality of man in the mass. It is a more sedate and affable *Tale of a Tub.*

Despite Hume's pious obsecrations to Theism, his view of human nature seems quite secular. Let us consider one passage in detail. Hume has been enlarging with some force on the apparent arbitrariness of life; he also recognizes the terror engendered in primitive man by that insecurity. Such terror is natural, but Hume insists that it is ignorant and superstitious. Primitive man has no understanding of the real causes of things, nor has he the leisure to contemplate the ultimate harmony of the cosmos; this is also true of contemporary mass man:

> Even at this day, and in EUROPE, ask any of the vulgar, why he believes in an omnipotent creator of the world; he will never mention the beauty of final causes, of which he is wholly ignorant: He will not hold out his hand, and bid you contemplate the suppleness and variety of joints in his fingers, their bending all one way, the counterpoise which they receive from the thumb, the softness and fleshy parts of the inside of his hand, with all the other circumstances, which render that member fit for the use, to which it was destined. To these he has been long accustomed; and he beholds them with listlessness and unconcern. He will tell you of the sudden and unexpected death of such a one: The fall and bruise of such another: The excessive drought of this season: The cold and rains of another (Section VI).

[12]*Monthly Review*, 16 (February 1757), 133.

How true an observation of human nature — but what are we to conclude from it? Hume is speaking here as a Theist for whom the teleological arguments for God are the compelling, philosophical proofs: all things in creation are adapted to their purpose and point to a divine architect. Yet even as he wrote that passage, he may have been fashioning, in the manuscript of the *Dialogues*, his derisive demolition of that argument. Nor need we stray beyond the passage itself. The very description of the hand, with its gratuitous and whimsical accumulation of detail, reads more like a parody of teleological arguments. Hume, one suspects, is mocking the rationalistic "proofs" of God. But if that is so, then is not the "vulgar" *right* to speak instead of the vicissitudes of nature? And is there not also a curious and probably deliberate inconsistency between Hume-the-Theist's confidence in cosmic harmony and Hume-the-observer-of-life's recognition that the world, for man, is insecure and violent? Such are the complexities of Hume's thought and style, compared with which the essay on miracles is merely brilliant persiflage. But I think *some* things can be concluded from the passage. Hume is using his hypothetical peasant, I believe, to elucidate the futile and abstruse "demonstrations" of God. Belief comes much more vividly and dramatically from the numinous experience — our sense of weakness, frailty, dependence. But Hume is assuredly *not* saying that such experience points to God or has any true religious value, for he abhors any conception of God tinged with the numinous: "Where the deity is represented as infinitely superior to mankind, this belief, though altogether just, is apt, when joined with superstitious terrors, to sink the human mind into the lowest submission and abasement, and to represent the monkish virtues of mortification, penance, humility, and passive suffering, as the only qualities which are acceptable to him" (Section X). Obviously God is superior to us, but we are to consider him so only philosophically; the emotional resonances of that recognition are superstitious and produce only evil effects. This then is a salient pattern winding its way through the *Natural History*: a recognition of the strength of religious fear, a secular interpretation of the source of that fear, a wholly

[218]

negative view of the effects of that fear on human behavior. Deists had long held such views, but when we add to them Hume's suave mockery of Theism — if such it be — we are left with the closest thing in the eighteenth century to pure agnosticism.

In the last three chapters Hume develops his conception of the holy and prescribes our response. Discussing "impious conceptions of the divine nature," Hume notes that the more intense a notion of the sacred men have, the more oppressive are their terrors. God must be viewed as perfect, yet his actions must seem capricious by merely human mensuration. Still, if he is omnipotent and also omniscient, if he can read our hearts, then we must needs praise him in our worship, despite our "gloomy apprehensions" about his motives:

> Here therefore is a kind of contradiction between the different principles of human nature, which enter into religion. Our natural terrors present the notion of a devillish and malicious deity: Our propensity to adulation leads us to acknowledge an excellent and divine. . . . Thus it may safely be affirmed, that popular religions are really . . . a species of daemonism; and the higher the deity is exalted in power and knowledge, the lower of course he is depressed in goodness and benevolence; whatever epithets of praise may be bestowed on him by his amazed adorers (Section XIII).

So in the popular (i.e., non-Theistic) religions there is an inherent and agonizing split: man is driven to fear and to worship God. How nearly Hume approaches the modern understanding of the numinous experience. Otto himself states that religions saturated with the dreadful and wayward aspects of the numen, and sawn from any moral base, lapse into demonism; but where an Otto would wish for a deepening and purifying of these very proper emotions of fear and dread, and their transmutation into a sense of the holy, Hume would exclude them altogether as irrational and subversive of true morality. Hume says that we are prompted to moral acts by the ties of nature and by a "sentiment of order and moral obligation" (here Hume again indulges a tautology, explaining moral behavior by presupposing a moral sentiment in our hearts). But the superstitious man cannot understand that "the most genuine method of serving the divinity is by promoting the happiness of his creatures." The superstitious man, driven daemonically, is not content with such acts, but performs those that serve no obvious purpose or are in fact contrary to his natural inclinations. This compulsion drags him into crimes, whose consequences are horror, remorse, and a perpetual turmoil in his soul. Much better is "manly, steady virtue, which either preserves us from disastrous, melancholy accidents, or teaches us to bear them. During such calm sunshine of the mind, these spectres of false divinity never make their appearance" (Section XIV).

Here on a more sophisticated level are the same prejudices bristling in the *History of England*. Surely it is inherent in an act of sacrifice that it be performed for no selfish or even utilitarian end. Hume fails to recognize this, or that there is a part of man that desires by deodands to witness to the wholly transcendent; and he assumes that when man does yield to such perverse desires, crime is the only result. So it may be, but if fewer crimes have been committed in the name of that humanitarianism and benevolence which Hume regards as "the most genuine method of serving the divinity," this can only be because that philosophy has more briefly obtained. But we are in a better position than Hume to know this. Hume despises that turbulence of spirit (the Pauline "fear and trembling") which according to most religious testimony occurs in any real encounter, any wrestling, with the transcendent. And naturally so: the whole notion of a wrestling god is degrading for Hume (VI), as is any anthropomorphism, which, he assumes, is merely a projection of our petty weaknesses and silly desires (III). He never considers here, as he never considers it when discussing our craving for wonder in the essay on miracles, whether such impulses may be a legitimate means of knowledge, however subject, like all things, to abuse and perversion. Hume really is the sort of thinker who decides that because we *wish* something were true, it can't be.

No more appealing, to be sure, is the opposite extreme of self-delusion. The Pascalian "reasons of the heart" can be wrenched into excuses for believing, and acting on, any absurdity. We are also in a good position — but no better a one than Hume's I suppose — to know *this*. Hume's dissection of the psychology of worship and its antagonistic forces of dread and reverence, his candid denomination of popular religion as daemonic — these go notably beyond anything in the routine religious writers of the day, whether conventional or Deistic. Once their implications are grasped, these sections of the *Natural History* ought to have been far more disconcerting to the believer than the lucubrations of the essay on miracles. Yet Hume's own views are rather narrow and, in a fundamental way, emotional. Alternative understandings are either ignored, as in the last chapters of the *Natural History*, or sneered down, as in the *History of England* and the essay on miracles; they are seldom refuted. One thinks of Augustine's meditation, in the *Confessions*, on the omniscience of God and the complexity, the inscrutability, of the human spirit. Such a passage is but a ragbag of nonsense for Hume, and dangerous nonsense at that, for it leads to daemonism and superstition. But where has the humanitarianism of this genial philosopher, "le bon David," taken us? Pragmatism aside, is his view of human nature more consonant with human experience than Augustine's? Hume's puerile diatribes against the doctrine of the Real Presence can be explained as the staunch empiricist's scorn of a belief that shamelessly defies sensory experience. Undoubtedly that doctrine does so.[13] But one wonders if Hume's boisterous loathing of that dogma was not urged on him by his detestation of a *deus praesens*, an active, living God, "ignobly" human in some of his characteristics, unfathomable in others. Such is not the god of the philosophers, but the god caught up in that "ghastly mythology" of crucifix-

---

[13]In a postscript in Glanvill's *Sadducismus Triumphatus*, Henry More, the great opponent of Hobbes, even as he defends belief in witches and spirits, refuses to credit "that gross, rank, and scandalous impossibility of *Transubstantiation*." More considered himself an empiricist.

ion and martyrdom to which Hume objects on the grounds of good taste. At the end of the *Natural History* Hume asserts that "the good, the great, the sublime, the ravishing are found eminently in the genuine principles of theism," just as "the base, the absurd, the mean, the terrifying will be equally discovered in religious fictions and chimeras." But the reader will ransack this work in vain to find one example of sublime or ravishing feeling which is not allied with superstition. In light of the *Dialogues* it seems clear that Theism itself had very little appeal, even for Hume's fastidious palate.

□

The *Dialogues concerning Natural Religion* is assuredly Hume's finest theological work. The participants are the skeptic Philo, the orthodox Demea, and the natural theologian Cleanthes. Some of Hume's contemporary critics associated Hume with Cleanthes, and plausibly, for he expounds the Theism that Hume seems to enforce in the *Natural History* and he sometimes argues like an intransigent empiricist; while Philo appears to embrace a Pyrrhonism to which Hume himself never clearly consents. Most early commentators, however, saw Philo as Hume's chief spokesman, and such is the consensus of modern scholars.[14] The speakers themselves are not always consistent, however: Philo sometimes talks like a Theist (though perhaps facetiously), Demea sometimes like a mystic or Fideist, sometimes like an a priorist theologian in the manner of Joseph Clarke, and Cleanthes sometimes like a Deist, sometimes like an a posteriorist theologian in the manner of Samuel Butler. The

[14]Early commentators identifying Philo with Hume were: Joseph Milner, *Gibbon's Account of Christianity* (1781), Thomas Hayter, *Remarks on Mr. Hume's Dialogues* (1780), review of the *Dialogues* in *Monthly Review*, 61 (November 1779). This is supported by E. C. Mossner, "The Enigma of Hume," *Mind*, 14 (1936), N. K. Smith in his edition of the *Dialogues*, and most other scholars. An interesting case for Hume as Cleanthes is given by James Noxan, "Hume's Agnosticism," in *Hume: A Collection of Critical Essays*, ed. V. C. Chappell (New York: Doubleday, 1966).

Dialogues opens with the complaisant confession that "Opposite sentiments, even without a decision, afford an agreeable amusement," and so it is quite possible that Hume aims at no ultimate verdict and is not wholly to be identified with any one of his disputants.

The general import of the *Dialogues* seems to be that no religious scheme or demonstration of God is immune from attack — a point Pascal would have appreciated — and that a tranquil, temperate skepticism is the sanest attitude — a conclusion from which Pascal, in the wager, dissents. The most famous part of the work is the assault conducted by Philo on one of the chief supporting structures of natural theology: the teleological argument, or argument from design. Refurbishing weapons used in an earlier essay in the *Enquiry*, Philo denies that we can demonstrate the existence of a Creator from our sense of a cosmic order or pattern. To do so is to argue by analogy, but because a watch requires a watchmaker does not mean that the universe had to have a Creator. The creation is unique, nothing can be properly compared with it. Not only is the analogy remote and failing in empirical evidence, but it is arbitrary. Why should we compare the universe to a watch when we might more aptly compare it to an organism? And if it be an organism, why then the ordering principle may be innate and not transcendent, as it is in vegetable growth. Nay more: our very sense of design may be too choosy and subjective. A more disinterested view of the universe will disclose such apparent evil and waste as to throw into grave doubt the craftsmanship of any divine architect.

Like the essay on miracles, these sections of the *Dialogues* have been celebrated as conclusive. Philo's concatenation of logic is acclaimed as "final and complete"; "Little, very little, remains of the 'religious hypothesis' after this assault"; it is "devastating"; it is the "definitive refutation" for "sophisticated audiences."[15] But of course this last remark might be judged tau-

---

[15]See: Smith, edition of *Dialogues*, 30; Gay, *Enlightenment*, I, 417; R. B. Schwartz, *Samuel Johnson and the Problem of Evil* (Madison: Univ. of Wisconsin Press, 1975), 11; Robert Hurlbutt III, *Hume, Newton, and the Design Argument* (Lincoln: Univ. of Nebraska Press, 1965), 189.

tological, the proof of one's sophistication being one's consenti-
ence with Philo. It is not my intention to enter very deeply into
this controversy, which is perhaps not strictly pertinent to my
subject. But I would note that some critics, with something
resembling sophistication, have been troubled by Philo's logic.
They argue, for example, that it is not self-evident that arguments from analogy are ipso facto invalid or feeble, even when
they tackle something that is unique (and one might quibble —
since Philo is fond of quibbling — that all things *are* unique).
Cosmologists reach conclusions about the universe in despite of
Philo. Anthropologists reach conclusions about the human race,
though it is the only race we know, and though we analogously
compare modern primitive people with our ancestors. Are we to
reject all this as vain? Philo argues that to postulate an entity to
account for something else is simply to compound the mystery,
but scientists do this all the time. The analogy, deliberately
ludicrous, that Philo constructs between the universe and an
animal or vegetable is to no purpose: principles of order are not
obviously innate or generated in the seed of a tree, for example;
and anyway, we must still explain the existence of the animal
or vegetable in the first place. Moreover, vegetation and generation can be plausibly seen as transmitting order, or as themselves orderly processes and hence as providing further evidence
for the argument from design. Hence, there may be nothing
innately fallacious in an argument by analogy, or intrinsically
silly about the argument from design. Then too, what Philo castigates as argument by analogy may actually be an inductive
argument, because it selects particular circumstances in the
world from which to argue; it is arguing from part to the whole,
which is done all the time, and which, by the way, Hume does
in the essay on miracles. It is perhaps really an argument from
experience, resting on our observation that many objects possessed of organization were designed. Philo is certainly right to
say that there is a vast difference between the universe and a
human artifact, and we may also agree that the greater the differences, the more enervated are any comparisons, analogies, or
inductions; but it has not been proved that the differences over-

throw the arguments.[16] These various objections to Philo may help us to understand a phenomenon that has puzzled many students of Hume: why in his own day, and even in our own, the argument from design — "a stubborn, troublesome ghost" in Peter Gay's revealing phrase — seems to hang on despite Hume's alleged triumph. It may also be that the tendency to see order in nature is more than merely a perverse atavism. It is too pervasive and pertinacious to be dismissed thus cavalierly, and indeed there is evidence that Hume himself never shook free from such beliefs.

I am not trying presumptuously to explode Hume but to suggest that like any other important book the *Dialogues* has stimulated, not finished off debate. It is curious that academics, who usually stress the *pursuit* of truth over its achievement, and for whom every argument is to be open-ended, are so hasty to find Hume definitive on religious matters. After all, Philo's arguments have wrought much. No one, no *sophisticated* theologian, after the *Dialogues*, could argue so confidently from design. It is at most a piece of evidence — rather a large chunk some would say — but not a conclusive proof. Hume's main purpose, I think, was not utterly to overthrow the argument from design, but to show that even if it were valid it furnishes us with no deity worth worshipping: it tells us nothing about his *moral* qualities. Even if one could demonstrate a Necessary Being, the philosophers' *ens necessarium*, nothing very compelling, nothing of the numinous, would be preserved. In this purpose I believe Hume has succeeded.

Hume is also to be praised for his discussion of evil in Parts X and XI. These are among the most powerful sections of the *Dialogues*, and they are a much more philosophical rebuttal of the optimism of *An Essay on Man* than Voltaire's *Candide*. No honest person, however pious, can blink a fact of human nature: that one can look at the evil in the world and conclude that

[16]See R. G. Swinburne, "The Argument from Design," *Philosophy*, 43 (1968), 199–211, and Leon Pearl, "Hume's Criticism of the Argument from Design," *The Monist*, 54 (1970), 270–84.

God, if he exists, is either inept or malicious. The existence of evil has checked religious faith in more people, I think, than the failure of rational proofs. The profoundest religious documents — *Job*, the *Gospels*, *Revelation* to cite examples from the Judaeo-Christian tradition — fully recognize the power of evil. Now in the *Dialogues* Cleanthes represents the Deistic view, and that of *An Essay on Man*, that evil is not so pervasive and that one should adopt a cheerful perspective. But his position is shown to be quite precarious. Philo of course sees much misery in the world, and Demea, who likes to expatiate on God's majesty and mystery in biblical language (see, e.g., Parts II, III), is happy to concur. By contemplating mundane wretchedness, he says, we are thrown into a religious frame of mind. Behind Demea hovers the approving shade of Augustine or Pascal. But Philo, although very subtle and careful, refrains from drawing that pious conclusion. In the old days, he counters, an effective rhetorician would point up the debility of human reason and "the absolute incomprehensibility of the Divine Nature, the great and universal misery and still greater wickedness of men . . . to promote superstition [i.e., religious awe]," but in an age of enlightenment such themes are more apt to foster skepticism (XI). In other words, the old arguments would work when they could engage a pre-established reverence in the audience, but once a tendency toward skepticism is started, such arguments will only further encourage it. This is a shrewd observation, and it condemns implicitly the aesthetics of terror and awe exploited a decade before the *Dialogues* was written by poets such as Thomson, Blair, and Young. Of course the continued popularity of those poets and the imminent vogue of the Gothic novel suggest either that Hume's point is not so astute as it seems, or that his age was not so enlightened as he thought. Nevertheless, his discussion of evil is a refreshing contrast to the bromides of *An Essay on Man* and its kin.

Hume is also adroit in setting Demea and Cleanthes at odds on those aspects of religion most odious to him. For example, strong in the Judaeo-Christian tradition is the notion of a God

utterly transcendent but not utterly unknowable; he is mysterious, but often described in an anthropomorphic manner. Had
Hume united in one character a sophisticated anthropomorphist
(after all, according to Christianity we are made in God's image
and he is a Person) and a sophisticated believer in the god of
thunder, Philo might have had a signal opponent. A Watts or a
Lowth might have provided Hume with a model. But for Hume
anthropomorphism is inherently primitive, naive, intolerable in
any refined view of the deity, and belief in a numinous god
leads to superstition and daemonism: this we have learned from
his other works. And so he splits up the concepts. He attributes
to Cleanthes an anthropomorphism that Demea rends as too
reductive and that Philo actually reduces to the absurd; and he
infects Demea, who is something of a jackass, with an obsession
with divine mystery and transcendence that is made to seem
evasive and finally nihilistic (Philo has great fun suggesting that
Demea's Fideism and his own skepticism are proximate; and in
a sense of course he is quite right). I do not mean that Hume is
clumsily loading the dice. Internal and external evidence alike
shows that he did not wish to set up straw men but to give
everyone intelligent arguments. No doubt Hume could not
really *conceive* of sophisticated versions of these beliefs, though
they were available for his use. But it remains that the qualities
normally accented in a numinous religion are separated and
thrown into intestine war, and they are represented less forcibly
than they might have been.

The concluding themes of the *Natural History* resonate again
at the end of the *Dialogues*. Cleanthes, as a last and very desperate resort, defends even a corrupt religion as better than none
(as an opiate of the people). But Philo sees it only as a force for
disruption. True religion, of course, is humanitarian and political: it is "to regulate the heart of men, humanize their conduct,
infuse the spirit of temperance, order, and obedience." Man is
more ably actuated by natural inclinations toward honesty and
benevolence than by religious systems, which are but the fertil-
izer of superstition and enthusiasm. Man is not even much sol-

aced by the corrupt religions, for they pander to his melancholy and gloomy moods, and in them "we find the tremendous images to predominate."

It is true; both fear and hope enter into religion; because both these passions, at different times, agitate the human mind, and each of them forms a species of divinity, suitable to itself. But when a man is in a chearful disposition, he is fit for business or company. . . . When melancholy, and dejected, he has nothing to do but brood upon the terrors of the invisible world, and to plunge himself still deeper in affliction.

To know God, says Seneca, *is to worship him*. All other worship is indeed absurd, superstitious, and even impious. It degrades him to the low condition of mankind, who are delighted with intreaty, solicitation, presents, and flattery. . . . Commonly it depresses the Deity far below the condition of mankind; and represents him as a capricious daemon, who exercises his power without reason and without humanity!

One could, of course, pick apart this conclusion: the confining of religion to ethics, the absolute distinction between natural inclinations and religious belief (have they no reciprocity of influence?), the inconsistencies (Philo will sometimes minimize the influence of religion on man, or enlarge it, according to his purpose), the sedulous selection of only the bad influences of religion — this from the same Philo who withered the argument from design because of its selective evidence! Both the *Natural History* and the *Dialogues* show that "strange mixture" so often found in intellectual geniuses and described so well by George Santayana in speaking of Bertrand Russell: "great ability and great disability: prodigious capacity and brilliance here — astonishing unconsciousness and want of perception there."

But the most striking thing in the conclusion is the motto from Seneca, "To know God is to worship him." It is easier to agree with this apophthegm than to say just what it means, for a great deal hangs on the word "know." The *onus* of the *Dialogues* is that we can know *nothing* significant about God. Even

that Theism to which Philo finally and most strangely subscribes yields knowledge of the Being only, and not the Nature,
of God — and there are good grounds for thinking that Hume is
not even a Theist! Seneca's slogan is inspiring — that is the purpose of a slogan. But on Hume's own terms, it is vacant. So the
conclusions of both his great works on religion are highly
ambiguous. At the end of the *Natural History* we hear, but are
shown nothing, of the raptures of Theism, and Theism itself,
between the lines, has been evacuated of meaning. It can only
be a very foolish or slovenly reader of the *Dialogues* who will
be soothed by the Senecan motto. Hume's god is far more inscrutable than Pascal's — *absconding* in the less appetizing acceptation of that word.

Hume is a Proteus who will not be wrestled into form and
tell us clearly what he knows. In temper he is very like the
more sophisticated Deists, and yet, of literary men at least, only
Dryden seventy years before saw so lucidly through the pretensions of that fugacious sect. Hume may have been an immanentist, attracted to the notion of some "original, inherent principle
of order somewhere, in thought or in matter" (*Dialogues,* VI);
but this is at best a shadowy belief and it illuminates nothing.
Perhaps he was a pure skeptic or Pyrrhonist, though if he were
it is odd that he should write and argue so indefatigably, and
anyway his works are so crammed with cocksure opinions that
he could never have been anything but a very impure Pyrrhonist. Despite great differences in thought and manner, Hume is
akin to Pascal in his sense of the limits of reason. But he is a
Pascal who will not take the wager, and it is to his credit that
he refused to sentimentalize or adulterate him, like Pope and
Young. One thing we can say: he was distinctly modern. Peter
Gay has called him the "complete modern pagan," and this is
rather wide of the mark, for the pagans had a strong sense of the
numinous. But Jung has defined modern man as a creature
whose "capacity to respond to numinous symbols and ideas" has
been destroyed or at least greatly eroded. Such is the modernism
of Hume, though for the same reason he is a most incomplete
pagan. Like Pope he recognizes the numinous only in its dae-

[229]

monic form. But he is much more consistent and perspicacious than Pope, and if he believed in any vital deity at all, I daresay it was Young's "devouring god." Hume was one of the first, and he remains one of the most sedulous and insinuating, to try to extirpate from the human consciousness all sense of the sacred and transcendent.

◻

The nimiety of information on Johnson, culled from his own works and from the profuse records of Boswell and other memorandists — some of it contradictory, erroneous, or obscure — makes it particularly hard to consider his views concisely but without distortion. He was, in addition, an unusually complicated person who could change his mind and, in conversation at least, deliberately argue a perverse or unpopular side to test his ratiocinative powers. We must remember, too, that Johnson regarded himself as a moralist, not a philosopher or theologian. In any event, there are several good recent discussions of Johnson on religion,[17] and I have no wish to plod over paths already dusty from academic feet. At the same time, Johnson's opinions, seen in the context of this study, and especially set next to Hume's, may acquire a fresh significance; and though I believe that the jejune stereotypes of Johnson as bully, John Bull, or bull-headed Church-of-England man have been adequately confuted, there is yet alive a feeling that he represents

[17]See: Walter Jackson Bate, *The Achievement of Samuel Johnson* (1955; rpt. New York: Oxford Univ. Press, 1961) and *Samuel Johnson* (New York: Harcourt Brace Jovanovich, 1977); Maurice J. Quinlan, *Samuel Johnson: A Layman's Religion* (Madison: Univ. of Wisconsin Press, 1964); Chester F. Chapin, *The Religious Thought of Samuel Johnson* (Ann Arbor: Univ. of Michigan Press, 1968); Robert Voitle, *Samuel Johnson the Moralist* (Cambridge, Mass.: Harvard Univ. Press, 1961); Richard B. Schwartz, *Samuel Johnson and the Problem of Evil* (Madison: Univ. of Wisconsin Press, 1975); Roger Sternbach, "Pascal and Dr. Johnson on Immortality," *Journal of the History of Ideas, 39* (1978). For an interesting survey of nineteenth- and twentieth-century stereotypes of Johnson's religious views, see Lionel Basney, "The Popular Image of Johnson's Religion," *Christianity and Culture, 25* (1976).

the reactionary, emotional, dogmatic, or defensive side of the latter eighteenth century, and that Hume is just the reverse of all that. There may be some truth here, as in most stereotypes, but it is "dashed and brewed with lies." In many ways Johnson was quite *au courant* and empirical, and his thoughts on such matters as Roman Catholicism or psychic phenomena are far less stodgy and doctrinaire than Hume's. Such things have not been sufficiently remarked, particularly in Hume scholarship; and Johnsonians, as a lot, seem lamentably innocent of Hume. First I shall rummage through Johnson's ideas generally as they relate to this study. I shall then take up an essay where Johnson does uncharacteristically argue theology at some length — the review of Soame Jenyns — and conclude with a glance at *The Vanity of Human Wishes* and *Rasselas*.

Johnson was often charged, even by some of his friends, with having a superstitious or credulous nature, and he himself sometimes admits as much; yet he was fundamentally an empiricist. "No man was more incredulous as to particular facts, which were at all extraordinary; and therefore no man was more scrupulously inquisitive, in order to discover the truth."[18] Thus speaks Boswell, and his own reports of Johnson on religion bear him out. For example, Johnson argues that no honest person can be a Deist, but Boswell in rebuttal cites Hume. Johnson insists, however, that Hume *had not* studied the evidence, that he himself confessed that "he had never read the New Testament with attention."[19] And there is not only scripture, but the weight of human testimony through the ages: "The Christian religion has very strong evidences. It, indeed, appears in some degree strange to reason; but in History we have undoubted facts, against which, in reasoning *à priori*, we have more arguments than we have for them; but then, testimony has great weight, and casts the balance."[20] This is Johnson's basic argument, repeated else-

[18]Boswell, *Life*, II, 247. The view is strongly supported by Mrs. Piozzi, despite her less amiable attitude toward Johnson; see *Johnsonian Miscellanies*, ed. G. B. Hill (Oxford, 1897), I, 241–45, 279.
[19]*Life*, II, 8–9.
[20]Ibid., I, 398.

where with some variations: we accept many things on testimony (e.g., that the British have vanquished the French in Canada) even though testimony of any kind is vulnerable; we make many crucial decisions in life without strictly "demonstrative reasoning" (e.g., our choice of spouse, profession); above all, we should seek truth in "human experience," to which is owed more deference than any theoretical book hatched in a solitary mind. Hence the unwarranted presumption of Hume: "a man who has so much conceit as to tell all mankind that they have been bubbled for ages, and he is the wise man who sees better than they."[21]

Although Johnson will sometimes refer to a First Cause, design, and so forth, his arguments are generally drawn from consensus or human testimony and experience, sources to which Hume often appeals. Even Johnson's quip on Hume's attitude toward death, so much resented by some of Hume's more humorless disciples, is in fact a witty exercise in Humean logic. When Boswell told him that Hume professed to face death calmly, Johnson responded: "It was not so, Sir. He had a vanity in being thought easy. It is more probable that he should assume the appearance of ease, than that so very improbable a thing should be, as a man not afraid of going . . . into an unknown state, and not being uneasy at leaving all he knew."[22] This is a parody, or rather a clever application, of Hume's argument from probability against believing testimony of the miraculous. Of course Johnson's conclusions in respect of Hume were probably wrong, but since he is mocking Hume's logic, he would likely have relished the error. Hume had snidely called belief in Christianity miraculous in itself. Now turning the tables, Johnson is in effect calling Hume's much vaunted tranquillity a miracle! This is all very offensive to some of Hume's adulators, who however seldom stick at calling Johnson a superstitious despot.

A similarly empirical attitude informs Johnson's views on the

---

[21]Ibid., 428; V, 47; I, 454; V, 29.

[22]Ibid., III, 153. Johnson speaks more violently about Hume in this regard in II, 106.

occult. It is astonishing, he remarks, that after so much human experience the question of specters seems hopeless of resolution. He censures John Wesley for not probing sufficiently into a case of an alleged ghost: this had been a good opportunity, he says, to try to settle an issue that is "one of the most important that can come before the human understanding." He himself constructs empirical criteria to distinguish an authentic from a merely fanciful spectral experience: the specter must tell the person something he himself could not know, which could come only by a preternatural agency, and which turns out to be true. Johnson also took an active part in the investigation, in 1762, of the famous Cock Lane Ghost, whose fraudulence he was instrumental in detecting. A Hume would never have bothered — yet it is not Hume who is censured for his closed-mindedness, but Johnson for his credulity! Some credulity, of course, there was. "His elevated wish for more and more evidence for spirit, in opposition to the groveling belief of materialism, led him to a love of such mysterious disquisitions." Thus Boswell. Johnson himself confesses he may be rather too eager to believe supernatural reports: "I am so glad to have every evidence of the spiritual world." When someone chides him: "You have evidence enough; good evidence, which needs not such support," Johnson answers simply, honestly: "I like to have more."[23] Such candid disclosures justify my epithet for Johnson, reverent empiricist.

On witchcraft, however, Johnson can be very skeptical. He observes in a note on *Macbeth* that most people take their opinions from what is in fashion, and that consequently in Shakespeare's time witches abounded: "prodigies are always seen in proportion as they are expected." The whole witch business was a "general infatuation," he decides, but his long note, an earlier version of which he wrote as a young man, shows considerable knowledge of witch lore. He is also skeptical when discussing magic in *The Tempest*. But some years later, in oral disputation, he contends that it is no more inconsistent with the idea of a

[23]See Ibid., III, 230, 297–98; I, 405–407; IV, 94, 298–99; II, 150.

Deity that there should be evil spirits, than that there should be any sort of evil. He appeals, typically, to human experience: "you have all mankind, rude and civilized, agreeing in the belief of the agency of preternatural powers. You must take the evidence: you must consider, that wise and great men have condemned witches to die." To be sure, Parliament has abolished the witchcraft laws — because the practice had ceased. "Why it ceased, we cannot tell, as we cannot tell the reason of many other things." Boswell notes elsewhere: "He admitted the influence of evil spirits upon our minds, and said, 'Nobody who believes the New Testament can deny it.'"[24]

Johnson was very cautious concerning miracles, agreeing with Hume that as a general proposition it *is* more likely that witnesses should be lying than that miracles occurred. But he points out that we have, in addition, the prophecies, which have been fulfilled, and that it is certainly conceivable that God might in special circumstances suspend the laws of nature in behalf of Christianity. Moreover, the Christian miracles "are attested by men who had no interest in deceiving us; but who, on the contrary, were told that they should suffer persecution, and did actually lay down their lives in confirmation of the truth of the facts which they asserted." In recounting the story of the Earl of Roscommon's presentiment of his father's death, Johnson concedes that the present age is skeptical, but notes that the tale was told by someone "who had no interest to deceive" and could not himself have been deceived. In a sermon Johnson allows that God may, "by special acts of providence," obviate bad deeds, "but this, whenever it is done, is a real, though not always a visible miracle, and is not to be expected in the ordinary occurrences of life, or the common transactions of the world."[25]

[24]See Johnson, *Works* (New Haven: Yale Univ. Press, 1968), VII, 122–23; VIII, 752–55; *Life*, V, 45–46; IV, 290.

[25]*Life*, III, 188; Johnson, *Lives of the Poets*, ed. G. B. Hill (Oxford: Oxford Univ. Press, 1905), I, 230–31; Sermon V in *Oxford Works* (London, 1825), IX, 335.

Johnson resumes the most important arguments of the Restoration believers in demons and miracles, appealing to empirical evidence, consensus, scripture. Like them, he refuses to explain away all testimony for the supernatural as proceeding from delusion or deceit. Like them, he argues that diabolic evil is no more inconsistent with a benign or omnipotent Deity than moral or physical evil. Like them, he believes in the possibility of divine intervention. Like them, he thinks that the investigation of psychic phenomena is legitimate and useful and may fortify religious belief — he is humble and honest enough to admit that he is not *above* needing such supports. But he also recognizes, like them, that the imagination is responsible for some uncanny experiences, that witnesses should be evaluated for their reliability and that empirical criteria should be set up to differentiate genuine from fanciful psychic phemomena. I see very little difference between Johnson and Glanvill, though of course Johnson is nothing so systematic, and in *some* moods more skeptical. In his *Life of Johnson* Sir John Hawkins wonders if Johnson had been at one time a "dabbler in demonology." I take it he means, not that Johnson had been an apprentice sorcerer, but that he may have browsed in Casaubon, Glanvill, or Hutchinson. Internal evidence shows that he had ruminated along the same lines, and the contrast between him and Hume, allowing for differences in style and temperament, is very like that between, say, More and Hobbes a century since.

In his later years and in most of his moods, Johnson was quite the ecumenist, finding good things to say about Presbyterianism, Methodism, and Roman Catholicism, though he himself was ever a staunch Anglican. "For my part, Sir, I think all Christians, whether Papists or Protestants, agree in the essential articles, and that their differences are trivial, and rather political than religious." He denies that there is any idolatry in the Roman Mass or worshipping of images or saints. Of course some ignorant Catholics may do these things, but the doctrine is sound enough, and the images are merely supplied as aids to devotion. "I would be a Papist if I could. I have fear enough; but an obstinate rationality prevents me. I shall never be a Papist, unless on the near approach of death, of which I have a very great terrour." Like Hume he is familiar with Tillotson's argument against the Real Presence; if God had never spoken figuratively, we might believe the literal import of Christ's phrase "this is my body," but since God does sometimes speak in clearly figurative language, we cannot say. But there is nothing of Hume's scorn and scurrility on the subject in Johnson, who concedes that "able men, indeed, have *said* they believed it" and who in a sermon hints that Communion is more than a memorial and a "means of grace." Like Hume Johnson opposes religious retreat or monasticism — man is a social being, and in solitude is too often a prey to his emotions and imagination; but again he never falls into the rant of Hume. He likes the idea of purgatory and judges generously Dryden's conversion to Rome: many "men of argument and study" have sincerely converted. On the minor poet Garth's similar conversion, he shrewdly remarks "that there is less distance than is thought between scepticism and popery, and that a mind wearied with perpetual doubt willingly seeks repose in the bosom of an infallible church." He differs from Hume on the crusades, terming them a "noble project." The crusaders have since been "defamed" only because they were unsuccessful. Glossing *1 Henry IV*, he justifies the "lawfulness and justice" of the holy wars — not, however, in the interests of propagating the gospel, but for self-defense, it being the aim of Mahometanism "to extirpate by the sword all other religions."[26]

The distinctions observed by Johnson between the official beliefs and the sometimes debased practices of the Roman Catholics, between the shared doctrines of Catholicism and Protestantism and their *political* differences: these are indispensable to any sophisticated and objective study of religious thought in

---

[26]*Life*, I, 405; III, 188; II, 104–105; IV, 289; V, 71; Sermon IX in *Oxford Works*, IX, 371–75. On spiritual retreat: *Life*, II, 10; V, 61–62; *Letters*, ed. R. W. Chapman (Oxford and London: Clarendon Press, 1952), III, 55; purgatory and Roman Catholicism: *Life*, I, 240; II, 104–105; *Lives of the Poets*, I, 377; II, 63; crusades: *Yale Works*, II, 431; VII, 455.

Johnson's time. But they are distinctions to which Hume seldom stoops in his flights of diatribe and raillery. On Roman Catholicism and the Real Presence Johnson shows a sensitivity that seems quite modern, and certainly moderate, when thrown against Hume's strident, seventeenth-century mockery. Like Hume, Johnson believes in man's social responsibility and so deprecates spiritual retreat. But Hume on the subject can only harangue us about hypocrisy and fanaticism. Johnson's strictures are far more probing psychologically, and he has a compassion for solitaries than one can only *wish* to find in Hume. Credulity and Christian partisanship may have underlain Johnson's defense of the crusades, but a stronger motive, I suspect, was his desire to shock fashionable opinion. Hume's aspersions, then as now, were safer than Johnson's apologies, but Johnson disdained to beat a dead horse.

In the previous chapter I noted Johnson's low opinion of the ability of the poetic imagination to express the sacred. This in itself suggests that he held a high doctrine of the holy, but it also means, if he was consistent in theory and practice, that there is little attempt to evoke the numinous in his own works. That is the case. But from his discursive remarks he seems to be quite orthodox. One essential trait of the Creator is that "he has a power to unmake or annihilate his creature." The "fear of the Lord" is the beginning of wisdom: we should preserve in our minds "a constant apprehension of the Divine presence, and a constant dread of divine displeasure"; we should participate in regular worship and also perform some "particular and unaccustomed acts of devotion." He can even see the wisdom of fasts and other austerities if we are moderate — another contrast with Hume. He shares Hume's mistrust of enthusiasm, defining it in the Dictionary as a "vain belief of private revelation; a vain confidence of divine favour or communication." But he understands the nature and importance of prayer and even allows that a certain amount of "fancy is to be admitted into religious offices," for it is "a faculty bestowed by our Creator, and it is reasonable that all his gifts should be used to his glory." Not for him Hume's intellectualized and ascetic, one might even say,

puritanical, preference for Spartanism. Although he denies
Hume's belief that religion "is best adapted to a gloomy and
melancholy state of mind," he does observe, doubtless thinking
of himself: "There are many good men whose fear of GOD pre-
dominates over their love."[27]

Johnson's fear of death is notorious, and it is often contrasted
invidiously with Hume's calmness. It is sometimes represented
as a sign of latent skepticism: that Johnson feared annihilation.
This cannot be entirely controverted but it seems clear to me
that Johnson feared damnation more than annihilation. Certainly he believed in hell, and reproached as egoistic the notion
that we can know we are saved; it is better to view salvation as
conditional. He was haunted by the parable of the talents, and
continually rebuked himself, in his Prayers and Meditations, for
indolence. He knew that he had been blessed with great gifts,
but did not know if he had employed them well; hence again
his dread of death. He defends belief in an afterlife on several
grounds: the soul must be immaterial since it has qualities
impossible to identify with matter; immortality vindicates
God's justice, since evil often triumphs here.[28] He is hopeful
that friendships may survive after death, though he admits that
neither scripture nor experience sheds much light on this matter. We have seen Pope's smug scorn for such hope, and can
well imagine Hume's. But the intellectuals' hypothesis of an
afterlife, usually an austere and static mystical communion,
may be no more valid or appealing than the vulgar rigmarole of
harps and wings. After all, our relationships are a part of our
personalities, and it is not reasonable, it is not theological, to
assume that we shall be *dehumanized* in the afterlife; *transformed*, yes. I have digressed briefly here for a purpose. Johnson's religious beliefs are sophisticated but very human. He
would not have scorned Hume's peasant with his talk of the
vicissitudes of life, but would have understood him very well.

[27]*Life*, IV, 30; *Oxford Works*, IX, 314–15 (Sermon III); Letters, I, 401;
Oxford Works, IX, 437 (Sermon XVI); *Life*, III, 339.
[28]On salvation: *Life*, IV, 278; on afterlife: *Oxford Works*, IX, 348 (Sermon
VI); 519 (Sermon XXV); *Life*, III, 317.

He was aware of the dangers of superstition and enthusiasm, but recoiled from the pallor of intellectualized religion. We are more than minds. We should fast, we should use our imagination in the worship of God. In his view of devotional exercises, in his hopes for the afterlife, Johnson would hang on to the whole man.

In February 1784 Johnson received a sudden and unexpected relief from dropsy which he seems to have viewed as miraculous and an instance of particular providence; it was accompanied by a profound tranquillity. In a prayer written on 5 December 1784, when he received his last communion, he expostulates: "forgive and accept my late conversion, enforce and accept my imperfect repentance." Contemporary Evangelicals quickly fastened on this curiosity to prove that Johnson had known the instantaneous sanctification so prized by that group, and the debate over what Johnson experienced and meant is still unresolved.[29] I do not think that he was referring to Evangelical conversion, though he found much to admire in Evangelicalism and Methodism. But there *is* evidence that Johnson had doubts, not about God and the afterlife, but about the efficacy of the Atonement, and those doubts may well have contributed to Johnson's rooted and persistent psychic turmoil. That the doubts were finally allayed seems clear. It is certain that he died in resignation and with a belief in personal providence.

If I have any thesis about Johnson, it is simply that he was struggling to preserve a reasonable, but reverent spirit in an age that he saw as increasingly diffident or overtly skeptical. Out of this struggle, it may be, came credulity, but its concomitants were insight, tolerance, and compassion. Johnson wrote in a sermon:

The prevailing spirit of the present age seems to be the spirit of skepticism and captiousness, of suspicion and distrust, a

[29]See Maurice J. Quinlan, *Samuel Johnson: A Layman's Religion* (Madison: Univ. of Wisconsin Press, 1964), 179–94, and Donald J. Greene, "Dr. Johnson's 'Late Conversion' A Reconsideration," in *Johnsonian Studies*, ed. Magdi Wahba (1962).

contempt of all authority, and a presumptuous confidence in private judgment; a dislike of all established forms, merely because they are established, and of old paths, because they are old. . . . The prejudice, to which many of the disorders of the present age, in which infidelity, superstition, and enthusiasm, seem contending for empire over us, may be justly ascribed, is an overfondness for novelty.[30]

Hume represented for Johnson not only the prevailing skeptical and captious spirit but the presumptuous confidence in private judgment. Johnson fulminates, like Hume, against superstition and enthusiasm. But to these Johnson adds a third, infidelity. All of them proceed from the modern, eighteenth-century man's restless and vain desire for change and novelty, his irrational flight from the experience of the past. In this way does Johnson link Hume's own prejudices with those Hume despised, and he reduces them all to the same dead level.

⌑

In 1757, when Hume's *Natural History of Religion* appeared, Johnson published his one protracted piece of dialectical reasoning, the long review of Soame Jenyns's *Free Inquiry into the Nature and Origin of Evil*.[31] The resemblances between the two works — and let us include the *Dialogues*, which Hume had substantially finished by then — are several and curious. Both Hume and Johnson measure theoretical speculation against empirical observation. Both attack dearly held conceptions, Hume the argument from design and the moral superiority of monotheism over polytheism, Johnson the idea of the chain-of-being and the a priori assertion of God's moral attributes. Both address the problem of evil without the routine dissemblings and equivocations, and in general exhibit a rigor of thought sel-

---

[30]*Oxford Works*, IX, 352–53 (Sermon VII).

[31]This review appeared in 1757 in three installments in *The Literary Magazine: or, Universal Review*, 13 (April 15), 171–75; 14 (May 15), 251–53; 15 (June 15), 301–36. All quotations are from this text.

dom achieved by contemporary Christian or deistic writers. Finally, just as Hume undermines Deism, so Johnson blows up a rationalized apologia for Christianity that is little more than clandestine Deism. Much of Jenyns's book is a dilation and dilution of *An Essay on Man*, and Johnson does not scruple to accuse him of a species of plagiarism.

But before examining the review we should note Johnson's long quarrel with *An Essay on Man*. In 1739 a youngish Samuel Johnson translated Crousaz's *Commentary* on Pope's theodicy, to which he appended some ample notes, his first extant exercise in real literary criticism. In these notes, which contrast agreeably with Crousaz's uliginous reflections, he censures Pope's theory of the "ruling passion" — that we are born with certain dispositions of temperament that direct us into different careers and so forth. Johnson opens his attack with empirical objections: people often change their inclinations as they age, and the inclinations themselves are often prompted by fortuitous happenings, "the Circumstances in which [the people] were placed, the objects which they first received Impressions from, the first Books they read, or the first Company they conversed with." Moreover, people do not commonly behave because "of any fix'd or unvaried Principle, but place their highest Felicity sometimes in one Object sometimes in another." Then he brings forth a moral objection: the theory is deterministic, it encourages us to acquiesce in our present humors even when it appears that we should struggle against them. Underlying both Johnson's empirical and moral criticism is this: the theory is presumptuous, too facile and reductive of the mystery of human existence. For that mystery Johnson had a respect, I should say a reverence — one recalls Browne's "the line of our dayes is drawne by night, and the various effects therein by a pencill that is invisible." More than forty years later, at the term and zenith of his career, Johnson renews these strictures in his *Life of Pope*, denouncing the theory of the ruling passion on the same grounds, and much more plainly charging Pope with intellectual arrogance and presumption. *An Essay on Man*, he decides, is a hotchpotch of commonplace notions and highly dubious conjectures. Johnson derides the theory of the chain of being and heaps on Pope an acidulous mixture of ironical praise and open ridicule: "This Essay affords an egregious instance of the predominance of genius, the dazzling splendour of imagery, and the seductive powers of eloquence. Never were penury of knowledge and vulgarity of sentiment so happily disguised."

Jenyns's book offends even more wonderfully than Pope's poem. I have argued earlier that Pope flutters between a high sense of the holy and the calm enticement of rationalism. In the main, Jenyns falls on the rationalistic side and, devoid of Pope's dazzling splendor and seductive powers, is yet more vulnerable. Johnson's review is more than an exquisite butchering of a mediocre book; it is a vehement attack on reductive rationalism expressing principles characteristic of Johnson from his earliest to his last literary criticism: reverence for the mystery of human experience and the holy, a distrust of mere speculation, and contempt for intellectual presumption.

Philosophically the most important part of Johnson's review is his dismantling of the chain of being. A. O. Lovejoy, the supreme modern authority on the concept, considers this critique to be the most profound of the early ones. But we should realise that the conception of the chain of being had been notably elaborated from the time of Browne. In the hands of Pope, Akenside, Jenyns and others it had become, not a pregnant metaphor of universal order and hierarchy illuminating man's unique dualism, but a quasi-scientific theory comprising yet another theory, the doctrine of plenitude. The doctrine of plenitude asserts that God, to exert his full power and fecundity, had perforce to create everything that *could* be created; thus every section of the scale of being is crammed with life, and we have a cosmos of inspissated vitality. This doctrine not only strives to exalt God (from one angle of course it is a hideous notion) but also explains certain evils of imperfection: there *had* to be such a creature as man, for if man were placed higher in the scale, and enjoyed angelic qualities, why then *some other* creature would occupy his place, and so on. Jenyns unreservedly, and as he found indiscreetly, milks the idea to explain all sorts of evil. For example, just as certain animals afford us amusement and,

[242]

to be sure, food, so Jenyns supposes that there may be beings above us "who may deceive, torment, or destroy us for the ends only of their own pleasure or utility." In this manner would Jenyns extenuate human misery.

Johnson's rebuttal is threefold. He argues empirically: observation shows us many apparent gaps in nature, as between man and the next highest animal. He argues philosophically: if the chain of being is a continuum, as the doctrine of plenitude insists, then between any two entities there must be an infinity of other entities. Yet that would make nonsense of any notion of a *chain* or *scale*, and since infinite division is endless division, the whole concept collapses into absurdity and irrelevance. He argues morally: whatever justifications may be contrived for evil as a "universal good," it remains that individuals still feel pain, and the theory that superior beings distract themselves with our agonies, or view them with supine indifference, is totally conjectural, affords us no real consolation, and is in truth a monstrous impiety. In a long but superbly sustained *reductio ad absurdum* Johnson more fully displays that daemonic cosmos which Jenyns, for very different reasons indeed, has let us glimpse. Here is a small part of it:

> As we drown whelps and kittens, they amuse themselves now and then with sinking a ship, and stand round the fields of *Blenheim* or the walls of *Prague*, as we encircle a cock-pit. As we shoot a bird flying, they take a man in the midst of his business or pleasure, and knock him down with an apoplexy. . . . Many a merry bout have these frolic beings at the vicissitudes of an ague, and good sport it is to see a man tumble with an epilepsy, and revive and tumble again, and all this he knows not why. . . . Perhaps now and then a merry being may place himself in such a situation as to enjoy at once all the varieties of an epidemical disease, or amuse his leisure with the tossings and contortions of every possible pain excited together.

Job had been tempted to believe in a creator as evil a responsible for such a universe as this, and only H have imagined a worse. *This* is the madness and bl proceeds, not from religious enthusiasm or superstition, but from "an overfondness for novelty." Jenyns, Johnson observes, hopes by such theories to stand "at the head of a new sect," though in truth he is but "a new example of human folly."

Johnson is no less severe than Hume would have been on Jenyns's ramshackle and zany theology. He ridicules Jenyns when he launches into half-baked theories of his own, like the one just mentioned, and he catches him out in tautological reasoning, as when he presupposes what later he tries to demonstrate: God's moral attributes. But he does praise Jenyns from time to time: when Jenyns concedes, for example, that we should not presume to ask God to explain himself, when he argues that our dread of death should be overcome by our hopes for the afterlife, when he insists that ethics must be complemented by religious faith. When Jenyns rather complacently admonishes us to choose those actions that promote our own and our fellows' happiness — also a favorite theme of Hume's, as we have seen — Johnson reflects: "it is not possible in many cases for most men . . . to determine what actions will ultimately produce happiness, and therefore it was proper that *Revelation* should lay down a rule to be followed invariably in opposition to appearances, and in every change of circumstances, by which we may be certain to promote the general felicity, and be set free from the dangerous temptation of *doing evil that good may come.*" Here is the same restless discontent with facile moral nostrums to which is owed his despisal of the ruling passion. Repeatedly he chides Jenyns (and he might have been thinking of Pope or Hume) for his eagerness "without any distrust of himself to tell us what has been hid from all former enquirers." Or again: "When this author presumes to speak of the universe, I would advise him a little to distrust his own faculties." Such presumption is not only unwarranted in fallible mankind, but renders disservice to the Deity: "Surely a man who seems not completely master of his own opinion, should have spoken more cautiously of omnipotence, nor have presumed to say what it could perform, or what it could prevent." Jenyns's theories are in fact "dogmatical limitations of omnipotence . . . [which] encourage impious presumption, or stimulate idle curiosity." In endeavoring to exalt God through the chain of being and the doctrine of plenitude, Jenyns is in fact bemeaning God; and he offends more than Job, for Job had only asked God for justification, but Jenyns officiously provides it *for* God. Not only are his conjectures fragile and foolish, but in their presumption and novelty they are apt to drop into sacrilege and daemonism.

Jenyns is not a total rationalist. He concedes that the evidences of Christianity "are not irresistible, because it was intended to induce, not to compel, and that it is obscure, because we want faculties to comprehend it," and he admits that religion has been corrupted by human wickedness. Johnson agrees: "All this is known, and all this is true, but why, we have not yet discovered":

> Thus, after having clambered with great labour from one step of argumentation to another, instead of rising into the light of knowledge, we are devolved back into dark ignorance, and all our effort ends in belief that for the evils of life there is some good reason, and in confession, that the reason cannot be found.

And so Johnson leaves us with this echo, distant and merely figurative, of the doctrine he has derided, the chain of being and man's queasy place on it. But the steps lead us nowhere, and man, for Pope "darkly wise," remains in dark ignorance. Yet this much Johnson is prepared to say, defending the prerogatives of the holy against the incursions of mortal impudence: "the magnificence of the universe adds nothing to the supreme Being. . . . and of happiness it does not appear that any is communicated from the Beings of a lower world to those of a higher."[32] But Jenyns, cheerily unmoved by anything Johnson

---

[32]At the end of his *Great Chain of Being* A. O. Lovejoy, lapsing into whig criticism and affirming his belief in an arbitrary and contingent universe — a belief he apparently thinks all moderns must share — calls Johnson to his support, citing his attack on the static concept of the chain of being. But Johnson was a staunch upholder of hierarchies. He attacks a rationalistic and presumptuous reformulation of the concept, but is not therefore to be enlisted in cause of modern existentialism. Johnson's thought, like Hume's, is high ceptible to over-simplifying.

has said, dismisses his demolition of the chain of being as "no more than a quibble on metaphysical terms," and observes of the devastating *reductio ad absurdum* that it is just like the reaction of a narrow-minded peasant, who stubbornly refuses to credit something because he cannot see it.[33] Such is the fate shared by Johnson with Hume: so deft is their iconoclasm, so penetrating their criticism of received opinions, that the dullards want even the wit to be embarrassed.

¤

Johnson's best known imaginative works are *The Vanity of Human Wishes* (1749) and *Rasselas* (1759). Both address similar themes: the inadequacy of human pleasures to satisfy our deeper needs. *Vanity*, modeled on Juvenal's tenth satire, is an inventory of various occupations or states of being, showing in each case their inability to yield happiness. Johnson's poem is appreciably more melancholy than Juvenal's, however, stressing from the start the pathos of the human condition and the daemonic impulsions of man. Life is a "Maze of Fate" of which, unlike Pope's "mighty maze," the plan is very indistinct. Man is wavering, betrayed by pride, treading dreary paths, pursuing happiness as "treach'rous Phantoms in the Mist": "How rarely Reason guides the stubborn Choice, / Rules the bold Hand, or prompts the suppliant Voice." Images of attack, invasion, subversion, prevail: fears invade (41); sickness invades (283–84), predatory "Time hovers o'er, impatient to destroy" (259). Man is doubly victimized: by such external threats as old age, disease, detraction, and by his own mental deception and delusion. Having enforced the vanity of seeking happiness in external things, Johnson offers one alternative to succumbing beast-like to one's fate:

> Petitions yet remain,
> Which Heav'n may hear, nor deem Religion vain.

[33]Soame Jenyns, *Works* (London, 1790), III, 7, 9.

Still raise for Good the supplicating Voice,
But leave to Heav'n the Measure and the Choice.
Safe in his Pow'r, whose Eyes discern afar
The secret Ambush of a specious Pray'r.
Implore his Aid, in his Decisions rest,
Secure whate'er he gives, he gives the best.

(349–56)

We should pray for mental tranquillity, controlled emotions, a resigned will; for love, patience and faith: "With these celestial Wisdom calms the Mind, / And makes the Happiness she does not find." So Johnson concludes.

And the conclusion is not unexpected. But the power of the poem stems rather from the treatment of the theme than the novelty of the sentiment. A comparison with the fourth epistle of *An Essay on Man* will help to illustrate this power and also cast further light on Johnson's distaste for that poem and for the mentality lurking behind it. Pope's fourth epistle is on a similar subject: he descants on the sources of happiness, gives some specimens of false sources (martial power, fame, and so on), concludes that it is found in an internal quality, Virtue. Although both poems are in the same meter and form, the tone could scarcely be more different. Compare with Johnson's terminal couplet, quoted above, Pope's description of happiness: "Fix'd to no spot is Happiness sincere; / 'Tis no where to be found, or ev'ry where; / 'Tis never to be bought, but always free" (IV, 15–17). Or consider these: "Take *Nature*'s path, and mad Opinion's leave, / All states can reach it [happiness], and all Heads conceive" (29–30); "Heav'n breathes thro' ev'ry member of the whole / One common Blessing [happiness], as one common Soul" (61–62); "See! the sole Bliss [happiness] Heav'n could on *all* bestow, / Which who but feels, can taste, but thinks, can know" (327–28). Pope's style and rhetoric make it seem simple to be happy — if only we knew so much as Pope. Happiness is everywhere, free, easy of access, rather like air; let us just take a deep breath. Let us just "take Nature's path," which is rather like advising a confused adolescent seeking an identity to "be himself."

[247]

But the point of *Vanity* is that happiness is not easy of access: human nature is too involuted, too prone to self-deception. What mortal can claim to be immune from the blandishments of fortune? Not Pope, surely! Even at our devotions we are vulnerable, "ambushed" by some pious-sounding but self-serving supplication. We are allowed no vacant, suasive formulas. To be sure, we are urged to trust to God, to believe that whatever he gives "he gives the best." But there is more than merely a verbal distinction between this and Pope's "Whatever is, is right!" The second has the triumphal ring of theodicy, the first puts it as a matter of faith, the substance of things *hoped* for. Note too the difference in Pope's attitude as it filters through his poem. When some malcontent objects in the fourth epistle that virtue sometimes starves "while Vice is fed," Pope responds a shade contemptuously: "What then? is the reward of Virtue, Bread?" (149–50). Inevitably Johnson would agree: No, it is not. Nevertheless, one could use a bit more compassion in Pope's reply and in his frothy dismissal of all those material evils we are to transcend. Johnson remarks in his review of Jenyns: "This author and *Pope* perhaps never saw the miseries which they imagine thus easy to be born." Defending God's reluctance to suspend his universal laws for individuals, Pope chides: "Think we like some weak Prince th' Eternal Cause, / Prone for his Fav'rites to reverse his Laws?" (121–22). After a moving enumeration of the miseries endured by a young scholar, Johnson advises him that even if he escapes disease and melancholy "Yet hope not Life from Grief or Danger free, / Nor think the Doom of Man revers'd for thee" (155–56). The point is similar, but in Johnson there is no appeal to abstractions, universal laws or an eternal cause; there is no contemptuous comparison with weak princes and favorites. There is only that weightiest of human experiences, the doom of man, which needs no analogies or abstractions. Even for someone so foolish as to fancy himself exempt Johnson has, not disdain, but compassion.

Pope — or at least the persona he projects in the poem, for he himself suffered great physical pain — seems far less sensitive than Johnson to the ultimate mystery and tragedy of life and its

Dionysian compulsions. Pope's deity is a contrivance of the intellect limited by those very laws he created; Pope's universe is a "mighty maze, but not without a plan"; Pope's typical stubborn man is a kind of fool or child who, if he will but comprehend the general pattern, can achieve happiness. Johnson's deity is personal (he can discern our specious prayers), but otherwise shadowy and reticent; Johnson's universe is a maze of fate, a bog, a mist, sometimes almost the infernal cosmos parodied in the Jenyns review, in which human beings, obsessed with love of money, fame, power, beauty, academic prestige, grope blindly and pathetically, their only hope lying, not in intellectual comprehension, but in humble prayer. Although the poem is in one way more formal than Pope's, with its heavier freight of abstractions and Latinisms, its taught and elliptical syntax, yet it seems to have more feeling. Johnson does not sequester himself from his suffering humanity — here is the disadvantage of Pope's Apollonian detachment — but avoids equally the cheap sentimentality of fifth-rate devotional poets and the perhaps equally easy intellectualism of *An Essay on Man*. His poem is not so quotable or aphoristic as Pope's, and rightly so; for there are some subjects upon which quotability is not to be reckoned a virtue. Not only is Johnson more aware of the irrationality of humankind and the impermanence of happiness, he is also the better empiricist. In reading *Vanity* one feels that Johnson has indeed "seen the miseries" under which, just like Pope, he urges us to be patient. I should also like to note the difference between Johnson and Akenside, Thomson, and Young, all three of whose major works reached their essential form just a few years before *Vanity*. These poets, like Pope, swing between intellectual argument and enthusiastic rhapsody or terror. But there is neither theodicy nor rhapsody nor terror in Johnson's poem — though there may be an implicit horror, always well controlled. As an empiricist he begins by showing the physical and psychological poverty of the human condition; as a devout empiricist he proposes the religious remedy, but with little theologizing and no tincture of enthusiasm. It is the method of Pascal, and it is one of the reasons why this poem, unlike the other philosophical-religious poems of the time, has continued to engage skeptics and Christians alike. The former may respect Johnson's insight, compassion, and candor. The latter will not be frustrated by theoretical constructions that have since been defecated or by crescendos of rhetoric that seem too naive or gross for our intricate and hesitant age.

◻

Loosely paraphrased, *Rasselas*, written just a decade later, seems to argue a similar theme. As the tale is more developed than the poem, it is not so dense. The nightmare maze of *Vanity* gives way to a greyer realm, no more happy or less foolish, but less compulsive and actively hostile. Set in Abyssinia and Egypt, *Rasselas*, like the other European Oriental tales, is rather a string of philosophical reflections than a story, and certainly the didactic element preponderates over narrative and characterization. The work has been compared with those novels of self-discovery or quest so popular in the last two centuries, but the resemblances are remote. Johnson's characters are endowed with too little psychology to make it a convincing novel of self-discovery, and though they are indeed on a quest, we know from the start that their quest is futile; they return at the end to the Happy Valley whence they fled to see the world. The world they have seen, learnt to be content with their lot (though in their imaginations they are still excogitating grandiose schemes — such is the persistence of that faculty), and so they malinger along into the final chapter, aptly titled "the conclusion, in which nothing is concluded."

Rasselas is better compared to an allegory such as *The Pilgrim's Progress*, one of Johnson's favorite works. As in *Rasselas*, the end of the quest is always known; as there, the characters are inalterable types; as there, the episodes are governed, not by realism, but by the moral intent of the author. But *Rasselas* was written some eighty years after the first part of *Pilgrim's Progress*, and the differences between the works tell us much about Johnson's age. In *Rasselas* the quest is couched in terms of happiness, not salvation, though mere hedonism is one of the first of its forms to be discarded. Rasselas notes in chapter two that animals live from moment to moment in apparent contentment, but that man is perpetually restless, longing to renew fatigued pleasures, and he reflects: "I can discover within me no power of perception which is not glutted with its proper pleasure, yet I do not feel myself delighted. Man has surely some latent sense for which this place affords no gratification, or he has some desires distinct from sense which must be satisfied before he can be happy." Many chapters later the great pyramid is shown to be the most awesome yet most disheartening symptom of this restless craving; it is "a monument of the insufficiency of human enjoyments." Pascal and Young, among many others, had drawn out the spiritual implications of this condition, but Johnson approaches the matter from the empirical or psychological angle, and there is nothing of Bunyan's explicit Christianity.

Then too, the structure of *Pilgrim's Progress* is linear, moving from the City of Destruction to the New Jerusalem. That of *Rasselas* is circular and confined by the secular world. The pilgrims in Johnson's tale, like blundering mankind in *Vanity*, must learn to seek a psychological state rather than a place. As the sagacious Imlac observes, "long journeys in search of truth are not commanded." The elusiveness of happiness is exacerbated by the "hunger of the imagination." This is exemplified by the semi-comic aeronaut in chapter six, of whom Rasselas remarks "your imagination prevails over your skill"; by the wise Imlac himself, who warming to his dissertation on the education and qualifications of a poet, falls into an "enthusiastic fit" and goes on to "aggrandize his own profession" (Ch. XI); by the stoic who fondly imagines that he is immune from human suffering (Ch. XVIII); but chiefly by the mad astronomer. Like Swift in *A Tale of a Tub*, Johnson here adumbrates the gradual usurpation of the reason by the fancy or imagination, and although his treatment is less colorful, perhaps, certainly less farcical and grotesque than Swift's, yet it is more subtle and compassionate. The astronomer is truly a man of genius; he also

[251]

has the social graces, and wears an appearance of sanity on most subjects. Slow was the progress of his infatuation that he could control the weather, and even at his most alienated he feels how outlandish his belief must seem to others. Having retreated from society, he is specially prey to this fantasy, and his cure lies in enticing him back into society, where by comparing his judgments with those of others, he is able to rectify the vagaries of his imagination. The astronomer's malady is a symptom of religious melancholy, and as such similar to that disparaged by Swift and Hume; but Johnson's sensitive development of his character blunts any satiric effect and highlights rather the pathos and potential tragedy of such daemonic obsession:

> "Ladies, said Imlac, to mock the heaviest of human afflictions is neither charitable nor wise. Few can attain this man's knowledge, and few practise his virtues; but all may suffer his calamity. Of the uncertainties of our present state, the most dreadful and alarming is the uncertain continuance of reason" (Ch. XLIII).

Restored to sanity, the mad astronomer confesses that his reason had been "subjugated by an uncontrolable and overwhelming idea." He has as it were, and by chance, yielded to a ruling passion that deprives his reason of its autonomy and fosters mental and social anarchy. This is Johnson's most illuminating, though implicit, attack on Pope's theory, showing that such obsessions are not implanted by nature, but engross one through fortuitous associations and through solitude, and that on the whole they are not constructive, but erode free will. In fairness to Pope, however, we must recall that his Eloisa is a more violent and theatrical embodiment of a similarly obsessive "idea." But what Pope dramatizes with detachment, and Swift and Hume savagely mock, Johnson lights up in its interiority and probes with a strangely modern dexterity.[34]

---

[34]Johnson's whole treatment is very similar to Burton's in *The Anatomy of Melancholy* (III, 4, Memb. 1, Subs. 2–5, and Memb. 2, Subs. 6), who recognizes that madmen may appear sane on most subjects, that solitude often aggravates

Inevitably *Rasselas* has been compared with *Candide*, published the same year but unavailable to Johnson before he finished his work. Both are oriental tales exhibiting the reticence of happiness and concluding on a note of resignation. As for the men themselves: both Voltaire and Johnson detested *An Essay on Man* (though in his salad days Voltaire had admired it); both had a keen sense of evil and an equally keen contempt for those who endeavored to excuse it or who generally pursued abstruse, metaphysical speculation — Voltaire had even, in his Philosophical Dictionary, attacked the notion of the *Chaine des Êtres Créés* in a more casual, but not a more sarcastic, vein than Johnson. But I believe that such critics as Joseph Wood Krutch go astray when they find that the tales enforce the same lesson. Krutch argues that the discussion of eternity in the penultimate chapter of *Rasselas* is merely Johnson's offering "to orthodoxy, as he always does, the tribute of formal profession," and that the "effective" (i.e., "real") moral, as distinguished from the "formal" moral, is the same as that of *Candide*.[35] Krutch's "effective" moral is that distilled by abstract paraphrase, perhaps, but it evaporates out the flavor of the book, which like *Vanity of Human Wishes* and the Jenyns review proclaims the necessary humility of man in face of the mystery of life. The final chapters of the two books, of which Krutch makes so much, are indeed similar, but it is a little odd that Johnson's penultimate chapter, if it is merely a routine tribute, should be more than thrice the length of the last. Voltaire's book is certainly a pungent if unphilosophical attack on Popean optimism; but it is much more than that, for as Boswell, Hume, and other contem-

madness, and that good counsel from friends will often overcome self-conceit and free the soul from its obsession; the book was a favorite of Johnson's. Thomas Gordon, *The Humourist* (London, 1724) tells the story of a mathematics professor who fancied his whiskers were emblems of virility. "In every other Respect our Physician was a well-bred Person, and which is as wonderful, *understood Latin*. But we see the *deepest Learning* is no Charm against the Spleen" (14).

[35]J. W. Krutch, *Samuel Johnson* (New York and Burlingame: Harcourt, Brace and World, 1963), 182–83.

poraries noticed, it is actually a satire on the belief in provi-dence.[36] In Johnson's terms, it attacks superstition and enthusi-asm but promotes infidelity. Moreover, the deistic and dispassionate ethical religion of El Dorado, of which Voltaire seems to approve and which may have been inspired by Swift's Houyhnhnms, is quite at odds with Johnson's own views and the implied values of *Rasselas*. Actually, the strongest thematic similarity is where Martin, who like Imlac has seen the world, tries to persuade Candide that there is very little happiness in it, and that even those who appear happy probably are not (*Candide*, XXIV; *Rasselas*, XVI). But bating occasional resemblances, the two works are quite dissimilar and reflect very different sides of the latter eighteenth century. Despite their disagree-ments, Voltaire and Pope remain temperamentally close, and *Candide*, sprightly and facile, is to *Rasselas* as *An Essay on Man* to the *Vanity of Human Wishes*.

Rasselas is the capital expression of Johnson's most character-istic thoughts. Originally to be entitled "The Choice of Life," it shows that "Very few . . . live by choice. Every man is placed in his present condition by causes which acted without his fore-sight, and with which he did not always willingly co-operate"(XVI). Philosophers encouraging us to live according to "reason" or "nature" would plaster over the realities of life with artful verbiage (XVIII, XXII). There is no ruling passion to motivate us, no rationalism to tutor us, no speculation to ensure our happiness. Work can bring pleasure, or at least an evanes-cent oblivion of discontent. Change, novelty, imaginative dwell-ing in the future or the past affords harmless escape and relief. On this theme Johnson is peculiarly Pascalian: "The truth is, that no mind is much employed upon the present: recollection and anticipation fill up almost all our moments" (XXX). "Such

---

[36]See Boswell, *Life*, I, 342; Hume, *New Letters*, ed. Raymond Klibansky and Ernest C. Mossner (Oxford: Oxford Univ. Press, 1954), 53: *Candide* "is full of Sprightliness & Impiety, & is indeed a Satyre upon Providence, under Pretext of criticizing the Leibnitian System." See also *Monthly Review*, 21 (1759), 84; *Critical Review*, 7 (1759), 550.

. . . is the state of life, that none are happy but by the anticipation of change: the change itself is nothing; when we have made it, the next wish is to change again" (XLVII). Like Pascal, he but exhibits this restlessness and leaves us to find the solution. That there is a solution we may be sure, but Johnson would only impress on us our ignorance and impotence. This pious empiricism is seen in Imlac's opinion on ghosts, which narrowly matches Johnson's own stated belief; its opening sentence, in fact, resembles Johnson's opening remarks on witchcraft cited earlier, where he speaks of its acceptance by people "rude and civilized" alike:

> There is no people, rude or learned, among whom apparitions of the dead are not related and believed. This opinion, which, perhaps, prevails as far as human nature is diffused, could become universal only by its truth: those, that never heard of one another, would not have agreed in a tale which nothing but experience can make credible. That it is doubted by single cavillers can very little weaken the general evidence, and some who deny it with their tongues confess it by their fears (XXXI).

The penultimate chapter to which I have already referred — usually passed over hastily by critics and mere readers — is occupied by Imlac's lengthy discourse "on the nature of the soul." This is one of the very few occasions when Johnson, in his printed works, touches on such a subject, and his mode of argument (I see no reason not to associate him with Imlac here) is most interesting.[37] The account is strictly philosophical: there is no invoking of revelation, no homily to the effect that the miseries of this life point to a celestial recompense. It is in fact an attempted rebuttal of that materialism circulating much more forcibly in France than in England, but with which Hume, as a form of immanentism, toys in his *Dialogues*. According to Imlac, "all the conclusions of reason enforce the immateriality

---

[37]Gwin J. Kolb discusses the intellectual background of this chapter in *Philological Quarterly*, 54, (1975), 357–69.

of mind, and all the notices of sense and investigations of science concur to prove the unconsciousness of matter." Of course materialists will contend that matter may have qualities unknown to us, including consciousness. But Imlac replies:

> "He who will determine ... against that which he knows, because there may be something which he knows not, he that can set hypothetical possibility against acknowledged certainty, is not to be admitted among reasonable beings. All that we know of matter is, that matter is inert, senseless and lifeless; and if this conviction cannot be opposed but by referring us to something that we know not, we have all the evidence that human intellect can admit. If that which is known may be over ruled by that which is unknown, no being, not omniscient, can arrive at certainty."

Here again is the reverent empiricism. It is then objected that Imlac may be limiting (like Jenyns) God's power; but Imlac responds that this is simply the ineluctable constraint of non-contradiction. Someone else contends that immateriality, even if granted, does not prove duration. Imlac concedes that our notions of immateriality are obscure, but argues that "Immateriality seems to imply a natural power of perpetual duration as a consequence of exemption from all causes of decay: whatever perishes, is destroyed by the solution of its contexture, and separation of its parts; nor can we conceive how that which has no parts, and therefore admits no solution, can be naturally corrupted or impaired." As its creator, God might of course annihilate the soul whenever he wished; however, "philosophy" shows that it cannot perish "by any inherent cause of decay, or principle of corruption." The group then decide, understandably, to think less on a choice of life and more on the choice of eternity.

This chapter is no furibund assault on free thought, but neither is it trite, or a mere fillup to orthodoxy. Had Johnson wished to propitiate that not always very discriminating goddess he might have expatiated, like Thomson, on the order and majesty of nature, like Young on the magnificence of the heavens, like Akenside or Pope on the fecundity of the First Cause. The chapter is, I think, deliberately arid and sober. Sense experience informs us that matter is unconscious; reason shows us that mind is immaterial. Materialists who identify mind with matter are speculatists asking us to accept their hypotheses in defiance of reason, of empirical observation, of intuition. I am not of course suggesting that Johnson's case is impervious to objection or that no assumptions underlie it. Some of the same arguments might be employed in behalf of the immortal souls of beasts, for example, which plunges us into chilly theological waters. But I *am* suggesting that it is consistent with the principles running throughout Johnson's thought: empirical, logical, mistrustful of speculation, but, withal, inclined toward the orthodox view. Throughout *Rasselas* Johnson has shown us the unsatisfactory nature of temporal pleasure. He has shown us that, psychologically, man seems made for another world. At the end he has given us non-biblical grounds for supposing that the cerebral part of us will not, indeed, perish with that body which we so incessantly endeavor to satisfy and sustain. This is no coaxing or wheedling of orthodoxy; but to have gone further would have been unduly to parochialize the lesson. Pope had inveighed against intellectual presumption in *An Essay on Man* but, in Johnson's view, had tumbled into it himself in his theological and metaphysical speculation. Having excoriated Jenyns two years before *Rasselas* for doing the same, Johnson was doubtless on guard against it himself. Hence the "conclusion, in which nothing is concluded."

No man can evade the tincture of his age, but some men are less conspicuously, less slavishly, *of* their age. Both Hume and Johnson could be inveterate ax-grinders, but they could also see through all the varieties of contemporary speculation. In both men there is even a reticence of assertion and resilience of thought. Both shared the general dislike of their age for enthusiasm, and neither could give himself to the fashionable moods pandered to by the mid-century poets. The Deism of Akenside and Thomson, compared with Hume's Theism, is glaring and amateur; Johnson returns to a sterner, tougher Pascal than

[257]

Young's. They are both superb craftsmen, masters of ironical and sinewy prose, and they never lose sight of the most imperative questions. I consider them to be the finest, strongest, yet least cluttered minds of eighteenth-century Britain — I do not say the most creative. Carlyle's characterizations of the two are sound, but the character of Johnson is especially apt: reverence, love, devout humility. The first and the last of these are seen in Johnson's refusal to simplify existence through the formulas of rationalism. And as for the middle term: the contempt of Pope, Swift, and Hume yields in Johnson to an unsentimental solicitude for man and a truly modern sense of the daemons that infest him. Reactionary in some of his views, Johnson had the one insight of modernism that is genuinely an enlargement of classical wisdom: that we are all of us in some measure alienated in mind, that we should compassionate our brothers even as we seek the truth. In this, Pope, Swift, and Hume, with their bracing indignation and scorn, are back with Aristophanes.

CHAPTER VII

Spiritual Horror in the
Novel: Richardson, Radcliffe,
Beckford, Lewis

In thoughts from the visions of the night, when deep sleep falleth upon
men, fear came upon me and trembling, which made all of my bones to
shake. Then a spirit passed before my face. The hair of my flesh stood
up. It stood still . . . an image was before mine eyes; there was silence;
and I heard a voice.

Job

If, when the Spirit of God passed before the face of Job [actually
Eliphaz], the hairs of his flesh stood up, might one not, ran the
argument, by raising the hair induce the vision?

J. M. S. TOMPKINS

PLENARY STUDIES of the Gothic novel get off to a
very lame start with an obligatory inspection of *The Castle of
Otranto*, published on Christmas Eve, 1764, and written by that
elsewhere very lively antiquary and epistolist Horace Walpole.
Such studies then try to explain the great popularity of that
uncommonly silly book by discovering that it was a long-
yearned-for reaction against arid and passionless neo-classicism.
Thus, even the best of the studies wind up contrasting the
Gothic writers with the earlier "Augustans" who "dared not
step outside the sparkling life of their trim and brilliant salons."
That timid and unrobust culture, we are also told, was dominated "in all essentials . . . by a strict concept of reason, that
banished the emotional aura of religion and reduced the Deity
to a clockwork Prime Mover of the Universe."[1]

[1]Devendra P. Varma, *The Gothic Flame* (1957; rpt. New York: Russell and
Russell, 1966), 23, 209, 210. Older standard studies are: Edith Birkhead, *The*

[259]

Richardson, Radcliffe, Beckford, Lewis

I have no wish to iterate what I have perhaps already too wearisomely urged — but I shall do so briefly. Many inventive and influential writers of the earlier period resisted the rationalizing of religion: Pascal, Glanvill, Dryden, Defoe. The taste for spectral narratives flourished in the late seventeenth, early eighteenth centuries; and in the 1720s Defoe, always on the watch for a good thing, voluminously gratified such taste. In the 1720s, too, Anthony Blackwall was finding religious awe and terror in the Holy Scriptures, and Thomson was writing the most terror-filled of his seasons, *Winter* and *Summer*. Pope had popped out of his trim salon as early as 1717 to give us the daemonic *Eloisa*, fully decorated with Gothic paraphernalia; and *A Tale of a Tub* was written when Swift had hardly got *into* a salon. Of course a writer such as Hume deplored all this and, intellectual that he was, ridiculed appeals to terror as antiquated just when *The Castle of Otranto* was about to be a gleam in its creator's eye. But Walpole — unfortunately perhaps — was much closer to the spirit of the age than was Hume.

At their best, the Gothic novels communicate a sense of the numinous, usually in its daemonic phase, though even the best of them have a penchant for sensationalism and shudder-for-shudder's-sake. Scholars have made much of their Continental sources, but the native element is strong and traces back to Shakespeare and the Jacobean dramatists. The novels catered for a need that had been met, between the Jacobean and Georgian eras, in a covert and truncated way by the Glanvillean anthologies and later, more genteelly, by poems such as those of Akenside, Blair, and Thomson. But the novels show a further abandonment of theological scaffolding, a tendency noted in earlier chapters. Their emphasis is commonly on the story and its effect, denuded of Glanvillean apologetics and, in large measure, the didacticism of the mid-century poets. The aesthetics of terror and awe elaborated by Dennis and Watts prepared the way

Tale of Terror (London: Constable, 1921); Eino Railo, *The Haunted Castle* (London: George Routledge, 1927), Montague Summers, *The Gothic Quest* (London: Fortune Press, 1938); J. M. S. Tompkins, *The Popular Novel in England, 1770–1800* (1932; rpt. Lincoln: Univ. of Nebraska Press, 1961), Chs. 6 and 7.

for these novels, or perhaps one should say, they diffused religious sanction for the moods indulged. But by the time that the novels reach their ascendancy, such pious hedging-about or shoring-up was apparently dispensable.

The aesthetics of the mid and late century did, however, attempt explanations for the form, even justifications, though both are couched more often in psychological than in religious terms. For example, Burke's important essay on the sublime, appearing in the late 1750s, develops a psychological aesthetics of horror: the very excitation of our minds, even by the horrible, yields pleasure. Richard Hurd's *Letters on Chivalry and Romance* (1762) furnishes an intelligent if often qualified defense of terrible and supernatural themes in literature, and I have discussed elsewhere James Usher's even more unabashed apology for terror in 1767. Hurd, still very much a classicist, stresses the aesthetic (or as he puts it, the "poetical") value of exciting such feelings, while Usher pitches his argument along avowedly religious, but still very psychological, lines. In 1773 Anna Laetitia Aikin expressly applies Burkean theory to the novels: "they ventilate the mind by sudden gusts of passion; and prevent the stagnation of thought by a fresh infusion of dissimilar ideas"; such tales stimulate our imagination, excite and gratify our curiosity, and give us the pleasure of contemplating new and prodigious objects. In the same year Sir William Chambers, the celebrated architect and orientalist — and tutor to William Beckford — advises that rude stretches of country, not amenable to beautification, "may easily be framed into scenes of terror, converted into noble pictures of sublimest cast," and hence capable of arousing strong, presumably pleasant, sensations in the spectator. And if the pious intentions of Watts or Dennis may seem to have been shuffled away, yet by the end of the century, at the very zenith of the Gothic novel, supernatural horror is lauded for promoting religious awe, the "sacred effects of holy fear."[2]

[2]See: J. and A. L. Aikin, *Miscellaneous Pieces, in Prose* (1773), 45–46, 123, 126; William Chambers, *Dissertation on Oriental Gardening* (1773), 130–31; Courtney Melmoth, *Family Secrets* (1797), quoted in J. M. S. Tompkins, *The Popular Novel*, 221.

Now my subject here is not, precisely, the Gothic novel; neither *Clarissa* nor *Vathek* can be so described. My concern is *spiritual horror* in the novel, a phrase at once more comprehensive, yet more to the point. To have spiritual horror, a work must be set in a supranatural or transcendent context integral to theme and characterization; overt supernaturalism is not strictly required, but often present. Fielding's *Tom Jones* is set in a Christian and providential universe, but the supranatural potentialities are not brought into play in such a manner as to produce spiritual horror; in *Clarissa* they are, though like Fielding's novel it lacks overt supernaturalism. It is now customary, by the way, among critics to distinguish between horror and terror. Terror, they say, fetches its power from evil that is obscure and only insinuated, horror from its blatant, even crude, manifestations. But neither Burke nor other eighteenth-century aestheticians draw such fine distinctions; and anyway the Latin *horrere*, which means "to bristle or to make the hairs stand on end from fear," compasses both the subtler and the grosser effects. So I shall stick to "spiritual horror," using "Gothic" to refer to the special ingredients or conventions employed in *some* novels aiming at spiritual horror. The novels I consider here also have at least one, possibly more, daemonic characters. Such characters are often, though by no means inevitably, evil, nor are all evil characters daemonic: Blifil in *Tom Jones* may be despicable, but he is not daemonic. In *Dichtung und Wahrheit* Goethe describes the type succinctly:

This daemonic character appears in its most *dreadful* form when it stands out dominatingly in some *man*. Such are not always the most remarkable men ... and they seldom have any goodness of heart to recommend them. But an incredible force goes forth from them and they exercise an incredible power over all creatures, nay, perhaps even over the elements. And who can say how far such an influence may not extend?[3]

---

[3]Goethe quoted in Otto, *Idea of the Holy*, 152.

Richardson, Radcliffe, Beckford, Lewis

I shall be centering on Richardson's *Clarissa*, not a Gothic novel but a spectacular if leisurely exercise in spiritual horror; on Radcliffe's *Italian*, a Richardsonian novel with all the Gothic trappings; on Beckford's *Vathek*, an oriental horror tale; on Lewis's *Monk*, the most exultantly lurid and full-blown example of the general type. But, like all the other scholars of the subject, I feel I must first take up *Otranto*. And while I am about it I should also like to look at a much later, but equally abortive and even more tedious specimen, Godwin's *St. Leon*. My reasons for this preluding digression will, I hope, become apparent.

⌑

The Castle of Otranto introduced into English literature the peculiar accouterments of Gothicism: the mysterious castle, the European and antique setting, the dungeons and ghosts, the ponderous tyrant and the oppressed innocents, the play of irregular and illicit passion. But the novel itself, for all its Gothicism, can scarcely be considered to produce spiritual horror. To be sure, that is a subjective feeling, and some contemporary criticism implies that people shuddered at it spontaneously and not out of complicity with fashion. At the same time, the *Monthly Review* denounces its civilized author "for re-establishing the barbarous superstitions of Gothic devilism. *Incredulus odi* is, or ought to be a charm against all such infatuation."[4] Surely an *incredulus odi* came as easily to a sophisticated eighteenth-century reader as to a modern one; its immediate popularity is due to its superficial novelty and an incongruous amenity of style. The supernatural effects are too perfunctory and devoid of atmosphere. The gigantic spectre of Alfonso distributing its gear and limbs about the castle, and at length shattering that mighty edifice, encroaches more on the ludicrous than on the sublime. The skeletal hermit that rebukes one of the erring characters conveys far less uncanny terror than, say, Crusoe's avenging

---

[4] *Monthly Review*, 32 (May 1765), 394.

[263]

angel forty-five years before. Manfred himself is no daemonic personality, but a domestic tyrant who merely rants and blusters and who, after a mechanical repentance at the end, has not even the strength of character to die. The *other* Manfred, Byron's in the play of that title, is perhaps the finest embodiment of the daemonic man: a complicated and aristocratic soul who would have had nothing but disdain for this petty and cowardly namesake. The novel appeals frequently to providence and the divine will, but with far less conviction and, I daresay, sincerity, than *Robinson Crusoe*. The work does, indeed, have a surrealistic quality in the dream-like sequence of its plot, the grotesque imagery of the enormous helmet, and so forth; this will give it some slight interest, perhaps, for the modern reader with his modish liking for the abnormal. It was, of course, a pioneering work, but seldom has a pioneer been more flaccid. Walpole might have learned something to his purpose from Defoe or Richardson, but he despised both writers as low-brow. *Otranto* can still be read — I do not say it is *readable* — only because it is short; had it been published thirty years later it might have been considered a parody, rather than the parent, of this interesting genre.

In 1799, a full generation after *Otranto*, the philosophical radical William Godwin published *St. Leon: a Tale of the Sixteenth Century*. Godwin's plot and theme was suggested to him by John Campbell's *Hermippus Redivivus* (1743), praised by Samuel Johnson as "very entertaining, as an account of the Hermetick philosophy." After a chain of misfortunes, a young French nobleman, St. Leon, meets a stranger with vaguely daemonic qualities: his voice is like sublime thunder; his "eyebeam sat upon your countenance, and seemed to look through you." But in his secretive fussiness and irascibility he is really more like the mad astronomer in *Rasselas;* he is like him, too, in his vaunted abilities: "The talent he possessed was one, upon which the fate of nations and of the human species might be made to depend. God had given it for the best and highest purposes. . . . It might overturn kingdoms." If only Rasselas's sister had been there to socialize him out of this obsession! But of

[264]

course he *does* have powers: to manufacture gold and to achieve corporeal immortality; and he passes on the secret of the *elixer vitae* to St. Leon. St. Leon, then, becomes an adept, a magician in the sense meant by Thomas Vaughan: he practices a high art and resents being perceived as a mere alchemist. But, as Vaughan had lamented a century and a half before, the *canaille* vulgarly misconceive such business. St. Leon is persecuted by them, and they savagely kill his faithful Negro servant Hector. His wife, a distinctly flattering portrait of the arabesque Mary Wollstonecraft, dies too, harassed and enervated by all these trying experiences; and St. Leon wonders, with reason, if he is *fatal:* "I seemed, like the far-famed tree of Java, to be destined to shelter only to destroy, and to prove a deadly poison to whatever sought refuge under my protecting branches." He is arrested by the Spanish Inquisition and remains for twelve years its prisoner, escaping just before his *auto-da-fé.* In his supervening adventures he brings misfortune on his daughters and son: "Still, still my evil genius pursued me, and blasted every concern in which I presumed to interfere." The novel ends abruptly and inconclusively.

Five years before, in *Caleb Williams,* Godwin had superbly rendered the feelings of daemonic persecution and paranoia through psychological means. But *St. Leon,* like *Otranto,* is chiefly interesting as an example of blighted potentialities. In making his central character a noble and essentially virtuous, philosophical magician he varies significantly the Gothic formula inherited from Walpole, and he was probably the first to try to adapt the genre to the themes of theurgical or white magic. Perhaps even more important, he delineates the daemonic or fatal man sympathetically. St. Leon is more and more estranged from his family and mankind. No oppressor, he is persecuted; and he is a persecuted *liberal* at that! In one scene the chief inquisitor inflicts on him a long harangue — Godwin might have raked it together out of Casaubon or Glanvill — which runs through all the standard arguments for the existence of devils and witches. The inquisitor explicitly attacks modern Sadducees (a term that had not been much employed for a century) and defends the exorcisms of Christ. St. Leon does not controvert any of this, but seems, Hume-like, to consider it mere papistical rubbish unworthy an answer. Instead, he uses his time to declaim in a very high-minded and monotonous way against the unfair legal practices of the Inquisition. That, of course, is the prime difficulty with the novel. It oscillates between violent action and dry, rationalistic, often very trite, philosophizing. There is even less atmosphere than in *Otranto,* St. Leon resolutely refusing to impart the details of his magic to us readers because, of course, he is an "adept" sworn to secrecy. It is all an egregious example of the novelist *telling* rather than showing, and so Godwin interminably, exanimatedly, tells us of St. Leon's mental and physical struggles through four volumes. I do not mention this work merely as an example of a poor Gothic novel, for in fact it shows much more thought and innovation than even the mediocre ones. But it also shows how unsuited was the material for the rationalist frame into which it is set, or rammed. It remained for Godwin's daughter to reconcile radical philosophy with preternatural terror in *Franken-stein. The Castle of Otranto* and *St. Leon* can both claim some originality and sporadic power, but they also show that the Gothic appointments alone — the mysterious locale, the supernatural hints, the daemonic characters — do not infallibly produce spiritual horror. They are but props needing to be invested with a certain amount of gusto and at least vicarious belief.

⊓

Samuel Richardson's *Clarissa* (1747–1748) was for many reasons immediately popular. Its high-minded heroine and flamboyant libertine-villain — the latter modeled on the rakes of Restoration comedy — its pathos and appeal to the cult of sensibility, assured it of a favorable reception. Its inordinate length and epistolary method were not then the stumbling blocks they are now. And of course its officially pious purpose was most unexceptionable. Its title page certifies that it will exhibit "the DISTRESSES that may attend the Misconduct Both of PARENTS and CHILDREN, in Relation to MARRIAGE," and Richardson further assures us in his preface that his novel will "investigate the highest and most important doctrines not only of morality but of Christianity." Contemporary criticism extols its theme in a manner very unencouraging to the modern reader, who after all needs as much encouragement as he can get. For example, one of the better early critics, Joseph Spence, in remarks endorsed by Richardson himself, thus abstracts its central moral: "That a Woman, even of the greatest Abilities, should not enter into any, even the most guarded, Correspondence with a Rake; and that if she once falls into his Power, she is undone."[5] This is really about as probing and definitive as the summary of the theme of *Othello* by that hater of Shakespeare, Thomas Rymer: that a young lady should look well to her handkerchief and never marry a blackamoor.

Later critics, disgusted by such jejune interpretations, have dismissed the moral and religious side of the novel as "little more than a veneer," concluding that Richardson "has at best a shallow notion of religion," and that he shared "the complacent piety of his age."[6] At the same time they have been able to find other levels in the novel of which the author himself was likely unaware. Thus the conflict between Clarissa and the aristocratic rake Lovelace has been viewed economically as the collision of bourgeois Puritanism and the old Cavalier ethic, with Clarissa herself "the heroic representative of all that is free and positive in the new individualism"; or the novel has been invested with mythical and archetypal import, and Clarissa becomes the "love goddess of the Puritan middle class" through whom is expressed that insight, first revealed to moderns by Freud, which identifies

---

[5]Spence, quoted in *Samuel Richardson, Clarissa; Preface, Hints of Prefaces, and Postscript*, introduced by R. F. Brissenden (Los Angeles: Univ. of California Press, 1964), 9.

[6]See: Mario Praz, *The Romantic Agony*, tr. Angus Davidson (1933; rpt. Cleveland and New York: World, 1963), 97; Ian Watt, *The Rise of the Novel*, 216.

the love and the death wish, eros and thanatos.[7] *Clarissa* is one
of the most intricate novels of the eighteenth, or any, century,
and Richardson was certainly one of those writers, like Shakespeare and Defoe, whose works are saturated with more meaning than they know. I am by no means skeptical of the economic, archetypal, or psychological interpretations. But I do
think that the religious purpose of the novel cannot be disre-
garded just because Richardson and his earlier admirers bungled
the job of explaining it. In his Postscript Richardson repines that
he "has lived to see scepticism and infidelity openly avowed,
and . . . the great doctrines of the gospel brought into question."[8]
Behind this novel lie the assaults on Sadduceeism of More,
Glanvill, and Casaubon: rebuttals that rely increasingly on narrative as they dispense with a well-wrought theological frame.
Richardson himself may be intolerably conventional when he
tries to gloze his moral; but as a reticulation of the holy and the
daemonic, in all their complication and ambiguity, *Clarissa* is
unsurpassed; and this despite its eschewing the explicitly supernatural. One of Richardson's best modern commentators, William M. Sale, Jr., sees him opposing the facile optimism of his
age, and compares him with Swift and Johnson in that regard.[9]
Certainly *Clarissa* is a study in daemonic personality and conflict played out against a theological backdrop quite untattered
by rationalism. *Mutatis mutandis,* its purpose is that of the
Glanvillean anthology.

 Clarissa is about the attempt of a family to force one of the
daughters to marry a suitor, Solmes, whom she loathes. Driven
desperate, Clarissa flees with the attractive if unprincipled

---

[7]See generally the discussions of *Clarissa* by Watt, Ch. 7, and by Dorothy
Van Ghent, *The English Novel* (1953; rpt. New York: Harper and Row, 1961),
45–63.

[8]All quotations are from the Everyman Library edition of *Clarissa* (London:
Dent, 1963), with references given by volume and letter number. To avoid
confusion, brackets in the original have been replaced with parentheses.

[9]William M. Sale, Jr., "From Pamela to Clarissa," in *The Age of Johnson*
(New Haven: Yale Univ. Press, 1964), 137.

Lovelace, who at length rapes her while she is drugged. She escapes from him, but unable to work a reconciliation with her family, enters into a decline from which she never recovers. Clarissa's brother and sister — called by her confidante, Miss Howe, in an uncharacteristic understatement, "narrow spirits" — are fiendishly implacable. They are envious of the very material favoritism shown to Clarissa by her grandfather, but the envy goes beyond avarice. As Miss Howe correctly observes: "The distance between you and them is immense. Their eyes ache to look up at you. What shades does your full day of merit cast upon them! Can you wonder, then, that they should embrace the first opportunity that offered, to endeavour to bring you down to their level?" (I, 27). Clarissa's sister terms her "witch" and speaks of her "witchcraft" (I, 15, 42): epithets not intended literally, but no less spiteful for that. One truly feels that they hate her for the same reason that Iago hates Cassio: "He hath a daily beauty in his life / That makes me ugly." Her mother is inobnoxious but asthenic, of no use to her. Her father, Clarissa says, is not naturally ill-tempered, but his more generous spirits have been "imprisoned" by the gout, which has soured him (I, 5); and anyway, he very early and idiotically abdicates his paternal authority in favor of the son. Miss Howe suggests that they are all of them possessed of evil spirits (II, 78). The disparity between Clarissa and her deplorable family is pronounced: one agrees with Lovelace, as the novel unfolds, that nature must have been "in a perverse humour" when she imposed such "sordid ties" on Clarissa (I, 31). But of course Clarissa is too dutiful to violate readily such ties, sanctioned as they are by the Fifth Commandment; and, indeed, she *cannot* easily violate them. The family is united, an *"embattled phalanx,"* according to her brother: "So you know your destiny," he tells her, "and have nothing to do but to yield to it" (I, 32). Clarissa herself admits toward the end: "there was a kind of fatality by which our whole family was impelled ... and which none of us were permitted to avoid" (IV, 77). A modern, disgruntled critic wonders why some adjacent family or conscientious magistrate failed to interfere with this persecution of Clarissa.[10] However plausible in terms of realism that objection may be, it ignores the daemonic persistence of the family, the scrupulous obedience of Clarissa, and the *fatality* behind it all. It is like wondering why one of Job's friends did not lend him some money so that he might go to a proper doctor and re-establish his family on a new footing; or why those very nasty doings at the Macbeths' went so long unexposed.

The family's means of "bringing her down" is the *nouveau riche* suitor Solmes, whom they would constrain her to marry. Immediately he comes on the stage, he is contrasted with both Clarissa and Lovelace: unlike them, he is ungenerous, indeed a "niggard" (I, 13). He is an "upstart" — economically, of course, but psychologically and even physically. On one occasion he is found near Clarissa "squatting" on a chair (like Milton's Satan ignobly squatting, a toad, at Eve's ear). He has "splay feet," and his manner of approach is cringing and contemptible (I, 16); he is sordid and base, even a *"monster"* (I, 17). His "understanding ... the glory of a man" is debased (I, 20); he has a habit of "gnawing" the head of his hazel stick as a dog might a bone (I, 21); he exhibits a "diabolical parsimony" (I, 32) and is despised by his tenants. Weak and contemptible in himself, yet he has the support of the family and like them shows a fiendish, or perhaps animal, pertinacity in the face of Clarissa's repeated denials and patent detestation. Now it is all very well to emphasize the economic side of this: for various reasons, from the point of view of the family, Solmes would make a profitable match for Clarissa. But without lapsing into ridiculous caricature (the references I have assembled here are rather subtly distributed throughout several letters), Richardson presents Solmes as essentially subhuman, hardly better than a Caliban, who would ascend, not merely the social and economic scale, but the very scale of life itself. Richardson is clearly implying that Solmes and the family, like true devils, wish to defy the divinely sanc-

---

[10]Brian W. Downs, *Richardson* (London: Routledge, 1928), 102.

tioned hierarchy; all of them have the Satanic loathing of the holy and the desire to defile it.

Compared with Solmes, Lovelace looks very good indeed. As Clarissa's sympathetic Cousin Dolly tells her, he is a "fine gentleman; Mr. Solmes was not worthy to *buckle his shoes*" (I, 78; italics in original). Neither drunkard nor gamester, he is a generous landlord loved by his unracked tenants; but we also know from the start that he possesses a haughty and violent temper. Like Clarissa he is generous and hates meanness, and early in his career in the novel we hear of his sparing a young girl in his power. Like Clarissa, too, he keeps busy and sleeps only six hours a day. Most important, perhaps, he is no religious skeptic despite his libertinism. His fellow-rake Belford — as yet unconverted here — speaks correctly for him: "Although we find religion against us, we have not yet presumed to make a religion to suit our practices. We despise those who do. And we know better than to be even *doubters*. In short, we believe a future state of rewards and punishments. But as we have so much youth and health in hand, we hope to have time for repentance" (II, 44). Unworthy to buckle his shoes, Solmes is his John Baptist; and Lovelace audaciously claims to be Clarissa's "redeemer" — from her "jailors and persecutors" (I, 94, 98), and later from her violent reaction to her father's curse: "I have given her a life her unnatural father had well-nigh taken away" (II, 53). His very first letter speaks of his awe of Clarissa, his view of her as an angel, a divinity (I, 31). But later, after he tricks Clarissa into fleeing with him from her garden, he ponders thus:

> Now ... if I could pull her down a little nearer to my own level; that is to say, could prevail upon her to do something that would argue *imperfection*, something *to repent of*; we should jog on much more equally, and be better able to comprehend one another; and so the comfort would be mutual, and the remorse not all on one side (II, 19).

Like the others, then, he would bring her down. He is thus an antitype or infernal parody of a redeemer whom Solmes, indeed,

[271]

came before, though it can hardly be said that he prepared the way. In the *Apocalypse* the garden of the Lamb replaces the lost garden of Eden; but Clarissa's garden, though replete with familial thorns, gives way to the far more unremitting however seemingly "liberal," confinement of Lovelace.

Of course "buckle his shoes," when Cousin Dolly uses the phrase, is a mere cliché. Similarly, Lovelace is first associated with the devil in a trite figure of speech: "Talk *of the devil* is an old saying," says Miss Howe as she reports that Lovelace, whom she has been writing about, has just come to see her (I, 12). Equally whimsical is her comment sometime later: "I believe indeed he is a devil in everything but his foot" (II, 29); or, speaking of his friends: "I see not but they are a set of *infernals*, and he the *Beelzebub*" (II, 65). Yet her tone becomes more serious as Lovelace's machinations and mendacities become more evident:

> I never had any faith in the stories that go current among country girls, of spectres, familiars, and demons; yet I see not any other way to account for this wretch's successful villainy, and for his means of working up his specious delusions, but by supposing (if he be not the devil himself) that he has a familiar constantly at his elbow (III, 88).

Here Richardson well employs his leisurely, epistolary method, for precisely as Miss Howe's comments on Lovelace's diabolism move from cliché to gravity, his own truly diabolic qualities gradually surface. He is of course prideful, and wishes to revenge himself on the sex because of an early, depressing experience with unrequited love (I, 31). But the diabolic characteristics go far beyond this. Like the devil (and Iago) he delights in working mischief out of materials already at hand in the human beings he is manipulating (e.g., the family's envy and malice, II, 28). He loves intrigue and enjoys assuming disguises or causing his confederates to do so (as the devil can take on any shape or grant his devotees that power). He arrogantly usurps the role of providence, seeing it as both a pleasure and duty to devise punishments for those who in his opinion deserve them (II, 14; III,

[272]

1, 3). Like a recording angel, he marks down the offenses of his enemies in his "vellum book" (III, 15). He expects any woman he might marry to worship him idolatrously (II, 108). Even as Miss Howe's devil comparisons remain casual, he revels in his own sadistic nature, likening himself repeatedly to a hunter after game (e.g., II, 71) and being ever-stimulated by Clarissa's recalcitrance: "Then weeping, she struggled vehemently to withdraw her hands, which all the while I held between mine. Her struggles! Oh, what additional charms . . . did her struggles give to every feature, every limb. . ." (II, 126). "I love, when I dig a pit, to have my prey tumble in with secure feet and open eyes; then a man can look down upon her, with an *O-ho, charmer, how came you there?*" (II, 28). When Clarissa first escapes him, he pursues her in disguise and, apprehending her:

> I threw open my great-coat, and, like the devil in
> Milton (an odd comparison though!)
>> I started up in my own form divine,
>> Touch'd by the beam of her celestial eye,
>> More potent than Ithuriel's spear—

The quotation is peculiarly apt, to be sure: "odd," as Lovelace puts it with typically unsubtle salaciousness. Clarissa then falls in a fit, and one of the by-standers, Lovelace tells us, affirms "that I was neither more nor less than the devil, and could not keep her eye from my foot; expecting, no doubt, every minute to see it discover itself to be cloven" (III, 5 — cf. Clarissa's similar remark, III, 2). What had been a cliché in Miss Howe, now takes on true horror; and Clarissa asks him if he has "entered into a compact with the grand deceiver" (III, 35; cf. III, 33).

Still, Lovelace is no pantomimic Mephistopheles, but a creation of some complexity with his own emotional and even religious dimension. Like Robinson Crusoe he has a prophetic dream (III, 43), on which he reflects to Belford:

> I shall always have a prodigious regard to dreams henceforward. I know not but I may write a book upon that subject; for my own experience will furnish out a great part of it.

[273]

Glanville of Witches, and Baxter's *History of Spirits and Apparitions*, and the *Royal Pedant's Demonology*, will be nothing at all to *Lovelace's Reveries* (III, 44).

Naturally Lovelace gets the titles wrong, and *reverie*, connoting as it does the delightful daydream, is scarcely commensurate with his portentous vision. But one of Lovelace's flaws is that he is a very bad critic. He has another dream where he sees Clarissa welcomed into heaven, like Elijah leaving behind her her robe, which is azure, stuck thick with silver stars; while he, annihilated by Clarissa's avenger, Cousin Morden, sinks to hell (IV, 56). Notwithstanding this presaging dream, he undertakes a truly daemonic pursuit of Clarissa, even beyond the verge of her death; and of course he precipitates the crisis with Morden, who mortally wounds him. He is driven, and as Belford advises him (but he will not listen): "thou wilt go on tempting danger and vengeance, till thou meetest with vengeance" (III, 116). Clarissa is fond of meditating on such verses as this from *Job:* "For the arrows of the Almighty are within me, the poison whereof drinketh up my spirit: the terrors of God do set themselves in array against me." Here is Lovelace-the-critic's interpretation:

I cannot help expressing my pleasure that by one or two verses of it (the *arrow*, Jack, and *what she feared being come upon her!*), I am encouraged to hope, what it will be very surprising to me if it do not happen; that is, in plain English, that the dear creature is in the way to be a mamma (IV, 10).

His obtuseness is nearly incredible when he misreads her penultimate note to him (IV, 60). In introspection of his own sin (IV, 154) he is absurdly superficial.

In great contrast to the awakened Robinson Crusoe, Lovelace has no capacity to interpret the will of providence or properly "read" spiritual language; like Solmes, though less obviously, he has a debased understanding. Richardson correctly refused to grant Lovelace any abrupt conversion, but he just as correctly made Lovelace a Christian rather than a skeptic. This infuriates some critics, who charge Richardson with "degrading good works below faith" and presenting in Lovelace a "limited-liability blackguardism."[11] But a true skeptic will not even notice the providential hints, much less read them aright; nor will he experience Lovelace's authentic spiritual horror and desire for expiation. Lovelace is a *diabolic mortal,* and even Richardson seems undecided as to which element more strongly prevails. In his Postscript he thus vindicates Lovelace's blend of religious feeling and daemonism: "are not the very devils, in Scripture, said to believe and tremble?" Yet in the next paragraph but one he allows that only if Lovelace had actually ridiculed religion would he have been "truly infernal." In any event, it is overstating to say that he is "the devil himself,"[12] for he has retained much more humanity than, for example, the demonically possessed Weston, the "unman," in C. S. Lewis's *Perelandra.* Lovelace is no demon, but a truly daemonic character, compelled by energies beyond his rational grasp: fascinating, dominating, egoistic, self-destructive. In my opinion one can even feel some sympathy for him at the end, for unlike an Iago, at whose feet Othello, too, looks inquiringly, he can suffer, if he cannot comprehend, and even seek to atone. More appalling, in my view, is the bullying persecutor of Clarissa, the whoremadam Mrs. Sinclair, whose death-agonies, however risibly overcharged, still evoke spiritual horror.

The Latin adjective *clarum* has the sense of "bright," "clear"; but it also connotes "celebrated," "illustrious." Its feminine superlative form lurks in Clarissa's name, and the several contiguous meanings should be held in mind. Clarissa is, to be sure, the ideal young woman, but she is also *renowned* for her virtue, industry, and piety; she is an exemplar. One of the first books that we hear she owns is *The Imitation of Christ* (I, 75). Only a very deep cynic could wonder whether her emulation of the holy is sincere. Early in her very first letter she is wishing for death (I, 2); early Miss Howe says she is fitter for the next world than for this (I, 10). She is just the opposite of Pope's libidinous

[11]Ibid., 79.
[12]Van Ghent, 51.

Eloisa: "Were ours a Roman Catholic family how much happier for me, that they [i.e., her family] thought a nunnery would answer all their views!" (I, 13). She effaces herself, is kindly, yet clearly occupies a higher plane; and when she first inadvertently suffers physical violence as a result of her family's persecution, the language, blunt and coarse, is starkly incongruous with her nature: "I . . . fell flat on my face into the other parlour" (I, 78). Yet the envy of her brother and sister is aroused as much by her reputation, her exemplariness, as by her actual possession of virtue and piety. An imperfect world seldom dotes on perfection when it sees it first-hand, and never when the example is much talked of. Clarissa's own nature is very intricate. She says herself that she has a masculine resolution as well as feminine submissiveness (I, 9, 19), and Lovelace's remark has insight: "her charming body is not equally organized. The unequal partners pull two ways; and the divinity within her tears her silken frame. But had the same soul informed a masculine body, never would there have been a truer hero" (II, 102). She is no pious Pollyanna, but quite early recognizes and laments the violation of hierarchical order and consequent disruption of familial relations: "Something is strangely wrong somewhere!" (I, 64). Confused and manipulated by Lovelace into escaping with him — her tragic error in Aristotle's terms — she later reflects:

> Thus terrified, I was got out of sight of the door in a very few minutes: and then, although quite breathless between running and apprehension, he put my arm under his, his drawn sword in the other hand, and hurried me on still faster: my voice, however, contradicting my action; crying No, no, no . . . (I, 94).

I do not push the comparison pedantically or with much conviction, but it is possible that an eighteenth-century reader of this passage might have called to mind Pope's famous lines, in his Spring pastoral, on the coquette Sylvia: "She runs, but hopes she does not run unseen, / While a kind Glance at her Pursuer flies, / How much at variance are her Feet and Eyes!" No one could say that there is a scintilla of ordinary flirtation in Clarissa; but there are other, possibly more alarming, types of indirectness and fugacity. Although her Christian name suggests "exemplary," her surname, Harlowe, is a near homonym for a very unsavory word.

Lovelace several times remarks that his "principal design is but to bring virtue to trial" (II, 92), and it is evident that Clarissa herself sees her situation under the aspect of Job. The similarities are tantalizing: like Job, she is an apparently righteous and exemplary person subjected to an apparently arbitrary infliction of providence; like Job, she may have been too self-conscious of her virtue. Even before the rape she reproaches herself for her vanity and "presumptuous self-security," but like Job she refuses to despair (II, 101). After the rape, in a heap of anomalous, nearly incoherent ramblings, she views herself as "humbled in the dust" because she delighted in the applause of the world (III, 33). Richardson ingeniously reproduces her papers in his text, her lines stabbing out in jagged angularities to show a discomposed frame of mind. But her humiliations are not done: she is thrown into prison: "Very well, said she, why should not all be of a piece? Why should not my wretchedness be complete?" (III, 105). Like Job's friends, her relatives frigidly moralize her sufferings and rebuke her offenses. Texts from *Job* assist her meditations. For her funeral sermon she appoints verses from *Job*, xv. 31, 32, 33, desiring that "the alterations of the words *her* and *she*, for *him* and *he*, may be allowable," and she goes on to give a pathetic sample of the feminizing of Eliphaz's reflections on vanity (IV, 146). By the middle of the eighteenth century several critics had argued for *Job* as a drama, and Richardson plainly states in his Postscript that he is writing a Christian tragedy.[13]

---

[13]See, for example, remarks on *Job* in Robert Lowth, *Lectures on the Sacred Poetry of the Hebrews* (1787 — original Latin version, 1753), and Anthony Blackwall, *The Sacred Classics Defended and Illustrated* (1725). Lovelace's confidant, Belford, reads Blackwall after his conversion from libertinism (IV, 3). Much earlier Donne had called *Job* a "tragicomedy," having in mind its epilogue.

But there are also differences, some slight, some profound. Clarissa suffers less physical violence than Job, yet physical suffering is very subjective, and Clarissa is a more delicate organism. Her family's refusal to let her attend public worship is, to her, Draconian. Her utter isolation from society, during a good part of the novel, is arguably more repulsive than anything in *Job*. In the world of Clarissa, her "falling flat on her face into the parlour" is more shocking than Job's boils; and her experience in the debtors' prison seems almost inconceivable. The rape, notwithstanding her near insensibility at the time, is as horrifying an infringing the self as anything Job undergoes. Under all this she exhibits much more patience than that voluble patriarch, and her humility is invigorated by reading the scriptures and meditation; no voice from the whirlwind is needed to teach her. She can read providence from the start, and long before her real trials begin she rebukes her spiritual pride and expects the chastisement of heaven (I, 82). And yet when Samuel Johnson's friend Mrs. Thrale praised Clarissa's perfection, he responded: "On the contrary, you may observe there is always something which she prefers to the truth."[14] Johnson, who admired the novel very much, omitted to elaborate, and critics have generally thought that he was talking about a tragic self-deception, or perhaps a reticence thrust upon her by the finical codes of the day. This may have been all he meant, but the comment does pop up in a discussion having to do with "attention to veracity," and it is quite possible that a reader of the novel, whether of Johnson's or modern time, will decide that Clarissa wears an evasiveness for which her society is not wholly to blame. That she is drawn more strongly to Lovelace than she will confess, any diligent reader must perceive. Her sense of self-importance and self-dignity *is* considerable, though not all readers will agree that it is excessive. Her famous, figurative letter to Lovelace is deceitful, howevermuch we favor the deceit; and her analysis of her family's cruelty (it proceeds,

---

[14] *Johnsonian Miscellanies*, I, 297.

she says, from their inordinate love for her and disappointment in her: III, 121), coming as it does toward the end, is unspeakably naive. Very early she has a prophetic dream in which Lovelace "carried me into a churchyard; and there, notwithstanding all my prayers and tears and protestations of innocence, stabbed me to the heart" (I, 84). One so pure as Clarissa might well overlook the sexual innuendo of this presentiment, but its menace is surely clear; yet it is to no avail. Perhaps the greatest question is, how seriously does Clarissa *wish* to evade her destiny? And along with that question, another: what, really, is her attitude toward her violation and her supervening decline?

On these matters we find equivocation. I have noted that Clarissa is longing for death from her very first letter, though, I believe, this death wish is not very pronounced till after her father's curse (II, 50). Modern readers may be repelled by Clarissa's scrupulous preparations for dying, her bringing the coffin into her room, contriving the insignia for her tomb, and so forth. This is not being "positive" or "healthy." But in other times it was considered healthy to provide for a holy dying, and Clarissa is an old-fashioned girl. Richardson was the printer for Young's *Night Thoughts*, and he is aiming at its not paltry audience here; with a little mental adjustment, one should not be bothered by these things alone. But there is more to it. When Clarissa says "I dwell on, I indulge (and, strictly speaking, I enjoy) the thoughts of death" (IV, 90), she is "preferring nothing to truth" in the parentheses; but the truth may be distressing. In all the appurtenances of religious horror later familiarized by the Gothic novel — the coffin, the tomb — she takes a nearly narcissistic pleasure. The last quarter of the book might almost be considered an *inverted* Gothicism. She delights in what normal people like Belford find repugnant, and the chaste but funereal lily is her emblem. To put it plainly, self-destructive melancholy is unchristian, and though Clarissa several times denies that she is melancholy, she does confess to Belford that she is dying from grief (IV, 106). Ophelia in *Hamlet* is similarly afflicted because of the death of her father; she loses the will to

[279]

live and is denominated a suicide by the "churlish" popish priests. Clarissa's competent doctor believes that her malady is mental, and he tells her, in a remark recalling a colleague's diagnosis of Lady Macbeth: "You must, in a great measure, be your own doctress" (III, 112).

Why indeed *does* she die? On the one hand, she has a high personal sense of virtue and loathes her violated self: love has ruined her "in *my* own eyes; and that is the same to me as if *all the world* knew it. Hinder me not from going whither my mysterious destiny shall lead me" (III, 38). It is, she says, her "*self*, this vile, this hated *self*" which she will "shake . . . off, if possible" (III, 67). The rape is seen as an *invasion* of self (e.g., III, 5), and even a demonic possession: before the rape Miss Howe predicts that "some man, or some *worse spirit in the shape of one* . . . was to be sent to invade you" (II, 78). After it Clarissa exclaims: "Who can *touch pitch and not be defiled?* He has made a bad spirit take possession of me, I think" (IV, 79). On the other hand, she is sufficiently orthodox theologically to affirm: "I bless God, it [the violation] has not tainted my mind; it has not hurt my morals. . . . The evil . . . is merely personal [i.e., physical rather than spiritual]. No credulity, no weakness, no want of vigilance have I to reproach myself with" (IV, 67). If it has tainted neither mind nor morals, where lies the spiritual defilement of self?

The references to demonic possession are merely figurative — like those in *Eloisa to Abelard*. But like Eloisa, like Lovelace, Clarissa is a daemonic character. It is true she has that "goodness of heart" denied to such characters by Goethe, but she also has their "incredible force" and "incredible power." Her influence on others is marked throughout the novel, and like St. Leon she is viewed with a kind of dread by her family. As an early critic perceptively noted, she is too "inflexibly right" to arouse as much sympathy in the reader as she might have done; she does not seem to need it.[15] She is never more clearly daemonic than

---

[15]Aikin, *Miscellaneous Pieces*, 207.

in the celebrated penknife scene (III, 53), where she is prepared to kill herself, trusting God's mercy, rather than to submit to that hoary fate-worse-than-death. In this passage is all the machinery, rusting even in Richardson's day and certainly rusty now, of romantic melodrama. Yet if one will enter into it, it is an episode of real power, a confrontation, or collision, of two daemonic persons. "She seemed to tread air, and to be all soul," Lovelace writes later; and he is reduced to impotence. But, however skulkingly, he has his way; and though Clarissa understands theology well enough to know that her will is inviolate, yet a possession, a defiling, has occurred. For a daemonic character, the loss or injury of the self is unsupportable, and so, despite her canonical, her dutiful, Christian disclaimers of melancholy, she effectively wills herself to die. Like Lovelace she has a sense of fatality, a pride of self, a power beyond her own knowing, a self-destructiveness. Like many a more humdrum creature, these personages are trapped by stereotypes of themselves; but unlike the rest of us, they have the energy to actualize those stereotypes. Thus they are their own victims, and each other's. A marriage between Clarissa and Lovelace might have been a marriage of heaven and hell; nevertheless there are points at which the holy and the daemonic touch, or more than touch, at least as they exist in human beings. Seldom has that entanglement been dramatized so well as in *Clarissa*.

When it comes to theory, Richardson embarrasses our sophistication; he is a little too obvious and puritanical, even prissy. In his Postscript, defending his decision to kill off Clarissa, he argues that he is writing a Christian tragedy, that poetic justice (according to Aristotle and Addison) need not be observed in true tragedy; that, anyway, Clarissa *does* receive poetic justice: it is only deferred till the next world. Critics make fun of Richardson's eating and having his cake here, and suggest, not always jocosely, that the only difference between this novel and his earlier *Pamela*, in which the heroine is rewarded for her virtue with a wealthy, ex-would-be-seducer husband, is that here Richardson is "merely post-dating the Reward and paying it in a different currency. . . . He substituted a transcendental

[281]

for a sublunary audit, and that was all."[16] But such a view, albeit sportive, is superficial. Like Wagner's Isolde, however different their characters else, Clarissa *has* to die to make artistic and psychological sense, and Richardson did right in this matter, however obnoxious his theoretical rationale. *Clarissa* is a study in spiritual horror and in the love of spiritual horror. The daemonic in Lovelace is, I think, expertly handled; but it can be well enough understood. The daemonic in Clarissa is complicated. Apparently more virtuous and patient even than Job, she is also more perplexing. Is there a point at which her loathing of her "vile self" and zealousness to die contradict Christian piety and saintliness? Her oblique and ethereal manner actually enhances her allure and incites Lovelace's lubricious fury; is she then somewhat responsible for his tragedy as well as her own? Is there a sense in which, as her sister says, she does exert, and not altogether unconsciously, a witchcraft upon others? Lovelace early remarks the disorganization of her constitution, the divinity within her tearing her body's silken frame. Is it too fanciful to think of Dryden's daemonic Achitophel, whose "fiery Soul ... working out its way, / Fretted the Pigmy Body to decay"? But then the more conventional reading will rather identify *Lovelace* with Achitophel, diabolic tempters both. There will always be those, a Walter Pater or a Duchamp, who sense something sinister, erotic, even perverted, behind the primly pious smile of the Mona Lisa. Some such intuition, it may be, inhabits Johnson's downright remark about Clarissa's preferences.

Between the typical modern reader and *Clarissa* there are probably too many, too heavy, obstacles to be removed: its length, its epistolary form, its excruciatingly slow yet cumulatively powerful development. But it would be too bad if this same typical reader should be put off merely by allegations of Richardson's superficiality, complacency, or priggishness. Rich-

[16]Downs, 76. On Richardson and poetic justice, see Ira Konigsberg, "The Tragedy of Clarissa," *Modern Language Quarterly* 27 (1966), 285–98, and R. D. Stock, *Samuel Johnson and Neoclassical Dramatic Theory*, 109–10.

ardson may indeed have wrought better than he knew, but he has sounded spiritual depths beyond the reach of most novelists. He is astonishingly modern in his minute probing of individual personalities with all their oscillations, divisions, and bafflements. It is no wonder that Johnson liked him.

◻

Ann Radcliffe is usually considered the grand mistress of the Gothic novel. Her romances appeared from 1789 through 1797, excluding an inferior work published posthumously. She excelled in the psychological Gothic, in which she was preceded by Clara Reeve, who was perhaps the first to join the Gothicism of Walpole with the situations, the heroines, and to some extent the manner, of Richardson. Radcliffe is also the best exemplar of the rationalized Gothic, for the supernatural is seldom permitted impolitely to intrude, and logical explanations, or those at least purporting to be logical, are typically offered at the term for everything seemingly uncanny. Radcliffe, like Richardson, lays great stress on emotion, personality, female psychology, and her heroines resemble Clarissa in that they are decorously sensitive and delicate but thrown into oppressive and even horrible situations. Wisely refraining from Richardson's cumbrous epistolary form, she is able to introduce into her novels much more description and atmosphere. And of course there is the Gothic paraphernalia to heighten things. There is also a more deliberate cultivation of moods of terror, awe, melancholy, obscure horror, the sublime. The daemonic character, too, is more assiduously worked up, and diffuses its influence through her novels more than Lovelace is ever allowed to do in *Clarissa*. Her plots are more sedulously, or at least succinctly, designed than Richardson's, but they are even less realistic, freely using the stock devices of coincidence, disguise, and sudden recognition. Radcliffe is more sentimental than Richardson and refuses to entangle herself in his subtleties and equivocations.

Although *The Mysteries of Udolpho* (1794) has always been her most popular work, Radcliffe's best is probably *The Italian*, *or the Confessional of the Black Penitents* (1797). Set in Italy, and chiefly in the areas of Naples and Rome, in the mid-eighteenth century, the novel focuses on two star-crossed lovers, Vivaldi and Ellena, who seem to have stepped, or been wrenched, out of *Romeo and Juliet*. Like Romeo, Vivaldi secretly observes Ellena in the evening at her open window; like Juliet, Ellena musingly breathes his name (I, 1), and, sometime later, voices her regret that his family opposes their match (her language, of course, is of the eighteenth century; she speaks of his family's "visionary prejudice").[17] Ellena is not only more derivative than Clarissa, she is also more sentimental. Clarissa may often prefer something to the truth, but Ellena shows definite intellectual constraints. When the evidence correctly suggests that Schedoni, who she thinks is her father, was about to murder her, Ellena carefully fashions another explanation of the evidence: "for she was less anxious to discover truth, than to release herself from horrible suppositions" (II, 10). Clarissa is at least willing to be uncomfortable in the face of an unpleasant truth; but as we shall see again, there is something mentally hedonistic in Ellena. Still, there is nothing *sinister* about her.

Radcliffe's characterization of the villain-monk Schedoni, however, is forcible and even intricate. It is probably an overstatement to call him a "unique portrait" and original contribution to Gothic fiction,[18] since congeners can be spotted in earlier novels, and prototypes in the Machiavellian schemers of Elizabethan and Jacobean tragedy. Nevertheless, Schedoni is effectively presented and certainly influenced further development of the type in Scott, Byron, and a host of nineteenth-century hacks; he remains one of the most memorable of the earlier daemonic figures. Notice how neatly he fits Goethe's description:

> Among his associates no one loved him, many disliked him, and more feared him. His figure was striking, but not so

[17]All quotations are from Ann Radcliffe, *The Italian, or the Confessional of the Black Penitents*, ed. Frederick Garber (London: Oxford Univ. Press, 1968); references are given by volume and chapter number.
[18]See Varma, 100, 119.

from grace; it was tall, and, though extremely thin, his limbs were large and uncouth, and as he stalked along, wrapt in the black garments of his order, there was something terrible in its air; something almost super-human. His cowl, too, as it threw a shade over the livid paleness of his face, encreased its severe character, and gave an effect to his large melancholy eye, which approached to horror. His was not the melancholy of a sensible and wounded heart, but apparently that of a gloomy and ferocious disposition. . . . An habitual gloom and severity prevailed over the deep lines of his countenance; and his eyes were so piercing that they seemed to penetrate, at a single glance, into the hearts of men, and to read their most secret thoughts; few persons could support their scrutiny, or even endure to meet them twice (I, 2).

But like a good Machiavel he can assume other moods and appearances when it is to his purpose. His origins are obscure, and more than the truth he delights in all the deviousness and involution of Italian intrigue. His "passions might impel him to the perpetration of almost any crime, how hideous soever," and he discerns "only evil in human nature" (I, 4). In manipulating Vivaldi's mother, the nefarious Marchesa, he employs the obliquities and innuendoes of an Iago (e.g., I, 4; II, 3–4). His conscience is not altogether defunct, but it can be aroused only in connection with his supposed daughter, Ellena (III, 1), for whom indeed he has an egoistic rather than paternal affection. His cell is gloomy, containing books "written in unknown characters" and some "instruments of torture" whose function baffles the pure-minded Vivaldi's understanding. Even at the end, when his story is out and he is incarcerated by the Inquisition, his glance yet retains "the destructive fascination . . . of the basilisk," and he can utter a "demoniacal sound of exultation" — "a sound so strange and horrible . . . so unlike any human voice, that every person in the chamber . . . struck with irresistible terror, endeavoured to make their way out of it" (III, 11).

But Schedoni, thus magnetic, thus terrifying, owns a weakness nearly as execrable as his innate malignity. He is unaesthetic; he wants taste and sensitivity. We note in the description

[285]

above that he is graceless and uncouth; we note that his melancholy is not of the benign or philosophical species so esteemed in Thomson's *Seasons*. Wherefore he cannot understand the good or sensitive people such as Ellena; he is callous; he confounds "delicacy of feeling with fatuity of mind, taste with caprice, and imagination with error." Yet he himself gives way "to illusions not less egregious, because they were less brilliant, than those which are incident to sentiment and feeling" (III, 2). Although references linking Schedoni with the devil are less obtrusive than those applied to Lovelace, on the whole the monk is a more daemonic character than the rake: he is more imperious, more awesome, more sinister; and, when he is not venting daemoniacal sounds, he is eerily taciturn (the garrulous and egoistic Lovelace always more than gratifies our curiosity). But like Lovelace he is a bad critic, he has not "sensibility."

Ellena and Vivaldi have such "sentiment and feeling." They have the *good* kind of melancholy, and are always responding to scenes with pleasing dread or dreadful pleasure, with pleasing sadness, with congenial melancholy or religious or holy awe. They are, in short, pious aesthetes; and had they been English, they would surely have been voracious readers of Thomson the connoisseur of gloom and Young the rhapsodist of night. But although well matched, they evince slightly different dispositions. Ellena is more apt to respond to natural scenes, Vivaldi to those tinged with the supernatural. She is a naturalist, he a supernaturalist (his great weakness, we are told, is a love of superstition); but in both of them terror and awe kindle a religious sense. Let us consider Ellena first.

Early in the novel Ellena is abducted in a very frightening manner, but even in those trying circumstances she has an eye for the scenery. And the scenery is quite terrific: the setting sun, a river plunging impetuous and foaming down the cliffs of a mountain, becoming momentarily calm, then lapsing "with thundering strength to the abyss, throwing its misty clouds of spray high in the air." The road on which she is traveling winds toward a fragile bridge "which, thrown across the chasm at an immense height, united two opposite cliffs, between which the whole cataract of the river descended." This bridge, seemingly suspended in the clouds, Ellena regards with an exalted awe surpassing the "dreadful pleasure" with which she had been contemplating the river itself. On the other side of the bridge, the road descends more tranquilly toward a "sunshine landscape." Radcliffe furnishes her own gloze on this scene: it represents a "passage through the vale of death to the bliss of eternity" (I, 6). But the exegesis is unequal to the stupendousness of the scene itself; like Richardson, Radcliffe is as poor at commentary as she excels in description. The modern student of literature will probably think of "Kubla Khan," or divers passages in *The Prelude* that juxtapose in like manner violence and energy with calm and tranquillity. These are images of a mysterious and active creation or, as in Coleridge's fragment, of human life. The student may see in Radcliffe's scene, not so much a "passage to eternity," as an attempt, through the emblem of the nebulous and gossamer bridge, to synthesize the terrifying and the comforting aspects of nature, and to stress the inadequacy of human understanding in the face of the sublime: "Tumult and peace, the darkness and the light, / . . . Characters of the great Apocalypse, / The types and symbols of Eternity" (*Prelude*, VI, 635, 638–39).

Somewhat later Ellena, confined in a dismal and oppressive convent, draws solace and refreshment from natural scenes:

> Here, gazing upon the stupendous imagery around her, looking, as it were, beyond the awful veil which obscures the features of the Deity, and conceals Him from the eyes of his creatures, dwelling as with a present God in the midst of his sublime works; with a mind thus elevated, how insignificant would appear to her the transactions, and the sufferings of this world! . . . Thus man, the giant who now held her in captivity, would shrink to the diminutiveness of a fairy (I, 8).

Here is that *numen praesens*, that quickening yet transcendent deity dimly known and dreaded by Hume's vulgar peasant in the *Natural History*; but here communicating itself to the refined and delicate Ellena. In a similar but not identical situation to Pope's Eloisa, she uses the scenery to invigorate her piety; but in Eloisa's less chaste spirit it only feeds despondency.

Vivaldi likes nature, too, but he prefers the more overtly uncanny or weird situations. For awhile he seems to be haunted by a monk — not, as it transpires, Schedoni — and although he has a sound enough head to despise "the common superstitions of his country," yet he is awed by this singular personage and titillates himself by thinking it preternatural. We are told, indeed, that he would have been "disappointed . . . to have descended suddenly from the region of fearful sublimity, to which he had soared — the world of terrible shadows — to the earth, on which he daily walked, and to an explanation simply natural" (I, 6). The grim convent where Ellena is immured inspires in him a "pleasing sadness," and its doleful church communicates a "sacred awe" (I, 11). The religious ruins and monuments of Rome summon up in him "a melancholy awe, a sacred enthusiasm, that withdrew him from himself" (II, 6). Such is the ecstasy that Vivaldi finds in eldritch, as Ellena in natural, scenes.

But although superstitious dread does once, briefly, actuate the evil Marchesa's conscience (II, 4), it is not in the least condoned. When the same enigmatic monk visits Vivaldi in the dungeons of the Inquisition (having come through secret passageways and avoided the notice of Vivaldi's guards), Vivaldi's superstitious awe is shown to be a bad temptation: "though his imagination inclined him to the marvellous, and to admit ideas which, filling and expanding all the faculties of the soul, produce feelings that partake of the sublime, he now resisted the propensity, and dismissed, as absurd, a supposition, which had begun to thrill his every nerve with horror" (III, 7). It is well that he resists the propensity, since he must have his wits, such as they are, about him in the ensuing scenes. Schedoni himself best analyses Vivaldi's "prevailing weakness" — a susceptibility to superstition. Vivaldi, sometimes a bit slow, exclaims: "What! does a monk call superstition a weakness!" But Schedoni, even while discommending Vivaldi's "ardent imagination," describes it most engagingly: "It may not willingly confine itself to the dull truths of this earth, but, eager to expand its faculties, to fill its capacity, and to experience its own peculiar delights, soars after new wonders into a world of its own!" (III, 11). Not that Schedoni himself, a keen psychologist, is ever victimized by it; he is no average monk! Like sublime natural scenery, superstitious fear encourages a pleasing dread and emancipation from the self; but because superstition is false, its pleasures are meretricious, *ad captandum vulgus.* Radcliffe's perspective is not really so far removed from Hume's. Hence Ellena, who as heroine must be more nearly perfect than Vivaldi, takes no delight in such fear; and Vivaldi must be purged of it.

The Italian has many strengths. The dramatic opening has been highly and rightly praised for its setting the tone of mystery and dread. Evoking true horror are the scenes at the assassin Spalatro's ghastly house, and Schedoni's near murder of Ellena there. Schedoni himself is a superbly drawn daemonic character, and several of Radcliffe's landscapes, if we enter into them with the proper spirit, are remarkable attempts to do that in which far greater writers have failed: to convey the numinous. There are moments when one feels that Wordsworth and Coleridge are better at that only because they came later, though it is true that Radcliffe's descriptions often encumber and clog the plot. Whether treating human or physical nature, she is adroit in applying the insight, popularized by Burke, that obscurity is an important part of the sublime. Schedoni's origin is mysterious, his cell contains books in an unknown tongue, torture instruments whose functions are indecipherable. Radcliffe's landscapes are often taken at twilight, as impressive for what they partly conceal as for what they show. The Inquisition scenes at the end have been depreciated as "unduly prolonged,"[19] but they seem to me at once horrifying, subtle, and realistic. On the one hand, the maze of corridors and dun-

---

[19]Ibid., 98. A contemporary critic finds the scenes implausible: *Critical Review*, 23 (June 1798), 168; and see Birkhead, *Tale of Terror*, 52. Tompkins, 279–83, discusses succinctly the late eighteenth-century attitudes toward the Inquisition.

[289]

geons, the sinuous passageways, the sable, face-concealing garb of the inquisitors, are all exquisitely nightmarish. On the other hand, although we hear groans, yet we see no tortures; and the tribunal of the Inquisition is painted with what one guesses to be creditable realism. The inquisitors chatter among themselves, fall out with one another, show slight confusion sometimes, are sometimes surprisingly candid and even humane, at other times petty: just like any group of administrators and bureaucrats! Naturally Vivaldi reprehends the unjust methods of the Inquisition — what less would one expect of an upright, right-thinking young man? — but the scenes are well sustained and never collapse into the monotonous descriptions and pedantic harangues of *St. Leon*.

But the implicit rationalism of Radcliffe is not altogether satisfying. Those readers are many who have grumbled at her terminal explanations (though I suppose she would accuse them of being Vivaldis). There is a problem in aesthetics, put very well by the *Quarterly Review* in 1810:

> ... we can believe, for example, in Macbeth's witches, and tremble at their spells; but had we been informed, at the conclusion of the piece, that they were only three of his wife's chambermaids disguised for the purpose of imposing on the Thane's credulity, it would have added little to the credibility of the story, and entirely deprived it of its interest.

The analogy is apt. One might add that such explanations would deprive *Macbeth* of much of its meaning as well as its interest. Radcliffe's own religious principles are unexceptionable but jejune. In *The Italian* they are best scented in her sketch of a *good* convent, that of the Daughters of Pity. Unlike the oppressive one in which Ellena had been imprisoned, this one is devout but free of superstition, intolerance, and enthusiasm. Its Superior is "neither gloomy, nor bigotted," and in her lectures "she seldom touched upon points of faith, but explained and enforced the moral duties, particularly such as ... tended to soften and harmonize the affections" (III, 4). Clearly this enlightened Superior has absorbed *The Natural History of Reli-*

gion; or some such book. She is a tolerant and benevolent moralist, not some zealot ranting about theology.

In this characterization there is something a trifle too easy. Indeed, there is something in the entire book, with its plethora of "pleasing" aweful, horrible, scenes, that is too self-indulgent, too intellectually slattern. There is one short but telling episode (I, 8) where Ellena, confined in the *bad* convent, is befriended by the one sympathetic nun there, Olivia, who many chapters later is of course discovered to be her mother. In Ellena's barren cell, when she is out, Olivia kindly leaves a chair and table, some books and flowers. On returning, "Ellena did not repress the grateful tears, which the generous feelings of Olivia excited; and she forbore, for some moments, to examine the books, that the pleasing emotions she experienced might not be interrupted." We see that Ellena is quite an epicure of feeling! That sentence is immediately followed by this one: "On looking into these books, however, she perceived, that some of them treated of mystical subjects, which she laid aside with disappointment." To savor emotions or lose oneself in a landscape is one thing; to buckle down and study mysticism quite another, apparently. She is greatly relieved, however, to find that there are some Italian poets among the rest of the books. Consistent with this perspective, which the author clearly shares with Ellena, we are told that the Daughters of Pity excel, not in contemplation or homiletics, but in music — not, we are reassured, the difficult or intricate sort, but rather the kind that "steals upon the heart, and awakens its sweetest and best affections" (III, 4). Such is the *good* convent: liberated from theological doctrine and odious asceticism, it stands for humanitarianism, social responsibility, benevolence. But for his sex, David Hume might have dwelt there with great propriety.

□

William Beckford's oriental tale, the *History of the Caliph Vathek* (1786), is neither Gothic nor, in length, a novel, but it has been classed as a transition between the more conventional

Gothic romances of Walpole, Reeve, and Radcliffe, and the less reticent, more lurid horror-romanticism of *The Monk* and its nineteenth-century exfoliations. Certainly it is a wonderful little study in daemonic horror and an exotic version of the Faust theme.[20] Beckford, an erratic and fabulously wealthy sybarite, was a genuine scholar of *res orientalia*, and though he was only twenty-one when he began *Vathek*, he was one of the first to catch the flavor of eastern fable and folklore. Actually, orientalism seems to have caught on before Gothicism: a French translation of the *Thousand and One Nights* was available by the first decade of the century, and Goldsmith's *Citizen of the World*, the many satiric oriental tales of Voltaire, Johnson's own *Rasselas*, nourished the vogue. But in respect of authenticity of tone, none of these approaches *Vathek*.

The story itself is simple enough. The opulent Caliph Vathek is motivated by hedonism, the *libido dominandi*, and some slight degree, it can hardly be underestimated, of intellectual curiosity. Encouraged in his desires by his mother Carathis, a redoubtable astrologer and witch, he abjures Mahomet, devotes himself to a malignant giaour, and promises to "adore the terrestrial influences." As recompense, he will be brought to the fabled Palace of Subterranean Fire, where he will receive talismans to render him omnipotent and the treasures of the pre-Adamite sultans. A stretch of episodes follows showing Vathek's decadence, egoism, and fatuous cruelty. He takes as his paramour the equally haughty and self-regarding Princess Nouronihar, and after ignoring an admonitory spirit sent by Mahomet, he and Nouronihar are led to the Palace of Subterranean Fire, are privileged to interview Eblis, an oriental Lucifer, are shown the treasures, and are doomed to wander forever and in anguish, their right hands placed over the eternally flaming hearts that their chests, turned transparent, disclose. The last two para-

---

[20]Beckford originally wrote it in French, though it first saw the light of day in the standard English translation of his onetime friend Samuel Henley. For a handy account of the rather complex biographical and textual problems associated with *Vathek*, see Robert J. Gemmett, *William Beckford* (Boston: Twayne, 1977). All quotations are from Richard Garnett's edition (1893), as reprinted in *Three Gothic Novels*, ed. E. F. Bleiler (New York: Dover, 1966).

graphs point the moral: this shall be the punishment "of unrestrained passions and atrocious deeds . . . of that blind curiosity, which would transgress those bounds the wisdom of the Creator has prescribed to human knowledge" (194).

But if the story is uncomplicated, the style and tone are troublesome. The tale begins with a description of Vathek:

> His figure was pleasing and majestic: but when he was angry, one of his eyes became so terrible, that no person could bear to behold it; and the wretch upon whom it was fixed instantly fell backward, and sometimes expired. For fear, however, of depopulating his dominions and making his palace desolate, he but rarely gave way to his anger (109).

Here is the penetrating, terrifying glance of the alchemist in *St. Leon*, Schedoni, and legions of daemonic hero-villains — but ludicrously hyperbolized. If it be thought that such hyperbole is only a trait of the oriental style, the last sentence communicates an ironic detachment reminiscent of Pope, Swift, or Voltaire. Note, too, the grotesqueness: it is just *one* of Vathek's eyes that is thus demolitionary. This sort of thing runs practically throughout the tale, and to ironic hyperbole we may add outright comedy — for example, when Nouronihar tricks Vathek's chief eunuch into falling into her bath (148–51); and burlesque, as when the Satanic giaour transforms himself into a ball and is propelled about the court by Vathek's increasingly frenzied subjects (121–22). Voltairean irony, gross exaggeration, grotesquerie, comedy, burlesque: few of these have been thought to comport with spiritual horror, and they explain H. P. Lovecraft's rather understated remark that "Beckford . . . lacks the essential mysticism which marks the acutest form of the weird."[21]

---

[21]H. P. Lovecraft, *Supernatural Horror in Literature* (New York: Ben Abramson, 1945), 37–38. This is a typical criticism. George Saintsbury, admiring *Vathek* as "an almost entire and perfect chrysolite," nevertheless charges it with "a lack of mystical vagueness" (*The Peace of the Augustans* [1916; rpt. London: Oxford Univ. Press, 1946], 174). On the other hand, Birkhead, *Tale of Terror*, 98, praises as powerful and distinctive its "definite precision of outline," with "no vague hints . . . no lurking shadows concealing untold horrors." *De gustibus.*

A leading authority on Beckford, Robert J. Gemmet, also makes Lovecraft's point, but elaborates:

> The best satirists of the eighteenth century allowed their sense of the grotesque to be generated internally from the work itself; Beckford, on the other hand, generates his "outside" the context of the tale; and he allows it to intrude upon the general serious character of the work. The humor is fundamentally incongruous to the tale and seems more impulsive than purposeful.[22]

This is a sophisticated distinction, but makes heavy weather of Beckford's irony. I should like to suggest that *Vathek* is more complex, or at least more proficiently complex, than these commentators allow. In the same place Gemmet writes: "Critics have frequently cited the book's mixture of the sacred and the profane, as when, for example, the caliph during the course of a dinner suddenly grows pious and calls in the same breath in which he recited his prayers for 'the Koran and the sugar.'" Gemmet goes on to remark the "bizarre associations," the "unexpected juxtapositions," which counteract the serious tone and incite "nervous giggles."

What actually happens in the episode referred to is this. Vathek has not had a very appetizing or satisfactory dinner for quite awhile, due to some misadventures on the road. Two dwarfs are brought before him fetching a large basket of fruit, and they recount a rather prolix story to the effect that Allah inspired them to seek out Vathek and provide him this nutriment: "Vathek, in the midst of this curious harangue, seized the basket; and, long before it was finished, the fruits had dissolved in his mouth. As he continued to eat, his piety increased; and, in the same breath, he recited his prayers and called for the Koran and sugar" (145–46). In the first place, Vathek does not "suddenly" grow pious; it is just the opposite, his piety mounting as he eats. The *point* of the episode is clear enough, though it may wear the appearance of complexity when exegetes try

[22]Gemmett, *Beckford*, 95–96.

pedestrianly to explain it. Even as the dwarfs retail their flattering but tedious account of Allah's concern for Vathek, Vathek has been unable to check his appetite; but *as* he satisfies that appetite, he begins to have a little time for piety — though the genuineness of even that tardy piety is questioned by his calling simultaneously for the Koran *and* sugar. The episode shows us something about Vathek that is quite consistent with what we have already seen, and it in no way disrupts the tone. The throwing together of the Koran and sugar illustrates, not a failure of style in Beckford, but Vathek's hedonism. It is Pope's trick, who in *The Rape of the Lock* shows Belinda's superficiality when he predicts that she may "Forget her pray'rs, or miss a Masquerade, / Or lose her Heart, or Necklace, at a Ball." Such things are of the same value for a flibbertigibbet such as Belinda, and no less perfunctory is Vathek's piety. Beckford's wit, no more than Pope's is "generated outside the context of the tale," and it is no more incongruous with its subject than Pope's. Pope wishes to show by clever juxtaposition that Belinda's principles are disheveled; Beckford is doing the same with respect to Vathek, though to be sure his caliph is infinitely more reprehensible than Pope's coquette.

I have labored this point, it may seem pedantically, because I think that much of the controversial humor in *Vathek* can be similarly resolved. From Edgar Allen Poe forward we have expected our weird stories to be totally weird. Poe's cardinal principle of composition was that a piece should be directed to a single, coherent effect. Poe could be facetious, sometimes very much in Beckford's vein; but he segregates his facetious from his uncanny stories. Lovecraft was Poe's professed disciple, and his own best stories have an admirable singleness of tone. So it is no wonder that he, and many modern critics, should object to humor in a weird tale as incongruous or, to speak jargonically, "generated" outside the context.

But it has not always been thus. Marlowe's *Dr. Faustus* is full of humor, often very raw, and though some fussy critics have laid the blame for those passages on ancillary hacks, Marlowe may well have written or at least tolerated them. Certainly they suit well enough Faustus's character, which is often ridiculous and clownish, and in no way do they detract from the religious horror of the conclusion. Mozart's *Don Giovanni*, which appeared a year after *Vathek*, shows a similar mingling of farcical and lofty music as the homicidal playboy is summoned to hell by the animated statue of the Commendatore; one notes that the jovial finale of the opera was often censured as incongruous by post-Poe, or let us just say, Romantic critics. For that matter, even Bryon's *Don Juan* shows an artful, and many would declare, successful, juxtaposition of ironic iconoclasm and serious Romantic drama. Pope never wrote more somber lines than those which close *The Dunciad*, a work full of farce and grotesquerie. Then of course there are all those tragedies of Shakespeare, the comic portions of which Johnson agilely defends against the prissy, narrow classicism of Voltaire. The truth of the matter is that humor can be properly, or maladroitly, introduced into a serious piece. Beckford quite appropriately directs his humor at Vathek, and there is no reason we should not laugh at the folly and damnation of a sadist.

Not only is the humor *not* incongruous or "impulsive" in *Vathek*, but it was deliberately injected, I believe, to hinder a grave misconception into which some critics have nevertheless managed to blunder. For example, Vathek and his company have been styled "individualists whose freedom of expression takes on the quality of heroism, even though they all meet with tragedy in the end. . . . they are also heroes, whether good or evil, in their striking roles and postures."[23] This is what comes of seeing the humor as extrinsic! What that humor shows us, to the point of redundancy, is that Vathek, in role or posture, is a dolt, a coward, a sadist, a buffoon, a crude blasphemer. His mother Carathis has a truly daemonic presence, and some of her necromantic rituals are recounted with shuddery detail; but Vathek himself is not even very intellectually curious: "He was fond of engaging in disputes with the learned, but did not allow them to push their opposition with warmth. He stopped with presents the mouths of those whose mouths could be stopped;

[23]Ibid., 148.

whilst others . . . he sent to prison to cool their blood, a remedy that often succeeded" (111). He and his horrendous mother are tyrannical rulers, cruelest to those who are most faithful to them, impervious to anyone's feelings but their own, deracinated from all normal, human allegiances. It is hard enough to see Marlowe's Faustus as a hero—he appears more often a low jester, a conceited magician who, but only with the devil's aid, can fetch strawberries from afar, an adolescent classicist mooning over a Helen of Troy who never says a word lest she spoil his infatuation. But Faustus is Prospero compared with Vathek, his mother, his paramour. These characters have no freedom of expression, but are slavish voluptuaries; they have the heroism of the bully; their end is not tragic but fitting, for there has been no waste, no corruption of the good, in *them*. As in Dante, their punishment suits the condition of their souls: to wander purposeless and frustrated, their hearts incandescent, in death as in life. Only the most relentless whig critic, determined to find heroic, free-speaking individualists everywhere, could so stretch his imagination as to glimpse them here!

Then too, the farcical elements retire at the end. The good genii sent by Mahomet admonishes Vathek and Nouronihar to repent, arguing, like Faustus's good angel, that there is still time. Even Vathek is momentarily "overawed," but "his pride prevailing," like Faustus he cannot believe that any grace is possible. They encounter the Luciferian Eblis: "a young man, whose noble and regular features seemed to have been tarnished by malignant vapours. In his large eyes appeared both pride and despair: his flowing hair retained some resemblance to that of an angel of light." He has a voice "more mild than might be imagined, but such as penetrated the soul and filled it with the deepest melancholy" (187–88). Eblis is the middle-aged Satan of *Paradise Lost* in his adolescence, less scarred, more complaisant. The description of his palace, the mournful adjuration of the Soliman, above all the view of the damned themselves, ring with true spiritual horror:

> In the midst of this immense hall, a vast multitude was incessantly passing, who severally kept their right hands on

[297]

their hearts, without once regarding anything around them: they had all the livid paleness of death. Their eyes, deep sunk in their sockets, resembled those phosphoric meteors that glimmer by night in places of interment. Some stalked slowly on, absorbed in profound reverie; some, shrieking with agony, ran furiously about like tigers wounded with poisoned arrows; whilst others, grinding their teeth in rage, foamed along more frantic than the wildest maniac. They all avoided each other; and, though surrounded by a multitude that no one could number, each wandered at random unheedful of the rest, as if alone on a desert where no foot had trodden (186–87).

In their eldritch and loathsome detail, such passages are certainly prophetic of *The Monk*. The farcical matter, having presumably stifled any sympathy we might have felt for Vathek, now properly recedes, and we are left with these luminous and horrifying images. There is not, it is true, the thrilling desperation here of Faustus's last speech, or the last scenes of *The Monk*; it is rather the more monotonous, and for some readers the more memorable, horror of Dante.

In the images, and their masterly deployment, much of the power of *Vathek* resides. The story opens with Vathek's luxurious five palaces of the senses and concludes in the horrible Palace of Subterranean Fire. At the beginning Vathek is building a Babel-like tower to escape the confines of the earth and conquer the stars; at the end he descends to the Halls of Eblis, which have a nightmarish, labyrinthine quality reminiscent of a Piranesi "prison-scape."[24] In the middle of the tale Nouronihar, having taken a narcotic powder to simulate death and escape the as yet undesired attentions of Vathek, experiences coldness at the heart; at the end, her heart and Vathek's are ignited perpetually (it has been shown that Beckford got this idea from an earlier work — but he has adapted and transformed it with Shakespearean ingenuity). Now it is true that Beckford

---

[24]See W. B. Carnochan, *Confinement and Flight* (Berkeley: Univ. of California Press, 1977), 135, 140–41.

lingers over the opulence and sensuality of his story with something bordering on indecency; and this trait, together with his own known narcissism, throws into doubt the seriousness of his moral. We have the same problem with *The Picture of Dorian Gray*. But the malignant and restless egoism of Vathek, the gorgeous horror of the settings, the anguished throng shunning one another (individualists indeed!), the flagrant hearts — these remain with us, however melodramatic they may seem when detached from the context; and how satisfactorily they suit the "official" moral! The same may be said of the central image of *Dorian Gray*.

In the *Episodes of Vathek* — separate stories that Beckford intended at one time to incorporate into the tale proper — like themes and imagery obtain. In the two stories that were completed, the evil protagonists apostasize from Islam and try to extirpate it; one character is converted to a satanic Zoroastrianism, and the other to an atheistic hedonism. Although in directness and economy *Vathek* is better off without these, the tales themselves have great narrative and descriptive vigor. The account of the Zoroastrian Hall of Fire, in the "Story of Prince Alasi," is nothing inferior to *Vathek* in its magnificence of horror:

> The flames sometimes shone with an unendurable brightness; sometimes they shed a blue and lurid light, making all surrounding objects appear even more hideous than they actually were.... From time to time we were enveloped in a whirlwind of sparks.... In the portion of the temple where we stood, the walls were hung with human hair of every colour; and, from space to space, human hair hung also in festoons from the pyramids of skulls chased in gold and ebony. Besides all this, the place was filled with the fumes of sulphur and bitumen, oppressing the brain and taking away the breath. I trembled; my legs seemed to give way.... 'Take me hence,' I whispered; 'take me from the sight of thy god.'[25]

[25]William Beckford, *The Episodes of Vathek*, tr. Sir Frank T. Marzials (Boston: Small, Maynard & Co., n. d.), 39–40.

Paul Elmer More's appraisal of *Vathek* is correct. Conceding the obvious, that as an artist Beckford is far below Goethe, More goes on to criticize the ending of Goethe's *Faust* as sentimental and pallid in its feebly humanitarian anticlimax; and he reserves for Beckford this praise: that he imaged "a great and everlasting truth better than Goethe or any other man of his age."[26] But Johnson, in his own oriental tale, has also left us a powerful image, if not so scarlet and acrid as Beckford's. Rasselas and his party leave the Happy Valley to seek true happiness. Persuaded of the vanity of human wishes by such sights as the pyramids, they return home rather more content, keeping busy, to be sure, but somewhat aimless: "driven along the stream of life without directing their course to any particular port." So Vathek, tired of his sensual palaces, abandons them for more complete pleasure. The vanity of his quest is enounced by the Soliman, and he, his mother, and his paramour, mingle perforce with the vagrant crowd. Needless to say, the aimlessness of Imlac and Rasselas is very different from that of the despairing Vathek; and Johnson, true to his anti-romantic temperament, not only refrains from exploiting the oriental exoticism and eroticism of the genre but shrewdly undercuts them: an Arab chieftain, for example, is bored out of mind with his harem. (Gemmet calls Johnson's handling of the genre "sterile"!) But his point, and for that matter Voltaire's in *Candide*, is not so different from Beckford's. *Rasselas*, *Candide*, and *Vathek* are the three greatest oriental tales, and they each in their way express two favored beliefs of the eighteenth century: that happiness is forever elusive, and that self-deception is the natural state of man.

◻

Matthew G. Lewis's hair-raiser *The Monk* was published in 1796, a decade after *Vathek* and one year before *The Italian*. Even more than *Vathek* it is the product of youth, having been

[26]P. E. More, *The Drift of Romanticism (Shelburne Essays, Eighth Series)* (Boston: Houghton Mifflin, 1913), 36.

written when Lewis was nineteen. Its extraordinary precocious-ness, and an occasional resemblance to German horror tales, has thrown its originality into doubt. A leading authority, arguing that two-thirds of it was filched from a German romance, even refers to it as a "German adaptation." But Lewis has been vin-dicated, the supposed source — such is fate — having been pla-giarized from him![27] It remains true, however, that *The Monk* introduced into English literature the intensely vivid, some-times lubricious and sadistic horror of Teutonic legend. Lewis was by nature freakish and aristocratic, like Beckford, and as an adolescent he spent some time in Germany (he was an early fan of Goethe's youthful *Werther*) and in revolutionary Paris of 1791. So there is a distinctly Continental air about *The Monk* that is due to more than its locale in Spain. Lewis's mother owned a copy of Glanvill's *Sadducismus Triumphatus*, and crit-ics, rummaging around to find something to say about the gen-esis of his remarkable novel, have decided that Glanvill must have tinged Lewis's juvenile imagination. But as I have observed earlier in this study, the *Sadducismus Triumphatus* is sober, far removed from the macabre phantasmagoria it is fancied to be by those who have not peered into it. In diabolic naughtiness and horror Lewis easily surpasses anything in the dainty and schol-arly Glanvill (who I daresay would have been mightily shocked by *The Monk*); and Lewis's accent on the literalness of the satanic pact, however proper to his theme, is essentially Conti-nental and very discordant with the substance and spirit of Glanvill's book.

The Monk, however, is concocted of English as well as Con-tinental ingredients. The epigraph of the first chapter is taken from *Measure for Measure* — the description of the prudish and puritanical Angelo — and that play is again quoted in Chapter 6, at a particularly important stage in the development of the monk, Ambrosio.[28] At his first appearance Ambrosio is very like

---

[27]Tompkins alleges Lewis's derivativeness, 245–46; but cf. Summers, *Gothic Quest*, 223–28, 298, and Railo, *Haunted Castle*, 345–46.

[28]All quotations are from the original text, as reprinted by Grove Press, New York, 1952 (rpt. 1959).

Angelo: still relatively young, reputedly devout, he enjoys a great renown for holiness; but he has only a cloistered virtue, never yet having been exposed to temptation. As it does for Angelo, that temptation arrives in the form of lust. Ambrosio yields, turns hypocrite, but remains outwardly a moral rigorist, showing no charity or compassion to others (the erring but sympathetic nun Agnes, hounded by Ambrosio, is comparable to both Julietta and Claudio in Shakespeare's play). Finally, like Angelo, Ambrosio becomes criminal. These similarities cluster in the first two chapters; it is clear that the young Lewis is using *Measure for Measure* as a spring to actuate his own work. He also casts an eye at *Paradise Lost*. Twice in Chapter 1 the virtuous Antonia is described like Eve, the stress on "her long fair hair, which descended in ringlets to her waist." The abbey-garden — the most beautiful spot in Madrid, we are told — is like Milton's Eden, and it is there that Rosario reveals "himself" to Ambrosio as Matilda, his infernal temptress; it is there, too, that Ambrosio is ominously bitten by a serpent "concealed among the roses" (Ch. 2). Other passages, at which I shall glance later, recall Pope's *Eloisa to Abelard*; and on at least three occasions Lewis seems to model scenes on *Clarissa*: Antonia's lover Lorenzo has a dream (Ch. 1) in which Antonia is seized by a monster; but the monster descends to hell and Antonia ascends to heaven leaving her robe behind, just like Clarissa in Lovelace's similar dream. In a roguish reversal of Clarissa's penknife scene, Matilda threatens to plunge a knife into her heart if Ambrosio *fails* to respond to her overtures (Ch. 2). Finally, Ambrosio plots to rape Antonia when she is drugged — though unlike Lovelace he is intercepted in this design (Ch. 8). I have mentioned these influences because most studies of *The Monk* have ignored or minimized the elements of native literature upon which Lewis so heavily relies. But soon and dexterously he imparts to his characters psychological and daemonic dimensions quite unlike anything in *Measure for Measure*, and begins to work up his own situations with great, perhaps excessive, confidence. *The Monk*, however derivative in its earlier sections, however slovenly in facture (and we shall soon see how slovenly it is!), has power and even distinction.

Richardson, Radcliffe, Beckford, Lewis

Like Schedoni after him, Ambrosio is obscure in his origins; like Schedoni, he is ascetic and severe, magnetic as a preacher. But he is not particularly sinister; indeed, Lewis rather stresses his youth and innocence in the ways of the world. His eyes are striking, of course, but: "Tranquillity reigned upon his smooth unwrinkled forehead; and content, expressed upon every feature, seemed to announce the man equally unacquainted with cares and crimes" (Ch. 1). Even before his actual fall, however, we are told that he is inwardly proud of his attainments; and he is so deficient in self-knowledge that Matilda, seeking to seduce him, operates easily on his vanity (Ch. 2). Matilda is much more the Machiavel than Ambrosio, who is described as naturally intelligent and even generous. But he has been corrupted by the superstitions of his Roman Catholic upbringing. Thus Lewis presents him as a person torn "between his real and acquired character": "his inborn genius darted a brilliant light upon subjects the most obscure; and almost instantaneously his superstition replunged them in darkness more profound than that from which they had just been rescued" (Ch. 6). The degrading corruptions of a superstitious education, together with the release, effected by Matilda, of long-pent sexual passions, explain his fall. Impelled by these he is driven to foul crimes, culminating in the abduction, forcible rape (in peculiarly ghastly surroundings), and murder of the virtuous but naive Antonia — whose mother he had earlier throttled! Ambrosio had first been tempted by Matilda, disguised as a boy and novitiate in the abbey (Ch. 2). Soon tiring of her, he falls for the first time *truly* in love: with Antonia; and Matilda, resigned at length to his indifference, further inflames his lust for Antonia by displaying her naked in her bath, in a magic mirror (Ch. 7). All of these scenes, and especially the final rape, were speedily denounced as obscene and pornographic — Coleridge was one of the most ferocious critics. Even some modern commentators have been appalled, nowadays a rare capacity. But the scenes are certainly justified by the context and theme — if such scenes are ever justified. The after-effects of unbridled lust, the loathing of self and the other, the stupefaction and remorse, are very adequately rendered in Chapter 11 and give *The Monk* a spiritual resonance altogether beyond *The Italian*, or for that matter, *Measure for Measure.*

Matilda is much more menacing and daemonic than Ambrosio. Having insinuated herself, disguised, into Ambrosio's abbey, she reveals herself in the garden where, like Satan with Eve, she formally begins her seduction. But like Satan, she has earlier tried to contaminate her victim's dreams. Ambrosio has long been used to meditating with great religious ardor on a painting of the Madonna hanging on a wall of his cell, and in one of his dreams he is torn between erotic desires for Matilda and devotion to that Madonna. That devotion itself is clearly infused with no little sexual desire, however suppressed. But it further transpires that Matilda, laying her plans far ahead, had arranged to have *herself* painted as that Madonna, and then to have the portrait introduced into the abbey. In this manner have the sacred and the profane been inextricably mixed in poor Ambrosio's imagination, and even his purest devotions irreparably polluted. I have noted that there is a like confusion in the mind of Pope's Eloisa between divine and profane "ideas" or images; and there is, I believe, a sub- or inverted-Eloisa theme in *The Monk.* Possibly there are even verbal echoes, as when Matilda, professing modesty at first to allay Ambrosio's suspicions, says: "I expect not to inspire you with a love like mine: I only wish for the liberty to be near you . . . to obtain . . . your friendship" (Ch. 2). In the same passage she goes on to say: "I look upon you as a saint: prove to me that you are no more than man, and I quit you with disgust." But after Ambrosio seems safely ensnared: "I love you no longer with the devotion which is paid to a saint. . . . Away with friendship!" And much later, like Eloisa in one of her erotic fits, she argues that Ambrosio's vows were "unnatural" and that "were love a crime, God never would have made it so sweet, so irresistable!" (Ch. 6).[29]

But the comparison is complicated. Matilda is the temptress here, whereas Abelard is presumably the seducer in Pope's poem, although he is singularly supine. Yet Matilda mimics

[29]Cf. *Eloisa to Abelard*, 60–72, 92, 342.

some of Eloisa's feelings in order to inveigle Ambrosio, who, like Eloisa, will soon decide that his abbey cramps his enlarged desires. After captivating him, Matilda reveals another side of her character:

> Now she assumed a sort of courage and manliness in her man-
> ners and discourse, but ill calculated to please him. She spoke
> no longer to insinuate, but command: he found himself
> unable to cope with her in argument, and was unwillingly
> obliged to confess the superiority of her judgment. . . . He
> regretted Rosario, the fond, the gentle, and submissive; he
> grieved that Matilda preferred the virtues of his sex to those
> of her own (Ch. 6).

As is well known, Lewis was homosexual, and there is doubtless material here to feed the musings of the armchair alienist. From a purely aesthetic point, however, the relation between the two is well handled. Matilda seizes the initiative and dominates Ambrosio throughout the novel. It is she who shows him the naked Antonia in the magic mirror and excites his lust for her beyond control. It is she who, awesomely garbed as sorceress-priestess, invokes the Demon and requires from him the charmed branch of myrtle that will enable Ambrosio to get at Antonia in her bed (Ch. 7). It is she who uncannily appears in Ambrosio's cell at the end to tempt him yet once more to sign the infernal pact, and who then disappears in an astonishing cloud of blue fire. So it is not really so surprising when in the final pages the Demon discloses to the wretched monk that Matilda is actually a succubus who had assumed female form; after all, she has carried out her plan of entangling Ambrosio in lust and sorcery with a nearly preternatural exactitude.

It is usually thought that Beckford paved the way for *The Monk* in his use of shocking, concrete imagery — such a contrast with Radcliffe's diffidence and diffuseness. The question of influence is not easily determined: we know, for example, that Lewis particularly admired Radcliffe's own *Mysteries of Udolpho*. What cannot be doubted is that the imagery of *The Monk* is charged with luminosity and vigor, and that it consists chiefly of the erotic, and of the physically and spiritually horrid. Since the key to effecting Ambrosio's downfall is his repressed sexual desire, the erotic material, though it has been scattered about with prodigality, would seem to be justified *ex hypothesi*. Except for the concluding passages, the horrible scenes are mostly connected with a sub-plot concerning the sadistic imprisonment of Agnes, a pregnant nun. She is drugged in such a way as to lead her to think she is dying (to teach her a lesson), then immured in a loathsome subterranean dungeon. She is forced to deliver her baby by herself; it soon dies; but she clings to its putrid corpse till she is released. She does recover to marry the repentant and aristocratic father of her child, but her account of her sufferings is crammed with imagery recalling and surpassing that of poets like Blair and Young:

> Sometimes I felt the bloated toad, hideous and pampered with the poisonous vapours of the dungeon, dragging his loathsome length along my bosom. Sometimes the quick cold lizard roused me, leaving his slimy track upon my face, and entangling itself in the tresses of my wild and matted hair. Often have I at waking found my fingers ringed with the long worms which bred in the corrupted flesh of my infant (Ch. 11).

Such descriptions are indulged more copiously than the theme demands; they are no doubt part of a youthful reaction against stodginess, perhaps against the feminine obliquity of Radcliffean terror. But if the desire for a shudder, even for vicarious nausea, is natural to humankind, then it must be owned that Lewis answers that need much more ably than any of the graveyard school of poets.

In his fashioning the end of the novel, however, Lewis cannot be entirely acquitted of some self-indulgence, though here, too, tastes will differ. A brief comparison with *The Italian*, published a year later, is instructive. To begin with, Radcliffe is distinctly superior to Lewis in her portrayal of the Inquisition. Lewis is much livelier than Godwin was to be in *St. Leon*, of course, but his inquisitors are amorphous, and the torture scenes, though more forthright than Radcliffe's, are curiously feckless. Yet the advantages are not all on Radcliffe's side. In *The Italian*, we recall, Vivaldi is visited in his dungeon cell by an enigmatic monk who, coming through a secret passage, seems at first to Vivaldi to be supernatural. But the monk is very real, and Vivaldi rightly represses his superstitious humor. At the end of *The Monk* both Matilda and Satan visit Ambrosio. Their manifestations are truly supernatural and give much more power to Lewis's conclusion than would have been provided by the inconsequent rationalism of Radcliffe. When first invoked by Matilda, the Demon had appeared in the semblance of "a youth seemingly scarce eighteen, the perfection of whose form and face was unrivalled. He was perfectly naked: a bright star sparkled upon his forehead, two crimson wings extended themselves from his shoulders, and his silken locks were confined by a band of many-coloured fires. . . . His form shone with dazzling glory" (Ch. 7). Ambrosio of course had been expecting something repulsive. Now, however:

> A swarthy darkness spread itself over his gigantic form: his hands and feet were armed with long talons. Fury glared in his eyes, which might have struck the bravest heart with terror. Over his huge shoulders waved two enormous sable wings: and his hair was supplied by living snakes, which twined themselves round his brows with frightful hissings (Ch. 12).

The first description may well have been prompted by Eblis in *Vathek*, and it is even more mild: a decadent rather than daemonic devil, a diabolic aesthete who at most bemuses. Since the idea is to seduce Ambrosio into sorcery, the representation is apt. The second description is straight out of hardcore folklore. The Demon now uses the tactics of terror, and, appalling Ambrosio with the prospect of a fiery death in the *auto-da-fé*, he constrains him to sign with his blood the fatal pact. Straightway he releases Ambrosio from prison, but sets him on the brink of a precipice whence, after some conclusory jibes, he raises him by driving his talons into the monk's head and hurls him down so that he rolls or bounces from ledge to ledge till at last, his body immedicably broken, he sprawls by a river bank, yet living. There for six days he endures the auxiliary torments of insects that sting his sores and eagles that extrude his eyes, till finally a rain swells the river and he is swept away despairing as well he might be.

This conclusion, uniting as it does spiritual and physical horror, seems to me to be appropriate and efficacious, though there will always be some to whom this sort of thing will not appeal. Ingenious is the parody of Satan's carrying Christ to a pinnacle; and the descent and excruciation of the monk is presented more vividly than that of Simon Magus in the apocryphal tale. But the effect is marred, for some it is even destroyed, by an anomalous and ill-judged string of *Oedipus*-like "discoveries" with which the Demon taunts Ambrosio just before his death: that Antonia whom he raped and murdered was his sister, that her mother, whom he also atrociously killed, was his mother too, that Matilda, whom he had loved, is in truth a succubus. For upon observing Ambrosio's infatuation with the portrait of the Madonna, the devil "bade a subordinate but crafty spirit assume a similar form." Finally, he tells him that if Ambrosio had resisted him but one more minute and refused to sign the pact, he would have been released from the Inquisition: for the guards who he fancied were coming to take him to the stake, in reality "came to signify your pardon."

Now Matilda's psychology, as limned earlier in the novel, is indubitably human; an authorial comment on her feelings in the middle of Chapter 6, along with several other passages, certifies her mortality. Had such passages been prescinded in revisal, the whole business would be more credible; for, as I have suggested, Matilda is certainly a daemonic character. But the passages remain, and Lewis stands convicted of an inconsistency almost as gross as some of Shakespeare's. Montague Summers, allowing that this discrepancy is "serious," adds: "I like to think that this vaunt of the demon is a mere oversight, and, in reading, I delete it—at least mentally—from the text."[30] I

---

[30]*Gothic Quest*, 221.

myself should like to delete the whole paragraph of "vaunts." There has been no preparation for the disclosure that Antonia and her mother are sister and mother to Ambrosio. The notion that he was about to be pardoned by the Inquisition is more wildly improbable than that Matilda was a succubus. One would rather believe that *all* of these last-minute discoveries are demonic fictions — the devil is prince of liars — devised to augment Ambrosio's agony. But naturally there is no warrant in the text to think them lies; and so they remain, obdurate symptoms of a talented and precocious author over-reaching himself in his efforts to contrive a "grand climax."

Then too, the morality of *The Monk* is very shifty. For example, we are told, in Lewis's authorial voice, that Ambrosio was wrong to trust that God would forgive his lapse from chastity early in the novel: "he forgot that, having pronounced those vows, incontinence, in laymen the most venial of errors, became in his person the most heinous of crimes" (Ch. 6). "Most heinous of crimes" seems a very severe phrase, particularly in view of Ambrosio's later delinquencies. After all, the sympathetic Agnes also violates such vows, and complains repeatedly of the dreariness of monastic life; there is evidently a laxer standard for women. Lewis's attitude toward superstition and the supernatural is more interesting but less consistent than Radcliffe's. We are instructed that superstition is Ambrosio's weak point — very like Vivaldi, but very different from that other monk, Schedoni. Yet almost immediately after Lewis makes this point, Ambrosio is persuaded by Matilda to join her in a diabolic invocation. Since the invocation is authentic, he might have been better off had he yielded to the wise impulses of his superstitious dread and abjured Matilda. Lewis's equivocation is even more ludicrously marked in the sub-story concerning Agnes. Agnes's family is derided by Agnes, by her lover Raymond, by Lewis himself, for their flagrantly superstitious natures. Now this family is haunted by the ghost of a Bleeding Nun which stirs abroad at stated intervals (it is a notoriously punctual specter). The lovers decide to have Agnes impersonate the Bleeding Nun at the proper time, so that everyone will be afraid and her lover can emancipate her from her despotic family. But Raymond, through a contretemps, abducts the *real* ghost instead, who gives him an osseous embrace and haunts him indefatigably till the Wandering Jew (who else?) comes along and exorcises her.

In a greater writer, these absurdities might be defended as pointing up profound complexities or different levels of meaning. But *The Monk* was hastily written by a wayward hand, and anyway many of the same lapses can be discerned in even the best Elizabethan drama. For all of its deficiencies, many of them sighted only on close inspection, *The Monk* is at the apogee of the Gothic novel. There is nothing before or since to compare with it in brilliance of conception and gusto of narration, in its "reckless mendacity," to use Edith Birkhead's apt phrase. Connoisseurs of the genre sometimes prefer Charles Maturin's *Melmoth the Wanderer*, published a quarter century later; but that long novel has always seemed to me pretentious and languid compared with *The Monk*. To be sure, far superior works were to engage Gothic themes, but these come from the Romantic poets and superlative craftsmen such as Poe, Hawthorne, the Brontës. A preference for Radcliffe is quite defensible; she is much more conscientious than Lewis. But this is a little like preferring the finest lemonade to second-rate champagne: are we to call such a palate fastidious or just fussy? Setting Lewis's novel next to Thomas Mann's *Doctor Faustus*, John Berryman finds the second "frivolous by comparison": it may show profound experience and subtle artistry, "but maybe the main thing is not there."[31] This remark brings to mind P. E. More's distinction between *Vathek* and Goethe's *Faust*. In both *Vathek* and *The Monk*, despite irksome irregularities of structure and style, the main thing is intact, the authentic, spiritual horror.

¤

" — Have you gone on with Udolpho?"
"Yes, I have been reading it ever since I woke; and I am got to the black veil."

[31]Berryman, introduction to the Grove Press edition of *The Monk*, 13–14.

"Are you indeed? How delightful! Oh! I would not tell you what is behind the black veil for the world! Are you not wild to know?"

"Oh! yes, quite; what can it be? — But do not tell me — I would not be told upon any account. I know it must be a skeleton, I am sure it is Laurentina's skeleton. Oh! I am delighted with the book! I should like to spend my whole life in reading it. . . ."

"Dear creature! . . . when you have finished Udolpho, we will read the Italian together; and I have made out a list of ten or twelve more of the same kind for you."

"Have you, indeed! How glad I am! — What are they all?"

"I will read you their names directly; here they are, in my pocket-book. Castle of Wolfenbach, Clermont, Mysterious Warnings, Necromancer of the Black Forest, Midnight Bell, Orphan of the Rhine, and Horrid Mysteries. These will last us some time."

"Yes, pretty well; but are they all horrid, are you sure they are all horrid?"

This is of course Jane Austen, ridiculing in *Northanger Abbey* — gently enough — the votaries of the Gothic vogue. And when one of the characters professes to have read *Mysteries of Udolpho* in two days, "my hair standing on end the whole time," one wonders if this is not very far indeed from Eliphaz's hair-raising encounter in *Job*, and if the whole business has not really got out of hand. It is all very well to connect such novels with earlier appeals to terror and awe, as I have done, and to rebuke those critics who chatter on about that "long period of sobriety in literature" against which these works are a "natural reaction."[32] Yet *Vathek* and *The Monk* are also very different from *Robinson Crusoe*, *Night Thoughts*, or even *Clarissa*. There is less piety and more brimstone, and latent in them are any number of inauspicious social and philosophical tendencies. It is significant that De Sade considered *The Monk* and its kindred "the inevitable outcome of the revolutionary upheavals experi-

---

[32]Tompkins, 221.

enced throughout the whole of Europe."[33] The sinister alterations and distortions worked by Lewis on the Clarissa and Eloisa
themes suggest that some new force is operating in the minds of
men — or at least some men. We know that Johnson admired
Clarissa, but it would be intensely interesting to have the reac-
tions of Johnson and Hume to the later novels. They might
well, like Austen, have dismissed them as shallow and immature, and Johnson would surely have complained that they have
too little of human nature in them; he praises Shakespeare for
dramatizing universal rather than eccentric passions. But would
Hume or Johnson have sensed beneath the surface anything
profound, anything ominous? Do these novels explore spiritual
feeling or do they trivialize it through grotesquerie and
sensationalism?

Personal taste is bound to govern any answer to that question.
"In the room the women come and go / Talking of Michelan-
gelo," writes T. S. Eliot, implying at once the inanity of the discussion and the transcendent excellence of the artist. The vapid
remarks of Austen's characters, in other words, must be
weighed against the judgment of a Coleridge, for example, on
The Mysteries of Udolpho: "the most interesting novel in the
English language." We must remember, too, that the devil himself is a sensationalist and a vulgarian; even the exquisite Max
Beerbohm must show him so in "Enoch Soames." For such traits
the film "The Exorcist" was much excoriated in some quarters,
mostly academic; but it is quite faithful to accounts of diabolic
possession, ancient and modern. Certainly many attended the
film for titillation and shock, but this need not embarrass others
who admired its vivid presentment of an old and theologically
respectable Weltanschauung. Even the more superficial audiences, at bottom, may have liked the film because its recreation
of the mystery and horror of evil seemed so much more satisfactory than the attenuated, imaginatively impoverished views
of establishment, twentieth-century pundits such as John
Dewey and Bertrand Russell. "The Exorcist" is comparable to

---

[33]De Sade, quoted in Varma, 150

The Monk in its superfoetation of horror; and like *The Monk* it engenders that *deisidaimonias* or daemonic dread that the modern audience, no less than the eighteenth-century reader, appears to crave. Alfred Hitchcock's "Spellbound," however, is more in the Radcliffean mode, with the terrors merely insinuated, and a rational solution furnished at the end. Now "Spellbound" is probably a better crafted film than "The Exorcist," even as *The Italian* is more artful than *The Monk*. But in "The Exorcist" the *main thing* is there. The popularity of both films and their innumerable progeny proves the pertinacity — I do not say the wholesomeness — of the taste for horror.

Excepting *Clarissa*, which I consider as fine a novel as any in the century, these are not works of the first class. But like Shakespeare's plays they can operate on different levels, and all of them attempt to exercise the imagination in those non-rational areas scorned and perhaps feared by the apostles of the Enlightenment. And if, as it has been argued, a deep spiritual understanding cannot be attained without an immediate and strong sense of evil, then these books have their place in our religious education. Between titillation and spiritual exercise, after all, there is but a wavering line, and *Macbeth* can be enjoyed for as many wrong reasons as *The Monk*. It is only that *The Monk* cannot be enjoyed for as many right ones.

CHAPTER VIII

Religious Love and Fear in Late Century Poetry: Smart, Wesley, Cowper, Blake

I form the light, and create darkness: I make peace, and create evil: I the Lord do all these things.

Isaiah

For man is between the pinchers while his soul is shaping and purifying.

CHRISTOPHER SMART

THE EARLY AESTHETICS of terror and awe, the bourgeoning cult of horror and the sublime: these throw some light on mid-century poets and late-century novelists. Since mine is neither a philosophical nor a social study, I have blinked the question whether these theories were propelling public taste and the writers who gratified it or were but canalizing that taste. We seem unable to sort out that matter with respect to our own time, and are not apt to settle it for the eighteenth century. It is no less difficult to say with any exactitude how these four poets connect with what has gone before. There is in all of them a less timid use of biblical themes, a less abashed emulation of biblical style. At mid-century Robert Lowth's intelligent book renewed interest in Hebrew poetry, especially the psalms. Smart was the first poet of stature to see in such poetry an alternative model to the neo-classical couplet and Miltonic blank verse; and in his best poems there is a kindred parallelism, repetitive and responsive structure, free-swinging cadence; in them there is also that scriptural anthropomorphism, elusiveness, and obscurity defended by Lowth as stimulating religious wonder. Blake was later to adapt several of these devices to his own peculiar

ends. Wesley and Cowper give a more personal and introspective turn to Watts's devotional lyric; and Cowper, at least,
imparts to it an hectic intensity. In their best work there is less
of the moral commentary so deplored now in Thomson or
Young.

The decay and abandonment of theological structures noted
elsewhere continues to be evident here. These are all, at their
best, affective poets aiming at producing moods. When theology
does erupt, it is either aberrant orthodoxy, as in Cowper, or a
decoction of heterodoxy, as in Blake. The "deistic evasion" so
alluring to Pope and Thomson is little caressed here. Smart and
Wesley are the poets of religious love, and both, not always happily, try to charge that love with awe. Religious fear preponderates in Cowper and Blake, who in their way are reacting, I
think, to the same tergiversations and anxieties lurking behind
Vathek and *The Monk*. The daemonic elements of the holy,
repressed by Pope, Akenside, and Thomson, partly intuited by
Defoe, Richardson, and Johnson, are much more directly
engaged by Cowper and Blake; only Hume had so bluntly
described them, and then for a very different purpose. Otto postulates a daemonic or non-moral phase in human understanding
of the holy. Cowper and Blake are the great poets of that mood:
in the former it is undesigned, the appalling fruit of his tainted
Calvinism; in the latter it seems deliberate.

That two of the four, Smart and Cowper, were gripped by a
mania or madness, that Blake was widely held to be mad: these
are titillating resemblances I shall not pursue. I greatly doubt
that either Blake or Smart was mad in any very true sense; even
the suicidal Cowper was no raving maniac, however grievous
and serried his psychic wounds. And although their poetry, like
anybody's good poetry, is colored by their personal experience
and temperament, it is absurd to consider it the luscious inad-
vertency of distrait minds. Nonetheless, like Beckford and
Lewis, these three were notably eccentric, and it is worth repeat-
ing that at their best none of them flirted with that compromise
between numinous feeling and rational theodicy so often
remarked, and nearly as often, perhaps ungenerously, reproved

in this study. There is little in them that a Voltaire could really admire. There is no triumph, no flourishing of the Enlightenment *here:* except, perhaps, with a grotesque tortuosity, in the Blake of *The French Revolution.* But Voltaire would have cared no more for Blake's version than for the real one.

◻

The Seasons, Night Thoughts, and *Clarissa* attained completion and prosperity in the 1740s. Christopher Smart, meanwhile, was beginning his short career as hack-writer and aspiring poet. His monomania took the form of compulsive, public praying and caused him to be confined, possibly with short intervals of liberty, from 1756 to 1763; he died in debtor's prison in 1771. His works are usually sorted into pre- and post-incarceration classes, with the *Jubilate Agno* having been written over the long period of confinement. Although his earlier poems had brought him some esteem, his later ones, even or especially the fine *Song to David,* were disdained and derided: partly because they were the issue of a notorious madman (but I think this reason is magnified by some modern critics[1]), and chiefly because their form and tone — not particularly their content — were greatly at odds with the verse then in fashion. The nineteenth century predictably prized his *Song* and found the madness a garnishment. Rossetti declares, airily ignoring slovenly efforts such as *The Rape of the Lock:* "This wonderful poem of Smart's is the only great accomplished poem of the last century.... of course I mean earlier than Blake or Coleridge."[2] But even this is less fervid than Browning's encomium of 1887:

> Such success
> Befell Smart only out of throngs between
> Milton and Keats that donned the singing dress —

[1]See, e.g., Sophia B. Blaydes, *Christopher Smart as a Poet of His Time* (The Hague, Paris: Mouton, 1966). A more balanced study is Moira Dearnley's *Poetry of Christopher Smart* (London: Routledge, 1969).
[2]Quoted in *The Athenaeum,* 3095 (19 Feb. 1887), 248.

Smart, Wesley, Cowper, Blake

> Smart, solely of such songmen, pierced the screen
> 'Twixt thing and word, lit language straight from soul.[3]

In Smart at his best there is no doubt a reckless immediacy that appealed much more to the generation of Matthew Arnold than did the formalities and fastidiousness and whimsy of the earlier poets. Even in the most ostentatiously personal of them, Young, the didactic reflections crowd round the few bright images and encumber them. Browning says Smart "pierced the screen / 'Twixt thing and word," and that seems to have been his own professed intention: "my talent is to give an impression upon words by punching, that when the reader casts his eye upon 'em, he takes up the image from the mould which I have made" (*Jubilate Agno*, XII, 42).[4]

In the earlier poems Smart endeavors indomitably to shake free of exhausted poetic forms while trying with no less industry to be popular: a very complicated ambition. *The Hop Garden* (1752) owes much to *The Seasons*, but it is more trifling, and it is inferior. *The Hilliad* (1753) emulates *The Dunciad* and shares something of its daemonic phantasmagoria; but it is a much feebler effort. His "Night Piece" (1750) and "Fair Recluse" (1751) are festooned with Gothicism and melancholy; *Il Penseroso, Eloisa to Abelard, Clarissa*, lie behind them, naturally overshadow them. So far Smart is something of a dabster, talented, imitative, spasmodic. More ambitious and more successful were his five verse-essays on the "Attributes of the Supreme Being." These were written to win the Seatonian Prize awarded annually by Cambridge to works on that irreproachable theme; and win it they did in 1751, 1752, 1754, and 1756. In style they derive from Milton and Thomson; in substance they argue the a posteriori apologetics of *An Essay on Man* and scores of other essays, in or out of meter: the harmony, beauty, and intricacy of creation show forth the glory of God. Imitative

[3]"With Christopher Smart," 110–14, in *Parleyings with Certain People of Importance in Their Day* (1887).

[4]All quotations are from *The Collected Poems of Christopher Smart*, ed. Norman Callan (London: Routledge, 1949).

as he is, Smart can sometimes rise to the occasion; but even then he owes his debts. One of his best passages, for example — in "On the Immensity of the Supreme Being" — seems to me to be closely modeled on lines six through thirteen of the celebrated first stanza of Dryden's Killigrew ode, quoted in Chapter II. There is the same trailing syntax of "Whether ... Or ... Or ... " clauses and a similar enumeration and contrast of parts of the cosmic hierarchy:

> Whether the mind along the spangled sky
> Measures her pathless walk, studious to view
> Thy works of vaster fabric, where the Planets
> Weave their harmonious rounds, their march directing
> Still faithful, still inconstant to the Sun;
> Or where the Comet thro' space infinite
> (Tho' whirling worlds oppose, and globes of fire)
> Darts, like a javelin, to his destin'd goal.
> Or where in Heav'n above the Heav'n of Heav'ns
> Burn brighter suns, and goodlier planets roll
> With Satellits more glorious — Thou art there.

There are elsewhere echoes of *An Essay on Man* too audible to be accidental.[5]

To be noted, however, is the enlarging space given to biblical and explicitly Christian matter. The first two poems often strike the rationalistic tone of Pope or Thomson; but in the third Smart refers plainly to the fall of man and original sin, in the fourth to the Old Testament miracles and Christ, and in the fifth and last he introduces David in his office as exorcist. The effect of David's harp is compared with that of Orpheus': he "Drove trembling Satan from the heart of Saul, / And quell'd the evil Angel." In the same year, 1756, Smart wrote a "Hymn to the Supreme Being: On Recovery from a Dangerous Fit of Illness,"

---

[5]Cf. Smart's apostrophe, in "On the Omniscience of the Supreme Being," "Go to, proud reas'ner, philosophic man," with Pope's "Go wondrous Creature! mount where Science guides" (*Essay on Man*, II, 19–30); the point of the two passages is the same, the irony similar, and both refer to Newton.

which is an epilogue to the Seatonian poems; it too supplies miracles and exorcists. Smart describes the sickness of King Hezekiah (*Isaiah* xxxviii) whose forefather had been David, who is ill like Saul, and who is miraculously cured by God. He mentions the New Testament miracles and Christ the Exorcist who "drove out Satan from the tortur'd soul." Now the Seatonian poems show some talent, but they are finally conventional, directed at the modish audience that relished Pope and Thomson. To have introduced into them miracles and exorcists bespeaks a scintilla at least of courage and independence. Were it not for the fact of Smart's confinement, the *Jubilate Agno* and *Song to David* would be seen more readily, not as exorbitant departures from his routine verse, but as more arresting treatments of favorite themes.

The *Jubilate Agno*, as amazing as it is interminable, was written in the late 1750s or early 1760s and not intended for publication. It was preserved in manuscript by two of William Cowper's friends, who hoped, probably vainly, that it might help them to understand and assuage *that* poet's derangement. Much of it is tedious and murky, but other parts are sensible enough, and it was very likely written during Smart's lucid intervals. His madness itself, after all, may have amounted to little more than compulsive praying complicated by chronic alcoholism. The observations of perceptive acquaintances such as Johnson and Mrs. Thrale (she compares him to the mad astronomer in *Rasselas:* sane in all things but his one obsession) suggest that he ought not to have been put away.[6] Smart took literally the scriptural admonition to pray without ceasing, and the *Jubilate* may be the poetic sequel of that literalism; more mundanely, it is an abbreviated spiritual journal or diary. It shares traits with even so dissimilar a work as Pope's *Essay:* an aphoristic style, and the theme of a loving God manifesting himself in the diver-

---

[6]See: Johnson in Boswell, *Life,* I, 397; Hester Lynch Piozzi (Mrs. Thrale), "Piozziana," *Gentleman's Magazine,* 186 (July 1849), 24; Katherine C. Balderston, ed., *Thraliana: The Diary of Mrs. Hester Lynch Thrale* (Oxford: Oxford Univ. Press, 1942), II, 728.

sity and order of his creation. Notwithstanding these resemblances, it is hard to imagine an admirer of Pope's poem admiring this one, at least with equal fervor; for it is one of the most unusual poems of the century before Blake. Taken as a whole it is disunified and monotonous; taken as it was probably composed, in smithereens, it can be quite charming, even haunting. The separate lines typically bring sundry persons or things together. Sometimes the ligatures are very obvious: "Let Balaam appear with an Ass, and bless the Lord his people and his creatures for a reward eternal" (I, 11). Some are startling, but on a moment's reflection show sense and even wit: "Let Johnson, house of Johnson rejoice with Omphalocarpa a kind of bur" (XXVII, 10). Still others seem quite whimsical or weird, either expressive of some connection known only to Smart, or, practicing one of Lowth's theories, deliberately arbitrary to convey the variety and enigma of the universe. And then there are sustained passages that have the delicate suggestiveness and traceries of meaning of some of the best modern verse:

> For GOD the father Almighty plays upon the HARP of
> stupendous magnitude and melody.
> For innumerable Angels fly out at every touch and his
> tune is a work of creation.
> For at that time malignity ceases and the devils
> themselves are at peace.
> For this time is perceptible to man by a remarkable
> stillness and serenity of soul.

(X, 25–28)

The earlier figures — Orpheus the divine harper, David the harper and exorcist, Christ the Healer and Exorcist — are now associated with the Godhead directly, and their sanative, restorative powers with the actual creation. Weird, not mad, is the image of the angels emanating from God's harp, and there is surely a wise artfulness in moving from the harp's stupendous melody to the stillness and serenity of soul. Here is devotional poetry with an uncommon luminousness and shimmer. The anthropomorphic note so blaring in Watts and disdained as crude by

Pope, Thomson, and Hume, is here more finely tuned; and heavenly harps have been rescued, however briefly, from their usual vulgarity.

Hebraic parallelism, repetition, synecdoche, and metonymy, together with the characteristic personal turn of the Psalmist, are expertly employed in this passage, itself a fine little poem:

> For THUNDER is the voice of God direct in verse and musick.
> For LIGHTNING is a glance of the glory of God.
> For Brimstone that is found at the times of thunder & lightning is worked up by the Adversary.
> For the voice is always for infinite good which he strives to impede.
> For the Devil can work coals into shapes to afflict the minds of those that will not pray.
> For the coffin and the cradle and the purse are all against a man.
> For the coffin is for the dead and death came by disobedience.
> For the cradle is for weakness and the child of man was originally strong from the womb.
> For the purse is for money and money is dead matter with the stamp of human vanity.
> For the adversary frequently sends these particular images out of the fire to those whom they concern.
> For the coffin is for me because I have nothing to do with it.
> For the cradle is for me because the old Dragon attacked me in it & [I] overcame in Christ.
> For the purse is for me because I have neither money nor human friends.
>
> (X, 50–62)

At the beginning, the passage links the tremendous, Sinaitic God to the brimstone of the Adversary; it is a truly daemonic deity from whose thunder and lightning the old Dragon finds materials for afflicting those who fail to pray. The Adversary is

[321]

the dark side of God—Smart returns to the old meaning of "satan," the one it had in *Job*. But convinced as he always was of God's love, Smart refuses to amplify this hint, and the passage goes on orthodox enough, glancing at the Fall and closing with confidence in Christ's redemption; a confidence, however, made more poignant and intimate by the simple pathos of the last line.

The theme of his poem is religious joy, but Smart can strike a somber tone when he wishes:

> For the devil hath most power in winter, because
>   darkness prevails.
> For the Longing of Women is the operation of the Devil
>   upon their conceptions.
> For the marking of their children is from the same cause
>   both of which are to be parried by prayer.
> For the laws of King James the first against Witchcraft
>   were wise, had it been of man to make laws.
> For there are witchces and wizards even now who are
>   spoken to by their familiars.
> For the visitation of their familiars is prevented by the
>   Lord's incarnation.
> For to conceive with intense diligence against one's
>   neighbour is a branch of witchcraft.
>
> (XI, 1–7)

Here is Smart at his most tantalizing, obscure, and elliptical. Is there, for example, a pun on "conceptions" in the second line, resumed in the last? What *is* Smart's attitude toward witchcraft? James's laws were wise; but directly Smart qualifies himself: "had it been of man to make laws." The witches "even now" can communicate with their familiars—whose "visitation," however, has been obviated by Christ. The passage affirms the devil's power at the beginning; the last line declares one branch of witchcraft, at least, to be natural human malice: unless, of course, as we have been advised earlier, the devil is operating on those conceptions. It is as though Glanvill and his opponents had been wrapped into one. Or perhaps there is nothing in the wrapping, but only a unity of surfaces. Such passages, the delight of a certain tribe of modern critics, are like onions, from which layer after layer can be stripped, and there is nothing at the core. Such is the modernity, among all the quaintnesses, of Smart.

Far less obscure is the *Song to David* (1763), though well into the twentieth century the absurd myth has been perpetuated, even by estimable scholars, that it was scratched with a key on the wainscot of Smart's madhouse during a fit of lunacy.[7] Actually, it employs more adroitly many of the devices he had rehearsed in the *Jubilate*, and although long it has been assembled with great scrupulousness. Contemporary reviewers were apathetic, however, dismissing it as "a fine piece of ruins" — a phrase that might well have been applied to the then unknown *Jubilate* but that shows a very faulty judgment of the *Song.* Boswell regarded it as "a very curious composition, being a strange mixture of *dun obscure* and glowing genius," but William Mason wrote to Gray: "I have seen his 'Song to David' & from thence conclude him as mad as ever."[8] Some modern critics profess amazement that the poem failed to achieve immediate acclaim, rightly enough pointing out that there is nothing very singular in its ideas. It has indeed one of the *last* interesting expressions of the chain of being. It promotes a loving Deity and a harmonious universe: nothing to set one agog, nothing, in fact, very different from the Seatonian poems of a decade or a dozen years before. It can only have been hostility and prejudice against Smart because of his notorious confinement that hindered the poem's success.

Style and tone impress people more than ideas, however, and in style and tone the *Song* is exceptional. The Hebraisms already noted in the *Jubilate*, the hymn-like meter, the febrile

[7]That tale was probably first promoted by *The Monthly Review*, 28 (April 1763), 321. George Saintsbury solemnly rehearses it in *The Peace of the Augustans* (1916; rpt. London: Oxford Univ. Press, 1946), 78–79.

[8]Boswell and Mason quoted in Edward G. Ainsworth and Charles E. Noyes, *Christopher Smart: a Biographical and Critical Study*, in *The University of Missouri Studies*, Vol. 17, 4 (1943), 87.

mood, the symbolism compiled out of occultism, neo-Platonism, Freemasonry: these would have a rather restricted appeal for a generation nourished on Pope or Thomson, for an old maid like Mason. Still, a modern reader may feel that Rossetti's praise, mentioned earlier, is inordinate, and that, after all, Boswell's tepid judgment is fair enough. The power of the *Song* depends on cumulative effect; it is a concatenation of climaxes surging toward a grand climax, a liturgy or incantation whose aim is to kindle religious awe and adoration. God's harp reappears (XXXVIII), and David is the grand exemplar of the religious poet, the supreme adorer — and, of course, the exorcist:

> Blest was the tenderness he felt
> When to his graceful harp he knelt,
> And did for audience call;
> When satan with his hand he quell'd,
> And in serene suspence he held
> The frantic throes of Saul.
>
> (XXVII)

Like the Seatonian poems, some of its passages recall earlier eighteenth-century poetry, but they are far less obsequious. For instance:

> For ADORATION, in the skies,
> The Lord's philosopher espies
> The Dog, the Ram, and Rose;
> The planet's ring, Orion's sword;
> Nor is his greatness less ador'd
> In the vile worm that glows.
>
> (LXVI)

is suggestive of *An Essay on Man*, I, 270–80, where Pope, celebrating God's omnipresence, moves from the sun and stars to the very small: "As full, as perfect, in a hair, as heart, / As full, as perfect, in vile Man that mourns, / As the rapt Seraph that adores and burns." Pope's passage is calmly majestic, celestially insouciant. Smart's stanza, with the two short couplets and distributed middle and end rhyme, sweeps us unfalteringly into jubilation. David sings, among other things,

> Of gems — their virtue and their price,
> Which hid in earth from man's device,
>   Their darts of lustre sheathe;
> The jasper of the master's stamp,
> The topaz blazing like a lamp
>   Among the mines beneath.
>
> (XXVI).

This may bring to mind the famous lines from Gray's *Elegy:*

> Full many a Gem of purest Ray serene,
>   The dark unfathom'd Caves of Ocean bear:
> Full many a Flower is born to blush unseen,
>   And waste its Sweetness on the desart Air.

But Gray's meaning is rather sentimental, and his analogy unapt: the gem and flower do not illustrate his theme of thwarted potential; they *achieve* their potential, but only are unseen. For Smart, the wonder of the gem and jasper in the mine is no whit diminished by their being hidden; the whole creation, whether or not seen by man, sings the benevolence and power of God. In the *Song*, as in the *Jubilate*, Smart has found a mode of expression authentically his own.

Unfortunately, Smart raised a great heap of verse after the *Jubilate* and the *Song:* hymns, Christianized translations of the Psalms. These are all unspeakably tedious, far less lively than even his most derivative earlier poems. The cornucopian veins discovered in his two best pieces he failed utterly to pursue. He is recalled today, thus, as the erratic author of two exceptional poems, who in his earlier phase must be reckoned a second-rate Thomson, and in his later, a failed or blighted Blake. Yet he did succeed, however fitfully, in conveying the awesomeness of divine love and the ambiguities of religious feeling. And he resolutely fastens, again and again, upon that element in Christian-

[325]

ity most troublesome, most mortifying, to his enlightened contemporaries: its exorcisms.

□

Whether the strange career of Smart was shaped more by his own instability of character or by the indecisiveness and inanition of his age it is hard to judge. Certainly Charles Wesley is equally a poet of divine love, more consistent but less brilliant than his slightly younger contemporary. His hymns are always compared with Watts's and found to be more personal and emotional than the congregationalism of the earlier writer. Owing to the exigencies of the form in which they worked, and a congeniality of religious perspective, there are nevertheless many resemblances between them; and much of what I have said of Watts can be applied to Wesley. But along with the greater personal tone there seems to be in Wesley a softening or sentimentalizing strain and at times, curiously, a connivance with rationalism. One of his most famous hymns, "Wrestling Jacob," adapts an unusually daemonic manifestation of the holy. But in *Genesis* xxxii. 29, the divine being refuses to tell Jacob his name, lest Jacob then have power over him; in Wesley the name, divulged freely, is Love: a word which he sprinkles with great verve but little numinous feeling throughout the second half of the hymn. Perhaps because of his Arminian leanings, Wesley seems addicted to such lenitives.

Not that Wesley shuns awesome themes such as Judgment, Heaven, and Hell. His "Thou Judge of quick and dead" is on the same subject as Watts's "To the Memory of . . . Gouge," where Watts strenuously identifies Christ with the Old Testament Jehovah and pours into his poem all the ferociousness of apocalyptic imagery: Christ's burning arrows wound and annihilate the atheist; Satan, bound to his chariot wheels, "foams and yells aloud." But it is a far less smouldering and flamboyant Christ in Wesley, and the account is larded with lackluster poetic diction such as "dazzling train":

> To pray, and wait the hour,
> That awful hour unknown,
> When, robed in majesty and power,
> Thou shalt from heaven come down,
> The immortal Son of man,
> To judge the human race,
> With all thy Father's dazzling train,
> With all thy glorious grace.
>
> (st. 2)[9]

In "Righteous God! whose vengeful phials" Wesley even drops into the ludicrously casual: "O conclude this mortal story, / Throw this universe aside!" Perhaps his best presentment of the apocalypse is in "By faith we find the place above":

> Then let the thundering trumpet sound,
> The latest lightning glare,
> The mountains melt, the solid ground
> Dissolve as liquid air;
>
> The huge celestial bodies roll,
> Amidst the general fire,
> And shrivel as a parchment-scroll,
> And all in smoke expire!
>
> (st. 3–4)

Even here the language tends to be routine, and the optimistic, personal note reverberates at the beginning and end (st. 1–2, 8). Unlike Watts, it is the New Testament Christ of love that is featured here and in the judgment hymns generally. In Watts's "To . . . Gouge" Christ wounds the fleeing atheist; in this hymn

---

[9]A standard collection of Methodist hymns was assembled by John Wesley and published in 1780 as *A Collection of Hymns, for the Use of the People Called Methodists;* all quotations are from an 1877 reissue.

[327]

Wesley apostrophizes: "Jesus, to thy dear wounds we flee." In "O that I could revere" Wesley treats "fearful love" and exclaims that if God's mercy cannot draw him to God, then "Thou by thy threatenings move, / And keep an abject soul in awe, / That will not yield to love." He speaks of God's sword, his own "sacred horror." But as usual the hymn terminates with an appeal to Christ's mercy and love. Wesley typically presents the reflections of the individual and repentant sinner, avoiding the cosmic and clamorous imagery so often plied by Watts. The effect produced in the reader or singer, far from being terror or awe, might rather be described as *shame*, that we should by our obstinacy compel the loving God to assert his grandeur. This I take to be a form of sentimentality, however one regards it as art or theology.

Wesley's "When Israel out of Egypt came" is thematically similar to Watts's "Law Given at Sinai," quoted elsewhere:

> The sea beheld his power, and fled,
>   Disparted by the wondrous rod;
> Jordan ran backward to its head,
>   And Sinai felt the incumbent God;
> The mountains skipped like frighted rams,
> The hills leapt after them as lambs!
>
> (st. 2)

Although these lines have a proper charm, the imagery is more reserved, and the shameless anthropomorphism of Watts is positively counteracted. Here we have to do with the "incumbent God" and, in the stanza following, with "nature's God": both formulaic and colorless phrases, and the second, at least, a favorite of the rationalist and Deist. Then, too, the moral prized out of the episode of *Exodus* is very different in the two poets. For Watts, it is the very drama itself of the tremendous and transcendent God manifesting himself through the miracle of the deliverance and the theophany at Sinai; and it is also, of course, the all-compelling force of the Law promulgated there. But Wesley conveys this lesson:

> Creation, varied by his hand,
>   The omnipotent Jehovah knows;
> The sea is turned to solid land,
>   The rock into a fountain flows;
> And all things, as they change, proclaim
>   The Lord eternally the same.

For Wesley, the story shows God's immutability compared with creation: a traditional view, to be sure (Augustine speaks of God as *Immutabilis mutans omnia*), but one particularly iterated by *An Essay on Man* and other rationalistically disposed theodicies. Wesley was no Deist, of course; nor is his theology to be impeached. But it is his bias that is intriguing. In this hymn he has minimized the elements of awe and anthropomorphism and closed with a moral reflection as agreeable to the Deists as to the Evangelicals. Elsewhere, when he must choose, he sacrifices awe and terror to love. For Wesley it is the individual, spiritual struggle, the reluctancy of our hearts, that is important, and which the events of the Exodus express historically. For Watts, the historical events themselves were the important thing; and just as in *Exodus* they were intended to engender awe and fear of the Lord in the rabble-like and rebellious children of Israel, so Watts tried to recreate that effect in his humanly lackadaisical congregation.

Both Watts and Wesley are affective poets attempting to induce a religious mood. But there is much more internalizing of the spiritual drama in Wesley, and very little terror. Awe is not wholly absent, but unlike Smart at his best, Wesley is not able to blend in jubilation the intimacy of spiritual love with the awe of a transcendent Deity. He commonly settled for love—and who shall blame him? But in settling for it he veers sometimes toward rationalism and sometimes toward sentimentality. Wesley knew his theology as well as Watts. The trouble is, I think, that his theology is less intellectually tranquil, more readily distracted, seemingly without an inner quiddity: like some of the passages in Smart's *Jubilate*, but more often disappointing than tantalizing.

◻

For many years William Cowper was one of England's most loved poets. *His* fits of insanity — far more intractable and unrelenting than Smart's — failed to hinder his popularity. The *Critical Review*, whose writers had earlier styled the *Song to David* a ruin, expresses the general approbation of Cowper's *Task*: "the religious and moral reflections with which it abounds, though sometimes the diction is not sufficiently elevated . . . possess the acuteness and depth of Young, and are often expressed with the energy of Shakespeare."[10] Satisfactorily applauded was his first volume, published in 1782 when he was 51 and presenting didactic poems on such subjects as "Truth," "Hope," and "Charity." His long, discursive poem, *The Task* (1785), won him fame. He managed, then, to become what the youthful Smart, toiling away at his Seatonian poems or pastiches, had been hoping vainly to be, a much caressed religious bard and moral teacher. But posterity, always unreliable, has recoiled upon his contemporary success. Cowper epitomizes for George Saintsbury many "qualities of the century — its placidity, its not altogether profound but at any rate not quite superficial meditativeness, its pleasantry." From this hedging condescension it is but a short step and fifty years to Paul Fussell's contemptuous dismissal (he is speaking of *The Task*): "The expression of effeminate, prudential cautions here in a rhetoric and prosody full of Miltonic associations demonstrates the kind of ultimate aesthetic incoherence which makes most of Cowper's work so entirely unrewarding."[11]

Aesthetic, and for that matter theological, incoherence lies at the heart of Cowper, sure enough. Like the odd *curriculum*

[10]*Critical Review*, 60 (Oct. 1785), 256.

[11]Saintsbury, *Peace of the Augustans*, 342; Paul Fussell, *The Rhetorical World of Augustan Humanism* (London: Oxford Univ. Press, 1965), 32–33.

vitae of Smart, it tells us something, but the message is blurred, about the situation of the religious poet at the fraying fag-end of the eighteenth century. Still, the charges of placidity, pleasantry (pulverizing term!), effeminate cautions: these apply to only one side of an unusually involuted personality. "Light and dark are never far apart in Cowper," declares a modern biographer; and one can ransack him to bolster, or smuggle in, nearly any thesis. His famous letters, for one critic, show forth "the century's most precious possession, Common Sense"; for another, they breathe out despondency and terror; for a third, they "are stricken with sterility . . . they lack the juices of life."[12] Over his dark side, naturally, I shall linger here, for it is my own theory that Cowper is the great portraitist of a daemonic god. Of course he would be indignant, perhaps even grieved, to hear the matter put so baldly; in his more "official" or public poems he veils, but not effaces, the portrait.

Out of Smart's madness issued the *Jubilate Agno*; out of Cowper's a short, ghastly poem, to be examined later, and his *Memoir*. In 1763, at the age of 32, Cowper had a nervous breakdown and tried three times to kill himself. Actual insanity supervened, after which the recuperating Cowper turned Evangelical. Around 1766, sequacious of the Evangelical mode, he wrote a narrative of his earlier life out of grace, recounting his despair, his attempts at suicide, his rebirth in Christ. There is nothing, so far as I can tell, technically unorthodox about its theology. Satan, God's enemy and Cowper's, toils indefatigably to trap him in despair. But Satan works very closely with God, seems almost, as in *Job*, to be working on a divine commission. Thus when Cowper falls ill with the smallpox at 13, this is seen as a deliberate and extraordinary punishment from God; and on recovering and lapsing into his old ways, "the devil seemed

---

[12]The "modern biographer" is Charles Ryskamp, *William Cowper of the Inner Temple, Esq.* (Cambridge, Eng.: Cambridge Univ. Press, 1959), 26. On Cowper's letters, see: Saintsbury, *Peace of Augustans*, 259; Kenneth MacLean, "William Cowper," in *The Age of Johnson*, 265; Lytton Strachey, *Literary Essays* (New York: Harcourt, 1949), 274.

rather to have gained than lost an advantage, so readily did I admit his suggestions and so passive was I under them" (367).[13] Many years later, immediately after God lifts Cowper's depression by an inspiring view of nature, Satan works evil out of good by persuading him "that I was indebted for my deliverance to nothing but a change of scene. . . . By this means he turned the blessing into a poison" (368). God himself moves in a sinister way. Providence opens up a position for the idle Cowper; but in preparing for it he is driven to distraction and madness: "It pleased the Lord to give me my heart's desire and with it an immediate punishment for my crime [of coveting the position]." Or again: "I at once accepted it [the offered position], but at the same time (such was the will of Him whose hand was in the whole matter) seemed to receive a dagger in my heart" (369). Not only does God seem a tempter and punisher, but even the Redeemer imprecates poor Cowper: "I particularly remember that the parable of the barren fig-tree was to me an inconceivable source of anguish; and I applied it to myself with a strong persuasion in my mind that when the Saviour pronounced a curse upon it he had me in his eye and pointed that curse directly at me" (375). With God, Christ, and Satan all leagued against him, it is no wonder that Cowper has nightmares of excommunication:

> One morning as I lay between sleeping and waking I seemed to myself to be walking in Westminster Abbey, waiting till prayers should begin; presently I thought I heard the minister's voice and hastened towards the choir; just as I was upon the point of entering, the iron gate under the organ was flung in my face with a jar that made the Abbey ring (376).

[13]"Memoir of William Cowper," ed. Maurice J. Quinlan, *Proceedings of the American Philosophical Society*, 97 (1953), 367; page references are given in the text. A more complete version has recently become available: James King, "Cowper's *Adelphi* Restored: The Excisions to Cowper's Narrative," *Review of English Studies*, 30 (August 1979), 291–305. The more complete Memoir contains several long demonic visions or hallucinations excised from the published versions; these are quoted entire in King, 302–304, who terms the manuscript "a more harrowing document" than the published accounts.

The imagery of the *Memoir* will be familiar to those acquainted with the later poetry. Anticipating the public examination for that dreaded position: "I looked forward to the approaching winter and regretted the flight of every moment which brought it nearer like a man borne away by a rapid torrent into a stormy sea whence he sees no possibility of returning" (371). He expostulates, in a passage pieced together out of *Job, Jonah*, and the *Psalms:*[14] "O Lord thou didst vex me with all thy storms, all thy billows went over me; thou didst run upon me like a giant in the night season, thou didst scare me with visions in the night season" (376). He expects "every moment that the earth would open her mouth and swallow me . . . the avenger of blood pursuing me, and the city of refuge out of reach and out of sight" (378). He endeavors to pray but cannot because of despair (376). "A sense of self-loathing and abhorrence ran through all my insanity" (378). But he *can* pray when he is sane (381).

The *Memoir* is an extraordinary and pathetic document of daemonic terror — all the more appalling in view of its having been written when Cowper thought he was in a state of grace! But for him there was never to be a city of refuge. The images of the castaway, the storm, being swallowed up, were forever to haunt or infest his mind and verse. If Smart's insanity took the form of obsessive prayer, Cowper's was a despairing melancholy that forestalled prayer; if Smart's produced jubilant religious love, Cowper's fostered daemonic fear. The pattern of exorcism in Smart yields in Cowper to excommunication; and in place of Smart's loving, healing Savior there is only the contumelious Christ, scorner of pharisees, curser of fig-trees; the avenger.

Cowper wrote his Olney Hymns in the early 1770s, and they were published by his friend and fellow-convert John Newton in 1779, along with some of Newton's own. The hymns often end on a formulaically solacing note: "A cheerful confidence I feel, / My well-placed hopes with joy I see";[15] and these termi-

---

[14]See Ryskamp, 175.

[15]"Jehovah-Jesus." All quotations are from *The Poetical Works of William Cowper*, ed. H. S. Milford (London: Oxford Univ. Press, 1934).

nations, together with the vehemently scriptural themes, may prompt the hasty reader to class them with Wesley's, an important collection of which appeared a year later. They also have a psychological twist that allies them to Wesley's; but they are typically more penetrating and acute. "The Contrite Heart," for example, treats religious love:

> I hear, but seem to hear in vain,
>   Insensible as steel;
> If ought is felt, 'tis only pain,
>   To find I cannot feel.
> . . . .
> Oh make this heart rejoice, or ache;
>   Decide this doubt for me;
> And if it be not broken, break,
>   And heal it, if it be.
>   (5–8, 21–24)

There is an echo here of Donne's famous sonnet on a similar theme, "Batter my heart, three-person'd God." Of course it wants Donne's robust turbulence of rhythm and image, but it is not without something of his personal and sophisticated intensity. Certainly the elusiveness of spiritual love is more shrewdly — at least more candidly — set forth than in Wesley. Even more subtle and disturbing is "Jehovah Our Righteousness":

> My GOD, how perfect are thy ways!
>   But mine polluted are;
> Sin twines itself about my praise,
>   And slides into my pray'r.
> . . . .
> This heart, a fountain of vile thoughts,
>   How does it overflow?
> While self upon the surface floats
>   Still bubbling from below.
>   (1–4, 13–16)

Although critics such as Fussell draw cogent distinctions between the sentimentality of Cowper and the manly humanism of Johnson, such passages as these show insights not unworthy *The Vanity of Human Wishes* — remember "The secret ambush of a specious prayer"? Yet it is true that the imagery is at once more intimate and more theatrical ("polluted," "fountain of vile thoughts"). Johnson's Latinate solemnity and reserve have been abandoned for self-scrutiny and self-reproach.

A gloomy persuasion of God's adverse judgment, a profusion of images of chastisement, sinking or fleeing, excommunication, all these the hymns share with the *Memoir*. "Old-Testament Gospel" draws its matter from *Exodus* and *Leviticus*, particularly the Passover and the Sinaitic covenant, and hence may be compared with Watts's "Law Given at Sinai" and Wesley's "When Israel out of Egypt came." Watts accentuates the cosmic significance of the episodes to arouse awe and terror, while Wesley uses them to illustrate divine immutability. But Cowper fastens on Moses and the scapegoat as types for Christ — a Christ who is not, as for Wesley, the loving Savior or, as for Smart, the Exorcist, but, of course, the suffering Outcast. A similar view of the excruciated Christ is vividly, almost indecently, portrayed in "Jesus Hasting to Suffer": "He longs to be baptiz'd with blood, / He pants to reach the cross." Cowper's best known *horrible* passage is at the beginning of "Praise for the Fountain Opened":

> There is a fountain fill'd with blood,
>   Drawn from EMMANUEL's veins;
> And sinners, plung'd beneath that flood,
>   Lose all their guilty stains.

Cowper likes fountain imagery, as we shall see. But that poem on the whole is not as repulsive as the less well known "Shining Light": "My former hopes are fled, / My terror now begins; / ... Ah whither shall I fly? / I hear the thunder roar," and so on. Here, no more than in the *Memoir*, can he find a city of refuge. On a daemonic theme, there is nothing in Wesley approaching this in *vivida vis animi*:

> My soul is sad and much dismay'd;
> See LORD, what legions of my foes,
> With fierce Apollyon at their head,
> My heav'nly pilgrimage oppose!

[335]

See, from the ever-burning lake
How like a smoky cloud they rise!
With horrid blasts my soul they shake,
With storms of blasphemies and lies.

Their fiery arrows reach the mark,
My throbbing heart with anguish tear;
Each lights upon a kindred spark,
And finds abundant fuel there.
("The Valley of the Shadow of Death," 1–12)

The theology here is precisely that of the seventeenth-century demonologists: there is an external diabolic onslaught, but it moves under the stress of an internal impetus. The punitive divinity, the castaway, are regular inhabitants of the *Olney Hymns*, as in "Welcome Cross"; and there is a pullulating imagery of storm, sinking, drowning.[16]

Cowper's most familiar hymn, written just before another bout of insanity, is undoubtedly "Light Shining Out of Darkness." I should like to quote it entire:

GOD moves in a mysterious way,
     His wonders to perform;
He plants his footsteps in the sea,
     And rides upon the storm.

Deep in unfathomable mines
     Of never failing skill;
He treasures up his bright designs,
     And works his sovereign will.

Ye fearful saints fresh courage take,
     The clouds ye so much dread
Are big with mercy, and shall break
     In blessings on your head.

[16]See: "Jehovah-Jireh," "Temptation," "Looking Upwards in a Storm," "Peace After a Storm," and, on the revengeful god, "Prayer for Children."

Judge not the LORD by feeble sense,
 But trust him for his grace;
Behind a frowning providence,
 He hides a smiling face.

His purposes will ripen fast,
 Unfolding ev'ry hour;
The bud may have a bitter taste,
 But sweet will be the flow'r.

Blind unbelief is sure to err,
 And scan his work in vain;
GOD is his own interpreter,
 And he will make it plain.

In aptitude and restraint of imagery and phrase, in poise of thought and structure, this is to me the capital hymn of the later eighteenth century. The first two stanzas, imperturbably eloquent, ably evoke God's ineffability and transcendence. God governs his creation but is not lost in it; the anthropomorphism is adumbrated just enough to suggest the fundamental theological point, that only God's footsteps are discerned in nature, but that his majesty is seen in the storm. Deep mines, an image of God's omnipresence and goodness in Smart, here represent his infinite wisdom. The third and fourth stanzas slide toward rational theodicy, but eschew triteness and unlike some theodicies confess that there *are* clouds and frowns. The storm imagery connects them with the first stanza; and the fourth, with its disparagement of sense and affirmation of grace, preserves them from rationalism and links them to the final stanza. The penultimate stanza switches the metaphor but suitably conveys the sureness of divine providence (to consider the organic metaphor a sly denial of God's free will would be an absurd literalism). The sixth returns to the opening theme: God's inscrutability. Far from being superficial, it has about it a Pascalian reticence. God's creation alone reveals nothing, if the heart be not already turned to him; full understanding comes from faith. Cowper has thus remained true to his Evangelical Christianity, yet has excluded the retributive imagery, the quivering psychological inventory, the infatuating terror. The symbolism is clear and therefore suited to a hymn. Religious love and decent religious fear are deftly blended. Of all of Cowper's shorter poems, this seems inferior only to "The Castaway" itself, a daemonic companion piece.

"Light Shining Out of Darkness" is regrettably untypical of the *Olney Hymns*. There is nothing, I think, patently unorthodox about them; to St. Paul can be traced the storm and castaway imagery (I *Cor.* ix. 25–27). Underlying many of them, to be sure, is the Evangelical obsession with Election and emotional Conversion; but the hymns seldom slip into blatant doctrine. Unmistakable, however, is the religious dread and terror: more psychological than Watts, much sharper than Wesley. To compare the hymns with the *Song to David* is also instructive. Both deal with the non-rational in religious experience, but the one evokes joyful wonder, the other fear and dread, at the divine arcanum. Taken in a concentrated dose, the hymns exert a hypnotic effect comparable to the *Song* but very different in nature. Critics have not scrupled to say, and to say plausibly, that the *Olney Hymns* are owing to a "feeling of hatred for God."[17] The formulaic conclusions, unlike Wesley's, do seem factitious. Only "Light Shining Out of Darkness" significantly departs from daemonism, and it is unpleasant to reflect that it was written just before a recrudescence of insanity. With that exception, the hymns are not highly successful. On one side, the involution and imagery are too indecorous for hymns; on the other, the tag-endings fracture that integrity of tone desirable in short poems. They are neither practical for public nor satisfactory for private devotion. But what a record of religious fear!

Coming half a dozen years after the *Olney Hymns, The Task* is the best of Cowper's longer, more formal poems and the best piece of blank verse after *The Seasons* and *Night Thoughts;* indeed, it did for its generation what those works did for theirs. Although *The Task* now and then chases after Thomsonian

---

[17]MacLean, "Cowper," *Age of Johnson,* 260

awe, it has a less pretentious and decorated style; gone are the sweeping storms and eerie glooms of *Winter* and *Summer*. Winter, it is true, drags itself throughout *The Task* — Cowper was fond of the season — but it is sedate, homely, and English. There are, however, disquieting undercurrents. God's power, even his apparent arbitrariness, are set forth in a fairly vivid account of a Sicilian earthquake. Naturally God is shown chastising sinners justly — for who is without sin? Still, many relatively innocuous people are annihilated during the course of instruction. Here is Cowper's explanation: "where all / Stand chargeable with guilt, and to the shafts / Of wrath obnoxious, God may choose his mark: / May punish, if he please, the less, to warn / The more malignant" (II, 154–58). A Pope or Thomson would never have accommodated that uncomfortable observation; the problem of earthquakes is taken up in *An Essay on Man*, I, 141–56, but how discordant, how impertinent, would Cowper's lines seem were they thrust into the middle of Pope's placid solution. And one can only imagine Voltaire's mocking contempt; that unflagging iconoclast had written several times on the subject of earthquakes, always in a distinctly different vein from both Pope and Cowper.

The outcast reappears in the most famous passage (III, 108–90). Cowper compares himself to "a stricken deer, that left the herd / Long since; with many an arrow deep infixt / My panting side was charg'd." He identifies himself with the wounded Christ, who heals him. Thenceforth he lives as a solitary, remarking the folly of men in seeking solid knowledge and durable contentment. Of course the whole passage is tinged with sentimentality, but it is also a moving reflection on the vanity of human wishes, resonating with notes from *Ecclesiastes* certainly, and perhaps from Pascal and Johnson. The outcast, still pensive and estranged, has glimpsed the sun behind the thundercloud. In a much later passage, enlarging, as it were, on the last stanza of "Light Shining Out of Darkness," Cowper argues that to fathom and enjoy God's works we must first know God. Those whose minds have not been touched by heaven can only contemplate "with stupid gaze / Of ignorance" the whole creation. The "unambiguous footsteps of the God" are evident only to those prepared to see them: "In vain thy creatures testify of thee / Till thou proclaim thyself." But when God does so proclaim himself:

> Then liberty, like day,
> Breaks on the soul, and by a flash from heav'n
> Fires all the faculties with glorious joy.
> . . . .
> In that blest moment Nature, throwing wide
> Her veil opaque, discloses with a smile
> The author of her beauties, who, retir'd
> Behind his own creation, works unseen
> By the impure. . . .
>
> (V, 883–85, 891–95)

Like Thomson, Cowper sees God's power in the revolving seasons; but he also recognizes that a pedestrian or skeptical view will intercept our sense of the marvelous: "All we behold is miracle; but, seen / So duly [i.e., routinely], all is miracle in vain" (VI, 132–33). Avoiding sectarian terminology, Cowper never mentions grace, but that clearly underlies his argument; we need God's own special revelation before we can truly see the wonders of creation or draw inferences about the Godhead. But the word *grace* must have worn too old fashioned a complexion even for Cowper; and later poets, Blake or Wordsworth, call it genius or imagination. Notably absent in *The Task* is the hitherto obtrusive chain of being: presumably because, unillumined by grace, we find the idea mere moonshine. Irrespective of terminology, *The Task* is considerably more orthodox, or, if one prefers, Augustinian, than *The Seasons*; and the *Critical Review* was quite right to connect Cowper with Young rather than Thomson. His view is well summarized by a modern apologist: "Nature never taught me that there exists a God of glory and of infinite majesty. I had to learn that in other ways. But nature gave the word *glory* a meaning for me."[18]

---

[18]C. S. Lewis, *The Four Loves* (New York: Harcourt Brace Jovanovich, 1960), 37.

The Task concludes with a presentment of the Apocalypse and a defense of the life of retirement. The Apocalypse is handled with some real energy — certainly it is far less awkward than a slightly earlier attempt in Cowper's poem "Truth." But even on this theme he cannot refrain, after this rapturous vision, from scowling at the corrupted present world. As in "Jehovah Our Righteousness," there is the insidious infiltration of evil, the pollution of heart and fountain:

> Here ev'ry drop of honey hides a sting,
> Worms wind themselves into our sweetest flow'rs;
> And ev'n the joy that haply some poor heart
> Derives from heav'n, pure as the fountain is,
> Is sullied in the stream, taking a taint
> From touch of human lips, at best impure.
>
> (VI, 830–35)

The formulaic tags of the *Olney Hymns* are paralleled in *The Task* by more sophisticated and grandiloquent acclamations of divine benevolence: "Thus heav'n-ward all things tend. For all were once / Perfect, and all must be at length restor'd. / So God has greatly purpos'd" (VI, 818–20). So God has purposed, but in Cowper the taint of human lips is very stubborn and refractory. Just as the *Olney Hymns* substitute psychological introspection and perturbation for Watts's cosmic terror, so *The Task* prefers domestic retirement and retreat to Thomson's cosmic sublime. It closes with a vindication of the voluntary outcast who disdains worldly turmoils: "His warfare is within. There unfatigu'd / His fervent spirit labours." But we have barely begun to peek into Cowper's warfare within.

Watts and Smart both wrote poems directly after a sickness. Cowper wrote several. The first, "R.S.S. Written in a Fit of Illness" (ca. 1755) erupts from an adolescent and frustrated love affair. The imagery is chimerical, strangely similar to Watts's "Hurry of the Spirits, in a Fever and Nervous Disorders." There is the same soaring, seeming escape and satisfaction, final vanquishment and falling into gulfs. Cowper's, rendered in insipid heroic couplets and pilfered diction, is less impressive; but even at this early date there are the images of caducity and annihilation, the polluted or polluting fountain:

> Thy [Delia's] arm supports me to the fountain's brink,
> Where, by some secret pow'r forbid to drink,
> Gasping with thirst, I view the tempting flood
> That flies my touch, or thickens into mud.
>
> (11–14)

Delia, his beloved's poetic name, sustains him and empowers him to soar; but between them "Abhorred forms, dire phantoms interpose," and the poem ends with the contrast between his own gloomy sorrow and the "Hope, joy, and peace" associated with Delia.

The "Lines Written During a Period of Insanity" came during or just after Cowper's first severe breakdown in 1763. The erotic nightmare of the earlier poem, the closing contrast, are turned into pure religious fear and terror, with no meliorating, formulaic tag:

> Man disavows, and Deity disowns me:
> Hell might afford my miseries a shelter;
> Therefore hell keeps her ever hungry mouths all
> > Bolted against me.
>
> Hard lot! encompass'd with a thousand dangers;
> Weary, faint, trembling with a thousand terrors;
> I'm called, if vanquish'd, to receive a sentence
> > Worse than Abiram's.
>
> *Him* the vindictive rod of angry justice
> Sent quick and howling to the centre headlong;
> *I*, fed with judgment, in a fleshly tomb, am
> > Buried above ground.
>
> (9–20)

The pelting, nerve-wracking thump of the Sapphics is most effective, and the imagery is as ghastly as anything in Cowper (earlier in the poem he declares that God will give him only "Hatred and vengeance," and that he is "Damn'd below Judas"). The conclusion resembles, but inverts, that of the erotic poem. There Delia, representing health and happiness, soars upward to her "native sky" leaving the poet in the depths. Here the rebellious Abiram, the ground opening beneath him, is dispatched living to Sheol (*Numbers* xvi); but his doom, ironically, is better than the poet's, who is condemned to remain alive, above ground, but without hope. The alliterating "fed" and "fleshly" seem peculiarly loathsome in context, and recall the earlier "hungry mouths" of hell. For such a creature, or rather automaton, hell would indeed be a desirable city of refuge; but even hell is bolted against him.

I have said that this poem avoids the formulaic tag, but it would be more nearly correct to see in both these poems another, daemonic formula: the despairing contrast. We find it again, many years later, in "To the Reverend Mr. Newton on His Return from Ramsgate" (1780). Newton, "tranquil and serene," is set against the poet who, "afflicted and dismay'd," views the rocks and threatening sea as portentous of his fate. He concludes:

> Your sea of troubles you have past,
>   And found the peaceful shore;
> I, tempest-toss'd, and wreck'd at last,
>   Come home to port no more.

In "Heu! Quam Remotus" (1774) Cowper laments being swept away from all that he has loved and that has sustained him:

> Et fluctuosum ceu mare volvitur,
> Dum commovebar mille timoribus,
>   Coactus in fauces Averni
>   Totus atro perii sub amne.
>   (13–16)

In one of his very last verses, "Montes Glaciales" (1799), he tells of icebergs that, sundered from shore, gradually disintegrate in the sea. The poem closes with the daemonic formula: the ice-

bergs, frigid, wandering directionless, liquescently doomed, are
contrasted with the floating island of Delos, warm and fructi-
ferous, the delight and protection of the god Apollo:

> Sic Delos dicitur olim,
> Insula, in Aegaeo fluitasse erratica ponto.
> Sed non ex glacie Delos; neque torpida Delum
> Bruma inter rupes genuit nudum sterilemque.
> Sed vestita herbis erat illa, ornataque nunquam
> Decidua lauro; et Delum dilexit Apollo.
> At vos, errones horrendi, et caligine digni
> Cimmeria, Deus idem odit.
> . . . .
> Ite! Redite! Timete moras; ni, leniter austro
> Spirante, et nitidas Phoebo jaculante sagittas
> Hostili vobis, pereatis gurgite misti!
>
> (41–48, 51–53)

The language is more relaxed in these poems than in the
"Lines," but it has an ominous quietude. In "Montes Glaciales"
it is assuredly Cowper who is the monstrous ice-mountain
slowly but irremediably, because of its own weight, fracturing
from the basal shore: odious to God, fit only for the densest darkness. The real subject governing *perii* in the earlier piece, and
pereatis in this, is the same: William Cowper.

Hard upon "Montes Glaciales" came Cowper's last and best
known poem, "The Castaway." Like the others after "Lines," it
is more subdued and detached, more indirect and figurative; but
its Calvinistic theme is clear. Cowper is the "destin'd wretch"
cut off from "effectual aid" or grace. Of course it closes with the
daemonic formula, here laced with an irony recalling but refin-
ing that of the "Lines": luckier than the poet is the sailor
washed from his ship and reluctantly abandoned by his helpless
friends to float awhile and to drown:

> No voice divine the storm allay'd,
>   No light propitious shone;
> When, snatch'd from all effectual aid,

We perish'd, each alone:
But I beneath a rougher sea,
And whelm'd in deeper gulphs than he.

It remains, nevertheless, that both have "perish'd." The *perii* and *pereatis* are resumed, one more time, in the English; then Cowper is silent. I consider this, along with "Light Shining Out of Darkness," to be his most flawless poem. As in the hymn, the religious terror is restrained, the phrasing and structure well supervised. The six-line stanzas — each actually a quatrain and a couplet — achieve a gravity free of Miltonisms or false notes or theatrics. But what a chasm yawns between the hymn and "The Castaway." In the hymn the fear of God's judgment has been counterpoised by confidence in his grace; here it is, not solaced but quieted, only by despair. The impersonal, deistic, watchmaker god has been seen lurking, perhaps one should say, reclining, behind "The Castaway."[19] But this is to draw a red herring across the trail to be marked from the *Memoir* to this last, solemn valediction. Here is no deistic, but a daemonic god, no watchmaker but a close watcher: the same deity who plunges in the dagger or, as Christ, curses Cowper like the fig tree; who can punish less evil people to tutor the worse; who loathes the poet as worse than Judas and *feeds* him with judgment, condemning him to a living death; who reifies him in the frigid and sterile shapelessness of ice. No longer merely the "stricken deer" or voluntary recluse of *The Task*, Cowper has regressed to the excommunicated wretch of the *Memoir*, thirty-six years before.

"The daemonic-divine object may appear to the mind an object of horror and dread, but at the same time it is no less something that allures with a potent charm, and the creature, who trembles before it, utterly cowed and cast down, has always at the same time the impulse to turn to it, nay even to make it somehow his own."[20] Such is the manner in which Cowper

[19]William N. Free, *William Cowper* (New York: Twayne, 1970), 170.
[20]Rudolf Otto, *The Idea of the Holy*, 31.

made it his own. The resolution of awe and love briefly effected in the "Light Shining Out of Darkness" could not be sustained. And awe, stripped altogether of love, becomes dread. David Hume had observed: "Our natural terrors present the notion of a devillish and malicious deity: Our propensity to adulation leads us to acknowledge an excellent and divine. Thus it may safely be affirmed, that popular religions are really . . . a species of daemonism; and the higher the deity is exalted in power and knowledge, the lower of course he is depressed in goodness and benevolence." The contrasting spectacle of Wesley and Cowper would seem uncommonly to vindicate this opinion. For Cowper, finally, the daemonic dread overwhelmed the love. He had a strong, clinging intuition, which theological instruction could never dislodge, that God had sentenced him to annihilation directly he died; and more, that God wished him to speed the approach of that sentence by means of suicide.[21] But Cowper's convoluted and morbid Christianity gave him insight as well as torment; like Hume he could see that natural religion is illusory and that the creation itself is theologically dumb. One can even fancy him, given a different bias and set of friends, as a discontented, melancholy Hume. Certainly the *Dialogues concerning Natural Religion* could have acquainted him with little that he had not already revolved in his heart. But after all, it was not doubt of God's existence — not that! — that drove Cowper into the gulf.

⊐

With Blake one must always begin with the mandatory platitudes: he was a highly idiosyncratic and eclectic thinker, a visionary, perhaps a very mystic; not, of course, mad. Or was he? A chorus of modern exegetes insist solemnly on his coherence, inner logic, and even orthodoxy. But there is something in this remark: "The men of Blake's day who called him mad

[21]See John D. Baird, "Cowper's Concept of Truth," *Studies in Eighteenth-Century Culture*, vol. 7 (Madison: Univ. of Wisconsin Press, 1978), 367–73.

were less glib than others who have since called him sane. For they did not miss the larger context of his discontent."[22] Many are the quarries from which Blake carved his ideas, and so it is not too hard, but rather too easy, to connect him with other philosophies. Rummaging in the shards of his thought, one readily grasps pieces of Gnosticism, Evangelicalism, seventeenth-century radical Protestantism, hermeticism. One can even find a sediment of Hume, whom he loathed. Like that supple skeptic, Blake attacked natural religion and Deism — and he surely shared his opinion of popery. Like Hume he found disagreeable the ideas of religious mystery, priestcraft, a transcendent Deity; with Hume he shared a congenital skepticism. He would very likely have seconded Hume's belief that "the higher the deity is exalted in power and knowledge, the lower of course he is depressed in goodness and benevolence"; but he would have rephrased the opening to this effect: the more the divine is *falsely separated* from the human. One can also see in him a traditional Christian extolling the new covenant of love over the old *lex talionis*. In Blake, certainly, the figure of Jesus is central and always revered — but this is a stumbling block for critics. Northrop Frye, for instance, argues for Blake's acceptance of "the central fact of Christianity, the identity of God and Man." But while Blake may have identified God and man, that is not the "central fact" of Christianity. Its central fact is the incarnation, and Frye's verbal sleight-of-hand cannot shuffle away the difference between identifying God and man, and believing in Christ as uniquely the embodiment of God. Mark Schorer is far more precise when he links Blake's Christology with those hazy modern theologies that focus on the humanity of Jesus and the divinity of man, thus substituting "for the traditional paradox

[22]J. Bronowski, *William Blake, 1757–1827* ([London]: Secker and Warburg, 1944), 14. Arguing for Blake's orthodoxy, normality, and coherence are critics such as Northrop Frye, *Fearful Symmetry* (1947; rpt. Boston: Beacon Press, 1962) and J. G. Davies, *The Theology of William Blake* (Oxford: Clarendon Press, 1948). More skeptical opinions on these points are found in Osbert Burdett's early but still valuable *William Blake* (New York: Macmillan, 1926) and D. G. James's *Romantic Comedy* (London: Oxford Univ. Press, 1948).

[347]

of the incarnation the easier idea of grace as the individual's awareness of his own sanctity."[23] But Blake is full of stumbling blocks, and they seem to multiply the more intently one peers at him.

On balance, Blake is more heterodox than orthodox. From his works, I believe, no totally coherent philosophy can be extorted; but certain patterns and themes do reappear, sometimes with a wearisome frequency. Imbedded in his thought is a dialectical structure foreshadowing, but finally very different from, Hegel's; but it also differs from the linear and hierarchical patterns of the Judaeo-Christian tradition. At work in him, too, are the immanentizing proclivities of the later eighteenth and the nineteenth century. Not only would he abolish the usual dualism of man-with-nature and a transcendent God, but he attacks the very notion obsessively, tirelessly, in the figures of Nobodaddy and Urizen. In Blake we have only man and nature, and we are not always very sure about nature. There is in him, then, a subjectivism, even a relativism, that seems far from orthodoxy. There is really no God but Man, he asserts, lapsing into the Marcionite heresy, and the demonic deities that terrorize man, such as Urizen, or the inspiriting beings that liberate him, such as Los or Orc, are but mental conceptions or projections. Thus Cowper's vindictive deity, Pascal's *deus absconditus*, Akenside's discreet architect, for examples, are merely mental or *human* images; and Blake applauds or condemns them according as they comport with his own ideal of a divinized, unified, loving humanity. Permeating the dialectical strain is a cyclicalism: the imaginative Orc *becomes* the petrific, legalistic, domineering Urizen, who must then be regenerated and so a new cycle

---

[23]Frye, *Fearful Symmetry*, 41; Mark Schorer, *William Blake: The Politics of Vision* (New York: Henry Holt, 1946), 138. See also Davies, Ch. 7 passim, and especially his remark, p. 110: "The term 'Incarnation' was never employed by Blake, probably because he considered it was apt to be confusing." A very unlikely reason for Blake's avoiding anything! Despite his tendentiousness, Thomas J. J. Altizer is closer to the truth about Blake's version of Christianity in *The New Apocalypse: The Radical Christian Vision of William Blake* ([East Lansing]: Michigan State Univ. Press, 1967).

begins. Finally, Blake believes that the physical creation is not only fallen but essentially evil. Does all this add up to orthodoxy, even conceding the ambiguity of that well-worn word and the equal elusiveness of Blake? Then too, let us consider the intellectual traditions to which Blake has been most successfully linked: Gnosticism, Origenism, hermeticism, Spinozism, Swedenborgism, radical Protestantism (Blake owes something, after all, to the likes of Lodowick Muggleton and Thomas Woolston, squinted at in an earlier chapter). This is no company of centrists. And then we must add to these considerations Blake's own style and symbolism: not entirely opaque, but assuredly very private, very inconsiderate of others, and apt to splinter, ramify, and circle back on itself as we trek through his longer poems. I doubt Blake would have liked to be revered for his thought — he was too sturdy a relativist for that; nor would he have enjoyed being painted as a man of orthodoxy and the center.[24]

But for all of the angularities and sinuosities of his thought and symbolism, Blake remains one of the ablest poets in delineating spiritual dread and awe. He can capture very well the terror of a daemonic deity, and this whether he wishes us to believe in the objective existence of such a being (as Cowper does) or to see it as a projection — it is not quite fair to say a *mere* projection — of our own nightmarish fears. Following Otto's theory one might argue that Blake is trying to return to the primitive numinous experience, where the mortal both dreads yet is fascinated by the daemonic-divine presence. Such feeling precedes the "rationalizing" of that experience by importing into it such ethical conceptions as good and evil. In what is the closest thing to a manifesto, his famous *Marriage of Heaven and*

[24]Idolatry of Blake reaches its zenith, one hopes, in Harold Bloom's *Blake's Apocalypse* (New York: Doubleday, 1963); he considers Blake's epics "the best poetry in England since Milton" (9). T. S. Eliot's brief but cogent observations have not been disarmed by all the eulogistic Blake criticism: that Blake was too eccentric and private to be a true classic and that, far from becoming too visionary, "Blake did not see enough, became too much occupied with ideas" (*Selected Essays* [New York: Harcourt, Brace, 1950], 278–80).

Hell (1790–1793), Blake states: "Without Contraries is no progression. Attraction and Repulsion, Reason and Energy, Love and Hate, are necessary to Human existence. From these contraries spring what the religious call Good & Evil."[25] For Blake these contraries, or as we might say polarities, do not drive toward some synthesis, but are perpetually needful. Now Otto accepts as inevitable the unfolding of ethical implications. But Blake, ever vigilant against the potential despotism and hypocrisy of moral codes, contemns the "religious" (i.e., conventional or simple-minded) dualism of good and evil. What he immediately goes on to say, discounting some iconoclastic fringe, is not highly unconventional: "Good is the passive that obeys Reason. Evil is the active springing from Energy." This is not so very different from Pope's scheme in *An Essay on Man*, in which two necessary principles operate within us, self-love to urge, and reason to restrain. Both Pope and Blake recognize the need for a permanent and creative tension between the Dionysian and Apollonian sides of human nature. But since for Blake, unlike Pope, God is man, then presumably in "God" himself these contraries must forever obtain. Such a view, quite incompatible with conventional or rationalized theodicies, is not incompatible with the primitive numinous experience as Otto describes it, as Defoe dramatizes it in *Robinson Crusoe*, and as a few scattered passages in the Old Testament, most notably the line from *Isaiah* heading this chapter, reveal it to be. Blake himself strikingly presents it in an illustration of *Job*, where the Jehovah-type head and torso, one arm pointing to the Book of the Law, concludes in the cloven hoof, and round which twines the snake; while Job recumbent tries to ward off the oppression of the daemonic-divine figure. Blake's illustration and Otto's exegesis of the *Book of Job* are singularly complementary. Printed

[25]All quotations are from *The Complete Writings of William Blake*, ed. Geoffrey Keynes (London: Oxford Univ. Press, 1966). In the discussion that follows I am especially indebted to Martin K. Nurmi's fine monographs and articles, particularly "On *The Marriage of Heaven and Hell*," in *Discussions of William Blake*, ed. John E. Grant (Boston: D. C. Heath, 1961), 93–101, and "Blake's Revisions of *The Tyger*," *PMLA* 71 (1956), 669–85.

5. William Blake, Illustration XI, *Illustrations of the Book of Job* (1825)

above the picture is Blake's adaptation of *II Corinthians*, xi. 14–15: "Satan himself is transformed into an Angel of Light & his Ministers into Ministers of Righteousness," but placed where it is the text has acquired innuendoes, subversive of orthodoxy, which would not have gladdened St. Paul. Othello glancing at Iago's feet, Clarissa at Lovelace's: they show themselves to be adherents of canonical theology, for whom the daemonic is tidily sequestered from the divine. Such is not Blake's scheme.

In Blake's juvenile prose poem, "Contemplation," the title character exclaims: "O man, how great, how little thou! O man, slave of each moment, lord of eternity!" This is the conventional if paradoxical dualism of Pascal, Pope, and Young, and I do not know that Blake ever certainly repudiates it. But he assails *other* conventional dualisms in the *Marriage:* the dualism separating soul from body ("The Voice of the Devil") or god from man: "All deities reside in the human breast"; "God only Acts & Is, in existing beings or Men." When perceived with imagination, Blake says, all things are holy or infinite: "If the doors of perception were cleansed every thing would appear to man as it is, infinite"; and King David, not precisely Smart's exorcist, expresses that cleansing imagination or "Poetic Genius." Blake agreed with Pascal, Hume, and Cowper that the divine is not self-evident in nature. But where Pascal and Cowper looked to grace, and Hume relaxed in tranquil incredulity, Blake espoused the creative and animating power of the human imagination. For this reason, notwithstanding the perpetual need of contraries, Blake puts himself more on the side of energy or the "Devil" than on the side of reason or the passive "Good": "The road of excess leads to the palace of wisdom"; "The tygers of wrath are wiser than the horses of instruction [Swift's calm and prudential Houyhnhnms?]" Both the tigers and the horses may be indispensable and complementary creatures, but Blake's predilection is clear. Milton, as a true, imaginative poet, is "of the Devil's party without knowing it." "Damn braces. Bless relaxes," Blake orders. The original religious experience is poetic and invests all things with the marvelous, he says, but at length "a system was formed, which some

[352]

took advantage of, & enslav'd the vulgar by attempting to realize or abstract the mental deities from their objects: thus began
Priesthood." Inexorably opposed by Blake is the objectifying,
systematizing, or moralizing of religion, whether at Sinai in the
divulgation of the stony Law, or in the arid and metallic
schemes of the Deists. Blake's own motto or slogan, "I must Create a System or be enslav'd by another Man's," expresses the
creative and imaginative, but also the personal or individual,
nature of all healthy systems. Of course Blake's "Satanism" is
ironic, his language satirical, sedulously hyperbolic. He is out to
shock, and he sides with the tigers because the tigers are the
underdogs; they have had a poor press in the (to Blake) phleg-
matic eighteenth century. Indeed one can sympathize with his
detestation of religious hypocrisy and prudery, his contempt,
very like Dr. Johnson's, for facile and ostentatious "solutions"
of the problem of evil. But if Blake cannot fairly be styled a
Satanist, he does trench on antinomianism. For Blake, "Desire"
is the Comforter or Paraclete whom Christ prays to the Father
to send; and by satisfaction of desire, not the moral law, shall
we enter into the kingdom of heaven.

Before trying to understand Blake's treatment of religious
fear, it will help us to consider first his attitude to the divine-
daemonic in Christ. In the *Marriage*, quite in accord with his
other asseverations, Blake declares that "Jesus was all virtue, and
acted from impulse, not from rules." Virtue is thus associated
with spontaneity and feeling rather than with observance of the
law. Blake is still harping on this point many years later in *The
Everlasting Gospel* (ca. 1818), where Christ and Christianity are
opposed to "Moral Virtue." Far from being gentle and submis-
sive, Jesus was a truant as a child, haughty as an adult. Nor is
he uniquely divine, for Blake informs him: "Thou art a Man,
God is no more, / Thine own Humanity learn to Adore" (c, 41–
42). In fine, he is a rebel whose sole message, Blake tells us in
his prose prologue, is "Forgiveness of Sins." When Christ saved
the prostitute from being stoned, the oppressive Sinaitic law was
repealed, and the Earth (i.e., all creation) received a divine revelation: "Good & Evil are no more! / Sinai's trumpets, cease to

[353]

roar!" (e, 21–22). Now this is not at all the implication of scripture, for Christ tells the prostitute to go and *sin* no more; hence
Blake's improvisation here is an important key to his thought.
Christ is an antinomian rebel; and since the only sin is repression of desire, Christ ought to have been born, not of a virgin,
but — as the scurrilous old legend had it — of a prostitute.[26] Blake
wants to abolish or deny moral evil; and Christ's lawlessness and
pardoning of lawlessness seems not only to do that but also to
divinize desire. In Blake's contemptuous dismissal of the false
stereotype of "Creeping Jesus" there is much to applaud. The
routinely, comfortably pious do usually avert their eyes from
Christ's daemonic traits. Only Watts and Cowper, of the authors
treated here, were alert to them; and Blake's account of Christ
dragging Satan at his chariot wheels (b, 32–44) is very like
Watts's in "To the Memory of . . . Gouge." But for Watts, even
more for Cowper, such qualities are charged with a moral vengeance obviously repugnant to Blake — at least, when he is not
thinking about political oppressors. The Christ who blighted the
fig tree and who prescribes the different fates of the sheep and
the goats is a daemonic Savior that might make *Blake* uncomfortable! It must be owned, of course, that Watts and even Cowper are closer to the view of Christ presented in scriptures than
is Blake in *The Everlasting Gospel.* Christ's recognition of the
reality of sin and hell, of the dualism of good and evil, of the
need and value of suffering and self-denial, is so obvious to even
a casual reader of the New Testament (and Blake was no merely
casual reader) that one hardly knows what to make of the
bizarre caricature on which Blake has lavished such vigorous
and infectious verse. One wonders, indeed, if Blake were not
hiding something from himself. He was ambivalent, I think, on
the daemonic-divine experience, sometimes seeing in it a liber-
ating, lustral energy, sometimes a repressive, humiliating deg-
radation. Like everyone else, he narrows Christ down to suit his
own philosophy, and since he feels compelled to revere Christ,

[26]See *The Everlasting Gospel,* i, 3–4. Blake had dealt with this idea earlier
in *Jerusalem,* Plate 61, where Mary justifies "sin" because it affords opportu-
nities of divine forgiveness and compassion (11–13).

he remarks in him only the emancipation from the law, not the judgment by a higher law. But the other, sinister, elements of the daemonic press forward in Urizen and, perhaps, the Tyger.

In *The Everlasting Gospel* Blake disdainfully links the stereotype of "Creeping Jesus" with the imbecile humility of "Lamb or Ass." In the much earlier poem "The Lamb," in *Songs of Innocence* (1789), there is a parody of the catechism in which a puerile speaker inquires of a little lamb "who made thee?" The speaker complacently answers his own question:

> Little Lamb, I'll tell thee,
> Little Lamb, I'll tell thee:
> He is called by thy name,
> For he calls himself a Lamb.
> He is meek, & he is mild;
> He became a little child.
>   (11–16)

One need not despise the speaker's attitude: what is nauseating in an adult may be touching in a child. After all "The Tyger," its famous companion piece in *Songs of Experience* (1794), was written some years later, and between the two Blake had consolidated his ideas in *The Marriage of Heaven and Hell*. Still, it is obvious that "The Lamb" gives but a partial and defective view of the holy. In *Vala, or the Four Zoas* (1795–1804), where Blake's theology is more fully declared, the Divine Lamb is associated with the land of Beulah, a relaxing retreat of sleep and dream not necessarily malign, but definitely not paradisal; it is a roadside stop, passively refreshing (Night I, 94–100). Of course this place is in fact a *state*, and like the state of childhood it must give way to a higher stage of consciousness. One must not choose to linger there, to cling as an adult to infantile conceptions of the divine. Read for itself alone, "The Lamb" is a charming expression of a naive love of the holy. Seen in the wider context of Blake's thought, the innocence of the lamb and speaker alike is pathetic:

> The Lamb thy riot dooms to bleed to day
> Had he thy *Reason*, would he skip and play?

> Pleas'd to the last, he crops the flow'ry food,
> And licks the hand just rais'd to shed his blood.
> > *(An Essay on Man*, I, 81–84)

Pope is arguing that man, reasoning from experience and observation, can conceptualize his own death; mercifully, the lamb cannot. But what is good for the lamb is not good for man: both his place on the chain of being, and the lamb's, show God's wisdom and justice. Now Blake loathed Pope's transcendent god and Pope's chain of being; but on this he would presumably agree. As he affirms in the *Marriage:* "One Law for the Lion & Ox is Oppression." Man is himself divine, and must not immure himself in the trusting and deferential sensibility of the lamb.

"The Tyger" owns a deceptive simplicity and will never be interpreted to everyone's satisfaction. Since the speaker in "The Lamb" appears to be artless and naive (i.e., it seems to be a persona, not Blake himself), there is some reason to dissociate Blake from the speaker of this poem as well. While mature and sophisticated, this personage is much less confident about the answers to the questions he asks. The speaker in "The Lamb" is indeed quite the little dogmatist, who has conned his catechism with commendable assiduity. But the questions posed by "The Tyger" are not those of the catechism, nor does the speaker expect to be answered directly. The questions are instead rhetorical, designed to reveal the awe and fear of the persona vis-à-vis the tiger and its supposed creator:

> And what shoulder, & what art,
> Could twist the sinews of thy heart?
> And when thy heart began to beat,
> What dread hand? & what dread feet?
>
> What the hammer? what the chain?
> In what furnace was thy brain?
> What the anvil? what dread grasp
> Dare its deadly terrors clasp?
> > (9–16)

In the penultimate stanza he expostulates: "Did he who made the Lamb make thee?" From a very different perspective, Jehovah had thus peremptorily addressed Job concerning Leviathan:

> Canst thou draw out leviathan with an hook? or his
>   tongue with a cord which thou lettest down?
> Canst thou put an hook into his nose? or bore his jaw
>   through with a thorn?
> . . . .
> Who can discover the face of his garment? or who can
>   come to him with his double bridle?
> Who can open the doors of his face? his teeth are terrible
>   round about.
> . . . .
> Out of his mouth go burning lamps, and sparks of fire
>   leap out.
> Out of his nostrils goeth smoke, as out of a seething pot
>   or cauldron.
> His breath kindleth coals, and a flame goeth out of his
>   mouth.
> . . . .
> The arrow cannot make him flee: slingstones are turned
>   with him into stubble.
> Darts are counted as stubble: he laugheth at the shaking
>   of a spear.
>
> (xli. 1–2, 13–14, 19–21, 28–29)

Similarly in "The Tyger" the stars — traditional emblems of God's might, but in Blake usually symbols of oppression — throw down their spears, signifying their submission to the tiger. Now in Blake, as we have already noticed in the *Marriage*, tigers are commonly a favorable symbol representing imaginative vision or wrathful, revolutionary energy.[27] It is very tempt-

---

[27]See: *Europe*, Plate 15; *Vala*, Night II, 35. In the *Visions of the Daughters of Albion* the jealous, miserly, or pitiless man binds himself beside the trudging ox and cuts himself off from imaginative vision and pleasure, represented by, among other things, "the glowing tyger, and the king of night" (Plate 8, 5).

ing to view "The Tyger" as a celebration of the glorious, tremendous power of the creator; and so it has been piously explicated. But that would bring it perilously close to *Job*. There Jehovah is the supreme and categorical Catechist, unamenable to cajoleries or evasions. He also is asking rhetorical questions, questions contrived to point up the transcendence of the Godhead, the infirmities of Job's humanity, the ineluctability of his submission. But Blake would have none of these notions, and the dread and fear impregnating "The Tyger" are elsewhere arraigned as the tools of Urizenic oppression. It is possible that just as the speaker in "The Lamb" was a child, so the speaker here is a conventionally minded "religious" person, terrorizing himself with mental projections of the tiger and its daemonic creator, much as Cowper terrorized himself with images of the avenging God and Christ. In the *Marriage* Blake and an Angel, who stands for mundane piety, see a vision that includes, among other items, "the head of Leviathan; his forehead was divided into streaks of green & purple like those on a tyger's forehead." At all this the Angel is daunted and flees, but Blake remains and sees a pleasant prospect. The point of this "Memorable Fancy" is that vision is subjective; the terrifying imagery brings together *Job* and "The Tyger"; the conventional Angel reacts like the speaker in "The Tyger." If the Lamb-speaker has rehearsed his childish catechism, the Tyger-speaker, perhaps, has succumbed to a daemonic dread equally thoughtless in its unimaginative correctitude. And there is something else very curious. Blake's own illustration for "The Tyger" shows a most innocuous, even harried and nervous, beast: is this how *Blake* sees it, and is he thus contrasting his view with that of the quavering Tyger-speaker, even as he had contrasted it earlier with the timorous Angel's?

But I do not push this point. The poem remains equivocal in its imagery, elliptical in its syntax, obscure in its intention. Blake revised it several times, and the revisals show great indecisiveness and ambivalence. It is clear that "The Tyger" evokes daemonic-divine fear, and it is natural, as Otto observes, for the creature to feel ambivalently about such experiences. It is also

[358]

pertinent to note that, while tigers appear infrequently in scripture, the lion occupies a secure place — but an ambiguous one, for it can be the emblem of the devil or Christ. As we have just seen, the tiger is elsewhere associated by Blake with Leviathan, which had itself long been linked with Orc, the monstrous and inscrutable whale, and whose jaws, from the Middle Ages onward, had symbolized hell-gate. Since Blake disbelieved in a transcendental deity, one is forced to conclude that the emotions of the Tyger-speaker are merely subjective, unattached to externalities. Hence the variance between the literal import of the text and Blake's illustration. But is "The Tyger" an exercise in fatuous self-terrorizing or cathartic, imaginative vision? That, of course, is a question prompted by any experience of the numinous, and Blake probably knew what he was doing when he left it unanswered.

Not so elusive are Blake's attitudes toward the jealous and dictatorial Old Testament God, earlier ridiculed as Nobodaddy (nobody's daddy) but more extensively caricatured as Urizen, a name that may have been intended to suggest "your reason" or "your horizon" (the Greek *horizon* signifies "bounding circle" or "limit"). Urizen is first mentioned in 1793 in two poems, the *Visions of the Daughters of Albion* and *America*. In the first he is apostrophized: "Creator of men! mistaken Demon of heaven! / Thy joys are tears, thy labour vain to form men to thine image" (Plate 5, 3–4). In *America* he is a composite of Jehovah (he is jealous, sends plagues on rebels) and Milton's Satan: "his jealous wings wav'd over the deep; / Weeping in dismal howling woe, he dark descended, howling / Around the smitten bands, clothed in tears & trembling, shudd'ring cold" (Pl. 16, 6–8). With a title parodying the biblical books of Moses, *The First Book of Urizen* (1794) is a full-dress attack on legalism in thought and religion. In it Urizen continues to be identified with the daemonic god of Sinai. Blake's illustration on the title page shows him with the stereotypical Jehovah's aged visage and long beard; the stony tablets of the law are erected behind him, but his eyes are shut in sleep, no doubt dotage, as he scribbles autonomously in his book. In the text he is surrounded by "cold

[359]

horrors"; ice, hail, and snow. His creation of the universe is an act of self-love that separates him from the other "Eternals." In so creating, Urizen himself descends into matter, actually *becomes* the physical creation, because that is all that he can see. Urizen is a multifarious symbol. He is the daemonic tyrant, enouncing from his book of brass "one command, one joy, one desire, / One curse, one weight, one measure / One King, one God, one Law" (Pl. 4, 38–40). He is the diabolical architect of *Genesis* i, clamping out of fear a rigid order on his creation, but he is also like Milton's Satan charting his path through Chaos (Pl. 20, 33–39). He is the hackneyed, slovenly creator producing faithless copies of himself, monstrous and fragmented distortions of the ideal (Pl. 23, 2–7). And he sickens at his own creations, seeing "That no flesh nor spirit could keep / His iron laws one moment" (Pl. 23, 25–26). He spins from out himself "a spider's web, moist, cold & dim," a "Net of Religion" that enmeshes his creation (Pl. 25, 9–22). But Urizen is also the creation itself, or rather he represents the fall of the Eternal and Universal Man into disunity and matter; and his birth-pangs (the poem has nine sections) are retailed with hideous precision.

Psychologically, Urizen stands for those aspects of the human mind favoring unimaginative or finite perception and resulting in religious legalism or arid, analytic rationalism. His universe is that of all who see it as dead, splintered, unglorified. He is an egoist and tyrant presiding over his own narrow, always potentially chaotic cosmos, which he has peopled with fractional, yet refractory, self-images. He calls to mind Dryden's Zimri in *Absalom and Achitophel,* a feeble figure who is "everything by fits and nothing long" and who cannot even rule the contemptible political factions that he forms. But he is even more like Swift's caricature of the solipsistic modern in the fable of the spider and the bee; and his universe is surely in the same neighborhood as the spider's, which is "nothing but dirt, spun out of [his] own entrails (the guts of modern brains)." Like Swift's spider, Urizen is keen on mathematics. But if Blake has fashioned a satanic Jehovah, thus reversing the import of the Sinaitic imagery of conventional poets such as Watts or Wesley, he has not wholly abandoned the Mosaic ideal. The poem concludes with Fuzon, one of Urizen's sons and a rebellious Orc-figure, summoning the rest of Urizen's children to break out of the "Egyptian bondage" of Urizen's world; and in the muddled sequel, *The Book of Ahania* (1795), the fuliginous images of *Exodus* are imposed favorably on Fuzon:

> Fuzon on a chariot iron-wing'd
> On spiked flames rose; his hot visage
> Flam'd furious; sparkles his hair & beard
> Shot down his wide bosom and shoulders.
> On clouds of smoke rages his chariot
> And his right hand burns red in its cloud
> Moulding into a vast Globe his wrath,
> As the thunder-stone is moulded.
>
> (Pl. 2, 1–8)

He is the "pillar of fire to Egypt," the liberator, trying (vainly) to destroy Urizen by his tigers. But then Fuzon, too, aspires to be a tyrant-god, and he is straightway annihilated by the Sinaitic rock (Pl. 3, 36–46). The Old Testament deity can be a god of stony law and piddling but tyrannic protocol, which Blake detests, or a god of emancipating energy, which Blake admires; and in his cyclical view they may be the same deity, or operation of the human mind, in different phases. No wonder the Tyger is an ambivalent emblem.

The First Book of Urizen, then, presupposes at the beginning (whenever that was) a state of unity and innocence; but selfishness in Urizen, one might say the incipience of thought or self-consciousness, precipitates a fall into legalism, rodomontade, disunity; and both Urizen and his world (sometimes they are described as one, for to Blake we are what, or how, we see) are disjointed, oppressive and oppressed. Fuzon tries with no little valiance to lead his brothers and sisters out of the Urizenic captivity. Now there are intriguing parallels between this account and Paul's in the intricate and convoluted seventh and eighth chapters of *Romans*. Although holy, the Mosaic law, Paul argues, came fraught with a knowledge of sin and, paradoxi-

cally, sin itself: for the law "Thou shalt not covet" fostered con-
cupiscence, not abnegation, in the apostle. He recalls the period
when he was alive without the law — Paul may be referring to
his own childhood before the dawning of self-consciousness (and
selfishness) or to the primeval innocence of the race, it hardly
matters — but when the law came, sin also came, and death. He
then describes his own state in bondage to sin, disunified, one
part warring against another (this is very like Blake). He develops this into his favorite dualism (which Blake loathed): the
warfare between the flesh and the spirit; and he notes that not
only human beings but "the whole creation groaneth and tra-
vaileth in pain together." He hopes that through Christ the
whole cosmos "shall be delivered from the bondage of corruption into the glorious liberty of God." For Paul, unlike Blake,
the law remains sacred; it was a means of instructing man in his
nature; yet Paul candidly records its sinister influence. Unlike
Blake, Paul accepts the consequent disunity or dualism in his
nature, enjoining patience and faith. But the pattern he traces is
not dissimilar to Blake's, and like Blake he sees himself, dead
yet reborn in the Son of God, as no longer under dominion of
the law; and he yearns for a new and glorified creation one with
man and forever freed of the bondage of sin and corruption. In
Jerusalem Blake describes the new and purged life in Christ in
very Pauline fashion: the One Man, the Universal Family, is
"Jesus the Christ; and he in us, and we in him / Live in perfect
harmony in Eden, the land of life" (Pl. 38, 20–21).

In the most central Christian writings themselves, then, there
is lurking an ambivalence toward the law. We are too apt to
satisfy ourselves with Christ's remark that he came to fulfill the
law; but when Christians try to explain in what way the law is
fulfilled, and what are its present claims, a swarm of difficulties
fly up. In the Old Testament, Satan is not the arch-fiend but
God's agent who accuses and punishes; since the Mosaic law
performs the same office, there *is* something satanic about it.
Now Blake is, to say the least, less circumspect than the apostle.
For him the law is irrefragably demonic, not holy; ergo, so must

be its promulgator. If the creation is corrupt (as Paul freely concedes), then, says Blake, it reflects on the inadequacies of its parent. Far from being patient under our splintering, we should, through imagination, retrieve our essential unity and divinity — and of course such "redemption" can occur at any moment of time, for we *are* what we see. Blake is possibly more consistent than Paul, who sees the debilities of the law but affirms its holiness, who laments the depravity of creation but preaches the goodness of the creator. It is, however, a consistency purchased at great price: the consistency (how curious to say this of Blake) of the systematic logician. Christ must be only the rebel; the law must be only demonic; the lapsed creation only corrupt. For all of the tantalizing similarities, Blake is radically different from Paul in his Marcionite subjectivism, his anti-nomianism, his Gnosticism with respect to the creation, his Pelagianism with respect to human redemption. There is religious fear aplenty in Blake, and that vividly evoked in all its primitive intensity. But all orthodox theological scaffolding — the labefaction of which I have noted in many mid-century writers — has been replaced with something new, something built out of the vestiges of religious heterodoxy and the fresh materials of secular humanism.

Of Blake's didactic or prophetic poems, *Vala, or The Four Zoas* is the best alembication of his ideas on the holy and the daemonic. It was revised incessantly for a long time (1795–1804), and the vagaries of Blake's thought, stretched over many years of altering, amending, and discarding, have conspired with innumerable textual problems to make a definitive interpretation quite impracticable. Yet the poem contains many familiar themes, many passages arousing or exuding divine-daemonic fear, and, at the end, a most exceptional apocalypse. Its subject is the Universal or Divine Man, who falls into sickness and self-division as one or another of his four elements or humors gains tyrannical ascendancy. It is the most elaborated and colorful of Blake's versions of the Urizen myth. In the earlier parts of the poem Urizen remains much as we have already seen him. Jehovah lurks in his language and in the sublime, circumambient imagery.

> "Am I not God?" said Urizen, "Who is Equal to me?
> "Do I not stretch the heavens abroad, or fold them up
>   like a garment?"
> He spoke, mustering his heavy clouds around him, black,
>   opake.
> Then thunders roll'd around & lightnings darted to &
>   fro;
>
>   (III, 106–109)

This might have come from *Job;* indeed, we are invited to think that it did. And the Universal Man expresses toward Urizen that awed creature-feeling and dependancy so pervasive in the Hebrew poem:

> "O I am nothing when I enter into judgment with thee.
> If thou withdraw thy breath I die & vanish into Hades;
> If thou dost lay thine hand upon me, behold I am silent;
> If thou withhold thine hand I perish like a fallen leaf.
> O I am nothing, & to nothing must return again.
> If thou withdraw thy breath, behold I am oblivion."
>
>   (III, 60–65)

But Urizen is demonic, a false god. Line 59 tells us that Man is "Idolatrous to his own Shadow" — because Urizen is in fact *his* conception or projection, not, as orthodoxy would have it, the other way around. Like, perhaps, the Tyger-speaker, Man is thus sick, alienated from himself and his own divinity.

Urizen is the demonic architect, and here is his creation:

> Thus were the stars of heaven created like a golden
>   chain.
> . . . .
> In sevens & tens & fifties, hundreds, thousands,
>   number'd all
> According to their various powers, subordinate to Urizen

[364]

> And to his sons in their degrees & to his beauteous
>   daughters,
> Travelling in silent majesty along their order'd ways
> In right lined paths outmeasur'd by proportions of
>   number, weight
> And measure.
> . . . .
>   . . . Such the period of many worlds.
> Others triangular, right angled course maintain. Others
>   obtuse,
> Acute, Scalene, in simple paths; but others move
> In intricate ways, biquadrate, Trapeziums, Rhombs,
>   Rhomboids,
> Paralellograms triple & quadruple, polygonic
> In their amazing hard subdu'd course in the vast deep.
>   (II, 266, 269–74, 281–86)

Here is our last glimpse of the chain of being, the harmonious, hierarchical cosmos whose eulogies we have traced from Browne through Pope and Young and Akenside to Smart. But Blake's is no eulogium. There is "silent majesty" to be sure; but the silence is imposed by despotism. The "order'd ways" and "right lined paths" are pursued, not in joyous celebration of the rational and masterly creator, but under the compulsion of the domineering, obsessively ratiocinative demon-god. The last several lines, with their rigmarole of ungainly and analytical jargon, satirize and parody the entire conception. The sequence of hard stresses in the last line caustically evokes the clockwork tedium of this marshaled universe. In fact, Blake's passage is no less a *reductio ad absurdum* than Johnson's review of Jenyns; and the chain of being, once golden, is now iron.

Urizen is clearly associated with religious hypocrisy and repression (VIIa, 108–34), and his temple is invested with true daemonic horror. The passage parodies the *Genesis* creation and Milton's report of the building of Pandaemonium; the temple itself represents the establishment of ecclesiastical tyranny,

[365]

priestcraft, and superstition (how Hume would have relished all this), and it is contrived "in the image of the [fallen] human heart" (VIIb, 18–38). Recalling Paul's phrase, Blake begins his description: "the Universal Empire groans." Recalling his own imagery in the *Book of Urizen*, he shows Urizen weaving his "Web of a Spider, dusky & cold . . . stretched direful" (VI, 244, 247). But Urizen shares his villainy with Vala, who represents another part of humanity out of control. She is a malignant female principle marked by cruel sensuality, rapacity, rampant, self-indulgent passion. She is, indeed, curiously like Pope's goddess of Dulness in *The Dunciad*, who is a daemonic non-entity, a vortex who, notwithstanding, retains a numinous power: "Her ample presence fills up all the place; / A veil of fogs dilates her awful face: / Great in her charms!" Similarly the female Vala is a "nameless shadowy Vortex," a shadow rearing "her dismal head . . . / With sighs & howlings & deep sobs" (VIIb, 125–27). Like Dulness, Vala causes stupefaction and intellectual death:

> Urizen sitting in his web of deceitful religion
> Felt the female death, a dull & numming stupor, such as ne'er
> Before assaulted the bright human form; he felt his pores
> Drink in the deadly dull delusion; horrors of Eternal Death
> Shot thro' him. Urizen sat stonied upon his rock.
>
> (VIII, 415–19)

At the end of *The Dunciad* Dulness infects all civilization with her contageous yawn. So Vala diffuses her influence through all creation; more and more feel her "stony stupor" till at length "in a living death the nameless shadow all things bound." Thus the Eighth Night of *Vala* ends, like the fourth book of Pope's poem, with the triumph of ignorance and solipsism and a profusion of images of fragmentation and disunity. In Pope the "dread Empire" of Chaos has been restored; in Blake the "Universal Empire" of Man has flown apart under the double assault of Urizenic despotism and Vala's Medusa-like stupefaction. Swift's spider and Pope's Dulness are both emblems of a bullying and galvanic egotism, relentless and rapacious: a seemingly unified daemonic force whose essence is vacuity, a disorganized multiplicity whose name is Legion. These characters reappear, transformed yet true to their former nature and function, in Blake's own dunciad, the seventh and eighth Nights of *Vala*.

Until the apocalyptic Ninth Night the maleficent powers prevail. Even the birth of a possible emancipator, Orc, is presented as a satanic Christmas, complete with choirs of demons singing him to his restlessness. The winter is hostile and fiendish: "The winds around on pointed rocks / Settled like bats innumerable, ready to fly abroad." The "terrible child" at length springs forth "In thunder, smoke & sullen flames, & howlings & fury & blood. / Soon as his burning Eyes were open'd on the Abyss, / The horrid trumpets of the deep bellow'd with bitter blasts. / The Enormous Demons woke & howl'd around the new born King" (V, 38–41). Like the Tyger and Fuzon, Orc is ambiguous and sinister. But the Ninth Night, subtitled "Being the Last Judgment," is Blake's inimitable apocalypse. He had been working on illustrations for Young's *Night Thoughts* while writing *Vala*, and like Young's his poem is divided into nine Nights of which the ninth is an apocalyptic culmination. The Eternal Man, awakening to his fragmented condition and surveying his inner turmoil, laments "In this dark world, a narrow house, I wander up & down" — even as Young had thus exclaimed on man's inner dualism: "At home a stranger, / Thought wanders up and down, surpriz'd, aghast." Of course Young is marveling at a dualism that he accepts with Pauline deference; the Eternal Man's recognition of his disunity, however, is the first stage in his reunification. The apocalypses of *Night Thoughts* and Cowper's *Task* are perhaps the best that British, eighteenth-century poetry affords, aside from Blake's. And actually Blake works fewer changes in the traditional theme than is his habit. Naturally the *ideas* are uniquely Blakean: Urizen, Vala, Orc, and the other lapsed creatures are regenerated; Urizen repents his petrific and repressive rationalism and is reconciled with the passions, or Vala, who in her purified state is called Luvah. The apocalypse presumably signifies the reunifying of the Eternal Man through the daedal exertions of the imagination; its theology is probably quite contradictious to that of the orthodox Last Judgment. In view of the cyclical pattern to which Blake commonly adheres (Orc petrifies into Urizen who must be revitalized as Orc, and so on), it is hard to see how this can be a *last* judgment at all.

But that is Blake's problem, not ours. In its imagery his apocalypse is traditional enough and extraordinarily vivid. Not since Dryden's Killigrew ode has there been such a mettlesome version of the resurrection of the dead, and here Dryden's baroque wit is replaced with religious terror:

> . . . the bursting Universe explodes.
> All things revers'd flew from their centers: rattling bones
> To bones Join: shaking convuls'd, the shivering clay
>   breathes:
> Each speck of dust to the Earth's center nestles round &
>   round
> In pangs of an Eternal Birth: in torment & awe & fear,
> All spirits deceas'd, let loose from reptile prisons, come in
>   shoals:
> Wild furies from the tyger's brain & from the lion's eyes,
> And from the ox & ass come moping terrors, from the
>   eagle
> And raven: numerous as the leaves of autumn, every
>   species
> Flock to the trumpet, mutt'ring over the sides of the
>   grave & crying
> In the fierce wind round heaving rocks & mountains
>   fill'd with groans.
>
> (IX, 230–40)

To be sure, Blake gives the event a political turn, which adds to the grisly horror: for the resurrected souls of those who had been oppressed furiously assault their resurrected oppressors. Christ, the "Cold babe," is the regenerating human imagination, and he "Stands in the furious air." A corrupt judge hides his face beneath his erstwhile prisoner's foot, beseeching the prisoner to intreat with the Lord for him; but there is no mercy:

> While he [the judge] speaks the flames roll on,
> And after the flames appears the Cloud of the Son of Man
> Descending from Jerusalem with power and great Glory.
> All nations look up to the Cloud & behold him who was
>   crucified.
> The Prisoner answers: "You scourg'd my father to death
>   before my face
> While I stood bound with cords & heavy chains. Your
>   hipocrisy
> Shall now avail you nought." So speaking he dash'd him
>   with his foot.

(IX, 271–77)

And after this terror, a long purgation: All human souls must be sown as seeds, reaped, the corn thrashed and the grapes crushed, to provide the Eternal Bread and Wine. The regenerate Urizen oversees the task, behind which lies an inchoate Blakean theology partly inspired by *Revelation*, xiv. 14–20. Thus the gloomy dunciad of the seventh and eighth nights is reversed. Blake's last line is an answer to the closing couplets of Pope's *Dunciad* and perhaps a distant echo of Young's last line, which had read: "And MIDNIGHT, *Universal* Midnight! reigns." Blake writes — and by "Science" he means true knowledge and understanding: "The dark Religions are departed & sweet Science reigns."

Blake was a superb poet of spiritual fear and, in the latter parts of Night IX, of apocalyptic joy and love. But it seems to me that terror was his favorite theme. With terror, certainly, his apocalypse is more suffused than are the versions of such more conventional poets as Young and Cowper. Dryden's presentment is very fine, but too facetious and jubilant to be very dreadful. We must really turn to Watts's account of the Last Judgment, or to Cowper's personal applications, to discover anything comparable, and these are not so developed or sustained as Blake's.

Blake's two later prophetic works, *Milton* and *Jerusalem*, are but supplementary. Urizen has been regenerated in *Vala;* wherefore in *Milton* (1804–1808) the demonic Jehovah figure is simply called Satan (the satiric, satanic inversions of the *Marriage* seem quite forgotten). But Satan's language and description replay the familiar parodies of the Old Testament (e.g., *Milton*, Pl. 9, 19–29). Although Blake somewhat shifts his terminology, Satan's tabernacle (Pl. 38, 29–49) stands for the same perversions as Urizen's temple in *Vala*. In *Jerusalem* (1804–1820) the corrupt and selfish part of humanity is represented by the Spectre, which Blake invests with diabolic and ghoulish qualities. The malign Vala reappears in this poem, and Stonehenge, for Blake an apt symbol both in name and physical appearance, is the center of her worship and her power (Pl. 66, 1–15). Like Urizen's temple and Satan's tabernacle — and Pope's throne of Dulness — it is the focus of all spiritual and intellectual negation. All of these places are charged with the numinous, but they exploit primitive fears to twist and constrict, finally to strangle, the human imagination. Such was Blake's prevailing view of the numinous experience, howsoever ambivalent he may have been about the Tyger. Despite the last line of *Vala*, the "dark religions" continued to haunt him; and one suspects, from his poetry, that he rather enjoyed the haunting.

◻

There is a proclivity in all of these poets to present non-rational facets of religious experience in an intensely personal or psychological manner; they all fasten on, but diversely use, biblical themes. But Blake takes these traits to the farthest verge in immanentism and subjectivism. Smart's celebration of the benevolent Deity becomes celebration of the Eternal Man; Cowper's vengeful Jehovah becomes the mentally projected Urizen or Satan. "All we behold is Miracle," declared Cowper; and how cordially Blake agreed! But rather than praying for grace to enable us to see the divine, he looks within to the poetic genius or imagination. Where Smart had glorified the chain of being, and Cowper had ignored it, Blake denounces it as diabolic. There, and in his despisal of rationalists and over-simplifiers, he finds an unexpected ally in Samuel Johnson. Blake's obsession with vitalism or energy may seem to distinguish him most from the others studied here; but he differs from them, as fundamentally, in his onslaught against the traditional dualisms: good and evil, god and man, spirit and body. None of them so sedulously strives to evoke the primeval numinous experience, although Defoe, Richardson, and Cowper venture into it, and Hume, temperamentally so immune, shows exceptional insight.

Stylistically Blake is an extremist, of course; and when one considers the feebleness of Smart's Seatonian essays and later verse, the conventionality of Wesley, the platitudinizing piety of Cowper's public pieces (I am not mentioning the really inferior versifiers), one can well understand Blake's contempt for the poetry of his age: "The languid strings do scarcely move! / The sound is forc'd, the notes are few!" But whether Blake's efforts, on the whole, are to be reckoned propitious is another matter. For all of the connections I have suggested between Urizen and Swift's modernist spider, I am sure Swift would consider Blake himself to be one of those indecipherable and enthusiastic Gnostics whom he ridicules in the *Tale of a Tub*: there is the same hispid and perverse symbolism, the same self-indulgence and disdain for the reader. Even his admirers might agree to apply to Blake Swift's remark on the modern philosophers, that they are controlled by "a peculiar String in the Harmony of Human Understanding" and are heard fully only by those tuned to the same frequency. But they might be less eager to apply the observation of Joshua Reynolds, Blake's loathed foe, in his seventh discourse on art: "A man who thinks he is guarding himself against prejudices by resisting the authority of others, leaves open every avenue to singularity, vanity, self-conceit, obstinacy, and many other vices, all tending to warp the judgment, and prevent the natural operation of his faculties." It is highly doubtful that *Vala* has more readers than *The Task* or *Jubilate Agno*. In Blake's time, indeed, the languid strings twanged vacantly and long; but the opinion of one intrepid critic is worth noting: "I am convinced that [Blake's] method when carried to its extreme is more disastrous to poetry than the most rigid convention of the century."[28] Blake's peculiar string is, certainly, *sui generis*, and it is not always ignominious to prefer languor.

But then of course Blake thought it *was* ignominious, for that is to dwell ever in the land of Beulah and the fleecy lamb. Blake avoids languor at all costs, therefore, and the costs are sometimes high. He delights chiefly in images of terror and strident howling, in gnashing and wrestling, in all the distressing contortions and repulsive habiliments of physical horror. Here is Blake describing the prisoners of the Bastille:

> In the tower named Bloody, a skeleton yellow remained
> in its chains on its couch
> Of stone, once a man who refus'd to sign papers of
> abhorrence; the eternal worm
> Crept in the skeleton.
> ·
> In the tower nam'd Order, an old man, whose white
> beard cover'd the stone floor like weeds
> On margin of the sea, shrivel'd up by heat of day and
> cold of night; his den was short
> And narrow as a grave dug for a child, with spiders' webs
> wove, and with slime
> Of ancient horrors cover'd, for snakes and scorpions are
> his companions. . . .
> (*The French Revolution*, 33–35, 38–41)

Blake was also capable of quieter, more ominous horror:

> The Senses roll themselves in fear,
> And the flat Earth becomes a Ball;
>
> The stars, sun, Moon, all shrink away,
> A desert vast without a bound,

[28]Paul Elmer More, "William Blake," in *Shelburne Essays (Fourth Series)* (New York and London: Putnam's, 1911), 229.

[372]

And nothing left to eat or drink,
And a dark desart all around.
(*The Mental Traveller*, 63–68)

Disencumbered from the operose Latinisms and furbelows of
Thomsonian verse, here is the naked cosmic fear. The lines are
free, too, of Blake's corrugated theology, and at such times, I
believe, his own peculiar string sounds most cleanly. A Shakespeare or a Sartre, or the Pope of *The Dunciad*, might easily
understand and feel such poetry; the notes, though few, are
true.

The Next Stage

Naturam expelles furca, tamen usque recurret.

HORACE

"It is a most interesting thing in popular religion, this tendency to fissiparate, to breed pairs of opposites: heaven and hell, God and Devil. I need hardly say that in my view no real dualism in the universe is admissible.... *Your* Devil and *your* God ... are both pictures of the same Force.... The next stage of emergent evolution, beckoning us forward, is God; the transcended stage behind, ejecting us, is the Devil.... The world leaps forward through great men and greatness always transcends mere moralism. When the leap has been made our 'diabolism' ... becomes the morality of the next stage."

C. S. LEWIS, *Perelandra*

SUCH IS THE IDEOLOGY of Weston, zealot of scientism, declaimed just before he is commandeered by Legion and falls to the ground in convulsions; for him, personally, the next stage is daemonianism. Like Blake, Weston denies the dualism of good and evil, disdains routine morality, venerates energy and force. With Jung, he conjectures that the holy and the daemonic, anciently joined and since divorced, may be reconciled in some new state as yet unexemplified in any sublunary cult. Weston, in fine, is one species of the modern sensibility, and has all the whig critic's confidence in progressive enlightenment and naturalism:

Edit and interpret the conclusions of modern science as tenderly as we like, it is still quite impossible for us to regard man as the child of God for whom the earth was created as a temporary habitation. Rather must we regard him as little more than a chance deposit on the surface of the world, carelessly thrown up between two ice ages by the same forces that rust iron and ripen corn.

[374]

Epilogue: The Next Stage

That is not Weston, but Carl Becker. And here is Professor F. W. Bateson:

> ... since the commonest intellectual honesty increasingly requires us to surrender the Christian after-life and its Triple Custodian, suitably de-supernaturalized, to cultural anthropology, we are now proportionately compelled to objectify our ethical ideals in some non-religious mode. . . .

Bateson goes on to imply that, for "intellectually honest" moderns, "orthodox Christianity can only be maintained by what amounts to a lie in the particular Christian's soul."[1]

But Weston's mission is more ambitious than that of most pedagogues; it is "to spread spirituality," to encourage the "majestic spectacle of . . . blind, inarticulate purposiveness thrusting its way upward and ever upward . . . towards spontaneity and spirituality." The ultimate stage is "*pure* spirit: the final vortex of self-thinking, self-originating activity." So the goddess of *The Dunciad* enjoys another triumph. Weston is more sanguine than Becker, who seems to despair of our knowing anything except some unspecified "ascertainable facts" that have supposedly mortified all traditional logic, philosophy, theology; henceforth we must be satisfied "to measure and master the world rather than to understand it." But Becker does not tell us how, lacking a theoretical frame or set of values, we can ascertain the facts in the first place, never mind their interpretation. Bateson, as one might expect of a devout Arnoldian, offers us "great literature" as the non-religious mode that will provide us in future with those "ethical ideals" hitherto derived from religion by our "pre-scientific ancestors." But Bateson fails to explain how ethical ideals, whether encountered in literature or elsewhere, are of themselves supposed to compel belief and action; nor does he assist those who may have trouble harmonizing the ethics of T. S. Eliot, Dylan Thomas, and Thomas

[1] Carl Becker, *The Heavenly City of the Eighteenth-Century Philosophers,* 14; F. W. Bateson, *Essays in Critical Dissent* (Tatowa, N.J.: Rowman and Littlefield, 1972), 193–94.

[375]

Hardy. Weston's next stage is vaporous enough, but Becker's and Bateson's seem no more internally coherent or adequate to human experience and aspiration. Bateson, it is true, has the candor to insinuate that modern Christians must be liars. Even Weston, haranguing the pious Ransom, was more politic than that.

But most whig or naturalist critics are less ambitious even than Becker and Bateson, contenting themselves with ritual celebrations of the final phase: the conquest of superstition by secularism. To be modern, says Peter Gay, "is to be cut off from the consolations of religion or metaphysics. . . . To be modern is to be compelled to face reality."[2] Note that for Gay religion is synonymous with consolation; this is a faulty synecdoche that, as we have seen, such critics have been so witless as to apply even to those *least* consoling of religionists, Pascal and Johnson. Note too that he assumes, like Becker, that "reality," the facts, is out there to be "faced," yet like Becker he has already sawn reality to fit snugly his positivism. Gay is a staunch disciple of Hume, and as foxy a practitioner of *petitio principii*. More than a century of strenuous epistemological speculation might never have elapsed, for him. Other, similar critics may sniff more keenly than he the contemporary pessimism, incertitude, and malaise; but such feelings, they tell us, are the reproaches of our own "bad conscience at having failed the Enlightenment."[3] And so the "party of humanity" has been let down by man! Surely this is the final, feeblest, rationalization of the twentieth-century *philosophe*, for whom the next stage must seem an appalling descent into irrationality, primitivism, and nostalgia.

The next stage, however, *cannot* be a relapse or retreat — that is too hideous a prospect for the naturalists to entertain; and so they din in our ears, with damnable iteration, "we can't go

[2]Peter Gay, *The Bridge of Criticism* (New York: Harper and Row, 1970), 10. "Voltaire" is speaking in this modern dialogue of the dead, but he represents Gay's view.

[3]Robert Anchor, *The Enlightenment Tradition* (New York: Harper and Row, 1967), 145.

back." Weston, for example, dismisses contemptuously "a few outworn theological technicalities with which organised religion has unhappily allowed itself to get incrusted" but to which no right-minded progressive can ever return: these are technicalities like original sin, the dualism between God and man, between the supernatural and the natural planes. A. O. Lovejoy enjoins us to accept the modern world-view, the "world of time and change" devoid of eternals. Becker insists that "since Whirl is king, we must start with the whirl, the mess of things as presented in experience." Marjorie Nicolson decides that although poets after Dante and Milton have tried to create a coherent world-view, yet "all the king's horses and all the king's men cannot put Humpty-Dumpty together again."[4] A dogma so tenaciously held and so seemingly sensible and pragmatic cannot easily be refuted. Of course there *is* the ingenuous response of T. S. Eliot, commenting on a recital of the "can't go back" litany in a famous critic: "What bothers me especially in Mr. [Middleton] Murry's fluid world is that Truth itself seems to change. . . . That I simply cannot understand. . . . 'We cannot return to St. Thomas,' he says. I do not see why not." In its deadpan simplicity, this has a quaint appeal. Then there is the psychoanalytic rebuttal of Norman Foerster: "Without seeking to rise above the age by doubting its assumptions . . . [academics and scholars] have entered into its skeptical current emotionally, experiencing a universal prejudice to universals of all sorts." Eric Voegelin's remark is an apt rejoinder to Bateson's obeisance to the Zeitgeist: "No one is obliged to take part in the spiritual crisis of a society; on the contrary, everyone is obliged to avoid this folly and live his life in order." Finally, C. S. Lewis, with his usual suppleness, retrieves the sediment of truth in the naturalist view while reproaching its conclusion: "Humanity does not pass through phases as a train passes through stations: being alive, it has the privilege of always moving yet never leav-

[4] A. O. Lovejoy, *The Great Chain of Being*, 329; Becker, *Heavenly City*, 16; Marjorie Nicolson, *The Breaking of the Circle* (New York and London: Columbia Univ. Press, 1962), 123.

ing anything behind. Whatever we have been, in some sort we are still."[5]

Still, the litany continues to be rehearsed with an hypnotic, or robotic, fidelity; for fundamental to this naturalism is the belief that human consciousness is more aware of the "facts" or "reality," that human reason is operating more capably nowadays than it has hitherto, that future stages of human development will further widen and refine our sensibilities. Derisive, "commonsensical" slogans such as "you can't put back the clock" (a strikingly unapt figure) cloak the emotional and self-serving nature of these articles of faith. The final question, notwithstanding, is this: did the Enlightenment and all that it signifies help to free man from the gods and demons that have infested his fancy, or did it instead dull and stupify one part of his brain, leaving the technological side to run rampant? It seems clear, at any rate, that certain things drop out of our consciousness, however valuable are its acquisitions. The old translators and exegetes of scripture had a better "feel" for many passages than have their modern counterparts, despite all the sophisticated panoply of twentieth-century scholarship; and Dryden or Pope, commenting on Homer, Virgil, and Juvenal, have an acumen and sagacity to which the present-day critic, however erudite and sensitive, is seldom equal. For Dryden and Pope were interpreting spiritual countrymen, but the typical modern critic is peering into an alien land.

Although truth may be one, it admits of gradations of importance; and the truth of the "can't go back" litany is so paltry and parochial as scarcely to warrant the complacency with which it is commonly intoned. I have no more quarrel with the whig philosophy than with any other that I cannot accept. But I find a shade distasteful its arrogance, determinism, and confor-

---

[5]T. S. Eliot, *The Criterion*, 6 (1927), 346–47; Norman Foerster, *The American Scholar* (1929; rpt. Port Washington, New York: Kennikat, 1965), 55–56; Eric Voegelin, *Science, Politics, and Gnosticism* (Chicago: H. Regnery, 1968), 22–23; C. S. Lewis, *The Allegory of Love* (1936; rpt. New York: Oxford Univ. Press, 1958), 1.

mity; and it is in those matters that the whig and the spiritist critic are equally culpable. The spiritist urges that certain time-spirits or climates of opinion obtain in various periods, and that all thinking people share that spirit. The whig critic declares that the skeptical or naturalistic outlook prevails in this age, and that all honest people must accept it; those who do not, far from being adulated as courageous iconoclasts, risk being accused of "lying in their souls." Both sorts of critics, when glancing backwards, are apt to praise only the partisans of the Enlightenment, for the Enlightenment "was the true greatness of the eighteenth century" whence began "the spread of the ideals of humanity."[6] To be sure, intellectuals living in the same time have much in common. Nor can it be denied that skepticism, so deftly plied by Hume and his votaries, has strongly colored nineteenth- and twentieth-century Christian apologetics, where natural theology, or elaborate systems such as Thomism, are distinctly shunned. Not for nothing does Newman adopt, as the epigraph for his *Grammar of Assent*, St. Ambrose's "Non in dialectica complacuit Deo salvum facere populum suum." P. E. More's best piece of apologetics is entitled *The* Sceptical *Approach to Religion*.[7] The hope of demonstrating the existence of God and the supernatural has been abandoned by most sophisticated apologists, who draw instead upon internal, personal, psychological evidence. William James's *Varieties of Religious Experience* — indeed, Otto's own *Idea of the Holy* — are perfect specimens of psychologically oriented, post-Humean theology. Otto's is sometimes adjudged conservative only because it treats the numinous, an experience that has not altogether fallen out of

---

[6]Alfred Cobban in *The Eighteenth Century*, ed. Alfred Cobban (London: Thames and Hudson, 1969), 341.

[7]The tone, thesis, and manner of proceeding of More's book are wholly obfuscated by Allen Guttman, who in his *Conservative Tradition in America* (New York: Oxford Univ. Press, 1967), 140, describes it as "an academic version of the confident placards posted at religious centers on college campuses: 'Is Christianity Outmoded?' (The answer is usually negative.)" This is a particularly nasty specimen of the absurdities foisted on tory thinkers by whig criticasters.

human consciousness, but which gives the fidgets to many modern theologians.[8] "Metaphysics will walk again only when it surrenders pretension to proof, and, as humbly as the Apostles' Creed, begins its words with: I believe!"[9]

For whig critics, the eighteenth century was the purgatory of the human mind: the fairies and enchantments were definitively expelled, and man was made ready for the wonder-working final stage of reason. But the century can also be seen as the cemetery of grandiose intellectual schemes; and its facetious gravedigger was David Hume, throwing up now the *caput mortuum* of natural theology, now the *disjecta membra* of rationalism. Modern theologians have done well to discard the vulnerable theodicies so luxuriant in that age. Modern students of religious literature may be struck more forcibly than their precursors by the insight and intellectual honesty of Pascal, Dryden, Johnson, and Cowper, all of whom penetrated the pretensions of Deism and natural theology. Modern observers, noting the welter of religious beliefs and cults, the proliferation of surrogate (and usually surly) political and sexual faiths and of quasi-scientific systems such as Marxism, the ardor with which new dogmas such as behaviorism, environmentalism, egalitarianism, are sold and bought, can see better than Voltaire that the desires supposedly regimented or expelled by the Enlightenment continue unabated and *will* be fed, with however scrappy and malodorous fare. Seldom has the smorgasbord of placebos been more depressingly copious. Far from lapsing into the deter-

---

[8]For example, the recent revisers of the 1928 *Book of Common Prayer* have expunged from the litany and the lectionary the most forcible references to the holy wrath of God; see Philip Edgcumbe Hughes, "The Prayer Book Under the Scalpel," *New Oxford Review*, 46, 5 (1979), 8–12. Because of its popularity, it is significant that Hans Küng's exhaustive *On Being a Christian*, tr. Edward Quinn (New York: Doubleday, 1976) never condescends to treat of the numinous, even hostilely! But any reader of Hume can surmise how distasteful and gauche must seem that experience to this demure theologian.

[9]O. K. Bouwsma, *Philosophical Essays* (Lincoln: Univ. of Nebraska Press, 1965), 83.

minism of Becker or Bateson, I would suggest that moderns have at least as much intellectual freedom as people of any age. If with Gay one believes in the cause of the Enlightenment, then naturally one should nurture and circulate its ideals. But if one's commitments lie elsewhere, surely one may internalize and advocate one's principles without having flung upon him the contumelious innuendo that he is lying in his soul. Such "paper bullets of the brain" are harmless enough of course, but bespeak an insularity and bravado strangely inconsonant with the whig ideals of tolerance and anti-dogmatism. Zeitgeists, historical processes, spiritual evolutionism: such abstractions or hypostatized entities are mere ghosts — less than ghosts — and should hold no terror for a truly enlightened mind. As for climates of opinion, Johnson somewhere declares that it is a very dull dog indeed who lets the weather dominate his moods. In future, after all, the intellectuals smugly siding with "history" may only be remembered, like the modish rationalist in *Rasselas*, as persons "that had co-operated with the present system."

To pontificate about the Enlightenment constituting the "true greatness" of the eighteenth century is merely to give one's tastes and predilections the semblance of authority. One of the fascinations of the period — call it a greatness if you will — lies in the efforts of many of its thinkers to fortify certain elements in the human consciousness against forces increasingly hostile and bold. I have said that I am reluctant to impose highly theoretical paradigms on the age. But certainly the importance of Calvinist Christianity, whether Evangelicalism or actual Dissent, must be asserted. It directly influenced Defoe, Richardson, Watts, the Wesleys (there tempered with Arminianism), Cowper; it lurks in the background of More, Casaubon, Glanvill, Dryden, Thomson, Young, Smart, Johnson and, in Augustinian guise, Pascal and Swift; upon even Hume and Blake it may be seen to operate, however deviously. But one should realize that Calvinism had left no little tinge on Anglicanism itself by the time of Browne, so that formal distinctions between Anglicans and Dissenters are often irrelevant theologically. It seems clear,

[381]

nonetheless, that Calvinism and its exfoliations were bracing preservatives, throughout the Age of Reason, of a sense of the holy and daemonic.

There is also, and from the start, an individualizing or custom-tailoring of belief that owes something to that same Calvinism but something else to the dilating skepticism of the age. Donne, in *The First Anniversary*, commented sardonically on each man's wishing to be his own phoenix, preferring private judgment to authority. But Browne, in a very different vein, finds that every man's reason is his best Oedipus, and Blake decides that "I must Create a System or be enslav'd by another Man's." Now Browne and Blake are not saying, *toto caelo*, the same things; but they are closer to each other in this, I think, than either is close to Donne. Separated as they are by a century and a half, both have retreated from systematic or dogmatic theology; both have been declared skeptical and intellectually capricious; both fabricated volatile and idiosyncratic styles to evoke numinous feelings. At the same time, the supernatural world owns in Browne a comfortable domesticity far to seek in Blake. For between Browne and Blake, finally, the differences overweigh the similarities. Peter Gay reckons people like Hume and Voltaire among the first moderns in their skeptical outlook and naturalism. But another face of modernism is discerned in Blake. Much in contemporary thought has been called (one wants a less pretentious term) Gnostic. The twentieth-century Gnostic views the world as an alien place, and he wills to transform reality into something of his own creation, to *become* the creator. He concocts a new theological or ideological scheme to replace that of the exploiting, despotic establishment. He repudiates the idea of a transcendent being as encroaching too rudely on human dignity — it is degrading, oppressive. He is apt to be an immanentist, to revere human reason, to conceive salvation in naturalistic terms, to feel that evil is not really a mystery and that it can be eradicated or overleapt; he lops away the "diabolic hypothesis" with Occam's possibly overused, certainly overrated, razor. Blake lies as much behind the modern, Gnostic intellectual, seen, for example, in *A Portrait of the Artist as a*

Epilogue: The Next Stage

Young Man, as Hume or Voltaire lie behind Bertrand Russell or John Dewey.[10] The licentious whimsy of Browne has yielded in Blake to an hectic, unmistakably up-to-date, intensity. Browne shifts at will onto the preternatural plane; Blake pursues it with the ferocity and determination of a congenital naturalist. The contrast suggests that something has indeed occurred in the consciousness of sensitive people — of *some* sensitive people — in the interval between Browne and Blake; but what happened may have been an astringency or contraction, rather than enlargement or advance. One is tempted to apply to the eighteenth century T. S. Eliot's wry observation on the twentieth, that it is "an age which advances progressively backwards."[11]

Assuredly the age was advancing progressively *inwards*. The pugnacious, robust theology of Donne becomes versatile and shifty in Browne; and while it may reappear in Dryden and to some extent Pascal, even there it is given a personal cast; we are offered thoughts or reflections, and the religion of a layman. The Restoration apologists of daemonianism tried to meet the skeptics on their own empirical grounds, and their tactics were neither asinine nor wholly futile. But in Defoe, and even more spectacularly in the later novelists, psychological narrative takes over; while eighteenth-century apologists such as Blackwall, Lowth, and Usher lay stress on the psychological efficacy, rather than the doctrinal or empirical necessity, of things supernatural and miraculous. Poets such as Watts, Thomson, and Young are also psychological at their best, trying to arouse the numinous sense; but their theological frames are either ramshackle or utterly commonplace. Pope, Swift, and Hume treat the experience only in its repulsive, daemonic aspect; they are often very adroit psychologically, but deliberately refrain from exciting the

---

[10]See Eric Voegelin, *Science, Politics, and Gnosticism*, and Thomas H. Landress, "James Joyce and Aesthetic Gnosticism," *Modern Age*, 23 (1979), 145–53. Latterly the Gnostic spirit has bourgeoned in literary criticism and aesthetics, under the aegis of Deconstructionalism. For a summary and rebuttal of the opinions of that sect, see Gerald Graff, *Literature Against Itself* (Chicago: Univ. of Chicago Press, 1979).

[11]T. S. Eliot, *Choruses from "The Rock,"* VII.

numinous in the reader. When Johnson can be coaxed into theoretical discussion, he greatly resembles the seventeenth-century apologists. In his writings he, too, touches mainly the daemonic side, and it was more than temperamental aversion, I think, that kept him from using his energies to contrive a systematic theology. He once remarked that he had thought of all of Hume's objections to Christianity when very young, implying that he had considered and rejected them. No doubt he did think of them early, but I am not sure that he shook entirely free of them. He is at his best, whether in the review of Jenyns or in his more imaginative works, when he turns to psychological experience. He reserves his most intense religious expressions for the wholly private *Prayers and Meditations*. Similarly intimate were Smart's *Jubilate Agno* and the most introspective lyrics of Cowper; and in both there is something of that ambivalence and obscurity that marks the pre-moral numinous experience. In Blake, of course, everything is psychological and inward; modern in one way, he has perhaps more ably captured the primitive daemonic than anyone else mentioned here. Again one wonders if this distending inwardness betokens progress toward some higher stage of consciousness and self-knowledge, or retrogression to the dunciadic nightmare of subjectivity, fragmentation, and solipsism.

There are, it would seem, as many "next stages" as there are "brave new worlds" of the Enlightenment. For Weston the next stage is a vortex of pure, self-originating spirit, an unmitigated dunciadic vision. For Blake it is the unified, regenerate, Divine Man. For the naturalist or whig it is the ultimate secularization of human consciousness; it is the true, complete, inwardly apprehended belief that: "unparented, unassisted and undirected by omniscient or benevolent authority, [man] must fend for himself, and with the aid of his own limited intelligence find his way in an indifferent universe."[12] For Jungians it may be the recombining of the holy and the daemonic in some new, more harmonious dance. At the beginning of this book I alluded

---

[12]Becker, *Heavenly City*, 15.

to the inability of the typical modern mind to grasp that complexity of imperiousness and grandeur, love and assurance, traditionally ascribed to the Divine Father. Many people are now sensing the inadequacy of the god without thunder, the god of the philosophers; but in trying to fuse the holy and the daemonic in some ineffably evolving dialectic they have merely substituted a modish system for an ancient and deeply rooted mystery. Doubtless they feel that the old mystery is a superstition; but every age has its own sly superstitions, although they are never called by that name till they have gone into the dustbin. Meanwhile the mystery hangs on.

In all these modern schemes the next stage denies or claims to transcend the dualism between the divine and the human; but this is a venerable aspiration, as old at least as the insinuations of the serpent in *Genesis*, or the architectural plans, never realized, for the Tower of Babel. And orthodox Christianity envisages it in the *Apocalypse*, with the edification of the City of God. The pattern remains eerily constant, however at variance are the descriptions of the next stage or the schedules of its arrival. For most of these thinkers the next stage is either a synthesis or an evolution of the former ones. But in *Revelation* the dualism of good and evil is irrefragably affirmed; it is just that the one defeats the other. Earlier in this study I stressed the difference between the Christian, and the Hegelian or Marxian, understanding of *Eloisa to Abelard.* This is the same difference, on a cosmic scale; and it is a signal difference because the Christian scheme avoids the cyclicalism, evolutionism, or dialectic so relished by modern Gnosticism and naturalism alike. In Christianity the holy and the daemonic, howsoever like dancers they may seem, are antagonists through all time. The next stage comes after that.

INDEX

Index

Blair, Robert, 190–92
Blake, William, 23, 59, 158n, 198, 314, 315, 340, 346–73, 382, 383, 384; Christology, 353–55; *First Book of Urizen*, 359–62; general religious views, 346–53; "Lamb" and "Tyger," 355–59; style, 371–73; *Vala*, 363–69
Blaydes, Sophia B., 316n
Bloom, Harold, 349n
Bolingbroke, Viscount, 118, 119, 121, 122, 130, 146, 160
Boswell, James, 189, 202, 203, 231–36 passim, 253, 323, 324
Boulton, Richard, 80
Bouwsma, O. K., 380n
Bovet, Richard, 90
Boyd, James R., 192n
Boyle, Robert, 106, 108
Bragge, Francis, 80
Bredvold, Louis I., 9, 14, 25n, 37n
Brewer, E. Cobham, 68n
Briggs, K. M., 66n, 67n
Bronowski, J., 347n
Brower, Reuben A., 134n
Browne, Thomas, 22, 25, 26–36, 39, 40, 42, 44, 45, 48, 49, 51, 59, 85, 98, 117, 125–26, 127, 132, 168, 172, 173, 188, 193, 382, 383; on dreams, 29–30; on dualism of man, 28–29; on miracles, 63–65; and mysticism, 27, 34–35; and new philosophy, 31; on predestination, 32–33; on spirit of God, 33–34; his style, 26–27, 35; on witchcraft, 61–63
Browning, Robert, 316
Bruno, Giordano, 10
Buckle, H. T., 30
Bunyan, John, 83n, 206, 209, 250–51
Burdett, Osbert, 347n
Burke, Edmund, 108, 261, 262
Burnet, Thomas, 106, 108
Burthogge, Richard, 91

Burton, Robert, 70, 133, 154, 196n, 252n
Butler, Joseph, 53, 120, 121, 195, 222
Butler, Samuel, 82
Butterfield, Herbert, 4
Byron, George Gordon, Lord, 60, 264, 296

Calmet, Augustin, 93, 96, 98, 134n
Calvinism, 71, 84, 86, 99n, 151, 163, 177, 178, 204, 315, 381
Campbell, George, 105n
Campbell, John, 264
Carlyle, Thomas, 202, 203, 258
Carnochan, W. B., 298n
Carter, Elizabeth, 130n
Cartesianism, 46, 75, 80, 88, 90, 97, 102, 103
Casaubon, Isaac, 84
Casaubon, Meric, 77, 78, 84–85, 90, 97, 204
Cassirer, Ernst, 4
chain of being, 28, 28n, 56, 125, 131, 132, 142, 171–73, 183, 192–94, 242–44, 253, 323, 340, 356, 365
Chambers, William, 261
Chapin, Chester, 119n, 202n
Charles I, 67
Chesterfield, Philip Dormer Stanhope, 137
Christ, 19, 78, 102, 132, 308, 318, 331, 332, 333, 335, 339, 345, 359, 362, 363; appeal to self-interest, 53, 197; daemonic aspects of, 353–55; and exorcism, 64, 71, 88, 96, 107, 319, 320; incarnation of, 347–48; and Last Judgment, 167, 326–28, 368–69; and miracles, 65, 68, 80, 81, 99–101, 104; resurrection of, 101, 103
Ciardi, John, 14, 15
Clarke, Samuel, 120, 139, 222
Cobban, Alfred, 379n

Index

[389]

Index

Epictetus, 46
Erasmus, Desiderius, 122
evangicalism, 239, 331, 338, 347, 381
Evelyn, John, 99n
Ewen, C. L'Estrange, 62n, 68n, 76
exorcism, 64, 71, 95, 96, 105, 107,
    266, 318–19, 324, 326. *See also*
    Christ and exorcism
"Exorcist, The," 312–13

Fairchild, H. N., 119n, 124n
Farmer, Hugh, 105n
fear, religious, *see* awe, daemonic,
    horror, terror
Fell, John, 106n
Fideism, 24–26, 38–39, 42
Fielding, Henry, 262
Fleetwood, William, 99n
Foerster, Norman, 7, 377
Francis of Assisi, 216
Free, William N., 345n
Freud, Sigmund, 267
Frye, Northrop, 347
Frye, Prosser Hall, 26n
Frye, Roland, 147n
Fujimura, Thomas H., 37n
Fuseli, Henry, 116, 139, 186
Fussell, Paul, 330, 334

Gay, Peter, 4, 5n, 12n, 210, 223n,
    225, 229, 376
Gemmet, Robert J., 294, 300
Gibbon, Edward, 103, 208
Gierson, Herbert J. C., 13
Gifford, George, 70n
Gildon, Charles, 113
Glanvill, Joseph, 75n, 77, 78, 80, 82,
    91, 93, 94, 95, 97, 98, 116, 158n;
    Sadducismus Triumphatus, 85–90,
    301
gnosticism, 157, 157n, 347, 349, 363,
    382–83, 385
Godwin, William: *St. Leon*, 263–
    66

Goethe, J. W. von, 262, 280, 300
Goldsmith, Oliver, 82, 292
Gordon, Thomas, 82, 84, 253n
Gosse, Edmund, 62
Gothic novel, 84, 109, 226, 259–67,
    279, 283, 310
Graff, George, 383n
Gray, Thomas, 325
Greene, Donald, 210n
Guttman, Allen, 379n

Hale, Matthew, 61
Hansen, Chadwick, 81n
Hart, Jeffrey, 119n, 170n, 177
Harth, Phillip, 26n, 27n, 37n
Havens, R. D., 189, 190
Hawkins, John, 235
Hayter, Thomas, 222n
Henley, Samuel, 292n
Henry VIII, 67
Herbert, George, 128–29
Herbert of Cherbury, Lord, 36,
    40
Hitchcock, Alfred, 313
Hobbes, Thomas, 28, 46, 51, 74–77,
    87, 88, 91, 97, 106, 215; on
    demonic possession, 70–71; on
    dreams, 29–30; on *Job*, 15
Hogarth, William, 110, 158–60, 162,
    208
holy, 21, 42, 47, 123, 128, 130, 149,
    160, 171, 179, 237, 271, 275, 355;
    defined, 19–20; and fear of the
    daemonic, 118, 219, 315, 326
Hopkins, Matthew, 67
horror, 184, 188, 191, 261, 262, 266,
    279, 282, 283, 289, 293, 299, 308,
    314, 372
Hughes, Philip Edgcumbe, 380n
Hume, David, 23, 78, 85, 86, 97, 99,
    101, 103–106, 204–30, 232, 253,
    260, 312, 346, 347, 352, 366, 380,
    383; compared with Johnson, 201–
    204, 236–41, 257–58; *Dialogues*

Index

concerning Natural Religion,
222–29; *History of England,* 205–
208; essay on miracles, 210–15;
miscellaneous essays, 208–10;
Natural History of Religion, 215–
22
Hunter, J. Paul, 110n
Huntley, F. L., 27
Hurd, Richard, 261
Hurlbutt, Robert, III, 223n
Hutchinson, Francis, 62, 75, 80–81,
97, 103
Huxley, Aldous, 9, 14

Innocent VIII, 67
Inquisition, 265, 266, 289–90,
306

James I, 67, 68, 158n, 322
James, D. G., 347n
James, William, 53, 379
Jansenists, 46
Jenyns, Soame, 240–46
Jesuits, 46, 54
Joan of Arc, 207
Job: compared with Clarissa, 277–78.
See also Bible: *Job*
Johnson, Samuel, 60, 169, 197, 208,
211, 230–58, 264, 278, 296, 312,
319, 371, 384; compared with
Hume, 201–204, 236–41, 257–58;
compared with Pope, 123, 130,
247–49; on religious verse, 164;
general religious views, 231–40;
Rasselas, 250–57, 292 300; review
on Jenyns, 240–46; *Vanity of
Human Wishes,* 246–50
Joyce, James, 190, 382–83
Jung, Carl, 17, 21, 22, 229, 374
Juvenal, 246

Kallich, Martin, 147n, 149n
Keats, John, 158n
Kierkegaard, S. A., 53

King, James, 332n
Kinsley, William, 145n
Kittredge, G. L., 7
Knight, G. Wilson, 119n
Kolb, Gwin J., 255n
Konigsburg, Ira, 282n
Kramnick, Isaac, 119n
Krutch, Joseph Wood, 253
Kuhn, Thomas S., 21
Küng, Hans, 380n

Laird, David, 210, 211
Landa, Louis A., 147n
Last Judgment, *see* Apocalypse
Laud, William, 207
Lea, Henry Charles, 67n
Leavis, F. R., 119n, 153
Leland, John, 105n
LeMahieu, D. L., 214n
Leventhal, Herbert, 63n
Lewis, C. S., 17, 21, 149, 153, 263,
275, 340n, 377
Lewis, M. G.: *The Monk,* 300–
310
Locke, John, 91
love, divine, 168–69, 315, 319, 323–
29, 334
Lovecraft, H. P., 86n, 116, 293, 295
Lovejoy, A. O., 28n, 242, 245n, 377
Lowth, Robert, 106, 108, 116, 198,
277n, 314, 320, 383
Lucretius, 10
Luther, Martin, 152, 205

Machen, Arthur, 17
Mack, Maynard, 119n, 128n
McKillop, A. D., 178n
McKnight, S. A., 75n
MacLean, Kenneth, 331n
MacLeish, Archibald, 14–15
magic, 63, 73, 74, 75n, 77, 204, 233,
265, 266
Malleus Maleficarum, 67, 68
Mann, Thomas, 310

[391]

Index

Index

Poe, Edgar Allen, 295
Pope, Alexander, 57, 60, 117, 118–46, 160, 161, 163, 165, 168, 169, 199, 315, 318n, 383; *Dunciad*, 139–46, 157, 172, 296, 366–67; *Eloisa to Abelard*, 131–37, 180, 252, 260, 275–76, 288, 304–305; *Essay on Man*, 118–19, 121–31, 177, 182, 193, 241–42, 247–49, 319, 324–25, 339, 350, 356; *Rape of the Lock*, 137–39, 295
Praz, Mario, 267n
predestination, 32–33
Price, Martin, 39n
Price, Richard, 105n, 106n
Protestantism, 38, 77, 98, 99, 100, 122, 158, 205, 235, 236, 347, 349
Providence, 72, 99, 104, 106, 110–14, 155, 182, 239, 254, 264, 272, 277, 278, 337
Prynne, William, 160
Pyrrho, 10

Radcliffe, Ann, 263, 283, 305, 307, 310; *The Italian*, 283–91
Railo, Eino, 301n
Ramsay, Allan, 83–84
Ramus, Petrus, 98
Ransom, John Crowe, 17, 18, 21
Raphael, 158n
rationalism, 3, 5, 10, 14, 24, 25, 35, 41, 66, 85, 96–97, 109, 118, 120, 131, 141, 170, 201, 214, 242, 326, 329
reason, 4, 30–31, 37–39, 49–51
Redwood, John, 5n
Reeve, Clara, 283
Reeves, James, 130n, 145n
Renault, Mary, 20
Revelation, 39, 40, 41, 48, 98, 120, 121, 130, 141, 147
Reynolds, Joshua, 371
Richardson, Samuel, 263, 264; *Clarissa*, 266–83, 313
Robertson, D. W., Jr., 134n

Roman Catholicism, 37, 38, 42, 66, 76, 108, 122, 151, 158, 205–206, 209, 216, 235, 236, 237, 303
Romanticism, 163, 203, 296
Romeo and Juliet, 284
Root, R. K., 119n
Rose, Elliot, 67n
Rossetti, D. G., 316, 324
Rowse, A. L., 153n, 155n
Royse, Josiah, 14
Russell, Bertrand, 228, 312, 383
Russell, Jeffrey Burton, 22n
Rymer, Thomas, 267
Ryskamp, Charles, 331n

Sacred, *see* holy
Sade, Marquis de, 45, 311
Saintsbury, George, 293n, 326n, 330, 331n
Sale, William M., Jr., 268
Santayana, George, 228
Satan, 69, 76, 91, 144, 176, 326, 331, 332, 354, 359, 370; in Bunyan, 83n; in Defoe, 91, 113, 114; in *Job* and O.T., 22, 322, 362; in Milton, 82, 270, 304, 360; in *Vathek*, 297. *See also* Devil
Schorer, Mark, 347
Schwartz, R. B., 223n
Scot, Reginald, 71, 74–77, 80, 81, 82, 87, 89, 91, 96, 97, 113; *Discoverie of Witchcraft*, 68–70
Scott, Walter, 41, 90
Scripture, *see* Bible
Seneca the younger, 228, 229
Sextus Empiricus, 10
Shadwell, Thomas, 83
Shaftesbury, Third Earl of, 120, 146, 169, 176
Shakespeare, William, 163, 296
Sherlock, Thomas, 101
Shumaker, Wayne, 7n, 21n, 67n
Sickels, E. M., 168n
Sinclair, George, 90, 94
Sitwell, E., 134n

Index

Index

LIBRARY OF CONGRESS CATALOGING IN PUBLICATION DATA

Stock, R. D. (Robert D.), 1941–
   The holy and the daemonic from Sir Thomas
Browne to William Blake.

   Includes index.
   1. English literature — Early modern, 1500–
1700 — History and criticism.   2. English
literature — 18th century — History and criticism.
3. Religion in literature.   I. Title.
PR439.R4S8   1982   820'.9'382   81-11974
ISBN 0-691-06495-4   AACR2

Robert D. Stock is Professor of English at the University of Nebraska.
His previous publications include *Samuel Johnson and Neoclassical
Dramatic Theory* (1973); *Samuel Johnson's Literary Criticism* (1974);
and *The New Humanists in Nebraska* (1979).